高等教育财经政法融通
系列教材

U0662364

MULTINATIONAL
CORPORATION OPERATION
AND MANAGEMENT

跨国公司经营
与管理

（双语版）

田毕飞◎主编

清华大学出版社

北京

内 容 简 介

本书主要介绍了跨国公司的基本概念、对外直接投资理论、跨国公司的具体职能管理、跨国公司在中国的发展现状、中国跨国公司的发展现状及全球跨国公司的未来发展趋势。

本书是湖北省来华留学全英文授课品牌课程及湖北省一流本科课程的配套教材，重点突出数字型跨国公司前沿及中国跨国公司特色。本书可作为国际经济与贸易、金融学、投资学、国际商务等经济学与管理学专业的高年级本科生与研究生相关课程的教材，也适合作为跨国公司从业人员的学习与培训资料。

图书在版编目（CIP）数据

跨国公司经营与管理：双语版：汉文、英文／田毕飞主编. -- 北京：清华大学出版社，2025.9.
（高等教育财经政法融通系列教材）. -- ISBN 978-7-302-70191-0

Ⅰ. F276.7

中国国家版本馆 CIP 数据核字第 20254Z3W85 号

责任编辑：张　伟
封面设计：李召霞
责任校对：王荣静
责任印制：宋　林

出版发行：清华大学出版社
　　　　网　　　址：https：//www.tup.com.cn，https：//www.wqxuetang.com
　　　　地　　　址：北京清华大学学研大厦 A 座　　　　邮　　编：100084
　　　　社 总 机：010-83470000　　　　　　　　　　邮　　购：010-62786544
　　　　投稿与读者服务：010-62776969，c-service@tup.tsinghua.edu.cn
　　　　质量反馈：010-62772015，zhiliang@tup.tsinghua.edu.cn
　　　　课件下载：https：//www.tup.com.cn，010-83470332
印 装 者：三河市铭诚印务有限公司
经　　销：全国新华书店
开　　本：185mm×260mm　　印　　张：18　　　　　字　　数：413 千字
版　　次：2025 年 9 月第 1 版　　　　　　　　　印　　次：2025 年 9 月第 1 次印刷
定　　价：59.00 元

产品编号：109276-01

前　言

目前，国内外有关"国际商务"的教材非常丰富，其篇章结构与内容也比较成熟。相较而言，有关"跨国公司经营与管理"的教材很少，且其篇章结构与内容很不一致，差别明显。究其原因，主要有以下两点：一是"国际商务"类教材的适用专业更广；二是与"国际商务"类教材的内容比较接近但主要适用于管理学专业的教材很多。为了帮助国际经济与贸易、金融学、投资学等经济学专业的学生更好地适应社会需要，编者一直致力于为学生们遴选优秀的国内外教材，以达到良好的授课效果。令人遗憾的是，编者至今未找到特别合适的教材，使得在过去20年的授课经历中，不得不先后更换了5本教材。作为国际经济与贸易等专业的核心必修课程之一，很多高校的"跨国经营管理"课程现已升级为双语或全英文教学。编者在过去几年曾以"跨国经营管理"（双语）课程为例主持完成了湖北省级教学研究项目"一流本科专业双语课程'雨课堂'建设研究"。该研究项目在突出"雨课堂"授课特色的同时，全面检视并更新了"跨国经营管理"（双语）课程的大纲、讲义、教案及题库等教辅材料。过去三年的授课实践证明，更新后的教辅材料达到了较好的授课效果。因此，编者决心以这些教辅材料为基础，自编教材并公开出版，以期惠及更多学生。

本书共有十章，可分为三部分。第一部分包括第一章至第三章，主要介绍跨国公司的基本概念及对外直接投资理论，旨在阐述跨国公司是什么、跨国公司为什么要对外直接投资以及为什么可以对外直接投资。第二部分包括第四章至第九章，主要介绍跨国公司的具体职能管理，包括战略管理、组织管理、营销管理、财务管理、供应链管理和人力资源管理，详细阐述了跨国公司如何进行对外直接投资管理。第三部分即第十章，主要介绍跨国公司在中国的发展现状及中国跨国公司的发展现状，同时展望跨国公司的未来发展趋势。

本书是集体智慧的结晶，共有5人参与了教材的编写。其中：田毕飞教授负责教材大纲的拟定与全书内容的统稿，并编写了教材的第一、五、六、七、九、十章，吴婷婷博士编写了第二章，盛月博士编写了第三章，吴英娜副教授编写了第四章，侯娱林博士编写了第八章。

本书是湖北省来华留学全英文授课品牌课程及湖北省一流本科课程的配套教材，汇集了编者20年的一线教学经验与素材，重点突出了数字型跨国公司前沿及中国跨国公司特色。本书可以直接用于"跨国经营管理"双语和全英文课程的教学，适用于国际经济与贸易、金融学、投资学、国际商务等经济学与管理学专业的高年级本科生与研究生教学，也适合跨国公司从业人员学习与参考。

限于篇幅，本书的很多内容以电子版形式呈现，请读者根据文中的二维码等提示查阅详细信息。本书在编写过程中参考了大量国内外文献及国际组织与国内官方网站的资料,相关出处已尽可能在脚注或参考文献中列示,在此向所有作者致谢,若有疏漏,敬请谅解。尽管编者已对全书进行反复打磨,但不当之处在所难免,敬请读者批评指正,以便再版时修订。

编　者

2024 年 11 月于晓南湖畔

目 录

第 一 章
Chapter 1

跨国公司概论
Introduction to Multinational Corporations

Learning Objectives
- To know the concept of multinational corporations
- To recognize the features and types of multinational corporations
- To be familiar with the generation and development of multinational corporations
- To understand the positive and negative effects of multinational corporations

第一节 跨国公司的概念
（The Concept of Multinational Corporations）

1. The term of multinational corporations

跨国公司最初是在西方发达国家产生和发展起来的一种企业实体。这些国家已经研究跨国公司几十年了，然而，迄今为止尚未形成统一名称。在英文文献中，有关跨国公司的名称多种多样，其中最常见的有四种：国际公司、多国公司、全球公司和跨国公司。这些名称虽然都表示从事跨国经营活动的企业，但其内涵却存在较大差别。这种差别源于跨国公司在不同发展阶段的演变历史，以及不同的企业跨国经营战略。

Multinational corporations（MNCs）were originally a type of corporate entity that emerged and developed in developed Western countries. These countries have studied MNCs for several decades. However, a unified name has not yet been formed. In English literature, there are various names for MNCs, among which four are the most common: international corporations, multinational corporations, global corporations, and transnational corporations. Although these names all refer to enterprises engaged in cross-border business activities, there are significant differences in their connotations. These differences arise from the evolution history of MNCs at different stages of development, as well as different corporate cross-border business strategies.

（1）International corporations

In the early stages of the development of MNCs, foreign business accounted for a relatively small proportion of all business, and enterprises mainly focused on the parent company's business in their home country. Foreign subsidiaries and branches usually

1

considered how to enhance the parent company's competitive strength and organize production and business activities, such as ensuring raw material supply, providing low-cost components, and increasing the overseas sales of their company's products. Compared to corporations whose business is completely limited to one country, these enterprises engaged in limited cross-border production and operation activities are called international corporations. This idea of conducting cross-border business based on the product lifecycle and focusing on the domestic market has formed the international business strategy of international corporations, also known as the international strategy. Implementing this strategy requires enterprises to have strong new product development capabilities, be able to successfully capture the domestic market, and effectively control and manage the transfer of product technology to overseas subsidiaries. Many large corporations in the United States, such as Procter & Gamble, General Electric, and Pfizer, adopted international strategies in their early stages of development.

(2) Multinational corporations

International corporations conducting cross-border business activities based on their home country market face significant challenges in adapting to changes in local market demand. And differences in culture, economic development level, business practices, and social systems between the home country and the host country also have serious impacts on the realization of their business goals. Especially when enterprises realize that products will be eliminated in the domestic market solely through export and that transferring outdated technology or equipment abroad will lose the opportunity for development, they expand the scale of outward direct investment. At this point, how to enhance the adaptability in various host countries has become a question that enterprises must consider when carrying out cross-border business activities. In order to ensure the success of cross-border business activities, enterprises need to formulate development strategies based on the specific characteristics of different host countries, adjust product structure, product performance or product packaging, and even adopt different management methods in subsidiaries of different host countries. This type of enterprise that conducts cross-border business activities based on the unique environment of different host countries is often referred to as a multinational corporation. The prominent feature of MNCs is their strong flexibility and adaptability in different host countries. The strategy adopted by such, also known as multinational strategy, focuses on the differences between host countries. Localization is the core content of a multinational strategy. Each subsidiary in the host country needs to improve the product technology provided by the parent company or develop new products based on local market demand, and make the most of local resources to meet the needs of the local market. Many large European corporations, such as Unilever, Philips, and Nestle, adopted a multinational strategy in their early stages of development. Multinational corporations developed rapidly in the 1950s and 1960s, as during this period, many countries generally adopted high tariff policies, and implementing the multinational strategy was an effective way to avoid switching taxes. However, by the 1970s, with the rise of global strategy, the position of multinational strategy had been shaken in many industries.

（3）Global corporations

In order to enhance the adaptability of multinational operations, multinational corporations usually need to establish a complete production and operation system in each host country, including product research and development, raw material and component procurement, production and assembly, warehousing, transportation and marketing, as well as after-sales service and all other production and operation links. If the market of the host country is small, it is difficult for foreign subsidiaries to achieve economies of scale. To improve efficiency in cross-border operations, companies must consider the markets of different countries in the world as a whole, that is, formulate cross-border business strategies from a global market perspective. This type of enterprise that conducts cross-border business activities targeting the global market is often referred to as a global corporation. Global corporations are committed to the production and operation of global products. The market for this type of product is a global market, and its demand arises from similar or convergent preferences among consumers in various countries. The cross-border business strategy of global corporations is global strategy, whose strategic goal is to improve efficiency through large-scale production and operation activities based on global coordination, thereby effectively establishing absolute cost advantages and occupying the global market. Coca Cola, Pepsi, Nike, and others are typical multinational corporations that adopt global strategies.

（4）Transnational corporations

The biggest cost of global corporations in their development is the reduction of the host country's specific environmental adaptability. The overall efficiency of cross-border operations and the adaptability to market changes in various host countries are two important goals that are difficult to balance simultaneously. Theoretically, a true multinational corporation should establish a global competitive advantage, which can achieve high overall cross-border operational efficiency, as well as greater flexibility and strong adaptability. From a global economic perspective, starting from the specific environment of each host country to carry out cross-border business activities is the dominant idea of the business strategy of multinational corporations. The relationship between the parent and subsidiary companies of multinational corporations is not simply a centralized and decentralized relationship, but rather different decision-making entities that depend on each other in an integrated global business network, ensuring the effective operation of multinational business activities through complex organizational management and coordination systems. Since the 1990s, more and more enterprises have been formulating and implementing strategies that balance efficiency and adaptability, namely transnational strategies, striving to develop into true MNCs. For example, McDonald's, KFC, Wallace, and others are well-known MNCs that balance efficiency and adaptability.

在国际公司、多国公司、全球公司和跨国公司这四种名称中，"多国公司"一词的使用最为普遍。从 20 世纪 60 年代到 80 年代，在西方的许多国家中，"多国公司"和"跨国公司"这两个词是混用的，而且用得比较多的还是"多国公司"一词。1973 年，联合国秘书处提供的一份题为《世界发展中的多国公司》的报告中，采用的是"多国公司"的提法。① 在次年讨论这份报告时，拉丁美洲国家的一些代表提出用"跨国公司"一词代替原来的"多国公司"。原因是在拉丁美洲一体化文化中，"多国公司"一词专指安第斯条约组织成员国联合创办和经营的公司。联合国经社理事会最终采纳了这个建议，并在联合国的有关文件中统一使用"跨国公司"一词。不过"多国公司"一词仍在学术界和企业界广泛使用。本书遵循这一传统，使用"多国公司"的称呼，泛指各种跨国企业。

Among the four names of international corporations, multinational corporations, global corporations, and transnational corporations, the term "multinational corporations" was most commonly used. In fact, from the 1960s to the 1980s, in many Western countries, the terms "multinational corporations" and "transnational corporations" were used interchangeably, and the term "multinational corporations" was used more frequently. In documents released by the United Nations, the term "transnational corporations" was uniformly used. However, the term "multinational corporations" is still widely used in the academic and business communities. This book follows this tradition, using the term "multinational corporations" to refer to various transnational corporations.

2. The definition of multinational corporations

（1）Structural criteria

凡采用"地区分布""生产或服务设施""所有权"等作为划分跨国经营与国内经营的标尺，都属于结构性标准。

Any use of "regional distribution", "production or service facilities", "ownership", etc. as the indicator for dividing cross-border operations from domestic operations belongs to structural criteria. The most famous example is Harvard Business School's Multinational Enterprise Project, which holds that a true MNC must have subsidiaries or affiliated enterprises in more than six countries. Raymond Vernon, the director of the project, believes that in the world's economic development, national sovereignty is powerless, while multinational corporations have made significant contributions, and he

---

① ［英］约翰·邓宁.多国企业,转引自联合国秘书处《世界发展中的多国公司》中译本.北京：商务印书馆,1975,附录Ⅱ.

has titled his work *Sovereignty at Bay*. Vernon points out in the book that multinational corporations typically have a fairly wide geographical distribution, and that a parent company cannot be included in the list of multinational corporations if it only has equity relationships with one or two countries outside its home base.

However, many international organizations, including the United Nations (UN) and the Organization for Economic Cooperation and Development (OECD), do not require MNCs to have their institutions located in more than six countries, but rather emphasize the need to have production or service facilities in two or more countries. It can be seen that MNCs emphasize the sum of production facilities, not just the combination of markets. That is to say, a company can be considered as a trading company only when it has import and export trade with many countries without having production or service facilities in these countries. If one owns production or service facilities but does not participate in business management, that is, they have property ownership but no management rights, it is simply an international holding company.

In western definition, ownership has two meanings: the form of ownership of assets and the country or countries which the enterprise belongs to, which is the nationality of the enterprise owner and senior management. Many international organizations do not attach great importance to forms of asset ownership, such as state-owned, private, cooperative or public-private partnerships, as well as partnerships and joint-stock companies. Only a few scholars believe that MNCs must be international monopolistic organizations and monopolistic capitalist ownership, while enterprises established by socialist countries abroad are an extension of public ownership and should not be referred to as MNCs. There are two different views on the issue of nationality of enterprises. Firstly, it is believed that the equity of transnational or multinational corporations should be owned by citizens of multiple countries, and the management rights should also be multinational. Secondly, it is believed that the characteristic of transnational or multinational corporations is "statelessness", that is, they do not belong to any country.

(2) Performance criteria

按跨国公司在全球经营业绩状况来界定跨国公司,主要是指企业的国外活动占整个公司业务份额,包括销售收入、资产总额、盈利额或公司雇员人数等达到一定标准才算得上是跨国公司。最常用的绩效指标是跨国程度指数。

When global business performance is used to define an MNC, it mainly refers to the proportion of its foreign activities in the entire company's business, including sales revenue, total assets, profits, or the number of employees. As Professor Raymond Vernon believes, the standard for MNCs is: companies with annual sales exceeding US $100 million. In 1993, the United Nations Conference on Trade and Development (UNCTAD) considered companies with a turnover of over US $1 billion to be MNCs, known as the "Billion Dollar Club". Among the performance criteria of the percentage of assets, sales revenue, production revenue, profits, and number of employees in the company's overseas business activities, overseas sales revenue or production revenue is mostly advocated as the main indicator, generally with a limit of 25%.

The most popular indicator to measure whether a company is an MNC is so called transnationality index, which is equal to (overseas assets/total assets + overseas sales/total sales + overseas employment/total number of employees)/3. Transnationality index is composed of the average of three ratios and is the average data used to measure the level of international participation of MNCs. It is a function of the degree to which a company's business activities are allocated abroad. The UN pointed out in the *World Investment Report 1998* that the theoretical framework for transnationality index (TNI) is based on the dichotomy between foreign and domestic activities, and that TNI is used to evaluate the degree to which the activities and interests of multinational corporations are involved in the domestic or foreign economy.

(3) UN criteria

1986 年,联合国跨国公司中心在其所发布的《跨国公司行为守则(草案)》中,将跨国公司界定为同时具有以下特点的企业:一是在两个或两个以上的国家拥有实体,不管这些实体的法律形式或经营领域是什么;二是在一个决策体系下经营,能通过一个或多个决策中心采取连贯策略和共同战略;三是各实体通过股权或其他方式互相联结,其中一个或多个实体有可能对其他实体施加重大影响,特别是同其他实体分享知识与资源,分担责任。

In 1973, the United Nations Secretariat defined multinational corporations as enterprises which control assets, mines, sales offices, and the like in two or more countries.[1] In 1974, the United Nations Commission on Transnational Corporations was established as an intergovernmental committee, and the United Nations Centre on Transnational Corporations (UNCTC) was also established as the secretariat of the United Nations Commission on Transnational Corporations, which was specifically responsible for handling UN affairs related to transnational corporations. In 1986, UNCTC redefined MNCs as enterprises that simultaneously possess the following characteristics in its draft code of conduct for MNCs: (a) comprising entities in two or more countries, regardless of the legal form or fields of activity of these entities; (b) which operate under a system of decision-making, permitting coherent policies and a common strategy through one or more decision-making centers; (c) in which the entities are so linked, by ownership or otherwise, that one or more of them may be able to exercise a significant influence over the activities of others, and, in particular, to share

---

[1] *The Impact of Multinational Corporations on Development and International Relations*. United Nations publication, Sales No. E. 74. Ⅱ. A. 5, 1973.

knowledge, resources and responsibilities with the others.

第二节　跨国公司的类型与特征
（Types and Characteristics of Multinational Corporations）

1. Types of multinational corporations

跨国公司的分类多种多样。按照经营内容分，跨国公司可分为资源型、制造型和服务型跨国公司。按照业务结构分，跨国公司可分为水平型、垂直型和混合型跨国公司。按照决策中心分，跨国公司可分为民族中心型、多国中心型、区域中心型和全球中心型跨国公司。按照国际化模式分，跨国公司可分为天生全球化企业和渐进型跨国公司。按照数据强度分，跨国公司可分为数字型跨国公司、信息与通信技术跨国公司和传统型跨国公司。

There are various types of MNCs. According to their business content, MNCs can be classified into resource-oriented, manufacturing-oriented, and service-oriented MNCs. According to their business structure, MNCs can be classified into horizontal, vertical, and mixed MNCs. According to the decision-making center, MNCs can be divided into ethnocentric, polycentric, regiocentric, and geocentric MNCs. According to internationalization models, MNCs can be divided into born-global firms and incremental MNCs. According to data intensity, MNCs can be divided into digital MNCs, ICT MNCs, and traditional MNCs.

（1）Classification by business content

① Resource-oriented MNCs. They are referring to MNCs whose main objective is to develop and utilize natural resources, which were the main types of early MNCs. The infamous British East India Company was a typical representative. While dumping British industrial products on a global scale, it also seized scarce resources such as tobacco, coal, ore, and fuel that Britain urgently needed from various countries around the world. It was an important tool for Britain to carry out colonial plunder, although the East India Company was not yet a modern MNC.

② Manufacturing-oriented MNCs. They are referring to MNCs that primarily engaged in the production and manufacturing of final and intermediate products, involving the manufacturing of steel, non-ferrous metals, chemical products, electromechanical products, durable consumer goods, etc. It is a type of MNC that rapidly developed during the recovery and reconstruction period of countries around the world after World War Ⅱ. The typical representatives include General Motors of the United States, Unilever of the United Kingdom, Panasonic Electric Company of Japan, etc.

③ Service-oriented MNCs. They are referring to MNCs that provide various services in the fields of trade, finance, transportation, communication, tourism, insurance, management, consulting, advertising, etc. The typical representatives include Citibank, PricewaterhouseCoopers, McKinsey & Company, etc. Service-oriented MNCs have developed rapidly since the 1970s for two reasons. One is that manufacturing-oriented MNCs have made significant outward direct investments in the service industry in order to share the development dividends of the service industry or achieve integrated production and service operations, leading to the emergence of a large number of service-oriented enterprises. Secondly, service-oriented MNCs have freed themselves from the positioning of providing services for manufacturing-oriented MNCs and actively and independently engage in outward direct investment.

(2) Classification by business structure

① Horizontal MNCs. They are referring to MNCs that operate or provide a single kind of product or service in a single field. The typical representatives include PepsiCo and McDonald's in the United States. This type of enterprises, regardless of where they set up branches, always produce or provide the same products or services as the company headquarters.

② Vertical MNCs. They are referring to MNCs that simultaneously engage in the upstream and downstream of a certain industry or produce products with different processing levels and process stages in a certain industry. The typical representatives include Royal Dutch Shell PLC and German Volkswagen. Shell focuses on the petroleum industry, with its business scope covering upstream oil exploration and extraction, midstream oil refining, and downstream oil transportation and sales, forming the entire industry chain of the petroleum industry. Although Volkswagen only produces cars, its global branches implement specialized division of labor, producing different parts of cars such as engines, gears, reducers, etc.

③ Mixed MNCs. They are referring to MNCs that engage in diversified operations, with each branch potentially producing products that are not closely related or even unrelated. The typical representatives include General Electric of the United States, Philips of the Netherlands, and others. General Electric is a world-renowned diversified enterprise, providing a wide range of products ranging from aviation engines to light bulbs and screws, many of which are even unrelated to each other. Philips is no exception, as it is a globally renowned home appliance company that also provides personal care and medical products, making it a typical hybrid MNC.

(3) Classification by decision center

民族中心型跨国公司,即以母国利益为中心进行经营决策的跨国公司。这类跨国公司往往处于国际化的早期,国际化业务有限,公司业务仍以国内为主,国外市场被视为国内市场的简单延伸。

① Ethnocentric MNCs. They are referring to MNCs that make business decisions centered around the interests of its home country. These multinational companies are often in the early stages of internationalization, with limited international business and their business still primarily focus on domestic markets. The foreign market is seen as a simple extension of the domestic market.

多元中心型跨国公司，即以各地分支机构的自身利益为中心进行经营决策的跨国公司。这类跨国公司的分支机构在全球分布广泛，经营活动丰富，主要采取的是本土化经营战略。在不违背母公司规定的前提下，各地的分支机构一切以本土利益为第一经营要义。

② Polycentric MNCs. They are referring to MNCs that make business decisions centered on the interests of its branches in various regions. The branches of such MNCs are widely distributed globally and have rich business activities, mainly adopting localization business strategies. On the premise of not violating the regulations of the parent company, local interests are the top priority for all branch structures in various regions.

区域中心型跨国公司，即以某一地区的分支机构利益为中心进行经营决策的跨国公司。这类跨国公司不是以一个国家或城市为决策单元，而是以包括多个地理上临近、文化上相似的国家的地区为考量单位，通常以设置区域总部的形式在全球开展经营活动，如北美、亚太、中东、北非、东南亚、大中华区等。

③ Regiocentric MNCs. They are referring to MNCs that make business decisions centered around the interests of its branch offices in a certain region. These MNCs are not based on a single country or city as their decision-making unit, but rather on regions that include multiple geographically adjacent and culturally similar countries. They conduct business activities globally by setting up regional headquarters, such as in North America, Asia Pacific, the Middle East, North Africa, Southeast Asia, Greater China, etc.

全球中心型跨国公司，即以公司总体利益最大化进行经营决策的跨国公司。这类跨国公司对国内外业务一视同仁，没有孰轻孰重的偏见。只要有利于公司总体利益，甚至可以牺牲母国或少数分支机构的利益。

④ Geocentric MNCs. They are referring to MNCs that make business decisions to maximize the overall interests of the company. These MNCs treat domestic and international business equally, without any bias of prioritization. As long as it benefits the overall interests of the company, they may even sacrifice the interests of the home country or a few branch offices.

(4) Classification by internationalization model

① Born-global firms. They are usually enterprises that have engaged in international business within three years of establishment and have overseas sales accounting for no less than 25%. With the progress of the Internet and communication technology and the arrival of the digital era, some enterprises can quickly carry out international business through cross-border e-commerce and other means, even if they are small in size, or even have only one person, and can even carry out transnational operations on their first day of establishment.

② Incremental MNCs. They are referring to MNCs that gradually carry out international business through continuous accumulation of experience and scale. This type of enterprise is a typical type of cross-border operation before the digital age. They often start with export with lower business risks, accumulate international experience and enterprise scale, gradually carry out licensing and joint venture operations, and ultimately choose sole proprietorship and outward direct investment.

(5) Classification by data intensity

According to *World Investment Report 2017* released by UNCTAD, the framework of the digital economy is shown in Figure 1-1. From Figure 1-1, it can be seen that MNCs can be divided into the following three categories based on digital intensity:

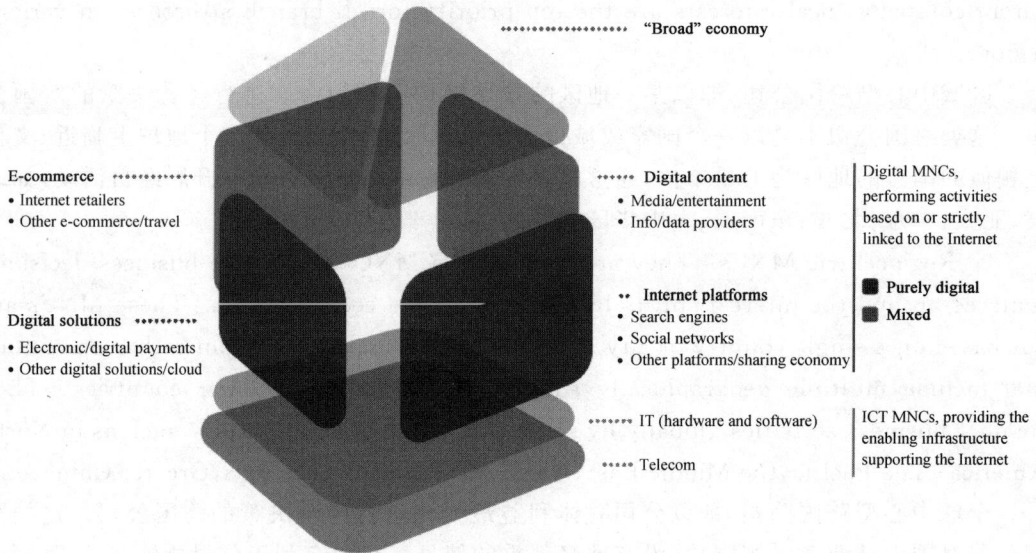

Figure 1-1　UNCTAD framework for mapping the digital economy
Source: UNCTAD, *World Investment Report 2017*

① Digital MNCs. In UNCTAD's analytical framework, digital firms include purely digital players (Internet platforms and providers of digital solutions) that operate entirely in a digital environment and "mixed" players (e-commerce and digital content) that combine a prominent digital dimension with a physical one.

Specifically, Internet platforms are companies providing digital services through Internet and cloud-based platforms, e.g. search engines and social networks. Sharing economy platforms such as transaction platforms (eBay) and open-source platforms (Red Hat) are also included. The category digital solutions (electronic and digital payments, other digital solutions in the cloud) describes a variety of players with core activities based on, or strictly linked to, Internet technologies, which include cloud hosting and computing, web hosting and email services, electronic and online payments, and digital solutions for business management and for financial applications (fintech).

Among the mixed players, e-commerce (Internet retailers, other e-commerce) consists of specialized and non-specialized online stores and online travel and booking agencies, focusing on fully online and online-born retailers. It also includes agencies specialized in online marketing and advertising. The last category in the scope of digital MNCs, digital content (digital media and entertainment, information and data providers), includes producers and providers of digital content, such as media (music, video, e-books and online magazines, online courses) and gaming ("classic" video games, online games, mobile games, multiplayer interactive games). It also captures "big data" providers, and providers of marketing and customer intelligence, as well as economic, business and credit information.

② ICT MNCs. They include IT companies providing hardware and software, as well as telecommunication firms. IT hardware and software cover the broad categories of manufacturers of ICT hardware (computer brands) and components (e. g. the semiconductor industry) as well as software houses and providers of auxiliary service. Telecom players are owners of the telecommunication infrastructure on which Internet data is carried.

③ Traditional MNCs. They are referring to the MNCs that are beyond the above MNCs, which may be the customers of digital technology or service rather than the providers or facilitators.

2. Characteristics of multinational corporations

(1) Business scale can be large or small

Incremental MNCs often have a large scale because they only engage in cross-border operations after a significant increase in the company's size, which in turn makes the enterprise even larger and wealthier. For example, if the sales of Walmart in the United States in 2024 were regarded as the GDP of a country, it would probably rank 25th in the world. However, there are also some small born-global firms, even with only one employee, that use cross-border e-commerce platforms to carry out cross-border operations from their inception. Therefore, business scale is no longer an important criterion for measuring MNCs.

(2) Competitive strategies are flexible and diverse

To compete in the international market, MNCs must develop competitive strategies tailored to the characteristics of different competitors in different host country markets. In the process of strategic formulation, it is necessary to consider both adaptability to the different operating environment of each host country and low-cost raw material sources and global economies of scale efficiency. It needs to consider both global competition conditions and the potential impact of strategic actions taken in one host country on other host countries. It is necessary to consider both the need for the headquarters of the company to coordinate economic activities scattered around the world through integrated leadership, and the autonomy required for external subsidiaries to respond flexibly to changes in local market demand. Therefore, the formulation and implementation of competitive strategies for MNCs are very complex, and many challenges, as well as many choices and factors that must be considered, are not involved in the process of domestic enterprises formulating and implementing competitive strategies.

(3) The development speed is getting faster and faster

In the digital economy era, digital MNCs, compared with ICT MNCs and traditional MNCs, are inclined to conduct foreign direct investment (FDI) with light asset, which can be measured by FDI asset-light index. It is defined at the level of the individual MNC as the ratio between the share of sales generated by foreign affiliates and the corresponding share of foreign assets. If the ratio is bigger than 1, it means the MNCs have achieved rapid growth in sales despite limited overseas assets, which reveals the reason why MNCs develop faster and faster in digital era. The direct reason for this phenomenon is the advancement of digital technologies such as 5G, cloud technology, and artificial intelligence. These technologies allow companies to invest a small amount of facilities overseas, even without the need for physical assets, to achieve cross-border operations, thereby accelerating the company's development.

(4) The global mindset is increasingly stronger

Regardless of the type of MNCs, all MNCs must have a global mindset and view the global market as a whole to carry out business activities in order to survive in the era of globalization. "Internationalization of the domestic market and domestication of the international market" are the concentrated manifestations of global thinking, while "thinking globally and acting locally" are the rational choices of many MNCs in their actual business activities.

第三节　跨国公司的产生与发展
(Generation and Development of Multinational Corporations)

1. The budding period before World War I

跨国公司不是普遍存在于任何社会之中,而是以社会化大生产和市场经济为特征的社会的产物。跨国公司也不是突然出现的,而是在市场及复杂的经济发展过程中逐渐形成的。

MNCs are not universally present in any society, but are products of a society characterized by mass production and market economy. MNCs do not suddenly emerge, but gradually form in the market and complex economic development process.

Before the Industrial Revolution, western capitalist countries engaged in overseas expansion based on three main motivations: the first is to meet domestic demand through trade and financial activities; the second is to acquire new territory or wealth; the third is to seek new channels for domestic capital export. Since the 15th century, maritime exploration activities aiming at discovering the new continent had gradually become active. These activities promoted the economic expansion of early capitalist countries and opened the prelude to cross-border production and operation. In the 16th and 17th centuries, there were significant improvements in transportation, the scope of cross-border trade activities expanded, and the relationships between trading partners of different countries shifted from irregular personal relationships to more reliance on formal commercial documents. During this period, outward foreign direct investment (OFDI) had two main purposes: firstly, to strengthen international trade activities; secondly, to strengthen overseas colonial rule and land development. However, compared to commodity trade, OFDI is negligible. Only the UK and France had a small amount of OFDI.

The Industrial Revolution significantly changed the foreign trade and colonial activities of capitalist countries. The external investment motivation of enterprises in these countries had also changed, shifting from promoting trade to seeking more raw materials and mineral resources for domestic industrial development. The introduction of the factory system had had a profound impact on the development of private enterprises and the formation of modern corporate management systems. At the same time, the Industrial Revolution led to the refinement of professional division of labor between and within enterprises, strengthening the role of technological progress, monetary capital, and management skills in socialized mass production. All of these laid the material foundation for cross-border operations, which in turn gave birth to MNCs. In 1865, Friedrich Bayer Chemical Company of Germany opened a factory in Albany, New York, USA to manufacture aniline. In 1866, the Swedish company Alfred Nobel opened a factory in Hamburg, Germany to manufacture explosives. In 1867, the American company Shengjia Sewing Machine established a sewing machine assembly plant in Glasgow, England. The above three companies are usually considered pioneers in modern OFDI.

There were two main motivations for early MNCs to engage in OFDI: firstly, to acquire new markets; secondly, to obtain new resources. Most OFDI targeting resources had flowed to developing countries, while OFDI targeting markets had flowed mostly between industrialized countries in Europe and America. In market-oriented OFDI, MNCs from different countries invested in different industries. The OFDI of British MNCs was concentrated in the processing and consumer goods industries. European MNCs focused on conducting cross-border production and business activities in the chemical and electrical engineering industries. The cross-border production and operation activities of American enterprises were mainly capital intensive large-scale production and assembly. By the eve of World War I in 1914, MNCs were increasingly conducting OFDI by setting up branch factories overseas. Moreover, in such investment, more emphasis was placed on utilizing the advantages of vertical or horizontal integration of production to reduce uncertainty in the intermediate product market.

2. The gradually maturing period between the two world wars

After World War I, the development of MNCs exhibited some completely different characteristics from the previous period.

Firstly, the growth of cross-border business activities in Western European countries was slow, while MNCs in the United States had made significant progress and gradually matured. The two world wars that mainly occurred in Europe resulted in European participating countries selling some overseas investment enterprises, especially a significant decrease in investment in the former Soviet Union. The severe economic crisis that occurred in 1929, as well as the prolonged economic depression that followed, further restricted the cross-border business activities of major capital exporting countries in Europe.

Secondly, the proportion of OFDI flowing to developing countries had increased. The direct investment activities of American MNCs in developing countries included new oil fields in Mexico and the Middle East, copper and iron mines in Africa, nitrates in Chile, bauxite in Guyana, and especially non-ferrous metals in South Africa. The UK had increased its investment in Commonwealth countries in an attempt to regain control of export markets lost due to the war. There was a notable surge of US investment in the UK, with 121 new manufacturing subsidiaries established in the 1920s, and 112 in the 1930s, of which 40% and 23% were acquisition entries, respectively. [1]

Lastly, diversified cross-border business models had led to the emergence of vertically integrated or diversified MNCs. The international economic and trade environment during this period was far inferior to that before 1914. Due to factors such as economic depression and war, many countries had raised tariffs and strengthened import controls. This prompted companies to replace export trade with cross-border production. During this period, the scale and quantity of internal transactions in multinational operations of enterprises increased significantly. Moreover, the growth of cross-border mergers and acquisitions was faster than that of newly established enterprises. This type of cross-border M&A activity was largely a strategy adopted by domestic oligopolistic monopolies in major capital exporting countries to strengthen their market position. One result was the rapid development of international cartels. [2]

3. The period of vigorous development after World War II

After World War II, a clear characteristic of the development of MNCs was the dominance of American MNCs. In 1960, the five largest foreign investment countries in

---

[1] Dunning, J. H., Lundan, S. M. (2008), *Multinational Enterprises and the Global Economy*, Edward Elgar Publishing Limited, Cheltenham, UK. P180.

[2] Dunning, J. H., Lundan, S. M. (2008), *Multinational Enterprises and the Global Economy*, Edward Elgar Publishing Limited, Cheltenham, UK. P184.

the world were the United States, the United Kingdom, the Netherlands, France, and Canada, with absolute cumulative investments of 31. 9 billion US dollars, 10. 8 billion US dollars, 7 billion US dollars, 4. 1 billion US dollars, and 2. 5 billion US dollars, respectively. The relative weights were 49％, 16. 6％, 10. 8％, 6. 3％, and 3. 8％. [1] The reason why the United States replaced Britain as the largest OFDI country was inseparable from the special political and economic environment of the post-war world. The participating countries in Western Europe focused their main energy on healing the wounds of war and rebuilding their homeland, with no time to pay more attention to the development of overseas investment. In order to restore domestic production as soon as possible, they even sold some foreign companies to raise funds. The United States, as the largest victorious country, took advantage of the opportunity to assist the participating countries in Western Europe in rebuilding and expanded its direct investment in these countries. During this period, important factors that prompted American companies to develop overseas through direct investment also included: a global shortage of dollars made American companies more inclined to produce and sell locally in other countries; the gap in labor costs between the United States and other countries was increasing; the implementation of antitrust policies in the United States had been strengthened domestically; and American companies were becoming more competitive in technology development and marketing. In Europe, MNCs from other major economically developed countries, except for the Confederation, also experienced recovery and varying degrees of development during this period. For example, by 1960, OFDI from the Netherlands and France had exceeded pre-war levels. [2]

From the industry distribution of OFDI, although there are differences in different countries, it is generally concentrated in manufacturing and resource-based industries. MNCs in the United States and the United Kingdom had seen a rapid increase on OFDI in the manufacturing industry. In 1960, 35％ of the OFDI of the two countries was in manufacturing, while in 1938, this proportion was only 25％. In the 1950s, OFDI from the Netherlands, France, and Switzerland was mostly concentrated in the manufacturing and service industries (finance and trade). [3] The investment based on obtaining the necessary resources for domestic production was another important feature of the development of MNCs during this period. The rapid economic development of developed Western countries after the war led to a significant increase in demand for resources. In

---

① Dunning, J. H. , Lundan, S. M. (2008), *Multinational Enterprises and the Global Economy*, Edward Elgar Publishing Limited, Cheltenham, UK. P174.

② Dunning, J. H. , Lundan, S. M. (2008), *Multinational Enterprises and the Global Economy*, Edward Elgar Publishing Limited, Cheltenham, UK. P185.

③ 同上。

order to ensure the supply of raw materials, energy and other resources required for domestic production, many MNCs invested in mining, oil and other industries in the host country to establish raw material production bases. For example, in 1950, the United States had the highest proportion of OFDI in the mining and oil industries. However, the direct investment activities of MNCs aimed at obtaining resources had gradually attracted the attention of host country governments. Some governments had implemented policies to impose restrictions, resulting in a decline in such investment activities in the 1960s and 1970s. A trend in the development of MNCs in the early post-war period was that OFDI flowed more towards developed countries. During the two world wars, the proportion of direct investment flowing to developed countries was approximately 33%, and by 1960 this proportion had risen to 67%. The investment focus of American MNCs was on Canada and Western Europe, while MNCs in the UK mainly developed towards Commonwealth countries among which Australia, Canada, and South Africa were investment priorities.[1]

Since the 1970s, the global economic landscape and business environment had undergone significant changes, which were as follows. First, Japan's economy developed into an economic powerhouse capable of competing with the United States and Europe. Second, the oil crisis in the early 1970s greatly elevated the position of oil exporting countries in the world economy. Third, some developing countries and emerging industrialized countries in Asia and Latin America were experiencing rapid economic development, forming new regional markets with enormous potential. With the end of the Cold War in 1989, the international trade and investment environment continued to improve, and the trend of global economic integration became increasingly evident, which had a direct impact on the development of MNCs. Both global corporations and truly MNCs developed during this period.

From the perspective of the flow of FDI by MNCs, there has been a significant increase from developed countries to developing countries from 1990—2022, as shown in Figure 1-2. The same story happened in terms of the flow of OFDI from different countries. As shown in Figure 1-3, although the flow of OFDI from developed countries is larger than that from developing countries in most years during the period of 1990—2022, the growth of the flow of OFDI from developing countries is greater and more dramatic.

近年来，发展中国家和新兴工业化国家的跨国公司有了长足的发展，特别是以中国为代表的金砖国家和新兴市场跨国公司发展迅猛，从无到有，从小到大，逐渐成为全球市场的重要参与者。随着改革开放政策的实施，特别是 2001 年加入世界贸易组织以来，中国

---

[1] Dunning, J. H., Lundan, S. M. (2008), *Multinational Enterprises and the Global Economy*, Edward Elgar Publishing Limited, Cheltenham, UK. P186.

Millions of dollars

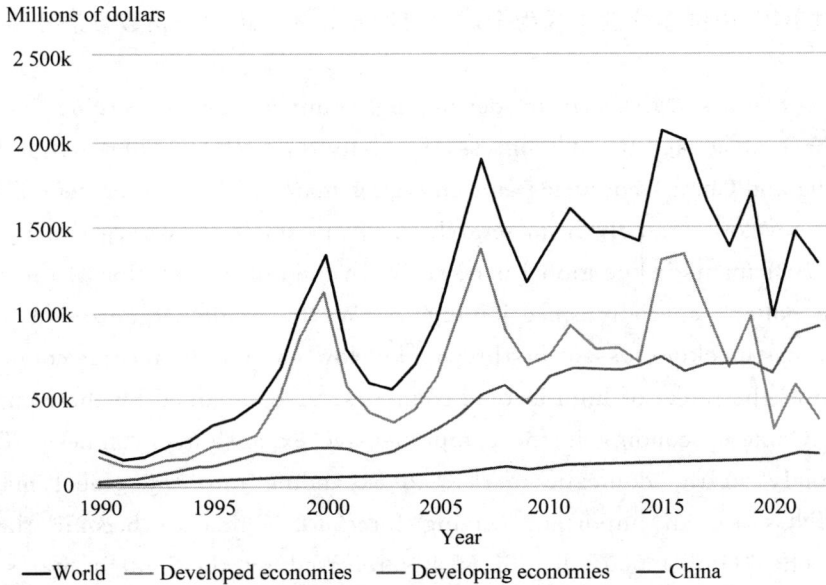

Figure 1-2　Trend of FDI flow，1990—2022

Source：UNCTAD，*World Investment Report 2023*

Millions of dollars

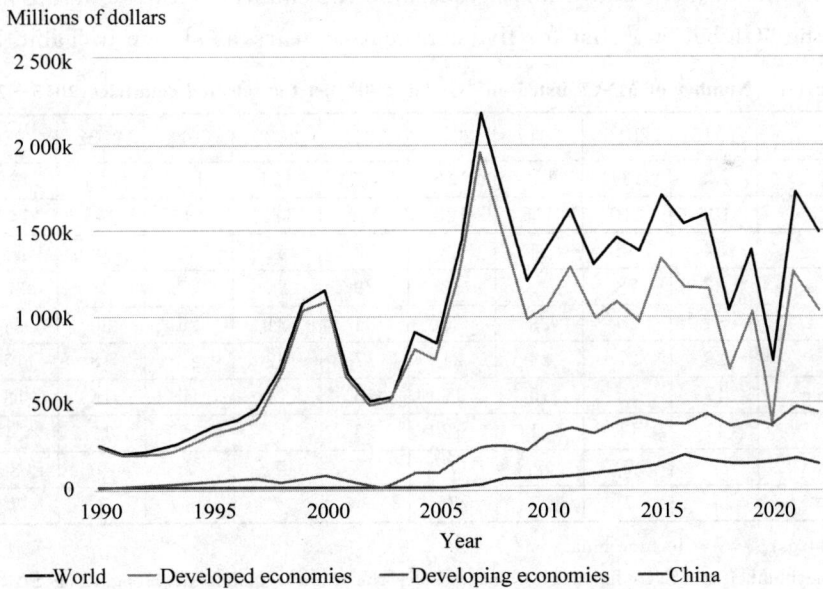

Figure 1-3　Trend of OFDI flow，1990—2022

Source：UNCTAD，*World Investment Report 2023*

从低收入国家快速跨过中低收入和中高收入的门槛，即将步入高收入国家行列。与中国经济全面崛起相伴随的，是中国跨国公司从仅专注国内市场到向全球市场的全面进发。中国跨国公司是中国成为"世界工厂"的重要推手。美国《财富》杂志连续多年发布的跨国公司世界 500 强榜单显示，2019—2023 年，包括香港和台湾地区在内的中国跨国公司上榜总数超过美国,中国连续五年成为全球上榜世界 500 强跨国公司数量最多的国家(参见表 1-1)。

In recent years,MNCs from developing countries and emerging industrialized countries have made significant progress,especially the BRICs (Abbreviation for Brazil, Russia,India and China) countries and emerging market MNCs represented by China, which have developed rapidly from scratch and from small to large,gradually becoming important participants in the global market. With the implementation of the reform and opening up policy,especially since joining the World Trade Organization (WTO) in 2001,China has quickly crossed the threshold of low-and middle-income countries and is about to enter the ranks of high-income countries. Accompanied by the comprehensive rise of the Chinese economy is the comprehensive expansion of Chinese MNCs from focusing solely on the domestic market to expanding into the global market. And Chinese MNCs are an important driving force for China to become the "Global Factory". The "Global 500" list of MNCs released by the United States magazine *Fortune* for several consecutive years shows that from 2019 to 2023,the total number of Chinese MNCs,including MNCs in Hong Kong SAR and Taiwan Province,has surpassed that of the United States,and China has become the country with the highest number of MNCs on the "Global 500" list for five consecutive years,as shown in Table 1-1.

Table 1-1　Number of MNCs listed on "Global 500" list for selected countries,2015—2024

	2015	2016	2017	2018	2019	2020	2021	2022	2023	2024
US	128	134	132	126	121	121	122	124	136	139
China	106	110	115	120	129	133	143	145	142	133
Japan	54	52	51	52	52	53	53	47	41	40
Germany	28	28	29	32	29	27	27	28	30	29
France	31	29	29	28	31	31	26	25	24	24
UK	29	27	24	21	17	22	22	18	15	17
South Korea	17	15	15	16	16	14	15	16	18	15
Canada	11	11	11	12	13	13	12	12	14	14
India	7	7	7	7	7	7	7	9	8	9
Brazil	7	7	7	7	8	7	6	7	9	9

Source:https://www.fortunechina.com/

Note:The number of MNCs listed by China includes the Chinese mainland;Hong Kong SAR,China;and Taiwan,China.

第四节　跨国公司的作用
(The Effect of Multinational Corporations)

跨国公司对东道国和母国既有积极影响,也有消极影响。这主要取决于对这种影响的分析是立足当下还是着眼长远,是静态分析还是动态分析。不论是对哪种影响的分析,都有大量的不同意见,这些争论可能永无休止。

MNCs can have both positive and negative effects on host and home countries. It mainly depends on the analysis of the effect types, such as short-run or long-run effect, and static or dynamic effect. No matter which type the effects belong to, there are always a lot of discussions, which may never end in the future.

1. Positive effects of multinational corporations

（1）Transfer capital

The FDI of MNCs promotes the cross-border flow of capital, which is not only beneficial for compensating for the lack of capital in host countries, especially developing countries, but also for achieving the goal of maximizing profits for MNCs. MNCs often have significant financial transactions between their wholly-owned or controlling subsidiaries in the host country and their parent companies. For example, if a subsidiary submits profits to the parent company, the parent company may make additional investments in the subsidiary. This cross-border transfer of capital reflects the characteristic of capital chasing profits, which helps to improve the international balance of payments of the host country.

（2）Spread technology

MNCs, in order to occupy the market in the host country, will bring advanced management experience and production technology from their home country to drive the host country. This allows enterprises in host countries, especially enterprises in developing countries, to observe, interact with, and ultimately master these experiences and technologies up close, thereby narrowing the technological gap between developed and developing countries. In some highly competitive industries, some MNCs from developed countries may even establish research and development centers in developing host countries, using the most advanced technology for the host country's market competition in the first time, which helps to improve the overall technological level of the host country.

（3）Create jobs

The FDI made by MNCs through the establishment of new enterprises undoubtedly creates new job opportunities and increases employment rates for the host country. Moreover, in order to achieve expected business performance, MNCs will also provide different levels of management and skill training to host country employees, which helps to improve the skill level and overall quality of host country workers. As of the end of 2022, the China-Pakistan Economic Corridor has brought a total of 25. 4 billion US dollars in direct investment to Pakistan and created 236,000 job opportunities. ①

---

① 中华人民共和国国务院新闻办公室. 共建"一带一路":构建人类命运共同体的重大实践(白皮书). 北京:人民出版社,2023.

（4）Increase tax

MNCs in the host country must pay various taxes in accordance with the relevant laws of the host country for their operating income, which increases the host country's fiscal revenue. This has been one of the main purposes for many countries, especially developing countries, to implement various preferential measures in recent years to attract foreign investment.

（5）Promote growth

MNCs, which rely on FDI as their basic means of operation, are the engines of global economic growth. Places where MNCs are more concentrated are usually also the places with the fastest economic growth. MNCs allocate resources globally by conducting intra company trade, greatly increasing the scale of global trade and improving resource allocation efficiency, making them an indispensable force for global economic growth. For example, the Mombasa Nairobi Railway invested and constructed by Chinese companies in Kenya has contributed 2% to Kenya's economic growth. [①]

2. Negative effects of multinational corporations

（1）Market monopoly

MNCs often have advantages in capital, technology, and talent compared to indigenous enterprises in the host country, and are in a competitive position in the local market. Due to the profit-driven nature of capital, MNCs may even use product quantity, quality, and price advantages to suppress indigenous enterprises in the host country, ultimately forcing indigenous enterprises to exit the market, thus forming a market monopoly situation. This not only is detrimental to the employment and taxation of the host country, but also harms consumer surplus, turning the host country into an economic colony.

（2）Deterioration of income and expenditure

The FDI of MNCs in the host country is usually accompanied by the outflow of capital from the home country, which worsens the international balance of payments situation of the home country. Meanwhile, direct investment by MNCs in host countries may also worsen their international balance of payments. On the one hand, if an MNCs' branch in the host country repatriates its operating profits back to its home country, it will reduce the available capital in the host country. On the other hand, if an MNCs' branch in the host country must purchase the necessary equipment or services for operation from other countries, it will expand the host country's imports and increase its international expenditures.

（3）Magnified risks

The FDI of MNCs often means the international transfer of industries, becoming an important driving force in shaping the global value chain, and gradually forming a situation where developed countries occupy the high-end of the value chain and developing countries are locked in the low-end and middle-end of the value chain. In the context of smooth global supply chains, countries around the world can generally benefit from industrial transfer and international division of labor, although the benefits of developed countries are significantly higher than those of developing countries. However, due to the impact of natural disasters, geopolitics, and the game of great powers, the global supply chain faces the risk of interruption, and decoupling and chain breaking seriously threaten the industrial security, economic security, and national security of various countries. The business activities of MNCs have significantly magnified national security risks.

（4）Sovereign erosion

In cross-border business activities, MNCs may use various resources to influence the policy-making of the host country in order to continuously obtain operating profits. And their most common approach is to use economic interests to exert pressure and coerce host countries into formulating policies favorable to MNCs through divestment. It is also a common practice to lobby policy makers in host countries through commercial bribery. These actions undoubtedly go beyond the scope of economic activities and erode the sovereignty of the host country. The various advertisements and promotions carried out by MNCs to promote product sales, once a cultural conflict arises, to some extent, also constitute cultural erosion of the host country and infringe upon the overall interests of its citizens.

（5）Economic collapse

MNCs gathering in large numbers in a host country may create pseudo prosperity for the local community as the host country's economy relies heavily on MNCs, gradually losing economic independence. When economic crises and other risks arise, MNCs flee one after another, and indigenous enterprises in the host country are weak and insufficient to support local economic development, causing the host country's economy to collapse instantly. Latin American countries, represented by Argentina, have long fallen into the "middle-income trap" and are unable to extricate themselves, which is the result of excessive reliance on MNCs and neglecting the development of local enterprises.

关键术语（Key Terms）

国际公司（international corporation）　　　全球公司（global corporation）

多国公司（multinational corporation）　　　跨国公司（transnational corporation）

跨国程度指数（transnationality index）

资源型跨国公司（resource-oriented MNC）

制造型跨国公司（manufacturing-oriented MNC）

服务型跨国公司（service-oriented MNC）

水平型跨国公司（horizontal MNC）

垂直型跨国公司（vertical MNC）

混合型跨国公司（mixed MNC）

民族中心型跨国公司（ethnocentric MNC）

多元中心型跨国公司（polycentric MNC）

区域中心型跨国公司（regiocentric MNC）

全球中心型跨国公司（geocentric MNC）

天生全球化企业（born-global firm）

渐进型跨国公司（incremental MNC）

数字型跨国公司（digital MNC）

信息与通信技术跨国公司（ICT MNC）

轻资产指数（asset-light index）

小结（Summary）

1. The names of transnational corporations include international corporations, multinational corporations, global corporations, etc. In this book, "multinational corporations" are used to refer to various transnational corporations. The definition of MNCs mainly includes structural criteria, business performance criteria, and United Nations criteria.

2. MNCs can be classified into resource-oriented MNCs, manufacturing-oriented MNCs, and service-oriented MNCs based on their business content; classified by business structure, they can be divided into horizontal MNCs, vertical MNCs, and mixed MNCs; according to the classification of decision-making centers, they can be divided into ethnocentric MNCs, polycentric MNCs, regiocentric MNCs, and geocentric MNCs; classified by internationalization model, they can be divided into born-global firms and incremental MNCs; classified by digital intensity, they can be divided into digital MNCs, ICT MNCs, and traditional MNCs. The characteristics of MNCs include: business scale can be large or small, competitive strategies are flexible and diverse, development speed is accelerating, and the global mindset is becoming stronger.

3. MNCs are not universally present in any society, but are products of a society characterized by socialized mass production and market economy. The period before World War I is commonly referred to as the embryonic stage of MNCs. During the two world wars, American MNCs made significant progress, with an increase in the proportion of global FDI flowing to developing countries and diversification of cross-border business operations. After World War II, American MNCs dominated, but in recent years, BRICs countries and emerging market MNCs represented by Chinese MNCs have developed rapidly and gradually become important participants in the global market.

4. MNCs can have both positive and negative effects. Positive effects include transferring capital, spreading technology, creating job opportunities, increasing taxation, and promoting growth; negative effects include market monopoly, deterioration of

income and expenditure, magnified risk, sovereignty erosion, and economic collapse.

延伸阅读（Further Readings）

习题（Exercises）

第二章
Chapter 2

跨国公司的对外直接投资
Foreign Direct Investment by Multinational Corporations

Learning Objectives

- To know the concept of foreign direct investment and its difference from foreign indirect investment
- To understand the motivation and prerequisite of foreign direct investment
- To recognize the different modes of foreign direct investment and their advantages and disadvantages
- To understand the different forms of legal organization of foreign direct investment

第一节　对外直接投资的含义
（The Concept of Foreign Direct Investment）

1. Definition of foreign direct investment

资本的国际流动就是国际投资。站在某个特定国家或企业的立场上,资本跨越国界从一经济体流出也称为对外投资。国际投资可分为对外直接投资和对外间接投资两种基本方式。对外间接投资也称国际间接投资、对外证券投资或国际金融投资,是指一国投资者不以获得国外企业经营管理权为核心,为获得资本增值或实施对外援助与开发而进行的国际证券投资和中长期国际资本借贷活动。对外直接投资又称国际直接投资、跨国直接投资或海外直接投资,是指一国投资者以获得国外企业经营管理权或控制权为核心,投入资金、技术等有形或无形的资产,在另一国设立企业从事生产经营活动的投资行为。一般认为,控制权是指投资者在直接投资企业中拥有股权数量在 10% 或以上,享有表决权并在企业经营管理中拥有发言权。

The international flow of capital is international investment, which refers to the outflow of capital from an economy across national borders from the perspective of a specific country or enterprise, also known as foreign investment. International investment can be divided into two basic forms: foreign direct investment (FDI) and foreign indirect investment (FII). Foreign indirect investment, also known as overseas indirect investment, foreign portfolio investment or international financial investment, refers to the investment conducted by a country's investors without obtaining foreign enterprises' operating right as the core, but aiming to achieve capital appreciation or the implementation of foreign aid and development of international portfolio investment activities and medium-and long-term international capital borrowing and lending activities. Foreign direct investment, also known as transnational direct investment or overseas direct investment, refers to the investment behavior of an investor in one country who, with the right to operate or control a foreign enterprise as its core, invests tangible or intangible assets such as capital and technology to set up an enterprise in another country to engage in production and business activities. Generally, control here means that the investor owns 10% or more of the equity in the direct investment enterprise, enjoys voting rights and has a say in the management of the enterprise.

Both the International Monetary Fund (IMF) in the sixth edition of the *Balance of Payments Manual* and the Organization for Economic Co-operation and Development (OECD) in the fourth edition of the definition of FDI agree that FDI reflects the objective of establishing a lasting interest by a resident enterprise in one economy (direct investor) in an enterprise (direct investment enterprise) that is resident in an economy other than that of the direct investor. The lasting interest implies the existence of a long-term relationship between the direct investor and the direct investment enterprise and a significant degree of influence on the management of the enterprise. The director indirect ownership of 10% or more of the voting power of an enterprise resident in one economy by an investor resident in another economy is evidence of such a relationship. The ownership of at least 10% of the voting power of the enterprise is regarded as the necessary evidence that the investor has sufficient influence to have an effective voice in its management.

跨国公司的国际投资往往采用对外直接投资的形式。相对仅有货币资本流动的对外间接投资而言，跨国公司的国际投资通常伴随着除了货币资本以外的生产技术、管理经验等要素流动，从而实现对世界市场以及全球资源的有效控制以及国际直接投资长期利益的获取。

International investment by MNCs often takes the form of FDI. Compared to FII that only involves the flow of monetary capital, international investment by MNCs is usually accompanied by the flow of factors such as production technology and managerial experience in addition to monetary capital, so as to achieve effective control over world markets and global resources and to reap the long-term benefits of international direct investment.

对外直接投资有三组重要概念：一是水平投资与垂直投资；二是投资流量与投资存量；三是外资流入和对外投资。

There are three important sets of terms for FDI. The first is horizontal FDI and vertical FDI. The second is FDI flows and FDI stocks. The last is inward FDI and outward FDI.

FDI can be divided into horizontal FDI and vertical FDI according to the production chain invested by investors. When an enterprise replicates its production activities in its home country in the host country through FDI, it is called horizontal FDI, which is generally used in industries such as machinery manufacturing. When the enterprise in the host country moves upstream or downstream in different production segments through FDI, it is called vertical FDI. If the enterprise invests in upstream activities of its own production in the host country, it is called upstream vertical FDI. If it invests in downstream activities of its own production in the host country, it is called downstream vertical FDI. Vertical FDI activities are mostly found in industries such as automobiles.

FDI flows and FDI stocks are two terms commonly used when discussing international direct investment. The flow of FDI refers to the amount of FDI undertaken over a given time period (usually one year), while the stock of FDI refers to the total accumulated value of foreign-owned assets at a given time.

Inward FDI and outward FDI are the FDI regarded from different directions. Inward FDI, also known as inflows of FDI, are the flows of FDI into a country. On the contrary, outward FDI, also known as outflows of FDI, are the flows of FDI out of a country.

2. Characteristics of FDI

(1) Establishment of physical enterprises

FDI is a major form of long-term capital flow, which requires investors to establish physical enterprise operating institutions in the host country and have direct contact with local customers, intermediaries, and governments. Investors not only have partial or full ownership of the invested enterprise, but also have control over the operation of the enterprise and directly participate in its management.

(2) More resource inputs

FDI requires greater resource investment, not only manifested in the international transfer of assets, but also in the international flow of capital with operating rights. Specifically, the investment includes capital production technology, business skills, and so on. There are both physical investments and monetary investments.

(3) Optimal location selection

FDI enables enterprise managers to invest in countries with unique comparative advantages to achieve global scale efficiency of the enterprise through effective allocation of production and operation links, to minimize production and operation costs, and to enhance enterprise performance.

(4) Greater risks

Compared to domestic investment, FDI faces greater risks and uncertainties as it requires the establishment of corporate entities abroad and is subject to specific circumstances in the host country like national risks. At the same time, investors also need to face and deal with the special social and cultural factors that exist in the host country's market.

3. Differences between FDI and FII

Both FDI and FII are profit-oriented. However, as two different investment modes, they are different in the following aspects:

(1) Control rights over the operation of the foreign enterprise

对外直接投资与对外间接投资最根本的区别在于投资者能否有效地控制海外企业的经营管理权。对外直接投资要求能有效控制海外企业的经营管理权,而对外间接投资一般通过国际证券市场进行,以获得利息、股息等为主要目的,不直接参与企业经营,对海外企业的经营管理没有控制权。通常来说,以投资者拥有国外企业股份数量的 10% 作为区分是否有控制权的标准。当拥有股份数量不足 10% 时视为对外间接投资,达到或超过10% 时则为对外直接投资。

The most fundamental difference between FDI and FII lies in whether the investors can effectively control the operation and management of the foreign enterprise. Foreign direct investors can effectively control the operation and management of foreign enterprises, while indirect foreign investment is generally conducted through the international securities market, with the main purpose of obtaining interest, dividends, etc. FII does not directly participate in the operation of foreign enterprises and have no control over the operation and management of foreign enterprises. Generally speaking, the criterion for distinguishing whether an investor has control is based on owning 10% of the shares of a foreign company. When the number of shares owned is less than 10%, it is considered as indirect external investment, and when it reaches or exceeds 10%, it is considered as direct external investment.

(2) Complexity of the forms of capital movement

Compared with that of FII, the form of capital movement of FDI is more complex. FDI is the external expansion of enterprise production and business activities, which not only involves the international flow of monetary capital, but also includes the international transfer and output of tangible and intangible assets such as capital, labor, machinery and equipment, intellectual property, etc. , which is relatively complex. FII, on the other hand, manifests itself only in the flow and transfer of international monetary capital, and its form of capital movement is relatively simple.

(3) Forms of benefits

The main source of benefits from FDI is the profit of the foreign enterprise, which varies with the operating conditions of the enterprise. Therefore, the income from FDI is mostly floating. However, the main benefits of FII are interest and dividends, which are relatively fixed.

（4）Risks for investors

Compared with FII, FDI carries greater risks. Because investors in FDI directly participate in the production and operation activities of enterprises, they are closely related to specific projects, whose cycle is generally long, resulting in a longer FDI cycle, and most of the returns from FDI are also floating. In addition, there are other unpredictable factors making FDI more risky. The investment cycle of FII is relatively short, and the returns are relatively fixed, making the risk of FII relatively small.

4. Sources of capital for FDI

随着跨国公司的发展，外商直接投资的资金来源渠道越来越多。在充分考虑融资成本、融资风险、东道国资本市场及相关政策法规之后，才能对合适的资金来源渠道做出判断和选择。跨国公司对外直接投资的资金来源通常可以分为内部融资和外部融资两大类。

With the development of MNCs, there are increasingly more sources of capital for FDI. Only after fully considering financing costs, financing risks, host country capital markets, and relevant policies and regulations can appropriate capital sources be judged and selected. Generally, the sources of capital for FDI by MNCs can be divided into two categories: internal financing and external financing.

（1）Internal financing

Internal financing is the accumulation of funds from within the MNCs and the use of profits after the distribution of dividends by the company and depreciation charges for investment. It mainly includes the following forms: share-raising, in which the parent company makes capital flow to the foreign subsidiary by purchasing its shares; lending by the parent company to the foreign subsidiary through its own capital or by the bank; mobilization of capital from other foreign subsidiaries; reinvestment of the profits of the foreign subsidiary, etc.

（2）External financing

External financing is financing from channels outside the MNC system, which are as follows. The first is financing in the home country. This financing channel covers issuing stocks and bonds in the home country's financial market, obtaining loans from government agencies, commercial banks and other financial institutions in the home country, and obtaining trade credits, special funds, etc., from the home country's government or other organizations. The second is financing in the host country. It includes issuing all kinds of securities in the financial market of the host country, obtaining all kinds of loans from the financial institutions of the host country, and obtaining funds from the assistance projects of the host country from the home country. The last is financing in the international financial market. For example, raise funds in the name of the home country in the third country, issue bonds in the international financial market, and obtain loans from international financial institutions.

第二节 对外直接投资的动因与条件
（The Motivation and Prerequisite of FDI）

1. Motivation of FDI

企业对外直接投资的动机有很多。著名国际商务学者约翰·邓宁将其归纳为四种类型,即资源寻求型、市场寻求型、效率寻求型以及战略资产寻求型,并且认为资源寻求型和市场寻求型是企业初始对外直接投资的两个必要动机,效率寻求型和战略资产寻求型是现有对外直接投资增长的主要方式,其目的在于促进企业区域或全球战略一体化。

There are many motivations for enterprises to conduct FDI. John Dunning, a renowned international business scholar, classified FDI motivation into four types, namely resource-seeking, market-seeking, efficiency-seeking, and strategic asset-seeking. Dunning argued that resource-seeking and market-seeking are two necessary motivations for initial FDI, while efficiency-seeking and strategic asset-seeking are main modalities for the growth of contemporary FDI, with the purpose of facilitating the integration of regional or global strategies of enterprises. Dunning also summarized the kind of variables that influenced the location decisions of MNCs in the 1970s and 1990s and, in doing so, completed the above classification of FDI motivation.

（1）Resource-seeking FDI

Resource-seeking FDI refers to investment made by MNCs in search of foreign resources of lower cost and better quality than those actually available at home. Resources include natural material resources, human resources, asset resources and information resources, and so on. According to MNCs' demand for resources, resource-seeking FDI can be mainly divided into three categories: FDI in natural resources like raw materials from abroad, driven by the motives of cost minimization and security of resource supply sources; FDI in resources like abundant and inexpensive labor force from abroad due to high cost of home country labor; FDI in resources such as technological know-how and management know-how from abroad due to demand for technological capabilities and marketing skills.

（2）Market-seeking FDI

Market-seeking FDI refers to the investment made by MNCs to develop or further expand their market share in the host country. There are several reasons for market-seeking FDI. First, the MNCs have to bypass tariff and non-tariff barriers in the host country's market and continue to serve it, replacing export trade. Second, the MNCs would like to get closer to upstream raw material or intermediate product suppliers and provide intermediate products or better services to downstream companies, following upstream and downstream enterprises to enter the host country. Third, the MNCs enter into host countries to better understand consumer preferences and thus better satisfy consumer demand in host countries. Fourth, FDI is made in the host country due to lower production and transaction costs compared to long-distance supply costs. Lastly, for the strategic purpose of global production and operation, the MNCs conduct FDI in the main markets where major competitors provide services.

（3）Efficiency-seeking FDI

效率寻求型FDI是指跨国公司为提高效率而进行的对外直接投资。跨国公司对已经实施的对外直接投资进行区域性或全球性的战略、效率投资调整，以使其全球性的生产经营网络更加合理。专业化跨国生产、各类资源的合理配置以及生产经营区位在全球范围内的优化提升了效率，使得跨国公司能够从规模经济、范围经济和风险分散中获利。

Efficiency-seeking FDI refers to FDI made by MNCs to improve their efficiency. MNCs make regional or global strategy and efficiency investment adjustments to their already implemented FDI in order to make their global production and operation networks more rational. Specialized cross-border production, the rational allocation of various types of resources and the optimization of production and operation locations on a global scale have enhanced efficiency, enabling MNCs to benefit from economies of scale, economies of scope and risk diversification. Efficiency-seeking FDI is divided into two main categories. One is FDI based on differences in the availability of traditional factor endowments and cost differences between countries. Another is FDI in countries with similar economic structures and income levels based on economies of scale and scope, as well as differences in consumer preferences and supply capacity.

（4）Strategic asset-seeking FDI

战略性资产主要包括研究与开发能力、商标和营销网络等，是对企业生存和长远发展具有战略意义的资源。战略资产寻求型FDI是指跨国公司通过收购境外公司资产进行的对外直接投资。其主要动机是通过升级收购方企业的全球资产组合，获取难以从外部市场获得或内部形成也需要较长时间的战略性资产，以维持或加强跨国公司所有权优势，从而推进跨国公司维持或提升全球竞争力的长期战略目标。这些收购多发生在电信、电子产品和商业服务等领域。

Strategic assets, which mainly include research and development capabilities, trademarks and marketing networks, are resources of strategic importance for the survival and long-term development of enterprises. Strategic asset-seeking FDI refers to FDI conducted by MNCs through the acquisition of assets of foreign firms. The main motive is to upgrade the acquirer's global asset portfolio, acquire strategic assets that are difficult to obtain from the external market or consuming a long time to form internally, and maintain or strengthen the investor's ownership advantage, so as to advance the MNCs' long-term strategic goal of maintaining or enhancing global competitiveness. These acquisitions tend to take place in industries such as telecommunications, electronics and business services.

2. Prerequisites of FDI

邓宁认为，只有当企业同时具备所有权优势、内部化优势以及区位优势时，才会对外直接投资。所有权优势是指企业独占无形资产和拥有规模经济所形成的优势；内部化优势是指企业为避免不完全市场给企业带来的影响将其资产或所有权内部化而拥有的优势；区位优势是指东道国在投资环境方面所拥有的优势，如东道国要素禀赋、政治法律制度等。

According to Dunning, only when a company has ownership advantages, internalization advantages, and location advantages at the same time, will it make FDI. [①]Ownership advantage refers to the advantage formed by enterprises monopolizing intangible assets and possessing economies of scale. Internalization advantage refers to the advantage that an enterprise possesses by internalizing its assets or ownership in order to avoid the impact of incomplete markets on the enterprise. Location advantage refers to the advantage that the host country possesses in terms of investment environment, such as the host country's resource endowment, political and legal system and so on.

Dunning believes that, "at any given moment of time, the more a country's enterprises possess specific ownership advantages, relative to enterprises of other nationalities, the greater the incentive they have to internalize rather than externalize their use; and the more they find it in their interest to exploit them from a foreign location, the more they (and the country as a whole) are likely to engage in FDI."[②]

当企业仅拥有所有权优势和内部化优势时，表明企业缺乏有利的投资场所，应当采取出口方式进入国际市场；当企业仅有所有权优势而无内部化优势和区位优势时，则表明企业拥有的无形资产优势无法内部应用，只能采取许可协议方式进入国际市场。

When a company only has ownership advantages and internalization advantages, it indicates that the company lacks favorable investment locations and should adopt an export approach to enter the international market. When a company only has ownership advantages without internalization and location advantages, it indicates that the intangible asset advantages the company possesses cannot be applied internally and that it can only enter the international market through licensing agreements. The available routes for the enterprise servicing markets are shown in Table 2-1.

Table 2-1　Available routes of servicing markets

		Advantages		
		Ownership	Internalization	(Foreign) Location
Routes of servicing markets	FDI	Yes	Yes	Yes
	Export	Yes	Yes	No
	Contractual resource transfers	Yes	No	No

Source: Dunning, J. H. (1981), Explaining the international direct investment position of countries: towards a dynamic or developmental approach. *Weltwirtschaftliches Archiv*, 117(1): 30-64.

---

① Dunning, J. H. (1979), Explaining changing patterns of international production: in defense of the eclectic theory. *Oxford Bulletin of Economics and Statistics*, 41(4): 269-295.

② Dunning, J. H. (1981), Explaining the international direct investment position of countries: towards a dynamic or developmental approach. *Weltwirtschaftliches Archiv*, 117(1): 30-64.

著名华人学者陆亚东认为,在数字时代,企业拥有的传统的所有权优势、内部化优势以及区位优势被弱化,而开放资源优势、链接优势及整合优势等新型优势得到增强。当跨国公司同时具备并利用这三种新优势时,能够使企业对外投资活动更有效率。[①]

The famous Chinese scholar Lu argues that, in the digital era, the traditional ownership advantage, internalization advantage, and location advantage of enterprises have been weakened, while new advantages such as open resource advantage, linkage advantage, and integration advantage have been enhanced. When MNCs simultaneously possess and utilize these three new advantages, they can make FDI activities more efficient.

第三节 对外直接投资的方式(Modes of FDI)

根据不同的标准,FDI 进入模式可分为独资和非独资、参股和非参股、绿地投资和跨境并购,如图 2-1 所示。

Based on different criteria, FDI entry modes can be divided into sole proprietorship and non-sole proprietorship, equity participation and non-equity participation, greenfield investment as well as cross-border mergers and acquisitions, as shown in Figure 2-1.

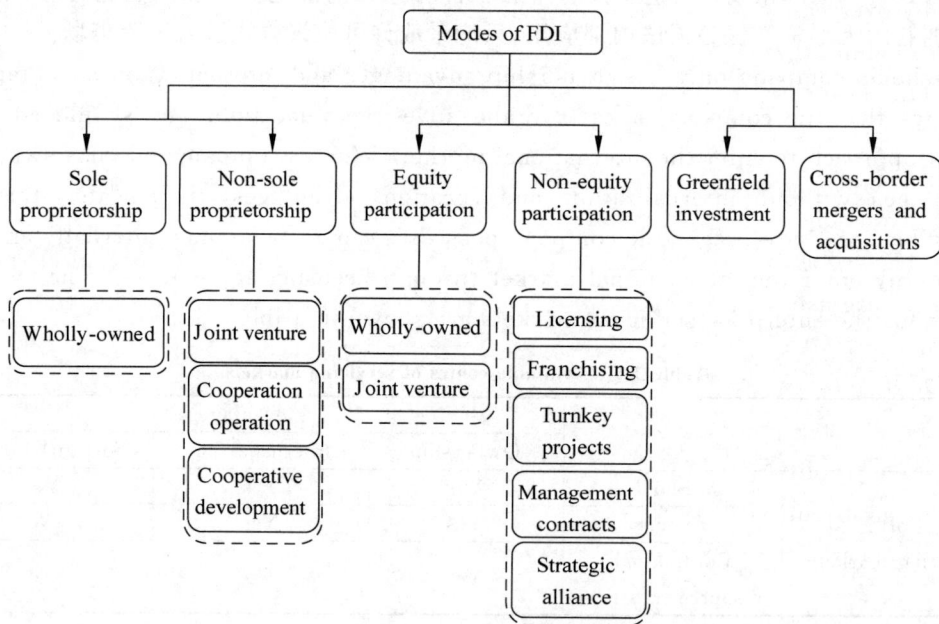

Figure 2-1　Modes of FDI

---

① Lu, Y. (2021), New OLI Advantages in Digital Globalization. *International Business Review*, 30(2): 101797.

1. Sole proprietorship and non-sole proprietorship

（1）Sole proprietorship entry mode

The sole proprietorship mode of entry is a way for MNCs to enter foreign markets by establishing, in accordance with the laws and policies of the host country and with the approval of the host country, a separate enterprise in the host country whose entire capital is owned by the MNC, which operates independently and is self-supporting. There are two main ways for MNCs to set up wholly owned overseas subsidiaries. One is to operate a new investment project in the host country, and the other is to implement mergers and acquisitions of the host country's companies.

There are several advantages of the sole proprietorship entry mode. First, it protects the firm's technological and commercial secrets, thus maintaining its competitive advantage in the host market. Second, MNCs have complete control over overseas wholly-owned subsidiaries, enabling them to make global strategic deployments and reduce internal conflicts and tensions. Third, under the global strategy of MNCs, it is possible for a country's overseas wholly-owned subsidiaries to specialize in producing certain components of the product line or final products, thereby achieving location and experience curve economy. Fourth, MNCs are able to independently control the profits earned by overseas wholly-owned subsidiaries in the host country.

Meanwhile, there are also some disadvantages of the sole proprietorship entry mode. On the one hand, it involves high capital investment and costs. On the other hand, it is subject to greater political and economic risks, and the MNCs have to bear the full costs and risks of the operation of the wholly owned subsidiaries.

（2）Non-sole proprietorship entry mode

非独资经营通常包括三种形式：合资经营、合作经营和合作开发。

There are usually three forms of non-sole proprietorship entry mode including joint venture operation, cooperation operation and cooperative development.

Joint venture is a business model in which MNCs, in accordance with relevant laws of the host country, jointly invest with host country enterprises, jointly operate, share risks, share profits and losses, and jointly share equity and management rights. Advantages of joint venture are as follows. Firstly, the participation of local enterprises makes it easier for the joint venture to be accepted by the host country consumers, obtain preferential treatment and reduce and avoid political risks like confiscation by the host country government. Secondly, it gives full play to the advantages of each investor in terms of capital, technology and sales, etc., and form a portfolio advantage. Shortcomings of joint ventures are as follows. Due to the dispersion of equity and management rights, the long-term and short-term interests of each investor are not consistent, and differences and contradictions are likely to arise in joint management, which is not conducive to the implementation of a unified and coordinated global strategy by MNCs. For those investors who have technological advantages, there is a risk of technology loss to the partner, which will be cultivated into a competitor in the future.

Cooperation operation refers to the mode of operation and cooperation in which MNCs and host country investors set up a cooperative economic organization in the host country in accordance with the laws of the host country on the basis of a signed contract, and the rights and obligations of each investor are stipulated in the contract through consultation between the parties. The cooperative economic organization set up by the cooperation is a contractual joint venture, which carries out investment, operation, management, profit distribution and risk bearing on the basis of the contract. It is generally consistent with joint ventures in terms of advantages and disadvantages, but due to its contractual provisions as the basis for cooperation among all parties, it can be more flexible in determining the form of the enterprise and can adapt to the needs of various investors.

Cooperative development refers to a mode of business cooperation in which a host country with natural resources makes use of MNCs' investment in the joint exploration and development of the country's natural resources by sharing risks and profits. Cooperative development applies to the development and production projects of large-scale natural resources such as oil, natural gas and coal. The host country of the resource owner takes the resources as the input for cooperation, the MNCs take capital, equipment and technology as the input for cooperation, and both parties share the profits according to the provisions of the contract. Compared with joint venture and cooperation operation, cooperative development involves the development and utilization of natural resources in the host country. It is therefore subject to strict management by the host country, and requires a large amount of investment capital, resulting in higher investment risks. At the same time, however, MNCs will also gain higher profits from successful exploration.

2. Equity and non-equity participation

(1) Equity participation

Equity participation refers to the direct investment method in which MNCs hold equity shares in their overseas subsidiaries based on ownership, and achieve effective control over the subsidiaries or projects through shareholding and control of the subsidiaries' operating rights. There are several forms of equity investment in MNCs, which include setting up a branch or a sale agency, establishing a processing and assembly plant, setting up a wholly-owned subsidiary or a joint venture. Among them, the wholly-owned subsidiary and joint venture are the two basic forms of equity investment.

Large MNCs in major developed countries tend to establish overseas subsidiaries as wholly-owned enterprises in order to exercise effective control over their subsidiaries, maintain their technological monopoly, operational decisions, product quality and trademark reputation, and thus maximize their overall profitability. The equity participation of joint ventures is mostly used to satisfy the requirements of developing host countries, thus reducing the political risk of MNC investment.

Compared with non-equity participation, on the one hand, equity participation allows MNCs to control their overseas subsidiaries more simply and effectively through equity without having to participate in all operational matters, thus reducing the burden on the enterprise. On the other hand, MNCs are able to flexibly choose the proportion of their equity participation and specific modes of participation in order to satisfy the development needs of the MNCs themselves and the host country's requirements.

（2）Non-equity participation

自 20 世纪 70 年代以来，非股权参与方式逐渐被广泛采用，主要是跨国公司为了应对发展中国家的国有化政策和外资逐步退出政策而采取的一种策略。非股权参与是指跨国公司依据东道国法律和政策，为东道国企业提供与股权没有直接联系的生产技术、管理咨询和销售渠道等，以取得某种程度的实际控制权进而实现本公司的经营目标的投资方式。相对于股权参与方式，跨国公司采取非股权参与的投资方式，虽然没有获得股权，但通过技术等优势也能够对东道国企业产生重要影响，因而跨国公司对东道国企业的控制程度没有降低，且能够降低经营风险并从中获取利润。非股权参与方式的具体形式很多，包括许可经营、特许经营、交钥匙工程、管理合同、战略联盟等。

Since the 1970s, non-equity participation has gradually been widely used, mainly as a strategy adopted by MNCs in response to the nationalization policy and the gradual exit of foreign capital from developing countries. Non-equity participation refers to the investment mode in which MNCs, in accordance with the laws and policies of the host country, provide host country enterprises with production technology, management consultancy and sales channels that are not directly linked to equity in order to gain a certain degree of actual control and achieve the company's business objectives. Compared with the equity participation mode, MNCs taking non-equity participation mode can also have an important impact on the host country enterprise through technology and other advantages though with no equity. As a result, the control of MNCs on the host country enterprise has not been reduced. In the meantime, it can reduce the business risk and benefit MNCs. Non-equity participation can take many forms, including licensing, franchising, turnkey project, management contract and strategic alliance.

Licensing, also known as a license contract, refers to a contractual form in which the technology licensor grants the technology licensee the right to use a certain technology, manufacture or sell a product for a specific period of time, and the technology licensee pays a certain royalty or usage fee. Usually, the transfer involves the right to use intangible assets rather than ownership. The advantages of a license agreement are as follows. Firstly, there is no need for MNCs to bear the high costs and risks in developing overseas markets. Generally, the licensee bears the necessary funds for overseas operations. Secondly, it reduces the risks brought by political instability in foreign markets to some extent. Finally, it helps MNCs to bypass investment barriers in foreign markets. The license agreement also has some shortcomings. Firstly, the licensee usually establishes its own manufacturing department, making it difficult for the licensor to realize the experience curve economy and regional economic benefits generated by centralized manufacturing. Secondly, if the licensee cannot allow the licensor to take away their own profits to support other licensees engaged in business activities in another country, the licensor cannot coordinate strategic actions between different countries. Thirdly, the licensor's authorization of technical know-how carries certain risks and may cultivate future competitors.

Franchising is essentially a special form of licensing, whereby an enterprise that has already achieved success in its operations not only transfers the right to use its intangible assets, such as trademarks, to the franchisee, but also insists that the franchisee agrees to abide strictly by the rules of how the enterprise will conduct its business and thereby expand its product sales or obtain royalty income. In other words, the franchiser transfers the full package of operation to the franchisee rather than a specific item such as the patent, trademark, or know-how. License agreements are mainly used in manufacturing businesses, whereas franchising is mainly used in service-based businesses, like McDonald's. The advantages of franchising and licensing agreements are relatively similar. Franchising reduces the costs and risks of entry into a foreign market and allows the franchisor to enter the target market in a shorter time. The disadvantages of franchising are the limited profitability of the franchisor, the lack of control over the franchisee and the possibility of fostering future competitors.

Turnkey project means that an MNC builds a factory or undertakes other engineering projects for the host country, and once the design, construction and testing of the production facilities are completed, the "key" of the ownership and management of the factory or project will be "handed over" to the user party in accordance with the contract, and the user party will take over to operate the plant or project. Once the contract is completed, the user party will get the "key" of all ready plant with normal production. Turnkey projects are also the means for MNCs to export process technology to other countries, and are mostly used in industries such as chemicals, oil refining and metal processing. The advantage of turnkey projects is that both contracting parties are able to fully exploit and profit from their core strengths. Particularly when FDI is regulated in the host country, MNCs are able to reap the rewards of know-how through turnkey projects, while user parties receive infrastructure projects designed for them by world-class firms. In addition, turnkey projects are less risky than traditional FDI. The disadvantages of turnkey projects are, on the one hand, the lack of long-term interest in the foreign market on the part of the enterprise adopting the turnkey project, which makes it less sustainable in the long term, and on the other hand, the fact that the turnkey project completes the contract through the sale of the technology, which may result in the flow of the process technology to a potential competitor, thus creating a capable competitor.

A management contract is a contract whereby a MNC with managerial advantages provides comprehensive management services to a host country enterprise without equity participation, and provides the services and receives the corresponding remuneration as stipulated in the contract for the duration of the contract. The management contract gives the MNC the right to manage the daily operations of the target enterprise abroad, either for the enterprise's entire business activities or only for a part of the target enterprise's activities or functions. By entering into a management contract, the MNC participates in and controls the production and operation of the target enterprise in the host country. Management contracts are mostly used in the service sector and are also more common in the public utility sector in developed and emerging market countries. The advantages of management contracts are that the provision of export management services by MNCs is conducive to the enterprises' understanding of the host country's market situation, expanding their influence in the host country's market, and that they carry lower business risks than investments in tangible assets. In addition, management contracts are conducive to upgrading the skills of workers and managers in host country firms. Management contracts in the public utility sector are conducive to upgrading public facilities in the host country. The main disadvantage of management contracts is that the recipient of the service is a similar enterprise, which tends to foster potential competitors.

A strategic alliance is a loose cooperative and competitive organization formed through various agreements between two or more enterprises in order to obtain their own sustainable competitive advantage in the market, achieve the purpose of common ownership of the market, cooperation in research, development and sharing of resources, and so on, and share the same advantages and risks. The strategic alliance focuses on "strategy" and does not take the pursuit of short-term profit maximization as its primary purpose, but is a strategic activity in line with the long-term plan of the enterprise. The strategic alliance of MNCs, also known as transnational strategic alliance, refers to the co-operative relationship established by two or more MNCs from different countries to achieve a certain strategic goal. Advantages of strategic alliance are as follows. First, it can share the cost of international investment and reduce risks and uncertainties. Second, it can provide firms with access to complementary assets and skills as well as learning opportunities that they would not be able to develop on their own. Third, it can provide access to different suppliers and distribution channels, which facilitate access to foreign markets. Fourth, it can help firms to set up useful industrial and technological standards. For the shortcomings of strategic alliances, on the one hand, in an alliance setting, the trust element of the partnership may be abused and the tendency of the collaborators to be more opportunistic is stronger; on the other hand, the alliance makes it easier for the collaborators to observe and imitate the firm's unique capabilities, with the risk of fostering competitors.

3. Greenfield investment as well as cross-border mergers and acquisitions

（1）Greenfield investment

绿地投资又称新建投资,是指跨国公司依照东道国法律或相关政策,在东道国境内出资设立全部或部分资产所有权归属外国投资者所有的企业的投资行为。绿地投资一般有两种形式:一是外国投资者投入全部资本,建立拥有全部控制权的独资企业;二是由外国投资者和东道国投资者共同出资,建立合资企业。

Greenfield investment, also known as new construction investment, refers to the investment behavior of an MNC that, in accordance with the laws or relevant policies of the host country, contributes to the establishment of an enterprise in the host country whose ownership of all or part of the assets belongs to the foreign investor. Greenfield investment generally has two forms. First, foreign investors put in all the capital to establish a wholly-owned enterprise with full control. Second, foreign investors and host country investors jointly fund the establishment of joint ventures.

Advantages of greenfield investment are as follows. First, greenfield investment can promote the host country's production capacity, employment and output growth, and is less likely to be restricted by the host country's laws and policies, and less likely to be resisted by local public. Second, compared with the acquisition of overseas enterprises, the procedures for establishing a new overseas enterprise are more simple. Third, enterprises set up by greenfield investment, especially joint ventures, often enjoy the preferential policies of the host country. Fourth, greenfield investment can accurately estimate the capital required for investment, and there is no problem of integration after the acquisition of the enterprise. Fifth, greenfield investment helps MNCs to select the production scale and investment location in line with their global strategic objectives.

Disadvantages of greenfield investment include the follows. First, greenfield investment has a long construction period, slow speed, lack of flexibility, and higher requirements on the financial strength of MNCs, which is not conducive to the rapid development of MNCs. Second, in the process of creating an enterprise, MNCs bear all the risks of greenfield investment, and there is a greater degree of uncertainty about the prospects for future revenues and profits. Third, after the creation of a new enterprise, MNCs need to develop the target market by themselves, which is not conducive to the rapid entry into the host country's market. Fourth, there is the possibility that competitors may seize the market through mergers and acquisitions and establish a strong market position, thus restricting the market potential of the newly established enterprise. Fifth, greenfield investment is adverse to the rapid cross-industry operation of MNCs and rapid diversification of products and services.

（2）Cross-border mergers and acquisitions

跨境并购是跨境兼并和跨境收购的总称，是指跨国公司为了达到某种目标，通过一定法律程序取得东道国目标企业全部或部分所有权的投资行为。其中，跨境兼并是指在东道国将当地或国外企业的资产及经营业务并入一家新的或已经存在的企业；跨境收购是指收购东道国当地或国外企业的资产或股份并获得占有与控制权。

Cross-border mergers and acquisitions（M&A）is a general term for cross-border mergers and cross-border acquisitions, which refers to the MNCs' investment behavior of acquiring all or part of the ownership of a target enterprise in the host country to achieve a certain goal through certain legal procedures. Among them, a cross-border merger refers to merging the assets and business operations of a local or foreign enterprise into a new or existing enterprise in the host country; a cross-border acquisition refers to acquiring the assets or shares of a local or foreign enterprise in the host country and obtaining the right of possession and control.

Advantages of cross-border M&A are as follows. Firstly, utilizing the target company's existing production equipment, technical personnel and skilled workers to acquire intangible assets such as technology, patents, and trademarks that are useful for the development of the acquiring company. At the same time, it can greatly shorten the project construction cycle and quickly establish business in the host country market. Secondly, by utilizing the existing sales channels of the target enterprise, it can quickly enter the local and foreign markets without going through the market development stage. Thirdly, through cross-border M&A, it can seize the first opportunity in the market and reduce competitors in the market. Fourthly, compared with greenfield investment, the risk of M&A is smaller. Fifthly, through cross-industry M&A, it can rapidly expand the scope of operation and location, increase the mode of operation, and promote the diversification of products and the expansion of the scale of production.

Disadvantages of cross-border M&A are as follows. First, it's hard for the MNCs to accurately assess the real situation of the acquired enterprise, which leads to the increase of the actual investment amount of the M&A target enterprise. Second, the relevant laws and policies of the host country may impose restrictions on the cross-border M&A activities. Third, the cross-border M&A activities will be boycotted by local public when the number and amount of the activities are too large. Fourth, the existence of the original contractual or traditional relationship of the acquired enterprise will hinder the post-M&A transformation. Fifth, there is the problem of post-merger integration.

第四节 对外直接投资的法律形式
(Forms of Legal Organization of FDI)

1. Parent company

母公司又称总公司,是指通过拥有其他公司一定数量的股权或通过协议方式能够实际控制、支配其他公司的人事、财务、业务等事项,并使其他公司成为自己的附属公司的公司。国际上也将母公司称为控股公司,但母公司不等同于只掌握股权而不从事业务经营的纯控股公司,而是指本身也经营其他业务活动,是独立法人,有自己的管理体系的混合控股公司或控股兼营业公司。母公司通过制定总的方针、政策、战略等对其世界各地的分支机构进行管理。

A parent company, also known as headquarters, refers to a company that can actually control and dominate the personnel, finance, business and other matters of other companies by owning a certain amount of equity in other companies or through agreements, and make other companies as its own subsidiaries. Internationally, the parent company is also referred to as a holding company, but the parent company is not equivalent to a pure holding company that only holds equity and does not engage in business operations. Instead, it refers to a mixed holding company or a holding and operating company that also operates other business activities, which is an independent legal entity, and has its own management system. The parent company manages its branches around the world by formulating general guidelines, policies and strategies. Parent companies have the following legal characteristics. First, the parent company actually controls the operational and management rights of the subsidiary company. Second, the parent company exercises control over the subsidiary through equity participation or non-equity arrangements. Third, the parent company has limited liability for the subsidiary to the extent of its capital contribution.

2. Branch company

A branch company of an MNC is a branch or affiliate of the parent company, which has no legal personality and is not legally or economically independent, but is only an integral part of the parent company. A branch company has the same legal entity as the parent company. A branch established in the host country is regarded as a "foreign company" and is not protected by local laws, but by the diplomatic protection of the home country. When a branch company withdraws from the host country, it can only sell its assets and cannot transfer its equity or merge with other companies. The legal characteristics of the branch company are as follows. Firstly, the branch company does not have legal personality and cannot assume responsibility independently, and all the consequences of its actions and responsibilities are borne by the parent company. Secondly, the branch company is authorized by the parent company to carry out its business, and it can only use the name and statute of the parent company. Finally, all the assets of the branch company belong to the parent company, and it does not have any independent property. A branch company is included in the parent company's balance sheet as an asset of the parent company, and the parent company has unlimited liability for the debts of the branch.

The advantages of setting up a branch include the following. Firstly, the establishment procedures are relatively simple, and only a small registration fee is required to obtain the business license of the country where it is located. Secondly, a branch company can enjoy the tax benefits because the subsidiary and the parent company belong to the same legal entity, so they pay less taxes abroad compared to the subsidiary. In addition, many countries' tax laws stipulate that if a foreign branch incurs losses, the amount of the losses can be deducted from the parent company's pre-tax profits, and the profits remitted by the foreign branch are generally not treated as dividends and are subject to profit remittance tax. Thirdly, a branch company is relatively easy to manage. The parent company can exercise comprehensive and direct leadership and control over the business activities of the branch company by controlling its management personnel. Finally, a branch company is less regulated by the host country in some sense. The host country does not have legal jurisdiction over the property of the subsidiary outside the host country, and it is more convenient for the branch to transfer property outside the host country.

The disadvantages of establishing a branch company are as follows. From the perspective of the parent company, firstly, the branch company must disclose all business activities and financial income and expenditure status of the parent company when registering, which damages the confidentiality of the parent company's business. Secondly, the parent company bears unlimited liability for the debts of the branch company, which is detrimental to the parent company. Finally, when the branch company withdraws, it can only sell its assets and cannot merge with other companies, which is not conducive to the development of the parent company. From the perspective of the branch company, on the one hand, the business of the branch is dominated by the parent company, which is not conducive to the creative play of the branch. On the other hand, branch companies are considered "foreign companies" in the host country, which is not conducive to local business operations. From the perspective of the home country, establishing a foreign branch will reduce tax revenue and be detrimental to the home country.

3. Subsidiary company

Subsidiaries are companies that are registered and incorporated under local law and are owned by the parent company in a certain percentage of shares or are effectively controlled by means of an agreement. A subsidiary is a complete company in its own right. The parent company has a controlling relationship with the subsidiary, but the subsidiary can operate independently and with greater autonomy in its business. The subsidiary is considered as a local company upon registration in the host country, governed by the laws of the host country and not subject to diplomatic protection by the government of the parent company. Subsidiaries are subject to tax when they remit profits as dividends and interest in the host country.

The main legal characteristics of a subsidiary include the following. Firstly, the subsidiary has independent legal personality. Subsidiaries are economically controlled by the parent company, but are independent legal entities with independent company names and articles of association, independent property, and are responsible for their own profits and losses. They can publicly issue stocks and borrow independently, engage in various economic and civil activities in their own name, and independently assume all consequences and responsibilities arising from the company's actions. Secondly, the subsidiary is actually controlled by the parent company in terms of economy and business, and can determine and control the composition of the subsidiary's board of directors. Thirdly, the parent company exercises actual control over the subsidiary based on equity or non-equity arrangements such as dominant agreements.

Advantages of establishing subsidiaries are as follows. Firstly, subsidiaries are regarded as local companies in the host country and are subject to fewer restrictions, which facilitates the development of business. Secondly, subsidiaries can independently take out loans from banks in the host country, which makes financing more convenient. Thirdly, subsidiaries have a greater degree of autonomy in operation, and they can give full play to their creativity in management. Fourthly, subsidiaries can flexibly choose the mode of recovery of their investment in the event that they terminate their business in the host country. The fifth advantage is that establishing subsidiaries in international tax havens is beneficial for the parent company to carry out tax avoidance activities.

Disadvantages of establishing subsidiaries include the following. Firstly, subsidiaries are independent legal persons in the host country, and the establishment procedures are relatively complicated and expensive. Secondly, subsidiaries need to understand the laws and regulations of the host country and set up administrative organizations in accordance with the provisions of the host country's company law, which increases administrative costs. Finally, subsidiaries are required to disclose their financial status, which increases competitive pressure. For joint venture subsidiaries, their business activities will be constrained by the shareholders of the host country.

4. Liaison office

A liaison office is a primary form of overseas enterprise set up by a parent company. It is a non-legal entity set up to further open up overseas markets, which does not constitute an enterprise. Generally speaking, a liaison office is only engaged in collecting information, liaising with customers and promoting products, but not in investing in production, accepting loans, negotiating contracts and fulfilling obligations. Similar to a branch company, a liaison office is not an independent legal entity and its registration procedures are relatively simple. Different from a branch company, a liaison office cannot directly conduct business in the host country and is not required to pay income tax to the host government.

关键术语（Key Terms）

对外直接投资（foreign direct investment）

对外间接投资（foreign indirect investment）

水平型对外直接投资（horizontal FDI）

垂直型对外直接投资（vertical FDI）

对外直接投资流量（FDI flow）

对外直接投资存量（FDI stock）

外资流入（inward FDI）

对外投资（outward FDI）

资源寻求型对外直接投资（resource-seeking FDI）

市场寻求型对外直接投资（market-seeking FDI）

效率寻求型对外直接投资（efficiency-seeking FDI）

战略资产寻求型对外直接投资（strategic asset-seeking FDI）

所有权优势（ownership advantage）

内部化优势（internalization advantage）

区位优势（location advantage）

开放资源优势（open resource advantage）

链接优势（linkage advantage）

整合优势（integration advantage）

独资（sole proprietorship）

合资企业（joint venture）

合作经营（cooperation operation）

合作开发（cooperative development）

许可经营（licensing）

特许经营（franchising）

交钥匙工程（turnkey project）

管理合同（management contract）

战略联盟（strategic alliance）

绿地投资（greenfield investment）

跨境并购（cross-border mergers and acquisitions）

母公司（parent company）

分公司（branch company）

子公司（subsidiary company）

联络办事处（liaison office）

小结（Summary）

1. International investment can be divided into two basic modes: foreign direct investment and indirect investment, and the fundamental difference between the two is whether the investor is able to control the operation of the enterprise. In addition, there are differences in the complexity of the form of capital movement, the specific form of returns, and the risk of investment. There are three important sets of terms for FDI: horizontal FDI and vertical FDI; FDI flows and FDI stocks; inward FDI and outward FDI. FDI is characterized by the establishment of physical enterprises, greater input of resources, optimal choice of location and greater risk. There are two sources of funds for

FDI: internal financing and external financing.

2. The motivations of FDI include resource-seeking, market-seeking, efficiency-seeking, and strategic asset-seeking. The prerequisite of FDI is that the enterprise should possess ownership advantage, internalization advantage and location advantage at the same time. In the digital age, enterprises also need to have three new advantages: open resource advantage, linkage advantage and integration advantage.

3. Modes of FDI can be classified into sole proprietorship and non-sole proprietorship, equity participation and non-equity participation, greenfield investment as well as cross-border mergers and acquisitions based on different criteria. Among them, non-sole proprietorship mode includes joint venture, cooperation operation, and cooperative development. Equity participation includes sole proprietorship and joint ventures, while non-equity participation mainly includes licensing, franchising, turnkey projects, management contracts and strategic alliances. Different FDI modes have different advantages and disadvantages.

4. The legal organizational forms of FDI include four types: parent company, branch company, subsidiary company, and liaison office. Different forms of legal organizations have their own characteristics as well as advantages and disadvantages.

延伸阅读(Further Readings)

习题(Exercises)

第三章 Chapter 3

跨国公司对外直接投资理论
Theories of Foreign Direct Investment by Multinational Corporations

Learning Objectives
- To understand the key theories of FDI by MNCs from developed countries
- To identify the theories explaining FDI by MNCs from developing countries
- To recognize the theories of FDI by MNCs from emerging economies
- To know similarities and differences of FDI motivations and strategies of MNCs from developed, developing, and emerging markets

第一节　发达国家跨国公司对外直接投资理论
（Theories of FDI by MNCs from Developed Countries）

1. Monopolistic advantage theory

垄断优势理论由史蒂夫·海默于 1960 年在其麻省理工学院博士论文《国内企业的国际经营：一项对外直接投资的研究》中提出。海默认为，跨国公司进行对外直接投资的原因是，它们在技术、管理、市场等方面拥有垄断优势，这些优势使它们能够在东道国市场上与当地企业竞争并获利。该理论得到了海默的博士论文指导老师金德尔伯格的补充，认为跨国公司的优势包括商标、营销技巧、专利技术、融资渠道、管理技能和规模经济等，这些优势的产生源于市场不完全。这一理论解释了跨国公司为何能在国际市场上长期生存和发展。

The monopolistic advantage theory is a cornerstone of international business and economy. The basic premise behind the theory is that firms are better off investing abroad than for simply exporting or licensing their products. Proposed by Hymer (1960) in his MIT PhD dissertation and later expanded by his supervisor Kindleberger, this theory offers an explanation of the following questions. Why do MNCs move abroad? What are their intentions? When do they establish foreign operations? The monopolistic advantage theory explains why and how MNCs expand and use their market power advantages to compete in international markets.

(1) Origin and development

Monopolistic advantage theory was first proposed by Stephen H. Hymer (November 15, 1934-February 2, 1974), a Canadian economist who focused on the research of MNCs. Hymer proposed monopolistic advantage theory in response to traditional international trade theories, like those of Adam Smith and David Ricardo, which failed to explain why U. S. firms preferred FDI over other international strategies. In 1960, Hymer submitted his doctoral dissertation titled *The International Operations of National Firms: A Study of Direct Foreign Investment*, which is regarded as the first modern theory of MNCs. In the dissertation, he argued that firms engage in FDI to exploit specific advantages unavailable to competitors, enabling them to maintain a monopolistic position globally.

Hymer believed that there are two kinds of long-term private international capital movements—direct investment and portfolio investment. Not everyone makes the distinction in quite the same way, but there is a great deal of similarity, and basically it is a question of who controls the enterprise in which the investment is made. If the investor directly controls the foreign enterprise, his investment is called a direct investment. If he does not control it, his investment is a portfolio investment. The theory of international capital movements predicts that capital will move in response to differences in interest-rates. However, this theory does not apply to direct investment and differences in interest-rates do not explain the movements of direct investment. Hymer suggested that direct investment is capital associated with the international operations of firms and that movements of direct investment are determined by the extent of international operations. International operations refer to the ownership and the control of enterprises in one country by firms in another country. Hymer pointed out that there are two main causes of international operations. For one thing, firms control enterprises in many countries in order to remove competition between them when the enterprises sell in the same market or sell to each other under conditions of imperfect competition. For another, firms undertake operations in a foreign country in order to appropriate fully the returns to certain abilities they possess. They choose this method instead of an alternative method like licensing because the imperfections in the market prevent the fullest realization of profits unless the firm exercises some control.

Several economists have built theories on Hymer's. Charles P. Kindleberger (October 12, 1910-July 7, 2003) critiqued and extended it by emphasizing market imperfections and the broader economic context. He explored how monopolistic advantages interact with global trade dynamics. Richard W. Johnson examined how firms choose investment locations based on their monopolistic advantages, while Richard E. Caves contributed insights from industrial organization, analyzing how distinctive capabilities shape international strategies. Together, these scholars refined and expanded

Hymer's foundational concepts in understanding MNC behavior.

（2）Core concepts and ideas

Monopolistic advantage theory builds on the idea that firms have unique assets or capabilities that allow them to compete in foreign markets. MNCs have disadvantages compared with local firms, including liabilities of foreignness, lack of local expertise and high costs of acquiring knowledge in new countries. But these are mitigated by the MNC's "monopolistic" advantages such as advanced technology, superior management skills, strong brand reputation and economies of scale. It's not just about having a product or service but having unique capabilities or assets that give the firm an edge.

These monopolistic advantages are created by market imperfections in the home market and are leveraged in the host country to maximize economic returns. According to Hymer, international markets are imperfect compared to domestic markets, so firms with monopolistic advantages can exploit these imperfections better. For example, a firm with advanced technology or specialized expertise can enter and succeed in a foreign market easier than a local competitor without such advantages.

Firms can choose their mode of internationalization, either by managing and controlling their foreign operations directly or through external arrangements such as licensing. Firms with monopolistic advantages usually prefer to internalize their operations to protect their proprietary knowledge and control their competitive edge. By setting up operations in another country, these firms can utilize their unique assets better and sustain their competitive position.

FDI involves equity investments like building a factory or acquiring a lasting interest in a firm abroad. FDI gives MNCs ownership and control over their foreign affiliates. MNCs choose FDI to utilize their monopolistic advantages which may include technological superiority, advanced manufacturing processes, strong brand names, valuable knowledge, patents, economies of scale or marketing skills. These advantages are firm-specific and cannot be bought by local competitors in the open market.

In conditions of perfect competition, local firms can benefit from inherent locational advantages and can acquire technology or other advantages from MNCs. However, monopolistic advantage theory departs from classical economic assumptions of perfect competition by recognizing market imperfections that create barriers for local firms. These imperfections prevent local competitors from acquiring the monopolistic advantages of MNCs. Hence, FDI is very attractive for MNCs as it gives them control over resources in foreign markets and monopoly power over local competitors. MNCs can earn monopolistic rents and profits that exceed the costs and disadvantages of international competition.

（3）Contributions and limitations

Hymer made an essential contribution by providing a theoretical basis for the motivation of MNCs in international expansion. It was a very important driver of thinking about MNCs as it stressed internal firm level advantages relative to external trade factors for explaining FDI. This has been one of the root ideas from which other researchers develop their own theories on FDI. As a result, Hymer is honored as "The Father of FDI".

Though Hymer discovered the monopolistic advantage and it became prevalent, this theory also has some restrictions. The chief criticisms of the monopolistic advantage theory are its inability to explain the source of monopolistic advantages, its static nature and that it assumes a larger firm is entering international markets for the first time. At the same time, despite the adjective "monopolistic", not all benefits derive from special advantages (which may simply represent greater efficiency and be Ricardian or supra-competitive), but rather could stem disproportionately, reasonably, and consistently from returns to scarcity-exploitation. Still, the theory is likely to be less pertinent for entrepreneurial firms or those competing in emerging markets who do not start out with monopoly benefits that are required for international success (and which often develop after a focal firm has already been syndicated into its first foreign market). Moreover, the theory cannot explain why FDI is always MNCs' entry mode of choice, or predict when an MNC with monopolistic advantages behaves differently regarding internationalization.

2. Product life cycle theory

产品生命周期理论由雷蒙德·弗农于 1966 年在其发表在《经济学季刊》上的论文《产品周期中的国际投资与国际贸易》中提出。该理论解释了产品从引入到退出市场的四个阶段(引入、增长、成熟、衰退)以及这些阶段对国际贸易和投资的影响。产品最初在技术领先的国家开发,随后生产逐步转移至具有成本优势的国家。该理论强调了全球供应链的形成,贸易和投资模式会随着产品生命周期的变化而调整。该理论最初认为产品生命周期只包括新产品、成熟产品和标准化产品三个阶段,后经过多次发展完善,将产品生命周期分为四个阶段。

The product life cycle (PLC) theory was developed by Vernon in the 1960s for tracking a typical journey of the products from their introduction on to decline in markets. The PLC theory also has implications on the international front in that product is evolved as it moves into various global stages of acceptance. According to PLC theory, a product will pass through life cycle stages from high export activity by the exporting country (conquering other countries), in terms of being first with absolute advantage in its production to being exported by other country competing on costs and prices. Specific growth theory naturally has this at its core or heart of the product life cycle (introduction→growth→maturity→decline). While the PLC conjectures facilitate identification of products as export goods, importables and those that can be produced abroad, this aids countries to develop policies designed to promote trade efficiency and economic wellbeing.

(1) Origin and development

Raymond Vernon (September 1, 1913-August 26, 1999) was an American economist. He observed that the Heckscher-Ohlin model, which focused on factor endowments like labor and capital, couldn't fully explain why certain products were produced in specific countries. Vernon proposed that products go through a life cycle with distinct stages, and their production locations shift as they mature. This theory was first introduced in his 1966 paper with the title *International Investment and International Trade in the Product Cycle* published on *Quarterly Journal of Economics*.

PLC refers to the market lifespan of a product, covering the entire journey from its introduction to its eventual exit from the market. Vernon believed that the product life cycle is similar to human life, going through stages of formation, growth, maturity, and decline. For products, this means moving through phases of introduction, growth, maturity, and decline. The timing and progression of these stages differ across countries with varying levels of technological advancement, leading to significant gaps and time differences. These time differences reflect the technological disparities between countries and highlight the competitive position of the same product in different markets. This, in turn, influences changes in international trade and investment. To categorize countries, Vernon grouped them into three groups: innovating countries (typically the most developed countries like the U. S.), other developed countries like European countries, and developing countries.

The theory was later developed by others such as Stephen Hymer, Staffan Linder, and Harry G. Johnson. However, the study begins with Vernon who wished to fill the gap between the neoclassical theories and the current trade dynamics.

(2) Core concepts and ideas

The PLC theory explains how a product evolves through different stages and how these stages affect international trade. The theory begins with production in a country with an absolute advantage and eventually shifts to countries with a comparative advantage as the product moves through its life cycle. This transition impacts trade patterns, influencing export strategies, foreign production, and ultimately, imports to the original country.

1) The product life cycle

There are four stages in a product's life cycle in respect to the PLC theory. The first is introduction stage. In this stage, the product is developed and produced domestically, with little international trade. The focus is on marketing the product within the home market and preparing for potential exports. The second is growth stage. As demand increases, the product begins to be exported. Companies may establish foreign production through licensing, joint ventures, or wholly owned subsidiaries to meet growing demand and participate in competition in international markets. The third is maturity stage. In this stage, sales stabilize, and competition intensifies. To remain profitable, firms may need to reduce prices, or shift production to developing countries where labor costs are lower, thereby extending the product's life cycle. The last is decline stage. As the product enters its decline phase, production typically moves to developing countries to minimize costs. Firms must prepare for the eventual phase-out of the product while looking for new market opportunities and products to maintain growth.

The PLC theory begins with the assumption that the enterprises in any one of the advanced countries of the world are not distinguishably different from those in any other advanced country, in terms of their access to scientific knowledge and their capacity to comprehend scientific principles. Producers in any market are more likely to be aware of the possibility of introducing new products in that market than producers located elsewhere would be. The United States market offers certain unique kinds of opportunities to those who are in a position to be aware of them. First, the United States market consists of consumers with an average income which is higher (except for a few anomalies like Kuwait) than that in any other national market. Second, the United States market is characterized by high unit labor costs and relatively unrationed capital compared with practically all other markets. In the early stages of introduction of a new product, producers are usually confronted with a number of critical, albeit transitory, conditions. The unstandardized nature of the design at this early stage carries with it a number of locational implications. First, producers at this stage are particularly concerned with the degree of freedom they have in changing their inputs. Second, the price elasticity of demand for the output of individual firms is comparatively low. Third, the need for swift and effective communication on the part of the producer with customers, suppliers, and even competitors is especially high at this stage. As the demand for a product expands, a certain degree of standardization usually takes place. This is not to say that efforts at product differentiation come to an end. On the contrary, such efforts may even intensify, as competitors try to avoid the full brunt of price competition. Once again, the change has locational implications. First of all, the need for flexibility declines. Second, concern about production cost begins to take the place of concern about product characteristics. Overall scarcity of capital in the less-developed countries will not prevent investment in facilities for the production of standardized products. There are two reasons why capital costs may not prove a barrier to such investment. First, the investment will occur in industries which require some significant labor inputs in the production process; but they will be concentrated in that subsector of the industry which produces highly standardized products capable of self-contained production establishments. Besides, even if the capital requirements for a particular plant are heavy, the cost of the capital need not prove a bar. Accordingly, one may say that from the entrepreneur's viewpoint certain systematic and predictable "imperfections" of the capital markets may reduce or eliminate the capital-shortage handicap which is characteristic of the less-developed countries; and, further, that as a result of the reduction or elimination such countries may find themselves in a position to compete effectively in the export of certain standardized capital-intensive goods.

2) Implications for international trade and investment

Vernon's PLC theory has significant implications for international trade and investment strategies. As a product progresses through its life cycle, production often shifts from high-cost developed countries to lower-cost developing countries, reflecting changes in comparative advantage. This cycle highlights how products evolve from local innovation to global standardization as competition and production dynamics shift.

Vernon initially divided products into three categories, namely, new product stage, maturing product stage, and standardized product stage, based on their stages in the product life cycle and how they behave in the international trade market. At the beginning, production occurs in the innovating country (e. g., the U. S.), followed by exports to other markets. Foreign production eventually begins, and, in the final stage, the product is imported back into the original market. These shifts in trade patterns are driven by market imperfections, consumer preferences, and technological differences across countries.

MNCs often use FDI to establish production facilities in key markets during the growth stage and relocate to lower-cost regions during the maturity stage. Strategically managing market entry and exit based on the product's life cycle can optimize profitability and market presence. Additionally, the theory highlights the importance of innovation in maintaining a competitive edge, as firms need to continually adapt to changing market conditions and stay ahead of competitors.

(3) Contributions and limitations

The PLC theory provides a useful framework for understanding how products evolve and how these changes affect international trade and investment. Initially, the innovating country gains an advantage through market proximity and innovation, but as production costs become more important, developing countries take the lead with their lower labor costs. The theory highlights shifting trade patterns over a product's life cycle and emphasizes the need for countries to focus on innovation and product development to stay competitive. It effectively explains mid-20th-century trade and investment trends, particularly in manufacturing industries, and remains a foundational concept in international business, integrating international trade and direct investment theories during corporate internationalization.

However, the theory has limitations in explaining modern market dynamics. One criticism is that the PLC's ability to predict the duration and progression of each stage is often unreliable. The model is viewed as static, not fully accounting for the continuous evolution of markets, products, and technologies. Process innovations can alter a product's characteristics and life cycle, prompting some MNCs to adopt diversified FDI strategies. Additionally, not all products follow the typical life cycle pattern—some may skip stages or experience multiple growth phases. Non-standardized products and those tailored for specific local markets may be produced abroad early on. Finally, in terms of international trade and investment, many MNCs no longer follow the traditional sequence of exporting first and then investing. Instead, they pursue strategic investment by directly entering potential foreign markets. The theory also struggles to address the growing complexity of international economic environments, including horizontal integration FDI between developed countries and the role of MNCs in intra-industry trade.

3. Internalization theory

内部化理论由彼得·巴克莱和马克·卡森于 1976 年在他们合著的《跨国公司的未来》中提出。该书解释了跨国公司为何选择对外直接投资而非出口或许可证转让。内部化理论认为,企业通过内部组织系统以较低成本在内部转移其优势,并将这一能力视为推动对外直接投资的主要动力。在市场不完善的情况下,为了实现整体利润最大化,企业倾向于将中间产品特别是知识产品在内部进行转移,以内部市场取代外部市场。通过这种方式,企业可以运用内部管理手段优化资源配置,避免市场不完善对经营效率的负面影响。

The internalization theory provides a framework for understanding why and how firms expand internationally through FDI rather than relying on external market transactions. It posits that MNCs internalize operations to overcome market imperfections such as inefficient resource coordination and difficulties in managing proprietary assets. By integrating vertically and horizontally, MNCs protect their competitive advantages and enhance efficiency. The theory emphasizes that internalization is particularly crucial for managing knowledge and intangible assets.

(1) Origin and development

The development of internalization theory is notably advanced by Peter J. Buckley and Mark Casson, who built upon earlier contributions from Hymer, Kindleberger, and Caves. Buckley and Casson introduced the theory in their 1976 book titled *The Future of the Multinational Enterprise*. They expanded the theory by integrating Coase's concept of the firm, viewing MNCs as a special case of multi-plant firms. Their model highlights how MNCs are both vertically and horizontally integrated, focusing on how internalization addresses market imperfections and manages the relationship between knowledge and intermediate goods. This approach provides a comprehensive framework for understanding FDI through internalization.

The theory is based on three very simple postulates. First, firms maximize profit in a world of imperfect markets. Second, when markets in intermediate products are imperfect, there is an incentive to bypass them by creating internal markets. This involves bringing under common ownership and control the activities which are linked by the market. Third, internalization of markets across national boundaries generates MNCs. Four main groups of factors are relevant to the internalization decision: (i) Industry-specific factors relating to the nature of the product and the structure of the external market; (ii) Region-specific factors relating to the geographical and social characteristics of the regions linked by the market; (iii) Nation-specific factors relating to the political and fiscal relations between the nations concerned; (iv) Firm-specific factors which reflect the ability of the management to organize an internal market. Prior to the World War Ⅱ, multinationality was a by-product of the internalization of intermediate-product markets in multistage production processes, and after the war, it is a by-product of the internalization of markets in knowledge. The industries where multinationality predominated in the pre-war period were for primary products such as food, minerals and oil. The markets where internalization was likely to be most advantageous were agricultural products, raw materials whose deposits are geographically concentrated, and intermediate products in capital-intensive manufacturing industries. The post-war pattern of FDI, in particular cross-investment between developed economies, may also be explained in terms of the internalization of knowledge.

(2) Core concepts and ideas

Internalization theory explains why firms choose FDI as a mode of international expansion to manage and control activities that would be inefficient or costly to handle through external markets. It views the firm as an alternative institution to markets. Instead of relying on external market transactions, firms internalize operations to manage production, distribution, and other activities within the organization. This approach helps firms address inefficiencies and reduce transaction costs associated with external markets.

1) Motivations for internalization: Compared to final product markets, market imperfections, such as coordination inefficiencies, market power, bargaining instabilities, pricing difficulties, government interventions, etc., are more pronounced for intermediate products, which include raw materials, components, assemblies, and various technologies, knowledge, and information closely related to the production of intermediate and final products. Firms internalize operations to overcome those market imperfections. These imperfections arise when market transactions are inefficient or costly, leading firms to prefer managing these transactions within the organization.

The theory contrasts internalization with market-based transactions. Internalization is preferred when it reduces the transaction costs and inefficiencies associated with external market transactions, particularly in complex or knowledge-intensive industries. This preference leads firms to establish subsidiaries or branches abroad rather than relying on third-party intermediaries.

2) Methods of internalization: The internalization theory emphasizes two types of integration within firms. One is vertical integration. Firms internalize activities along their supply chain. For example, a company might control both the production and distribution of its products to ensure quality, reduce costs, and maintain control over critical inputs. The other is horizontal integration. Firms internalize related activities and proprietary assets within the organization. This involves managing various aspects of production or service delivery in-house, rather than outsourcing these functions to external firms. Firms may enhance efficiency and maintain control over critical aspects of their operations through either vertical or horizontal integration.

3) Benefits of internalization: Advantages of internalization include control and efficiency, as well as knowledge protection. By internalizing operations, firms aim to minimize transaction costs such as search costs, bargaining costs, and enforcement costs, which can be high in external markets. By managing activities within the organization, firms can reduce transaction costs, improve coordination, and better control the quality and processes associated with their products or services. Internalization also helps firms safeguard their proprietary knowledge and technologies. By investing directly in foreign markets, they reduce the risk of losing control over valuable intellectual property or competitive advantages that could occur if they relied on external partners through licensing or franchising.

(3) Contributions and limitations

Internalization theory is crucial for understanding why firms prefer to invest directly in foreign markets and manage certain activities internally rather than outsourcing or licensing them. By internalizing operations, firms can protect proprietary knowledge, improve efficiency, and better coordinate global activities, thus maximizing profits and maintaining a competitive edge. The theory helps explain the strategic decisions of MNCs in a globalized economy.

Despite its importance, internalization theory has several limitations. It primarily addresses the motives and basis for MNCs' FDI from a microeconomic viewpoint, overlooking the international economic environment and macroeconomic factors. The theory also fails to cover the timing, direction, and roles of parent companies and subsidiaries in international operations. Additionally, it explains vertical integration but lacks insight into horizontal integration and diversification strategies. Finally, it does not thoroughly explain the sources of MNCs' organizational and management capabilities related to internalization, unlike theories such as monopoly advantage theory and PLC theory.

4. Marginal industry expansion theory

边际产业扩张理论,也称为投资比较优势理论,由日本经济学家小岛清于 1978 年在其专著《对外直接投资:跨国公司经营的日本模式》中系统性提出。该理论基于比较优势理论,强调对外直接投资应从本国已失去或即将失去比较优势的边际产业开始。边际产业通常是那些竞争压力大、利润率缩小的成熟产业,难以在母国继续保持盈利。通过对外直接投资将这些产业转移到生产成本较低、需求增长较快的国家,既能利用东道国的成本优势,又能促进其工业和经济发展,同时为母国释放资源,推动创新和高增长产业的发展。

The marginal industry expansion theory, also known as the theory of comparative advantage to investment, provides insights into the optimal strategy for FDI by focusing on marginal industries. It holds that the transfer of the "marginal industry" in which the home country loses its comparative advantage will drive the export of capital goods and intermediate products to the host country; that is, the relationship between FDI and foreign trade is complementary. The theory's relevance lies in its application of the principle of comparative advantage to guide investment decisions and its implications for economic development.

（1）Origin and development

The marginal industry expansion theory was proposed by Japanese economist Kiyoshi Kojima (May 22, 1920-January 7, 2010) in his 1978 book titled *Direct Foreign Investment: A Japanese Model of Multinational Business Operations*. Kojima's theory originated during a period of significant economic transition and globalization, when Japan was expanding its international economic presence, and the theory provided a framework to optimize the impact of Japanese FDI. This theory applies the principle of comparative advantage from international trade theory to analyze the distribution and regional structure of Japanese FDI during the 1950s to 1970s, and its relationship with imports and exports. It also effectively explains Japan's FDI practices in the 1960s and 1970s.

In his book, Kojima pointed out that Japan should undertake FDI in an industry which is becoming comparatively disadvantageous in Japan and at the same time has the potential of becoming comparatively advantageous in the host country. If an industry of the host country having potential comparative advantage, which has not been able to achieve its comparative advantage with low costs as it lacks technology, capital and management skill, were to become an industry of comparative advantage, it would develop as a new export industry in the host country. In response to this, Japan should enlarge another industry in which it has comparative advantages so that the capital and labor force of the industry which undertook direct investment abroad are transferred to this promising industry. This adjustment would upgrade the industrial structures of both Japan and the host country and could enlarge harmonious trade between them. FDI of this type would create more complementary and profitable trade than with no FDI.

This is "Japanese-type, trade-oriented direct FDI", which is totally different from "American-type, trade-substituted FDI". Thus, the most important criterion in undertaking FDI should be to take into consideration the present and potential pattern of comparative advantages between investing and host countries and to undertake direct foreign investment from the investing country's comparatively disadvantageous industry. This is trade-oriented investment and will bring about upgrading structural adjustment on both sides and changes in the composition of exports and imports. According to Kojima, MNCs achieve two types of economies of scale: the first are "genuine economies of scale", which contribute to savings of real resources; the second are "pseudo-economies of scale", which result in increased profits for the corporations, but with no corresponding savings in real resources. Hence, the most important rules for ensuring the developmental effect of FDI seem to be: (i) free trade; (ii) big MNCs are to compete freely instead of exhibiting monopolistic or oligopolistic behavior; and (iii) FDI plays the role of a "tutor" with a certain rule of fade-out.

(2) Core concepts and ideas

The marginal industry expansion theory explains how industries in developed economies gradually expand into international markets, particularly into developing economies. The theory, grounded in the broader context of international trade and economic development, emphasizes the role of marginal industries. Marginal industries are those in which the investing country is either experiencing or will soon experience a loss of comparative advantages. These industries may be mature or in the later stages of their product life cycle, where competitive pressures and shrinking margins make it difficult to sustain profitability in their home market.

Central to this theory is the idea that as industries approach the margins of profitability in developed countries, they begin to seek out locations where production costs are lower, and market demand is growing. By expanding into developing economies, these industries can exploit cost advantages, such as cheaper labor and raw materials, while also tapping into emerging consumer markets. This expansion is often facilitated by FDI, which allows firms to establish production facilities and distribution networks, and conduct sales operations in these new markets.

The marginal industry expansion theory applies the principle of comparative advantage to FDI, advocating for investment in sectors where the home country's comparative advantage is waning. Firms in declining industries in advanced economies shift their operations to countries that possess a relative advantage in producing the goods or services at a lower cost. This shift allows firms to exploit the comparative advantages of the host country, thereby contributing to structural economic transformation in both the home and host countries. In the home country, the migration of marginal industries frees up resources for investment in more innovative and high-growth sectors. In the host country, the influx of capital, technology, and expertise associated with foreign investment fosters industrial development and economic growth.

The theory suggests that FDI should begin with industries where the investing country is experiencing or is about to experience comparative disadvantage, and then progressively target other sectors. This strategy not only promotes the smooth transition of the investing country but also supports the development of emerging industries in the host country. Investing in marginal industries can help the host country reveal or enhance its comparative advantages, which may not be fully realized due to a lack of capital, technology, or management skills. This can widen the comparative cost gap between the two countries, creating conditions for more and greater trade benefits. This approach leverages the comparative advantage principle to enhance both the investing and host countries' economic outcomes.

（3）Contributions and limitations

The marginal industry expansion theory provides a dynamic perspective on how declining or peripheral industries in developed countries seek new opportunities through international expansion and foster economic growth in both investing and host countries. The theory highlights the benefits of targeted investment and technology transfer. It emphasizes practical steps for maintaining economic efficiency and fostering development. Its insights can guide investment decisions and policy formulation, particularly in the context of emerging markets and shifting global economic dynamics. Furthermore, the theory effectively analyzes the distinct characteristics of the U. S. and Japanese FDI in the 1960s and 1970s, and it partially explains the reasons behind the U. S. trade deficit.

However, the theory also acknowledges its limitations. First, although it effectively reflects the characteristics of Japanese FDI in the 1960s and 1970s, it fails to explain the motivations behind Japanese direct investment in major developed countries after the 1980s. Second, it does not account for FDI between developed countries with similar factor endowments, nor does it clarify the motives of increasingly advanced enterprises from developing countries investing in developed economies. Lastly, the proposed policy recommendations are not only inconsistent with the global strategies of MNCs but also overly idealistic regarding specific policies for direct investment in developing countries.

5. Eclectic theory of international production

国际生产折衷理论又称 OLI 范式，由约翰·邓宁于 1981 年在其专著《国际生产与跨国公司》中系统性提出。该理论整合了所有权优势、区位优势和内部化优势三个核心因素，解释了跨国公司对外直接投资的动因和条件。该理论强调企业在具备独特的资产和技术优势（所有权特定优势）以及通过内部化降低交易成本的能力（内部化优势）后，如果东道国市场环境有利（区位优势），企业就会选择进行对外直接投资。

The eclectic theory of international production, also known as the OLI (ownership, location, internalization) paradigm, was proposed by Dunning to address and integrate various aspects of international business and FDI. This theory offers a comprehensive framework for understanding why and how firms engage in international production and FDI. Dunning's work sought to provide a more holistic understanding of FDI by incorporating three key factors: ownership, location, and internalization.

(1) Origin and development

The economist John Dunning (June 26, 1927-January 29, 2009) introduced the eclectic theory in his book titled *International Production and the Multinational Enterprise* in 1981 to explain why companies choose to invest in foreign countries rather than simply exporting their products or licensing their technology. Dunning aimed to address this gap by combining elements from various existing theories into a unified framework. His work sought to provide a more holistic understanding of FDI by incorporating three key factors: ownership, location, and internalization. The eclectic paradigm has since become a foundational concept in international business studies, widely used to understand the complex factors influencing global investment decisions.

In the early 1980s, Dunning advanced the eclectic theory of international production by incorporating a dynamic approach. He examined the relationship between FDI and economic development stages in 67 countries from 1967 to 1978 and proposed the investment development path theory which outlines how a country's FDI evolves as its economy develops. It identifies four stages of the investment development path as follows. In the initial stage, countries lack firm-specific and internalization advantages, resulting in minimal FDI. In the second stage, improved investment environments attract increased FDI inflows and some outbound investments. By the third stage, as countries develop firm-specific advantages, they see foreign FDI in sectors with strong location advantages and increase outbound FDI in sectors with strong firm-specific advantages. In the fourth stage, outbound FDI surpasses inflows, reflecting strong domestic advantages and a focus on leveraging foreign location benefits.

Since the late 1980s, Dunning has refined his eclectic theory to better account for changes in MNCs' behavior amid economic globalization. He introduced a distinction between two sources of ownership advantages: asset advantages (existing before multinational activities) and transaction advantages (enhanced through internalization). This distinction clarifies the OLI framework and explains strategic shifts. Dunning also identified four FDI motivations: resource-seeking, market-seeking, efficiency-seeking, and strategic asset-seeking, highlighting the rise of strategic asset-seeking, where firms prioritize acquiring key assets like technology to boost global competitiveness. Additionally, he expanded the OLI framework to include the effects of multinational alliances and global networks, examining the role of firm interactions, global network governance, and the spatial clustering of firms on ownership, internalization, and location advantages.

(2) Core concepts and ideas

The eclectic theory of international production theory explains the factors that determine a firm's decision to engage in FDI and to conduct operations in international markets. It integrates three core components: ownership, location, and internalization.

1) Ownership advantages (O): Ownership advantages refer to the unique assets and capabilities that a firm possesses, which provide it with a competitive edge in the international market. These can include proprietary technology, brand reputation, managerial skills, and organizational capabilities. Firms are more likely to engage in FDI if they have substantial ownership advantages that they want to exploit abroad. These advantages help firms overcome the disadvantages they face relative to local competitors in foreign markets.

2) Location advantages (L): Location advantages pertain to the benefits that a firm can derive from operating in a specific geographic location. These benefits can include access to natural resources, labor costs, market size, infrastructure, and local regulations. Firms will choose to invest in a particular location if it offers significant advantages compared to other locations. These advantages might include lower production costs, favorable trade conditions, or proximity to key markets.

3) Internalization advantages (I): Internalization advantages relate to the benefits firms gain by internalizing operations rather than outsourcing or licensing them to external entities. This involves managing and controlling foreign operations within the firm. Firms are more likely to engage in FDI if they can achieve efficiencies and control by internalizing operations. This includes avoiding transaction costs and protecting proprietary knowledge.

The eclectic theory integrates these three components into a coherent framework, arguing that firms will engage in international production if they have significant ownership advantages, find attractive locations, and can benefit from internalizing operations. The interplay of these factors determines the firm's decision to undertake FDI.

The eclectic theory offers the basis for a general explanation of international production. As shown in Table 3-1, Dunning related the main types of foreign activities by MNCs to the presence or absence of the OLI advantages underpinning these activities. Such a matrix can be used as a starting-point for an examination of both the industrial and geographical composition of FDI.

Table 3-1　Types of international production: some determining factors

Types of international production	(O) Ownership advantages (the "why" of MNC activity)	(L) Location advantages (the "where" of production)	(I) Internalization advantages (the "how" of involvement)	Strategic goals of MNCs	Illustration of types of activity that favor MNCs
Natural resource-seeking	Capital, technology, access to markets; complementary assets; size and bargaining strengths	Possession of natural resources, and related transport and communications infrastructure; tax and other incentives	To ensure stability of supplies at right price; to control markets	To gain privileged access to resources vis-à-vis competitors	(a) Oil, copper, bauxite, bananas, pineapples, cocoa, hotels (b) Export processing, labor-intensive products or processes (c) Offshoring of some services
Market-seeking	Capital, technology, information, management and organizational skills; surplus R&D and other capacity; economies of scale; ability to generate brand loyalty	Material and labor costs; market size and characteristics; government policy (e. g. with respect to regulations, import controls, and investment incentives, etc.)	A desire to reduce transaction or information costs, buyer ignorance or uncertainty; to protect property rights	To protect existing markets, counteract behavior of competitors; to preclude rivals or potential rivals from entering new markets	Computers, pharmaceuticals, motor vehicles, cigarettes, processed foods, airlines, financial services
Efficiency-seeking (a) of products (b) of processes	As above, but also access to markets; economies of scope, geographical diversification and/or clustering, and international sourcing of inputs	(a) Economies of product or process specialization and concentration (b) Low labor costs; incentives to local production by host governments; a favorable business environment	(a) As for second category, plus gains from economies of common governance (b) The economies of vertical integration and horizontal diversification	As part of regional or global product rationalization and/or to gain advantages of process specialization	(a) Motor vehicles, electrical appliances, business services, some R&D (b) Consumer electronics, textiles and clothing, pharmaceuticals

| Strategic asset-seeking | Any of first three that offer opportunities for synergy with existing assets | Any of first three that offer technology, organizational, and other assets in which a firm is deficient | Economies of common governance; improved, competitive or strategic advantages; to reduce or spread risks | To strengthen global innovatory or production competitiveness; to gain new product lines or markets | Knowledge-intensive industries that record a high ratio of fixed to overhead costs and which offer substantial economies of scale, synergy or market access |

Source：Dunning，J. H. ，Lundan，S. M. （2008），*Multinational Enterprises and the Global Economy*，Edward Elgar Publishing Limited，Cheltenham，UK. P104-105.

（3）Contributions and limitations

The eclectic theory of international production combines multiple related theories into a cohesive framework. It effectively explains various aspects of international business activities and offers practical guidance for MNCs entering global markets. Compared to traditional theories，it provides robust theoretical and practical insights. And with Dunning's updates in the late 1980，its explanatory and predictive capabilities regarding multinational operations was significantly enhanced.

Nevertheless，as economic globalization and the complexity of multinational activities increase，the theory's limitations have become more apparent. It struggles to account for the rapid FDI behavior of developing countries，especially those without all three advantages，when investing in developed economies. Additionally，its focus on micro-level analysis limits its ability to address macro-level FDI motives across different countries. It also emphasizes cost analysis while overlooking revenue considerations，which are crucial for firms evaluating market entry options like technology transfer，export trade，and FDI. Future development of the eclectic theory may involve expanding the OLI paradigm with new variables，incorporating dynamic elements，and integrating macro-level and revenue-based analysis.

第二节　发展中国家跨国公司对外直接投资理论
（Theories of FDI by MNCs from Developing Countries）

1. Small-scale technology theory

小规模技术理论由刘易斯·威尔斯于1983年在其专著《第三世界跨国公司：发展中国家对外投资的兴起》中系统提出，旨在解释发展中国家如何在全球经济中积极进行对外投资。该理论主要强调发展中国家跨国公司的竞争优势包括三个方面：一是劳动密集型小规模生产技术，适应小市场需求；二是在国外生产民族产品，满足同种族团体的需求；三是低价营销战略，通过低生产成本和物美价廉的产品抢占市场份额。这一理论为分析发展中国家企业在国际化初期如何在国际竞争中争得一席之地提供了重要参考。

Small-scale technology theory was advanced by Louis T. Wells Jr. in the early 1980s as a significant contribution to understanding FDI from developing countries. The theory was developed in response to the growing evidence that developing countries were not merely passive participants in the global economy but were actively investing and competing internationally. It highlighted how these firms could exploit specific competitive advantages, such as cost efficiency and targeted market strategies, to overcome their limited advanced technology and financial resources and thrive in international markets. His theory addressed a gap in existing international investment theories that predominantly focused on large-scale, advanced technologies and the financial capabilities of developed countries.

(1) Origin and development

During the late 20th century, the rise of MNCs from developing countries began to challenge the traditional view that only firms from developed countries could successfully compete on a global scale. Louis T. Wells Jr. observed that these firms in developing countries, despite lacking advanced technologies and substantial financial resources, were increasingly engaging in FDI. To explain this phenomenon, Louis T. Wells Jr. , in his 1983 seminal work *Third World Multinational Companies: The Rise of Foreign Investments from Developing Countries*, proposed that these firms often used small-scale technologies tailored to niche markets and ethnic communities abroad.

This theory examines the comparative advantages of these countries' firms in FDI and explores differences between MNCs from developing and developed countries and how these differences impact their international business activities. Wells argued that traditional theories of international investment have a major flaw in not accounting for competitive advantages in small-scale technology. Such technology, though not modern, can still provide competitive advantages, mainly due to lower production costs tightly connected to the market characteristics of these countries, which can facilitate competitive FDI from developing country firms.

(2) Core concepts and ideas

Wells identified several competitive advantages for FDI from developing countries, despite their relatively limited advanced technology and financial resources compared to developed nations.

1) Small-scale technology for niche markets: Developing countries often utilize small-scale technologies designed for niche markets with limited demand in low-income areas. These technologies, which are suitable for small production runs, align well with the market characteristics of developing countries, enabling them to compete effectively where large-scale technologies cannot.

2) Ethnic market demand: A significant portion of FDI from developing countries targets ethnic communities abroad, particularly in countries with large diaspora

populations. These investments focus on ethnic-specific products and services, catering to the distinct needs of these communities.

3) Cost competitiveness: Despite less advanced technology, firms from developing countries remain competitive due to their low production costs. They often choose locations with lower wage levels and less stringent market requirements, which helps reduce production expenses and enhance their market share.

（3）Contributions and limitations

Wells' small-scale technology theory is considered as an innovative approach for studying FDI from developing countries, offering insights into how these firms leverage market characteristics and competitive advantages. It provides a valuable perspective on why and how MNCs from developing countries invest abroad.

However, the theory has its limitations. It primarily focuses on "second-tier" technologies and cannot fully account for new FDI trends observed since the 1990s, where developing country investments have increasingly involved larger scale operations and technological innovations. Consequently, some developing countries now engage in high-tech FDI, expanding beyond the scope of small-scale technologies.

2. Technology localization theory

技术地方化理论由英国经济学家桑加亚·拉奥于 1983 年在其专著《新跨国公司：第三世界企业的传播》中系统提出，解释了发展中国家跨国公司的竞争优势和投资动机。该理论认为，发展中国家通过在不同环境中本地化技术知识、改造进口技术和产品、结合当地供需条件进行创新，从而形成独特的竞争优势。这些创新活动不仅提高了经济效益，还使企业在国际市场上具备竞争力。这一理论突破了以往模型的局限，强调技术不仅要适应本地环境，还需不断改进以更好满足本地市场需求，进而推动经济发展并提升企业在全球市场的竞争力。

Technology localization theory builds on earlier theories as Wells' small-scale technology theory, by offering a more refined view of how technology can be adapted in developing countries. It argues that MNCs from these regions can compete effectively in both local and global markets by customizing technology to suit local environments and consumer preferences. The theory highlights how MNCs from developing countries not only adapt imported technologies but also enhance them to align with local resources, product quality, and preferences, giving them a competitive advantage. The approach addresses the limitations of previous models by focusing on the adaptation and improvement of technologies for local markets.

（1）Origin and development

Technology localization theory was introduced by Professor Sanjaya Lall (December 13, 1940-June 18, 2005) of Oxford University in his 1983 work *The New Multinationals: The Spread of Third World Enterprises*. This theory originated as a response to earlier theories on FDI and technology transfer. Lall critiqued Wells' small-scale technology theory by arguing that small-scale technology does not fully represent the technological capabilities of MNCs from developing countries. Instead, he suggested that the competitive advantage of MNCs from developing countries often stems from their innovative activities and adaptation of technology to local conditions, making it more suitable for the domestic market and leveraging local resources. This involves not just adopting existing technologies but innovating and improving them to meet specific local needs and conditions. Lall's research focused on firms in economies like India, Brazil, and Argentina, demonstrating that these companies could achieve significant technological and market successes through such localized adaptations.

(2) Core concepts and ideas

Lall believed that there are certain conditions under which it is theoretically possible that firms operating with generally "lower" levels of technology and skills can establish a proprietary advantage which is exploitable by FDI. Once the process of technical innovation starts in third world countries, it is not necessary that this advantage can be exploited only in other third world countries. Specific innovations (adaptations or breakthroughs) may endow a third world firm with an edge which can be exploited in developed countries by FDI, though the strength of local competition and the differences in market/cultural conditions are bound to make this fairly exceptional. These proprietary advantages of MNCs from the third world may be strengthened by two factors. First, they may have access to exceptionally cheap skilled manpower in their home country. Second, they may belong to large, diversified conglomerate groups run by traditional business families, which are institutions not commonly found now in developed countries. This conglomerate ownership may give them certain special advantages in terms of financial, managerial, and technical resources.

Lall's research on MNCs from India, Brazil, and Argentina shows that these companies often go beyond relying on small-scale, labor-intensive technologies. For example, Indian MNCs have advanced into technology-intensive sectors like software, leveraging both imported technologies and local innovation. Brazilian MNCs excel in areas of construction and energy, which do not align with Wells' model of small-scale production. Argentine MNCs, known for their robust R&D capabilities, frequently collaborate with large MNCs from developed countries.

Lall highlighted several distinct advantages for MNCs from developing countries. First, these MNCs excel in localized technological adaptation, modifying technologies to suit local environments and creating innovations tailored to specific conditions rather than simply imitating existing models. Second, by adjusting products to align with local economic conditions and consumer preferences, MNCs from developing countries gain competitive edges. Third, integrating with local supply chains enhances the efficiency of localized technologies, further boosting competitiveness. Additionally, the expansive and varied domestic markets in developing countries enable MNCs to develop technologies that are competitive both locally and internationally. Last, investments in countries with similar languages and cultures can further amplify these specific advantages.

(3) Contributions and limitations

Technology localization theory emphasizes that the competitive advantages of MNCs from developing countries come from their ability to innovate and adapt technologies to local conditions. This theory highlights that their advantages are relative rather than absolute, reflecting better alignment with local markets compared to MNCs from developed countries, and more advanced technologies compared to those in less developed countries.

However, Lall acknowledged that this theory primarily addresses surface phenomena and does not fully explore the micro-level technological development of MNCs from developing countries. It provides a broad view of how innovation and adaptation contribute to competitive advantages, but lacks a detailed explanation of how these companies compete on a global scale.

3. Technology innovation and industry upgrading theory

技术创新和产业升级理论由英国学者约翰·坎特韦尔和他的博士生帕兹·托兰惕诺于1990年在《技术积累与第三世界跨国公司》中提出，并由帕兹·托兰惕诺于1993年在其专著《技术创新与第三世界跨国公司》中进一步完善。该理论解释了发展中国家跨国公司如何通过对外直接投资增强技术能力和产业竞争力。该理论认为，发展中国家跨国公司通过积累和改进现有技术，推动产业升级，从基础技术领域向先进技术领域转型，从而提升其国际竞争力。该理论基于技术累积论，强调了技术积累与对外直接投资增长之间的紧密联系，指出技术进步是推动发展中国家产业升级和全球竞争力提升的关键因素。

The technology innovation and industry upgrading theory, also known as the technology accumulation and technological change theory, developed by John A. Cantwell and Paz Estrella E. Tolentino, explains how developing country MNCs use FDI to enhance their technological capabilities and industrial competitiveness. It suggests that these MNCs improve their technological proficiency through accumulating and adapting existing technologies to promote industry upgrading. This process allows them to transition from basic to advanced technology sectors and better compete internationally. The theory underscores the link between technological growth and increased FDI in developing countries.

(1) Origin and development

The technology innovation and industry upgrading theory was proposed by John A. Cantwell and Paz Estrella E. Tolentino from the University of Reading in their work *Technological Accumulation and Third World Multinationals* in 1990, and developed by Paz Estrella E. Tolentino in the book *Technological Innovation and Third World*

Multinationals in 1993. This theory originated from their observations of the evolving international investment patterns of developing countries, particularly the newly industrializing economies. During this period, these countries began to increasingly engage in FDI as part of their economic development strategies.

Cantwell and Tolentino noticed that, unlike traditional views which depicted developing countries as mere recipients of foreign technology, these countries were also becoming active investors. They found that as MNCs from developing countries invested abroad, they were not only transferring capital but also acquiring and adapting advanced technologies. This adaptation and accumulation of technology were critical for upgrading their domestic industries and improving their global competitiveness.

This led to the development of the technology innovation and industry upgrading theory. This theory explains the FDI behavior of developing countries from the perspective of technological accumulation, asserting that improvements in technological capabilities directly correlate with increased FDI. It posits that the existing level of technological capability is a crucial factor in shaping international production activities and the pace of FDI growth.

(2) Core concepts and ideas

The theory introduces two fundamental propositions:

First, the enhancement of technological capabilities in MNCs from developing countries is a continuous accumulation process that drives the upgrading of their industrial structures. Cantwell and Tolentino argue that historically, technological accumulation has been a key driver of economic development, forming the core motivation behind industrial and corporate advancement. However, while developed countries innovate through extensive R&D investments to develop cutting-edge technologies, MNCs from developing countries rely on a limited R&D capacity and leverage their "learning experience" and organizational capabilities to adapt and develop existing technologies.

Second, the improvement in technological capabilities of MNCs from developing countries is directly related to their increase in FDI. The existing level of technology influences their international production activities and determines the form and rate of FDI. Cantwell and Tolentino believe that FDI of MNCs from developing countries is significantly influenced by their domestic industry structures and endogenous technological innovation capabilities. MNCs in developing countries initially import technology and adapt it to the local market, gradually enhancing their technological innovation and production management skills, which boosts their international competitiveness and increases FDI.

（3）Contributions and limitations

The technology innovation and industry upgrading theory provides a framework for understanding how developing countries advance technologically and industrially through FDI. It highlights how these countries leverage foreign technologies to build their own capabilities and upgrade industries, emphasizing the role of technological accumulation and innovation in moving from low-tech to high-tech sectors.

While the theory is widely recognized for explaining FDI patterns in developing countries and regions, particularly in emerging Asian economies from the mid-1980s, it primarily focuses on how MNCs use accumulated advantages. It does not fully explain how these firms gain competitive advantages in FDI and international operations. As a result, it falls short in accounting for the strong competitive performance of MNCs from these regions in high-tech sectors such as semiconductors, computers, biotechnology, and electronic information since the 1990s.

4. Investment development path theory

投资发展路径理论由约翰·邓宁于1981年在其论文《解释各国的国际直接投资地位：一个动态或发展的视角》中提出。该理论阐释了一个国家的对外直接投资与经济发展之间的动态关系。该理论将国家发展过程分为五个阶段，认为随着经济的进步，外资的流入促进了本土企业能力的提升，并推动经济发展。在初始阶段，国家主要依赖内资以增强工业能力；随着外资的流入及不断增加，国内企业开始向外投资，展示出更强的国际竞争力；到后期，国家逐渐成为净资本出口国，寻求全球机会和战略资产。这一理论强调政府政策和跨国公司的战略在塑造投资路径中的重要性。

Investment development path（IDP）theory explains the relationship between a country's FDI position and its economic development over time. It suggests that foreign MNCs enhance local firms' capabilities, contributing to economic progress. The model divides this progression into five stages, showing that inward FDI stimulates and develops the host economy, facilitating its transition through these stages. Initially, countries attract FDI to build their industries. Then, as the countries develop, they begin investing abroad, demonstrating increased international competitiveness. In later stages, they become net capital exporters, seeking global opportunities and strategic assets, reflecting a shift from being an FDI recipient to an FDI investor.

（1）Origin and development

The IDP theory, first presented by John Dunning in his 1981 paper *Explaining the International Direct Investment Position of Countries*: *Towards a Dynamic or Developmental Approach*, is an extension of his eclectic paradigm. In his paper, he conducted an empirical analysis of the relationship between FDI and economic development stages in 67 countries between 1967 and 1978. He found that the scale of a country's international investment is closely related to its level of economic development—the higher the per capita gross national product, the greater the net outward FDI. Dunning also proposed that the tendency for OFDI from developing countries depends on the country's stage of economic development, as well as its ownership advantages, internalization advantages, and location advantages. On the above basis, he then proposed the IDP theory which illustrates the dynamic relationship between FDI and the level of development of a given country. The theory was later revised and refined multiple times by Dunning and Rajneesh Narula.

(2) Core concepts and ideas

The IDP model illustrates how a country's economic development influences its FDI patterns. It suggests that the balance of inward and outward FDI evolves as the economy develops. The model consists of five stages, highlighting the dynamic nature of FDI and its role in economic progress, as shown in Figure 3-1. Additionally, it underscores the significance of government policies and MNCs' strategies in shaping a country's investment path.

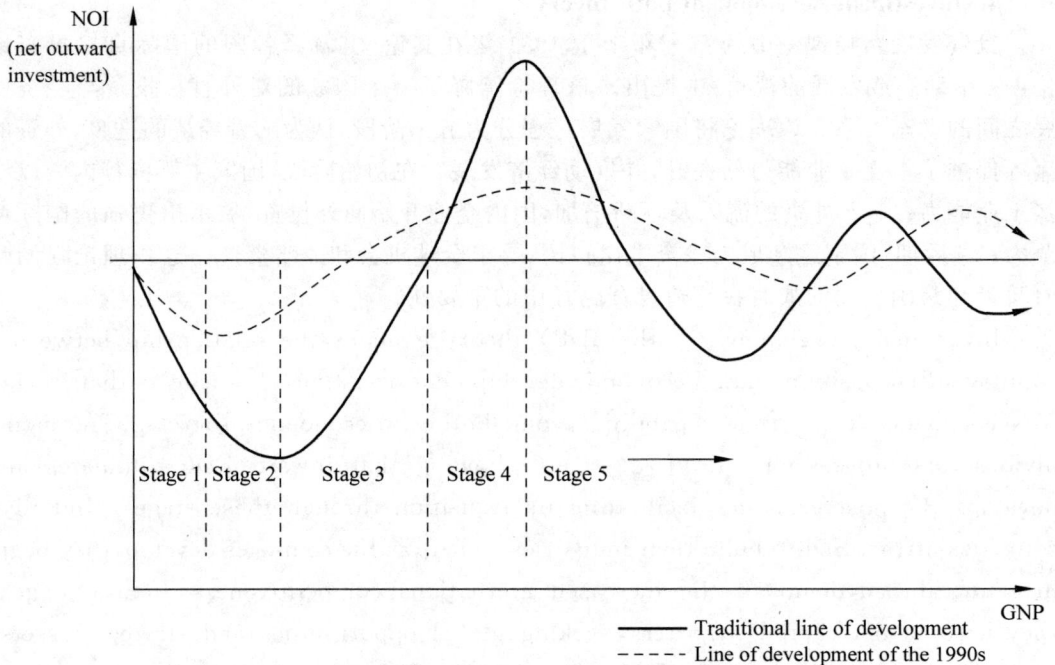

Figure 3-1　The pattern of the Investment Development Path

Source: Dunning, J. H. (1993), *Multinational Enterprises and the Global Economy*, Wokingham, Berkshire: Addison-Wesley.

1) Stage 1: At the initial stage, the domestic market generally lacks sufficient domestic capital and technological expertise for outbound investment because of poor infrastructure, misdirected government policies, low income per capita and inadequate education of the labor force. Foreign investors are mainly attracted by natural resources. Domestic firms have few ownership advantages and minimal outward

investment. Hence, the country acts as a net importer of foreign capital, with its focus on utilizing inward FDI to enhance domestic industry capabilities. The government's key role at this stage is to improve infrastructure and workforce training. Policies should be implemented to reduce market failures, which may include import protection and export subsidies. However, these measures do not enhance the technological level of the country's industry.

2) Stage 2: In the second stage, inward FDI begins to increase as the domestic market functions work more efficiently and attract more foreign firms, especially in low technology, labor-intensive manufacturing. If government policies effectively stimulate technological accumulation, they will create more advanced ownership advantages, initially within the sector that supports the primary industry. Firms in this supporting sector will begin to use their skills to produce moderately knowledge-intensive consumer goods, leading to an increase in outward investment. This outward investment occurs in two ways: to access new markets for slightly advanced products in less developed neighboring countries and to acquire technology in more developed countries. The extent of OFDI also depends on the country's trade policies. While net inward investment increases during the second stage, it starts to stabilize as domestic firms enter new markets.

3) Stage 3: As competition increases among firms producing standardized goods due to rising incomes, higher productivity leads to increased wages, making the country less attractive for labor-intensive investments. Domestic firms develop new ownership advantages, weakening foreign firms' positions, which drives outward direct investment as these firms establish affiliates in less developed countries to access markets for their advanced products. While inward investment may not decline, it shifts from labor-intensive production to more efficient processes that leverage human capital and technology fostered by public policies. Foreign firms transfer their unique assets from advanced markets to stay competitive. Additionally, inward direct investment through local asset acquisitions rises, including investment from domestic firms in developed countries. Some local firms evolve into MNCs, relying less on government support, though some may still seek assistance for foreign investments. Meanwhile, governments aim to attract inward investment in industries with limited ownership advantages.

4) Stage 4: The fourth stage begins when outward direct investment matches inward direct investment, after which outward investment grows faster. With lower capital costs than labor, the domestic market is dominated by firms leveraging their developed assets to compete against foreign companies and penetrate their markets. Inward direct investment mainly seeks assets from other stage 4 countries, with some from less developed countries driven by market opportunities. Outward investment increases as firms move less competitive assets to developing markets, internalizing

ownership advantages to bypass trade barriers. This leads to heightened intra-industry production and trade among similar MNCs. Government policies in this stage aim to maintain market efficiency through adjustments in location-bound assets and technological capabilities, supporting infant industries while phasing out uncompetitive ones.

5) Stage 5: In the fifth stage, advanced industrial countries primarily conduct transactions within MNCs. As markets and location-bound assets align, investments are more evenly distributed, leading to fluctuations around a zero net outward investment level. For MNCs, national borders become less significant, and transactions occur globally. This shift requires management to focus on organizing and allocating advantages. Economies transition from varied products based on factor endowments to economies of scale in differentiated goods, resulting in similar economic structures. To maintain their position, countries must enhance human and technological capital. Inward investments come from lower-stage countries seeking markets and knowledge, as well as from stage 4 or 5 countries rationalizing operations. Firms improve ownership advantages through strategic asset-seeking investments, including cross-border mergers and acquisitions (M&A) or alliances.

(3) Contributions and limitations

The IDP theory has a significant contribution to understanding the relationship between a country's economic development and its FDI patterns. It provides a structured and comprehensive framework to analyze how FDI evolves with economic development. By integrating the eclectic paradigm, the theory offers a robust explanation for why firms invest abroad. It also highlights the importance of government policies in attracting and managing FDI, making it useful for policymakers and researchers in economic planning.

However, the theory has limitations. It may not fully account for unique country-specific factors such as natural resources, size, and unique economic policies that significantly shape FDI patterns. Additionally, evolving global business dynamics and political reforms can create inconsistencies in its application. The assumption of free capital markets and openness to trade further limits the theory's relevance in certain developing countries.

第三节　新兴市场国家跨国公司对外直接投资理论 （Theories of FDI by MNCs from Emerging Markets）

1. Institutional theory

制度理论主要研究组织在特定制度环境中的运作与发展,强调法律、法规、文化和习俗等制度因素对组织行为和结构的影响。该理论认为,组织不仅为了提高效率和实现目标而行动和调整结构,更是为了获得合法性和稳定性。制度理论的出现反映了组织与其制度环境之间复杂互动的关系日益受到关注,提供了理解不同环境下组织行为的有力框架。特别是在全球化背景下,制度理论在新兴市场跨国公司国际化战略中的应用愈发显著,揭示了制度因素在这些公司国际扩展动机中的重要作用,包括制度支持和制度规避等。该理论的代表人物是著名华人管理学家彭维刚,其观点集中体现在发表于 2008 年的论文《基于制度的国际商务战略:聚焦新兴经济体》中。

The institutional theory has garnered significant attention in academic field recently. This theory primarily studies how organizations operate and develop within specific institutional environments. It emphasizes the impact of institutions,such as laws,regulations,culture,and customs,on organizational behavior and structure. According to this theory,organizations behave and structure themselves not only to improve efficiency or achieve goals but also to gain legitimacy and stability. Overall,the emergence of institutional theory reflects a growing recognition of the complex interplay between organizations and their institutional contexts,providing a robust framework for understanding organizational behavior across diverse environments.

(1) Origin and development

Institutional theory emerged from interdisciplinary influences,particularly sociology, economics,and organizational studies. Its origins can be traced to Max Weber's work on legitimacy and authority,further developed by scholars like Talcott Parsons and Philip Selznick. In the 1980s,the "New Institutionalism" movement gained traction through the efforts of W. Richard Scott,John W. Meyer,and Brian Rowan,who examined how organizations adopt structures and practices not just for efficiency but also to gain legitimacy within their environments. This emphasis on legitimacy became a core aspect of institutional theory,especially in contexts with varying institutional pressures.

Traditionally, institutional factors were often neglected in MNCs theories. However,as globalization advanced,recent studies have begun to explore the role of institutions in the internationalization strategies of MNCs,particularly those from emerging markets,highlighting how institutional factors shape these strategies and expanding the relevance of institutional theory. This theory was typically developed by famous Chinese management expert Mike W. Peng in his paper *An Institution-Based View of International Business Strategy: A Focus on Emerging Economies* published in 2008.

(2) Core concepts and ideas

Institutional theory argues that,although the industry-and resource-based views are insightful,they largely ignore the formal and informal institutional underpinning that provides the context of competition among industries and firms studied with these lenses. Institutions are much more than background conditions. Instead,institutions directly determine what arrows a firm has in its quiver as it struggles to formulate and implement strategy and to create competitive advantage.

Institutional theory suggests that the institution-based view represents the third leg of a strategy tripod, overcomes the long-standing criticisms of the industry-based and resource-based views' lack of attention to contexts, and contributes significant new insights as part of the broader intellectual movement centered on new institutionalism.

Institutional theory holds that for emerging market multinational corporations (EMNCs), institutional factors significantly influence the formulation and implementation of corporate strategies, rather than serving merely as a contextual backdrop. The theory emphasizes the impact of institutional factors on the international expansion motives of EMNCs, which mainly include the following:

1) Institutions as structures of stability: Institutions provide a framework that imbues organizations with meaning and continuity. This includes regulative elements (laws and regulations), normative aspects (values and norms), and cognitive dimensions (shared beliefs and understandings).

2) Institutional support: This concept refers to the favorable policies and practices instituted by home governments that facilitate the international expansion of firms, such as tax reductions, financial incentives, financial subsidies, and supportive regulatory frameworks that encourage businesses to enter foreign markets. Khanna and Palepu highlighted that emerging economies often face institutional voids during economic liberalization and institutional transformation. These voids create opportunities for EMNCs to leverage unique advantages like government support. By transferring these advantages to similar markets, EMNCs can gain a competitive edge over MNCs from developed countries.

3) Institutional escape: This theory highlights that EMNCs may pursue international expansion as a strategic means to circumvent the institutional constraints imposed by their home markets. This strategy allows firms to capitalize on more favorable institutional environments abroad, thereby enhancing their competitive positioning. Institutional arbitrage refers to leveraging the advantages of well-established institutions abroad to benefit the enterprise, essentially representing another facet of institutional escape.

(3) Contributions and limitations

Institutional theory provides insights into the behaviors and strategies of EMNCs during their international expansion amid diverse institutional landscapes. It explains how EMNCs leverage institutional voids and develop unique capabilities to compete globally, as well as how institutional factors affect their ownership and control decisions, especially in markets with varying levels of development.

However, the theory has its limitations. Critics point out that existing research often emphasizes formal institutions while neglecting informal ones, such as industry norms and cultural customs. This gap is particularly relevant when examining the transition of EMNCs from the "going out" phase to the "going in" phase.

2. Springboard theory

跳板理论由著名华人学者陆亚东及加拿大学者罗莎莉·佟于 2007 年在他们合作发表的论文《新兴市场企业的国际扩张：一个跳板视角》中首次提出,阐释了新兴市场跨国公司如何利用国际扩张作为战略手段,以克服国内的限制和竞争劣势。该理论认为,这些企业通过海外投资寻求技术、专业知识和市场准入等战略资产,旨在增强自身能力并提升全球影响力。新兴市场跨国公司通常采取高风险、高控制的进入模式和积极的选址策略,以规避国内制约,抓住国际机会。该理论强调了新兴市场企业在全球扩张中所面临的独特挑战与动机,展示了它们如何通过收购关键资源、增强全球竞争力,有效应对市场和制度约束。

The springboard theory, developed by Yadong Luo and Rosalie L Tung, explains how EMNCs leverage international expansion as a strategic response to overcome domestic limitations and competitive disadvantages. By seeking strategic assets, such as technology, expertise, and market access, through foreign investments, these firms aim to enhance their capabilities and establish a stronger global presence. The theory posits that EMNCs often pursue high-risk, high-control entry modes and aggressive location choices, enabling them to bypass domestic constraints and capitalize on international opportunities.

（1）Origin and development

The springboard theory is shaped by several key factors influencing EMNCs in the early 21st century. First, rapid globalization has led EMNCs to expand internationally at unprecedented rates, showcasing their unique trajectories compared to established MNCs. Second, these firms often face resource limitations, lacking advanced technologies, strong brands, and skilled talents, which poses challenges that traditional MNC theories fail to address. Third, weak institutional environments in many emerging markets hinder competitiveness, necessitating the acquisition of resources from abroad. Fourth, many EMNCs adopt proactive internationalization strategies, engaging in high-risk entry modes like cross-border mergers and acquisitions, in contrast to the cautious approaches of established firms.

Existing international business theories fall short in explaining the unique strategies and challenges of EMNCs, highlighting the need for new frameworks. The rise of EMNCs prompts key questions about how they overcome inherent disadvantages to achieve international success, fueling the search for fresh theoretical insights. The springboard theory, first presented by Luo and Tung in their 2007 paper *International Expansion of Emerging Market Enterprises: A Springboard Perspective* in particular, sheds light on the rapid internationalization of EMNCs, addressing their specific challenges and strategies in a globalized economy. It deepens our understanding of how these firms navigate their environments and acquire crucial resources for growth. In 2018, Luo and Tung published another paper with the title *A General Theory of Springboard MNEs* to improve the springboard theory by comparing it with the other main established theories on MNCs.

（2）Core concepts and ideas

The primary motivations driving EMNCs to expand internationally include compensation for competitive disadvantages, overcoming latecomer disadvantages, and counter-attacking global competitors. EMNCs seek to mitigate their competitive weaknesses by acquiring advanced technologies, global brands, and managerial expertise through international ventures. These firms aim to bridge the gap with established global competitors by aggressively entering foreign markets and leveraging strategic assets. They often expand internationally to challenge and counteract the dominance of global competitors in their home markets.

The springboard theory highlights several strategic processes and behaviors characteristic of EMNCs including asset-seeking investments, risk-taking and aggressive expansion, and integration with domestic operations, as shown in Figure 3-2. EMNCs actively pursue mergers, acquisitions, and partnerships to acquire strategic assets that enhance their competitive position. These firms are noted for their bold and sometimes high-risk investments in foreign markets, reflecting their proactive approach to internationalization. The international activities of EMNCs are closely integrated with their domestic operations, creating a recursive process where gains from abroad are reinvested at home.

The outcomes of the international expansion strategies of EMNCs, as proposed by the springboard theory, include enhanced global competitiveness and navigating institutional and market constraints. By acquiring critical resources and capabilities, EMNCs can significantly improve their global competitiveness and reduce vulnerabilities associated with their home country constraints. The theory underscores how EMNCs navigate and mitigate institutional and market constraints in their home countries through strategic international expansion.

（3）Contributions and limitations

The springboard theory enriches existing international business frameworks by focusing on the unique strategies and rapid expansion dynamics of emerging market firms, demonstrating how they leverage international markets to reposition themselves competitively both domestically and globally. Luo and Tung's theory significantly advances the understanding of EMNCs' international growth, explaining key motives such as acquiring strategic resources, overcoming domestic constraints, and competing globally. It highlights how EMNCs use international expansion as a "springboard" to acquire critical assets, emphasizing their aggressive and risk-taking behavior necessary to

Motivations of EM MNEs
- Asset seeking
- Opportunity seeking

Reasons encouraging them to spring
- Home government support for going global
- Willingness of global players to share or sell strategic resources
- Offshore availability of standardized technology
- Desire to hit the core and key international markets
- Entrepreneurial leadership

Springboard perspective
Systematically and recursively use international expansion as a springboard to:
- Compensate their competitive weaknesses
- Overcome their latecomer disadvantage
- Counter-attack global competitors
- Bypass stringent trade barriers into advanced markets
- Alleviate domestic institutional and market constraints
- Secure preferential treatments from home governments
- Exploit competitive advantage in other emerging and developing countries

Reasons impelling them to spring
- Their late mover position in international markets
- Strong foothold of global rivals in their backyard
- Fast change of technological and market landscape
- Shortened life cycle of industries and products
- Their deficiencies in core competencies and strategic assets

Unique activities
- Inward internationalization
- Risk-taking entry modes (acquisitions or greenfield)
- Path departure in location selection
- Radical in investment size and commitment

Unique challenges
- Poor corporate governance
- Post-spring integration and organization difficulties
- Lack of global experience, managerial competence and professional expertise
- Weak product/process innovation

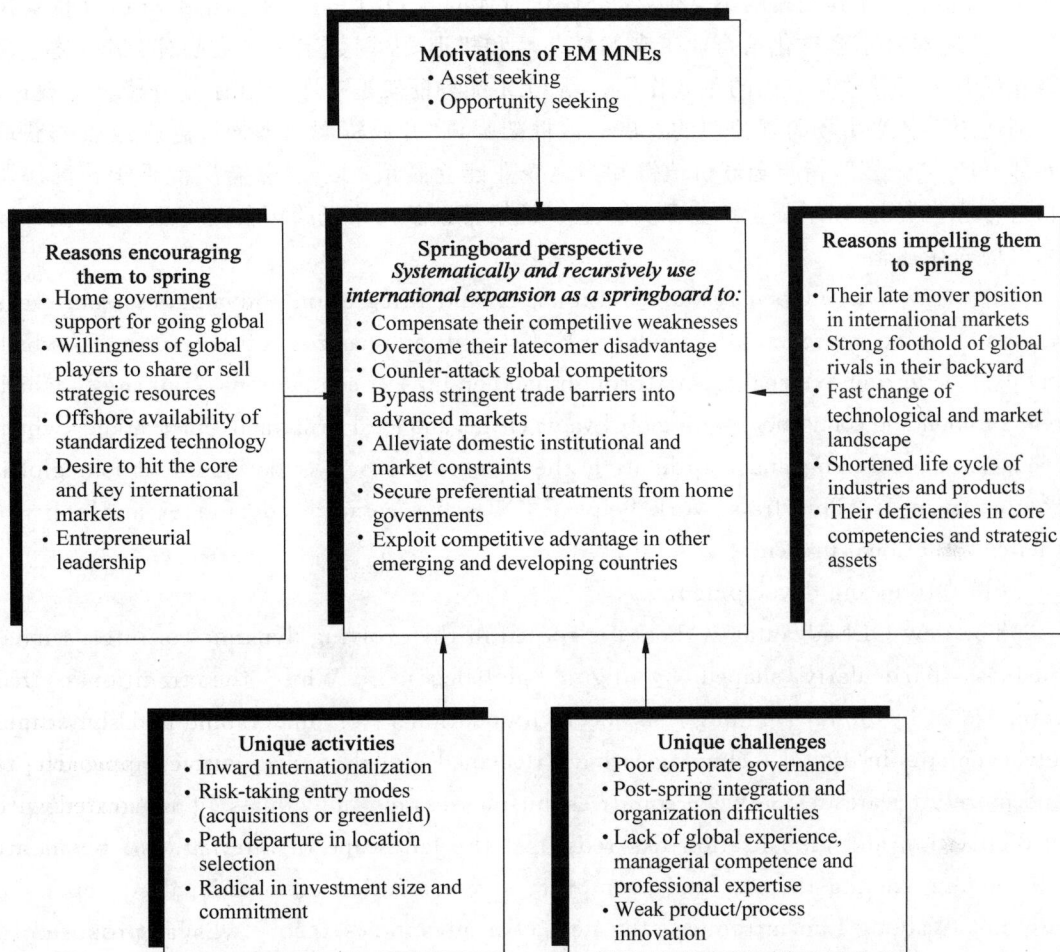

Figure 3-2　International expansion of EMNCs：a springboard perspective

Source：Luo，Y. and Tung，R. L. （2007）. International Expansion of Emerging Market Enterprises：A Springboard Perspective，*Journal of International Business Studies*，38（4）：481-498.

overcome latecomer disadvantages. The theory also offers a contextual view of the challenges and opportunities EMNCs face in global markets.

However，the theory has limitations. It overgeneralizes EMNCs' behaviors，as not all firms engage in springboarding，and more empirical evidences are needed to validate its claims. Additionally，the varying rates of success across firms，industries，and countries suggest the need for further refinement. The theory's complexity and the evolving nature of global markets may also necessitate continuous updates to remain relevant. While the springboard theory offers valuable insights into EMNC internationalization strategies，it requires further empirical support and refinement to address these challenges.

3. New OLI advantages

随着数字全球化的迅猛发展，传统的 OLI 模型面临挑战。在此背景下，华人学者陆亚东于 2021 年在其发表的论文《数字全球化时代的新 OLI 范式》中提出了新 OLI 优势理论，旨在应对数字全球化给企业带来的复杂性和机遇，强调数字工具在加速创新、建立网络和提升运营效率等方面的重要作用。新 OLI 优势框架是对邓宁原有 OLI 模型的改进，特别适用于新兴市场跨国公司的发展。该框架强调"开放资源"，即通过合作或收购获取外部资产；"链接"，指与全球价值链和当地企业建立联系；以及"整合"，侧重于跨国协调和组合这些资源，以增强全球竞争力。这一框架帮助新兴市场跨国公司克服劣势，提升国际市场的存在感。

The new OLI（Open resources, Linkages, and Integration）advantages framework adapts Dunning's original OLI model to EMNCs. It emphasizes "open resources", which involves acquiring external assets through partnerships or acquisitions, "linkages", which refers to building connections with global value chains and local firms, and "integration", which focuses on combining and coordinating these resources across borders to boost global competitiveness. This framework helps EMNCs overcome disadvantages and enhance their international presence.

（1）Origin and development

The new OLI advantages theory is rooted in the evolving dynamics of international business, particularly shaped by digital globalization. While the traditional OLI framework by John Dunning has been foundational for understanding FDI, rapid advancements in digital technologies have reshaped global connectivity, creating deeper and more intricate ties between countries, businesses, and individuals. This convergence of digitization and globalization has redefined the landscape of international business, challenging existing theories and prompting a re-evaluation of traditional concepts. In response, Yadong Luo introduced the new OLI advantages theory which stresses open resources, linkages, and integration in his paper *New OLI Advantages in Digital Globalization* in 2021. These revised advantages adapt the original framework to address the complexities and opportunities of digital globalization, enabling MNCs to enhance speed, flexibility, coordination, and efficiency in both interfirm and intrafirm activities.

（2）Core concepts and ideas

Luo's reinterpretation of the OLI framework introduces "open resources, linkages, and integration（new OLI）", specifically tailored to the strategies of EMNCs, offering a more flexible view of how these firms catch up in global markets. The framework includes three core components.

1）Open resource advantage：This emphasizes how firms can tap into open resources like digital platforms and open-source technologies, much like finding shortcuts on a map to reach their destination faster. By using these digital tools, MNCs gain access to global innovation, data, and real-time information, overcoming traditional barriers such as distance and cost.

2）Linkage advantage：This focuses on the ability of EMNCs to forge strong networks with global value chains and partners，similar to building bridges that connect different islands of knowledge and opportunity. These digital connections allow firms to share knowledge，innovate，and access new markets quickly.

3）Integration advantage：This highlights how companies can integrate digital technologies into their operations，akin to fine-tuning an engine for better performance. Digital connectivity enables MNCs to coordinate internal processes more efficiently， improving their speed，flexibility，and overall operational effectiveness.

（3）Contributions and limitations

The new OLI advantages enhance our understanding of MNCs in the context of digital globalization by complementing the traditional OLI model. This framework incorporates a resource-orchestration perspective，emphasizing how firms can effectively manage digital resources to boost their internationalization efforts. It specifically addresses how EMNCs can leverage linkage advantages to overcome latecomer disadvantages by facilitating access to networks and knowledge transfer.

However，the new OLI framework has limitations. Some researchers argue that it overlooks additional advantages relevant to digital platform firms，particularly the significance of information and knowledge assets. While Luo's framework is comprehensive， scholars suggest it should be refined to capture the nuances of digital platforms and emerging business models.

In summary，Luo's new OLI advantages theory provides valuable insights into international business strategy in the digital era，but ongoing researches and refinement are essential to fully understand the complexities of digital globalization.

关键术语（Key Terms）

垄断优势（monopolistic advantage）
市场不完善（market imperfections）
垄断优势理论（monopolistic advantage theory）
产品生命周期（product life cycle）
产品生命周期理论（product life cycle theory）
比较优势（comparative advantage）
内部化（internalization）
市场无效率（market inefficiency）
垂直整合（vertical integration）
水平整合（horizontal integration）
内部化理论（internalization theory）
边际产业（marginal industry）

边际产业扩张理论（marginal industry expansion theory）
国际生产折衷理论（eclectic theory of international production）
OLI 范式（OLI paradigm）
利基市场（niche markets）
小规模技术理论（small-scale technology theory）
技术地方化理论（technology localization theory）
本地化技术适应（localized technology adaptation）

引进技术提升(imported technology enhancement)

技术创新和产业升级理论(technology innovation and industry upgrading theory)

投资发展路径理论(investment development path theory)

新兴市场跨国公司(EMNCs)

制度理论(institutional theory)

制度环境(institutional environment)

制度支持(institutional support)

制度规避(institutional escape)

高风险进入模式(high-risk entry modes)

跳板理论(springboard theory)

新 OLI 范式(open resources,linkages,and integration advantages framework)

小结(Summary)

1. Theories of FDI by MNCs from developed countries include monopolistic advantage theory, product life cycle theory, internalization theory, marginal industry expansion theory, and eclectic theory of international production. The monopolistic advantage theory explains that MNCs invest abroad to exploit their unique advantages such as technology, management skills, and economies of scale. The product life cycle theory describes how products evolve through stages from introduction to decline, influencing international trade and investment patterns. The internalization theory focuses on why firms prefer FDI over exporting or licensing, emphasizing the reduction of transaction costs and protection of proprietary knowledge. The marginal industry expansion theory suggests that FDI should start with industries where the home country is losing its comparative advantage, benefiting both the home and host countries economically. Lastly, the eclectic theory of international production integrates ownership, location, and internalization to explain why and how firms engage in international production and FDI.

2. Theories explaining FDI by MNCs from developing countries cover small-scale technology theory, technology localization theory, technology innovation and industry upgrading theory, and investment development path theory. The small-scale technology theory highlights how developing countries use labor-intensive, small-scale production to compete internationally. The technology localization theory explains how these firms adapt and innovate imported technologies to gain a competitive edge. The technology innovation and industry upgrading theory explains how these countries accumulate and adapt existing technologies to enhance their industrial capabilities and competitiveness. Lastly, the investment development path theory outlines the dynamic relationship between a country's economic development and its FDI patterns, emphasizing the role of government policies and strategic investments in shaping this path.

3. Theories of FDI by MNCs from emerging markets include three main theories: institutional theory, springboard theory, and new OLI advantages. The institutional theory examines how institutional factors like laws, regulations, and cultural norms

influence the international strategies of EMNCs. The springboard theory explains how EMNCs use international expansion to overcome domestic constraints and competitive disadvantages by acquiring strategic assets abroad. The new OLI advantages theory, which adapts Dunning's original OLI framework to the digital era, emphasizes open resources, linkages, and integration to enhance EMNCs' global competitiveness.

延伸阅读（Further Readings）

习题（Exercises）

第 四 章
Chapter 4

跨国公司的战略管理
Strategic Management of Multinational Corporations

Learning Objectives

- To explain the concept of strategy and strategic management
- To understand how pressures for cost reductions and local responsiveness influence multinational corporations' strategic choice
- To identify and choose the different strategies for competing globally

第一节 跨国公司战略及其战略管理
（Multinational Corporations' Strategy and Strategic Management）

战略管理是组织设定目标、制定实现这些目标的战略,然后分配资源以确保这些战略成功实施的过程。这是一个动态且迭代的过程,要求组织不断评估并适应变化的环境。战略管理的核心是做出与组织使命、愿景和价值观相符的明智决策。对于跨国公司来说,战略管理更加复杂,因为它们的运营具有全球性质。跨国公司必须在多个法律体系、文化规范、经济状况和竞争格局中开展经营管理活动。

Strategic management is the process by which organizations set goals, develop strategies to achieve those goals, and then allocate resources to ensure the successful implementation of those strategies. It is a dynamic and iterative process that requires organizations to continuously evaluate and adapt to changing environments. At the heart of strategic management is the ability to make informed decisions that align with an organization's mission, vision, and values.

For MNCs, strategic management is even more complex due to the global nature of their operations. MNCs must navigate multiple legal systems, cultural norms, economic conditions, and competitive landscapes.

1. The concept of strategy

在商业环境中,战略指的是公司为实现其目标并保持相对于竞争对手的竞争优势而制定的长期计划和行动。它包括公司在市场中的定位、超越竞争对手的方法,以及为未来设定的目标。好的战略能够将组织资源、能力和行动与商业环境的变化动态进行协调。对于跨国公司来说,由于其运营的全球性质,战略为公司提供了一个路线图,以应对全球市场的复杂性,是企业规划进入新市场、跨境管理运营和在全球范围内竞争的框架。

(1) What is strategy?

Strategy, in a business context, refers to the long-term plan and actions of a company to achieve its objectives and to maintain a competitive advantage over its rivals. It encompasses the way a company positions itself in the market, the methods it uses to outperform its competitors, and the goals it sets for the future. A well-crafted strategy aligns an organization's resources, capabilities, and actions with the changing dynamics of the business environment.

At its core, strategy involves making choices about which markets to compete in, how to compete, and the unique value proposition that will attract customers. It includes decisions about product development, marketing, operations, finance, and human resources, all of which are coordinated to support the overall direction of the company.

(2) Strategy and MNCs

For an MNC, strategy is even more complex due to the global nature of its operations. It plays a pivotal role in the internationalization of companies, providing a roadmap for companies to navigate the complexities of global markets. It is the framework within which companies plan their approach to entering new markets, managing operations across borders, and competing on a global scale.

In the context of internationalization, strategy helps companies identify the most lucrative markets, align their resources, and leverage their competitive advantages. It involves assessing the external environment, including political, economic, social, and technological factors, as well as understanding the competitive landscape and consumer behavior in target markets.

As the rise of companies from emerging markets, many Chinese companies become successful with their international strategies. Haier, a leading home appliances manufacturer, embarked on a gradual international expansion strategy, which they summarized as "going out, getting in, and going up". Another notable case is Huawei's international strategy, which involved a phased approach to global expansion. Huawei started by targeting emerging markets and then gradually entered developed markets through strategic partnerships, localization strategies, and a strong focus on research and development. Lenovo's international strategy, on the other hand, was more rapid and acquisition-driven. Their acquisition of IBM's PC business allowed them to quickly enter global markets and gain access to new technologies and brand recognition. These strategies highlight the importance of adapting to local market conditions, leveraging global resources, and maintaining a long-term perspective when expanding internationally. They also underscore the need for a flexible approach that can respond to changing global market dynamics and the ability to integrate global operations with local market needs.

（3）MNCs' strategy and management

A well-crafted international strategy allows companies to make informed decisions about market entry modes, whether through exports, joint ventures, wholly-owned subsidiaries, or greenfield investments. It also guides the development of localized products and services that cater to the specific needs and preferences of consumers in different countries.

Furthermore, strategy is crucial for managing the supply chain effectively on an international level. It helps companies optimize their operations, reduce costs, and ensure a steady flow of goods and services across borders. This includes decisions about where to source raw materials, where to manufacture products, and how to distribute them to various markets.

In terms of human resource management, international strategy informs decisions about staffing, training, and managing a multicultural workforce. It addresses the challenges of cultural diversity and ensures that the company's values and practices are aligned with local norms and regulations.

Risk management is another critical aspect where strategy comes into play. International companies face a variety of risks, from currency fluctuations and political instability to legal and regulatory changes. A robust international strategy anticipates these risks and develops mitigation plans to safeguard the company's interests.

Lastly, an effective international strategy fosters innovation and adaptability, enabling companies to respond quickly to changes in the global business environment. It encourages the development of new technologies, business models, and processes that can be leveraged across markets.

In summary, strategy is the cornerstone of successful internationalization. It enables companies to expand their reach, optimize their operations, manage risks, and innovate in a way that is both sustainable and profitable. Effective strategic management is crucial for MNCs to navigate the complexities of international markets, optimize their global operations, and sustain their competitive advantage in the long term.

2. Levels of strategy

在战略管理领域，战略概念在组织内各个层级得到应用，每个层级都有其独特的焦点和目标。三个主要的战略层级是公司战略、业务战略和职能战略。每个层级在指导公司的方向和运营、确保一致性以及促进整体成功方面都扮演着至关重要的角色。

In the realm of strategic management, the concept of strategy is applied at various levels within an organization, each with its own focus and objectives. The three primary levels of strategy are corporate strategy, business strategy, and functional strategy. Each level plays a critical role in guiding the direction and operations of a company, ensuring alignment, and contributing to the overall success. Table 4-1 demonstrates the decision hierarchy, scope, content and major impacts of strategies at these levels.

Table 4-1 Levels of strategy

	Corporate strategy	Business strategy	Functional strategy
Decision hierarchy	Top management	Division level management	Function level managers
Scope	Corporate strategy is the highest level of strategy, involving the long-term development and overall direction of the entire company.	Business strategy focuses on specific business units or product lines, such as a division or a subsidiary.	Functional strategy is the most specific, targeting various functional departments within the organization.
Content	It includes determining the company's business scope, market positioning, resource allocation, diversification and internationalization strategies, mergers and acquisitions, and restructuring.	It involves how to compete in a particular market or industry, including market segmentation, target market selection, product positioning, competitive strategies (such as cost leadership, differentiation, or focus strategies), etc.	It includes how to support and implement corporate and business strategies through specific functional activities, such as marketing strategies, supply chain management, talent recruitment and training, product development, etc.
Impact	It determines the company's overall goals and vision, as well as how to achieve these goals through different business units.	Business strategy directly affects the competitiveness and market performance of business units.	Functional strategy directly affects the daily operational efficiency and effectiveness of the organization.

（1）Corporate strategy

公司战略是最高层次的战略。公司战略可以被定义为公司高层管理为实现可持续的竞争优势并确保组织的长期生存和增长所采取的一系列决策和行动。它涉及对整个组织的范围和方向做出决策。公司战略塑造了公司的基本性质，影响着从其文化到其投资决策的一切。

Corporate strategy, also known as company strategy, is the highest level of strategic planning. Corporate strategy can be defined as the set of decisions and actions that are taken by a company's top management to achieve sustainable competitive advantage and ensure the long-term viability and growth of the organization. It involves making decisions about the scope and direction of the entire organization. Corporate strategy shapes the fundamental nature of the company, influencing everything from its culture to its investment decisions. It answers the fundamental questions of what business the company is in, which markets to serve, and how to compete. It encompasses decisions about diversification, growth, and the allocation of resources across different business units or product lines.

Key aspects of corporate strategy include: determining the organization's purpose and goals; deciding on the organizational structure and governance; allocating resources across different business units or divisions; identifying and pursuing strategic initiatives that align with the company's mission.

Corporate strategy decisions are typically made at the highest levels of the organization, often by the CEO, the board of directors, and the executive team. These decisions require a deep understanding of the company's capabilities, the competitive landscape, and the broader economic and political environment. They also require a long-term perspective and a willingness to take risks to achieve significant gains.

（2）Business strategy

业务战略，也称为竞争战略，是在公司内部的单个业务单元或产品线层面上运作的。它关注的是特定业务如何在其市场中竞争以实现其目标。

Business strategy, also referred to as competitive strategy, operates at the level of individual business units or product lines within a company. It is concerned with how a specific business will compete in its market to achieve its objectives. Business strategy is about creating a sustainable competitive advantage by differentiating the business from its competitors or by achieving a cost leadership position.

Key elements of business strategy include: market positioning, which involves identifying a unique value proposition that appeals to a specific target market; competitive advantage, which could be based on factors such as product quality, innovation, brand reputation, customer service, or price; strategic alliances or partnerships that can enhance market access or technological capabilities; market entry and exit decisions, which are based on the attractiveness of the market and the business's ability to compete effectively.

Business strategies are developed by the leaders of each business unit, often in consultation with corporate headquarters, and are tailored to the specific needs and opportunities of the market in which the business operates.

（3）Functional strategy

职能战略是三个层次中最具操作性的，它专注于业务单元内的具体职能或部门。它将公司战略和业务战略转化为可执行的计划，指导组织的日常工作。每个职能领域，如市场营销、财务、人力资源、运营以及研究与开发，都会制定自己的战略来支持整体目标。

Functional strategy is the most operational of the three levels and focuses on the specific functions or departments within a business unit. It translates the corporate and business strategies into actionable plans that guide the day-to-day operations of the organization. Each functional area, such as marketing, finance, human resources, operations, and research and development, develops its own strategy to support the overall objectives.

Functional strategies typically include: marketing strategies that outline how to promote the company's products, acquire and retain customers, and build brand loyalty; financial strategies that involve capital budgeting, investment decisions, and risk management; human resource strategies that focus on talent acquisition, development, and retention; operational strategies that aim to improve efficiency, quality, and customer satisfaction; R&D strategies that drive innovation and the development of new products or services.

Functional strategies are developed by the managers of each department in alignment with the business strategy and are critical for the effective execution of the company's plans.

(4) Integration of the three levels

这三个层次的战略相互依赖,必须相互协调一致,组织才能有效地实现其目标。公司战略提供总体方向,业务战略为每个单元定义竞争方法,职能战略确保运营活动支持更广泛的战略目标。每个层次的战略都有其独特的焦点,但它们必须协同工作,推动公司朝着其愿景和目标前进。在竞争激烈且不断变化的商业环境中,三个层次上的有效战略管理对于长期成功至关重要。

The three levels of strategy are interdependent and must be aligned for the organization to achieve its goals effectively. Corporate strategy provides the overall direction, business strategy defines the competitive approach for each unit, and functional strategy ensures that the operational activities support the broader strategic objectives. If a company's corporate strategy is to focus on innovation, the business strategy for a particular unit might involve entering new markets with unique products. The functional strategies would then support this by investing in R&D, launching creative marketing campaigns, and ensuring that operations are agile enough to adapt to new product development cycles.

Corporate strategy, business strategy, and functional strategy form a hierarchical framework that guides an organization's decisions and actions. Each level has its unique focus, but they must work in concert to drive the company towards its vision and objectives. Effective strategic management at all three levels is essential for long-term success in a competitive and dynamic business environment.

For instance, Haier's corporate strategy is characterized by a focus on innovation and quality, which has been a cornerstone since Zhang Ruimin. Haier has also embraced a "renovator" role, aiming to transform not just its products but also the traditional manufacturing model through the use of digital platforms and a culture of continuous improvement. Operationally, Haier has adopted a user-centric business strategy, emphasizing rapid response to market demands and a high level of customization. This strategy is supported by a unique management approach known as "Rendanheyi", which encourages employee entrepreneurship and autonomy within the company. Haier has also been a pioneer in the Internet of Things (IoT), creating smart home ecosystems that integrate various appliances and services, enhancing user experience and loyalty. Functionally, Haier has implemented strategies that support its corporate and business objectives. For instance, its research and development strategy focuses on creating innovative products that meet specific consumer needs, while its marketing strategy leverages digital platforms to engage with customers and collect feedback. Haier's success in integrating these strategies is evident in its ability to adapt to changing market conditions and consumer preferences. The company's corporate vision of becoming a global leader in smart home solutions is supported by business strategies that focus on innovation and customer-centricity. Functional strategies are aligned with these objectives, ensuring that all departments contribute to the company's overarching goals.

3. The strategic management process

战略管理是组织为设定目标、制定战略和做出决策而进行的重要过程，这些决策将强化企业的竞争优势，保障企业的长期成功。

Strategic management is a critical process that organizations undertake to set goals, develop strategies, and make decisions that will enhance their competitive advantage and ensure long-term success. It involves a continuous cycle of assessment, planning, implementation, and control. Figure 4-1 illustrates the stages and processes involved in strategic management.

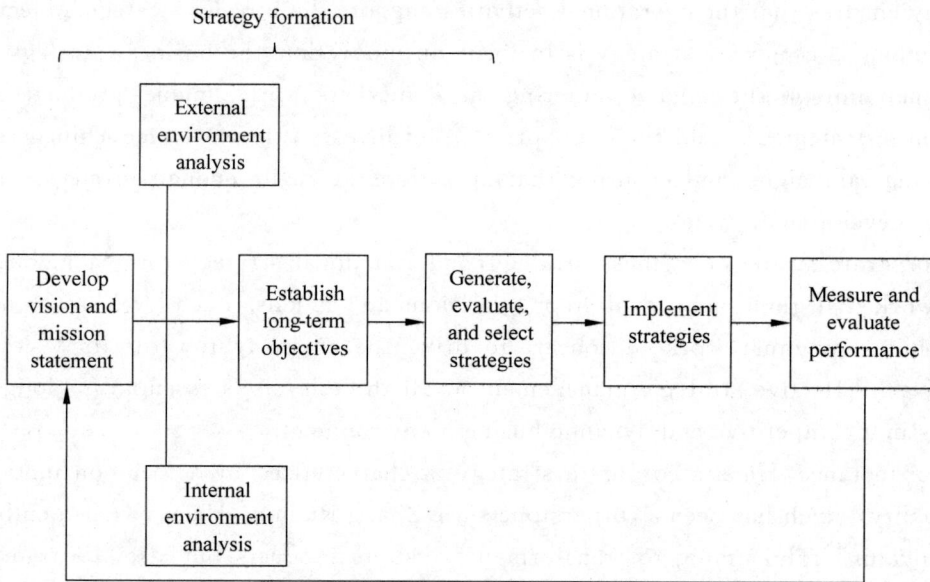

Figure 4-1 A comprehensive strategic management model

(1) Strategy formulation

制定战略需要回答三个重要问题：公司目前在哪？公司欲去何方？公司如何去？企业的使命、愿景、目标、现有战略和内外部环境说明了企业的现状。跨国公司通常在明确自己的长期目标后制定、评估和选择国际化战略。

When developing a corporate strategy plan, there are three important questions to answer. Where is the company now? Where will the company go? How is the company going to get there? The answers to the above three questions are embedded in the steps of strategy formulation. Strategy formulation is the starting point of the strategic management process, requiring the company to clarify its existing vision, mission, long-term goals, and strategy. It also requires an in-depth analysis of the external environment (opportunities and threats) and the internal environment (strengths and weaknesses) to understand a company's present situation and condition. In practice, goal formulation often precedes the external and internal environment analysis. MNCs pursue a variety of goals. When generating, evaluating and selecting strategies, companies also need to consider how to allocate resources, whether to diversify or internationalize, and whether to expand business through mergers and acquisitions or joint ventures. Decisions made at this stage will have a profound impact on the future development of the enterprise.

Key success factors for strategy formulation include: accurate information gathering, ensuring that the data and information collected are accurate and up-to-date for effective analysis; comprehensive environmental scanning, including a thorough analysis of both internal and external environments to identify all potential opportunities and threats; communicating with all key stakeholders to ensure their needs and expectations are understood and considered; developing a clear and inspiring vision and mission to provide direction for the organization; encouraging innovative thinking to develop unique and effective strategies; ensuring that resources such as funds, personnel, and technology are allocated effectively where they are most needed; strategic planning should have a certain degree of flexibility to adapt to changing market and environment; alignment of strategy with goals, ensuring that the strategies formulated are aligned with the organization's vision, mission, and goals.

(2) Strategy implementation

在制定战略之后，公司需要通过具体的行动计划来实施它们。这包括设定年度目标、制定政策、激励员工以及分配资源，以确保所制定的战略得到有效执行。战略实施的关键是确保所有部门和员工都朝着既定的战略目标工作，并且有效利用资源。

After formulating strategies, companies need to implement them through specific action plans. This includes setting annual goals, developing policies, motivating employees, and allocating resources to ensure that the formulated strategies are effectively carried out. The key to strategic implementation is to ensure that all departments and employees work towards the established strategic goals and that resources are used effectively.

Key success factors for strategy implementation include: strong leadership, which is crucial for driving the implementation of strategy; clear communication, ensuring that all employees understand the strategic objectives and their roles in achieving these objectives; ensuring that strategic projects are completed on time, within budget, and to quality standards through effective project management practices; employee engagement and commitment, which is the key to successful implementation; regularly monitoring and evaluating the progress of strategic implementation to make timely adjustments and improvements.

（3）Strategy evaluation

战略评估是战略管理过程的最后阶段，主要包括监控和评估实施结果。企业需要定期检查战略实施的有效性，确保战略目标的实现，并根据内外部环境条件的变化调整战略。

Strategy evaluation is the final stage of the strategic management process, involving monitoring and evaluating the results of implementation. Companies need to regularly check the effectiveness of strategic implementation, ensure the achievement of strategic goals, and adjust strategies according to changes in the market and internal conditions.

Key success factors for strategy evaluation include: setting clear performance metrics to measure the effectiveness of strategic implementation; making decisions based on evidence using collected data and feedback; learning from the implementation process and continuously improving the strategic management process; being able to quickly adapt to changes in the external environment and adjust strategies accordingly.

Throughout the strategic management process, the vision and decision-making ability of business leaders are crucial. They need to be forward-thinking, understand the development trends of the market and technology, and be able to flexibly adjust strategies to cope with the constantly changing environment. At the same time, they also need to ensure that there are sufficient resources to support the implementation of strategies and be able to motivate team members to work towards common goals.

Strategic decisions not only affect the current operations of a company but also determine its future direction and competitiveness. Therefore, companies need to continuously evaluate and adjust their strategies to ensure they maintain an advantage in the fierce market competition.

第二节　跨国公司战略目标与途径
（Strategic Goals and Means of Multinational Corporations）

全球战略不仅仅是一系列国际运营的集合，而是跨国公司为管理跨境运营而采取的一种经过深思熟虑的方法。它涉及利用全球活动整合所带来的竞争优势以及对本地市场需求的响应能力。在制定全球战略时，跨国公司必须考虑三个主要的战略目标：运营效率、风险管理和保持创新和适应性的学习能力。实现以上这些目标需要跨国公司具有一定的竞争优势，而跨国公司通常可以利用国家差异、规模经济以及协同效应或范围经济来建立自己的竞争优势。成功的全球战略的关键在于如何协调这些不同的目标和途径。

Global strategy is not merely a collection of international operations but a deliberate approach that MNCs adopt to manage their operations across borders. It involves leveraging the competitive advantages that arise from the global integration of activities and the responsiveness to local market demands. The concept has gained prominence as the world has become more interconnected, and companies have recognized the need to go beyond domestic markets to achieve economies of scale, diversify risks, and tap into new sources of innovation.

There are three primary strategic objectives that MNCs must consider when developing their global strategies. First, MNCs must strive to optimize the efficiency of their operations by reducing costs and improving the value of their outputs. This involves configuring the value chain in a way that maximizes the use of resources and minimizes waste. Second, MNCs operate in a diverse set of environments, each with its own set of risks. These risks can be macroeconomic, policy-related, competitive, or resource-based. A global strategy must take into account these risks and develop mechanisms to mitigate them. Third, in an ever-changing global landscape, MNCs must continuously innovate and adapt to stay ahead. MNCs usually have three tools for developing competitive advantages to optimize the MNCs' achievement of these different and, sometimes, conflicting goals. These tools are: exploiting differences in input and output markets in different countries, exploiting economies of scale, and exploiting economies of scope. The key to a successful global strategy is to manage the interactions between these different goals and means.

1. The dominant goal: achieving efficiency

效率是跨国公司的主要战略目标之一,在全球战略中的整合—响应框架能很好地反映这一效率目标。竞争环境、经济状况、技术进步、监管变化和客户需求等各种内外部因素形成了跨国公司降低成本的压力。能够成功降低成本的公司通常可以通过以较低的价格提供产品或服务、提高盈利能力或将节省的资金重新投资到其他战略领域(如研发或市场营销)来获得竞争优势。对本地响应的压力指的是跨国公司需要调整其产品、服务和商业实践,以满足其运营的本地市场的独特偏好、文化规范、法律要求和市场条件。

Efficiency, in business context, can be defined as the optimal use of resources to produce the maximum output with the minimum input. It is a dominant strategic goal. In the field of global strategy, this efficiency perspective has been reflected in the widespread use of the integration-responsiveness framework.

(1) Forces for global integration

Various internal and external forces always compel companies to minimize their expenses and improve efficiency. These pressures can stem from competitive dynamics, economic conditions, technological advancements, regulatory changes, and customer demands. Companies that can successfully reduce costs often gain a competitive advantage by offering products or services at lower prices, improving profitability, or reinvesting savings into other strategic areas such as research and development or marketing. According to Theodore Levitt, globalization has combined technological, social, and economic developments to create a unified world marketplace in which companies must capture global-scale economies to remain competitive. Although this argument is somewhat extreme and one-sided, in a global industry, a company's competitive position in one country is strongly affected by its position in other countries. Thus, the different countries in which an MNC operates can be linked to each other. This could be, economies of scale are particularly high in a specific industry, leading to the necessity of internationally standardized products. Alternatively, it could result from comparative cost advantages of a country that offer an incentive to specialize the activities of certain foreign subsidiaries, leading to interdependence between the worldwide activities. Necessity for worldwide learning, in order to exploit knowledge companywide that has been created in a particular country or the situation in which relevant actors around the MNC (e. g. customers, competitors, and suppliers) are the same in different foreign markets, enhances the requirement and the potential to coordinate closely the different international activities. These interdependencies between countries (which vary by industry) are called forces for global integration.

The forces for global integration can be divided into four categories: market drivers, cost drivers, governmental drivers, and competitive drivers. First of all, homogenous customer needs in the different markets may create opportunities to sell standardized products. With common customer needs, marketing becomes transferable across countries. Globalization suggests that different cultures become more similar, and lifestyles and tastes converge worldwide. From a cost perspective, different industries may have different incentives to standardize, but the greater the potential economies of scale and the steeper the experience curve, the more likely an industry is to turn global. While global sourcing efficiencies might be given in an industry, leading to concentration of supply and manufacturing, intercountry differences in labor costs and factor endowments might make concentration of production useful. Over the last few decades, logistics costs have generally been decreasing, making global integration easier to achieve. Many governmental drivers also have an influence on the need for globalization in an industry. For example, uniform technical standards are necessary for product standardization, and liberal trading regulations with low tariff and nontariff barriers to trade, and common market regulations are drivers for globalization, making cross-border trade easier. As the most important competitive driver, global competitors enhance the need for global integration. Only companies that manage their worldwide operations as interdependent units can implement a coordinated strategy and use a competitive strategy sometimes called "global chess", i. e. responding to threats in one market by reactions in other markets. Additionally, large MNCs offering the same products and brands around the world also promote the convergence of tastes and customer demands. International networks in production, market and innovation that also enhance the interdependence of countries and markets emerge in the presence of many MNCs.

(2) Forces for local responsiveness

Alternatively, depending on the industry, companies are facing another set of influence factors that make local responsiveness necessary. An MNC operates in heterogeneous conditions in many different host countries. The local unit in each country deals with different local customers and host governments, different market and distribution structures, and different competitors. Multinational flexibility, i. e. the ability of a company to exploit the opportunities that arise from this heterogeneity, is necessary. This contingency condition for MNCs is referred to as the forces for local responsiveness.

This pressure arises from the recognition that a one-size-fits-all approach is often not effective in a global business environment where diversity and local specificity are the norms. This might be caused by profound cultural differences in tastes, different environmental conditions (climate, topography, etc.), or different income levels and income distribution, among many other factors. A different structure of the distributive sector might make adaptations to the distribution strategy necessary. A different competitive situation in different markets might also force a company to change its strategy, adapting it to the local market conditions. Similarly, protectionism by governments often leads to the need to produce locally and/or adapt products to specific markets. While the need for adaptation has occurred at the country level in the past, it now increasingly occurs at the level of regional integration areas such as the EU.

Local responsiveness can also become necessary or beneficial due to either different labor conditions, e. g. labor cost or skill level, that require adaptation of production processes to optimize efficiency, or the availability or non-availability of suppliers. A low number of potential suppliers might make a higher level of vertical integration in the production steps more or less efficient due to a lack of alternatives. Different work attitudes that may be rooted in different cultures might make different leadership styles more or less effective in different countries.

2. Other strategic objectives

(1) Managing risks

战略管理的更广泛目标是创造价值,这不仅取决于特定资产预期产生的回报,还取决于过程中承担的风险。跨国公司面临的主要风险包括宏观经济风险、政治或政策风险、竞争风险和资源风险。管理风险的战略任务是在特定战略决策的背景下考虑这些不同类型的风险。

While efficiency is clearly a dominant strategic objective, it is not the only one. The broader objective of strategic management is to create value which is determined not only by the returns that specific assets are expected to generate, but also by the risks assumed in the process. First, an MNC faces certain macroeconomic risks which include cataclysmic events such as wars and natural calamities, and equilibrium seeking or even random movements in wage rates, interest rates, exchange rates, commodity prices, and so on. Second, the MNC faces political or policy risks, which arise from policy actions of national governments and not from either long-term equilibrium-seeking forces of global markets, or short-term random fluctuations in economic variables. Third, a company also faces certain competitive risks arising from the uncertainties of competitors' responses to its own strategies. The implications are complex in the context of global strategies since the responses of competitors may take place in many different forms and in many different markets. Finally, an MNC also faces resource risks. This is the risk that the adopted strategy requires resources that the MNC does not have and cannot acquire, for example, lack of appropriate technology, managerial talent, or capital.

The strategy of an MNC often assumes that appropriate resources will be acquired as the strategy unfolds. Yet the initial conditions on which the plans for on-going resource acquisition and development have been based may change over time. The strategic task of managing risks is to consider these different kinds of risks jointly in the context of particular strategic decisions.

(2) Innovation, learning and adaptation

基于核心竞争力，跨国公司能够通过在全球市场利用其技术、品牌或管理能力优势创造更多的盈利。与国内公司相比，多元化的国际环境为跨国公司建立核心竞争力提供重要助力，跨国经营的公司能够有更多机会发展多元化的能力，有更多的学习和创新机会。但是多元化的国际环境本身并不能保证公司学习能力的提升，跨国公司需要建立合适的制度将国际化经营带来的学习潜力变为现实。

With its core competencies a company can go abroad to make more profits by exploiting its technology, or brand name, or management capabilities in different countries around the world. The core competencies of the MNCs always reside at the center of these activities. To build core competencies, a key asset is the diversity of environments in which MNCs operate. This diversity exposes it to multiple stimuli, allows it to develop diverse capabilities, and provides it with a broader learning opportunity than is available to a purely domestic company. The enhanced organizational learning that results from the diversity internalized by the MNCs may be a key explanator of its ongoing success, while its initial stock of knowledge may well be the strength that allows it to create such organizational diversity in the first place.

The mere existence of diversity, however, does not enhance learning, but only creates the potential for learning. To exploit this potential, the MNCs must consider learning as an explicit objective, and must create mechanisms and systems for such learning to take place. Both centralization and decentralization may impede learning. In a more centralized company, diverse learning may not take place either because the subsidiaries may not possess appropriate sensing, analyzing, and responding capabilities to learn from their local environments, or because the centralized decision processes may be insensitive to knowledge accumulated outside the corporate headquarters. Other companies, in which the subsidiaries may enjoy very high levels of local resources and autonomy, may similarly fail to exploit global learning benefits because of their inability to transfer and synthesize knowledge and expertise developed in different organizational components.

3. Means: sources of competitive advantages

(1) National differences: location economies

根据比较优势原则,不同国家拥有不同的生产要素禀赋,在缺乏有效市场的情况下,这导致了国家间生产要素成本的差异。跨国公司可以将价值链各项活动按照其不同的要素密集度分布在经济、政治和文化条件最有利于该项活动的区位来实现区位经济。不同国家的消费者口味和偏好可能不同,分销系统、政府法规或不同促销策略和其他营销技术的有效性也可能不同。跨国公司可以通过调整其产品以适应每个国家市场的独特要求来增加其价值。各国的比较优势和禀赋差异也会发生变化。

From the perspective of input markets, according to the principle of comparative advantage, different countries have different factor endowments, and in the absence of efficient markets this leads to inter-country differences in factor costs. Different activities of the company, such as R&D, production, marketing, etc. , have different factor intensities. A company can therefore gain cost advantages by locating value creation activities where economic, political, and cultural conditions are most conducive to the performance of that activity. Companies that successfully do this can realize location economies which arise from performing a value creation activity in the optimal location for that activity, wherever in the world that might be.

National differences may also exist in output markets. Customer tastes and preferences may be different in different countries, as may be distribution systems, government regulations, or the effectiveness of different promotion strategies and other marketing techniques. An MNC can increase its value by tailoring its offerings to fit the unique requirements in each national market.

MNCs that take advantage of location economies create a global web of value creation activities. From a strategic perspective, managers need to take a dynamic view of comparative advantage and national differences. For example, the availability and cost of capital change, as do the technology and the wages of skilled and unskilled labor. Comparative advantages change, and a primary objective of the industrial policies of many countries is to encourage such changes. This dynamic feature of comparative advantage and national differences add considerable complexity to the strategic considerations of the MNCs.

(2) Scale economies

国际扩张还可以让公司获得规模经济或通过大规模生产实现单位成本的降低。规模经济指的是当企业增加其产量水平时所经历的成本优势。这些优势源于将固定成本分摊到更大的产量上，从而使得单位产量的平均成本下降。规模经济带来的动态收益是经验或学习效应。经验曲线的基本前提是，随着公司在生产产品方面的经验增加，由于工人熟练度提高、生产流程更高效以及设备利用率提高等因素，其单位生产成本通常会降低。能够最快地沿着经验曲线向下移动的公司将拥有竞争优势。更高的产量帮助公司挖掘规模效益，也让它积累知识，这使公司沿着学习曲线向下移动时成本逐渐降低。

Expanding internationally can also allow companies to gain scale economies or reductions in unit costs by producing in large volumes. Scale economies refer to the cost advantages that a business experiences when it increases its level of output. These advantages arise due to the spreading of fixed costs over a larger volume of production, which in turn leads to a decrease in the average cost per unit of output. The concept is fundamental in economics and business strategy, as it helps explain why larger companies can often produce goods or services at a lower per-unit cost than smaller companies. Its primary implication for strategy is that a company must expand the volume of its output so as to achieve available scale benefits. Car manufacturers like Toyota and General Motors benefit from scale economies by producing a large number of same models, which can spread the costs of setting up assembly lines over many units, thus reducing the cost per car.

A more dynamic benefit of scale is described as the experience or learning effect. The fundamental premise of the experience curve is that as a company gains experience in producing a product, its costs per unit of production typically decrease. This is due to factors such as increased worker proficiency, more efficient production processes, and better utilization of equipment. Companies that can move down the experience curve the fastest will have a competitive advantage. So, a company will be motivated to produce, using a single plant to serve the global market, as a means of getting down the curve rapidly. The higher volume that helps a company to exploit scale benefits also allows it to accumulate learning, and this leads to progressive cost reduction as the company moves down its learning curve. Therefore, learning effect suggests that as workers and organizations become more familiar with a task, they become more efficient at performing it. This learning can lead to productivity improvements and cost savings.

（3）Scope economies

范围经济指的是公司在多个市场运营或生产多种产品或服务时能够实现的成本优势。范围经济的第一个来源是多元化公司能够在相同或不同的价值链中共享投资和成本的能力；范围经济的第二个来源是共享的外部关系：与客户、供应商、分销商、政府和其他机构的关系；以及知识资产的共享。

Scope economies refer to the cost advantages that a company can achieve when it operates in multiple markets or produces multiple products or services. Tech giants like Apple or Samsung design and manufacture a range of electronic devices, sharing R&D, design expertise, and distribution channels. Retailers like Walmart or Amazon sell a wide variety of products, using their purchasing power and distribution networks to reduce costs.

These economies arise when a diversified company can share resources, skills, or activities across different products or business units, thereby reducing the overall costs of production or operation. A technology company that produces both smartphones and computers might be able to use the same design and engineering team, software, and retail distribution channels, reducing the overall costs of each product. A second important source of scope economies is shared external relations with customers, suppliers, distributors, governments, and other institutions. A multinational bank like Bank of China can provide relatively more effective service to a company expanding overseas than can a local bank from China. Leveraging subsidiary skills is another important way to develop competitive advantages since shared knowledge is the third important source of scope economies. Skills that are developed in the home market or one subsidiary can be transferred to other markets.

Scope economies can be a significant source of competitive advantage, but they also require effective management to ensure that the benefits of diversification are realized without creating complexity that offsets the cost savings. While both scale economies and scope economies are about achieving cost efficiencies, they do so in different ways—through increased output for the former and through the strategic combination of diverse products or services for the latter. Companies often seek to leverage both types of economies to enhance their competitive position.

4. Strategic trade-offs

The strategic task of managing globally is to use all three sources of competitive advantage to optimize efficiency, risk and learning simultaneously in a world-wide business. The key to a successful global strategy is to manage the interactions between these different goals and means. Table 4-2 offers some ideas of how to map means and ends.

Table 4-2 Strategic mapping of MNCs

Sources of competitive advantage	National differences	Scale economies	Scope economies
Achieving efficiency in current operations	Benefiting from current operation differences in factor costs: wages and cost of capital	Expanding and exploiting potential scale economies in each activity	Sharing of investments and costs across products, markets and businesses

The complexity of global strategic management makes it the manager's task to find out how to build a multidimensional and flexible strategy that is robust to the global environment dynamics. This, however, is not always possible because there are certain inherent contradictions between different strategic objectives and between different sources of competitive advantage.

For instance, the popular distinction between global integration and local responsiveness. Forces for global integration require that the company should carefully separate different value chain activities, and should locate each activity at the most efficient level of scale in the location where the activity can be carried out at the lowest cost. Each activity should then be integrated and managed interdependently so as to exploit available scope economies. In essence, it requires a strategy to maximize efficiency of current operations. Such a standardized strategy may, however, reduce MNCs' capability to adapt to different market demands or regulations. What is more, it also increases both endogenous and exogenous risks for the company. Global scale of certain activities may result in the company's costs being concentrated in a few countries, while its revenues accrue globally, from sales in many different countries. This increases operating exposure of the company to the vicissitudes of exchange rate movements because of the mismatch between the currencies in which revenues are obtained and those in which costs are incurred.

第三节　跨国公司的基本战略
(Basic Strategies for Multinational Corporations)

在全球化市场中竞争的公司通常面临两种类型的竞争压力——全球整合和本土响应,这些压力影响它们利用国家差异、规模经济和范围经济的能力。全球整合能够给跨国公司带来规模经济,通常要求跨国公司集中协调和控制分散在全球的各项活动。而本地响应或差异化的需求意味着跨国公司需要适应各地的不同口味和政府法规的问题。本地响应的压力意味着跨国公司可能无法从区位经济、规模经济和学习效应中实现全部好处,通常需要跨国公司对当地条件做出让步和调整。跨国公司在面临这两种压力的不同情况时,通常有四种基本的国际战略选择,即国际化战略、全球化战略、多国战略和跨国战略。

In dealing with environmental complexities and uncertainties, MNCs have a range of alternative strategic choices. Because there are some similarities as well as differences among markets of different countries, the choice of strategy is made on the basis of these similarities and differences. An emphasis on similarities calls for producing products that can be sold globally without modifications. To take advantage of the differences among markets of different countries would necessitate strategies that treat each market based on its own merits. Therefore, each market is considered a unique business opportunity that requires a response to its special characteristics and demands. With efficiency as the dominant strategic goal, in terms of strategy, therefore, the choice is between global integration and local responsiveness.

Companies that compete in the global market typically face two types of competitive pressure that affect their ability to exploit national differences, scale economies and scope economies. They face pressure for global integration and pressure to be locally responsive. Integration pressures include the importance of multinational customers, the presence of multinational competitors, investment intensity, technology intensity, pressures for cost reduction, universal needs and access to raw materials and energy. Local responsiveness pressures include differences in customer needs, differences in distribution channels, availability of substitutes and the need to adapt, market structure and host government demands.

Figure 4-2 demonstrates four basic situations in relation to the degrees of global integration and local responsiveness. Moving up the vertical axis indicates a greater pressure for integration. Global integration generates scale economies and capitalizes on further lowering unit costs, which could also occur by reaping the benefits of centralized coordination and control of geographically dispersed activities. The horizontal axis measures the need for MNCs to respond to local responsiveness or differentiation. This requires MNCs to address local tastes and government regulations, which means a decentralized coordination and control for these MNCs.

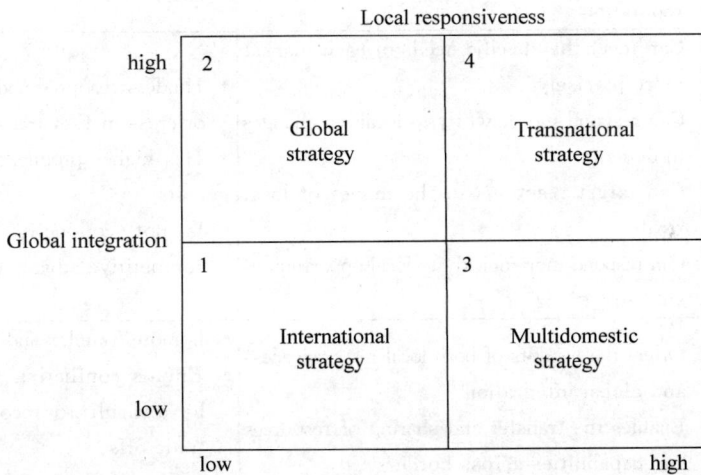

Figure 4-2　Global integration vs. local responsiveness

Pressures for local responsiveness imply that it may not be possible for an MNC to realize the full benefits from location economies, scale economies and learning effects. It may not be possible to serve the global market from a single low-cost location, providing a globally standardized product or service, and marketing it globally to attain cost reduction. Concessions and adaptations often have to be made to local conditions.

How do differences in the strength of pressures for global integration versus those for local responsiveness affect the MNCs' choice of strategy? The most popular framework for studying international strategy in MNCs is the Integration-Responsiveness (IR) framework, which is developed and applied by Bartlett and Ghoshal. The situations in these four quadrants in Figure 4-2 lead to four basic strategies respectively, international, global, multidomestic or localization, and transnational. Each strategy makes sense in certain situations depending on which pressures a company is facing. The advantages and disadvantages are summarized in Table 4-3.

Table 4-3　Advantages and disadvantages of four basic international strategies

Strategy	Advantages	Disadvantages
International	• Has lower costs due to little need to address local needs • Requires less international experience	• Can be blindsided by an unexpectedly international and local innovative rival
Global	• Has lower costs due to economies of scale, scope and location • Can lead to greater efficiencies due to the ability to transfer best practices across markets • Increases innovation from knowledge sharing and capability transfer • Offers the benefit of a global brand and reputation	• Cannot address local needs precisely • Is less responsive to changes in local market conditions • Involves higher transportation costs and tariffs • Has higher coordination and integration costs
Multidomestic	• Can meet the specific needs of each market more precisely • Can respond more swiftly to localized changes in demand • Can target reactions to the moves of local rivals • Can respond more quickly to local opportunities and threats	• Hinders resource and capability sharing or cross-market transfers • Has higher production and distribution costs • Is not conducive to a worldwide competitive advantage
Transnational	• Offers the benefits of both local responsiveness and global integration • Enables the transfer and sharing of resources and capabilities across borders • Provides the benefits of flexible coordination	• Is more complex and harder to implement • Entails conflicting goals, which may be difficult to reconcile and require trade-offs • Involves more costly and time-consuming implementation

1. International strategy

采用国际化战略的企业通常在国际市场销售的产品与国内市场相差无几。这类跨国公司面临的全球整合压力和本土响应压力都很小，能够将国内市场的竞争优势转移到海外市场，海外市场的同类竞争者也比较少。

MNCs find themselves fortunate in quadrant 1 (Figure 4-2) where pressures are low for both global integration and local responsiveness. An international strategy involves taking products that were initially produced for the domestic market and then selling them internationally. It leverages an MNC's core competencies in foreign markets and allows limited local customization. Procter and Gamble has used this strategy and so has Microsoft. This strategy is characterized by increased standardization of products and service. Since the international strategy requires a low level of global integration and local market adaptation, and its implementation costs are not significantly high, it is preferable among small companies. Those small companies focusing on domestic businesses have relatively less international business experience and thus tend to replicate their domestic business strategies when they involve in foreign operations through an exporting or a sales office.

An international strategy works well when a company has a core competence that foreign rivals lack and industry conditions do not demand high degrees of global integration or local responsiveness. MNCs pursuing an international strategy are often selling a product that serves universal needs, but do not face significant competitors, and thus are not confronted with pressures to reduce their cost structure. They have followed a similar growth pattern as they expanded overseas and tend to establish manufacturing and marketing functions in each major markets. The resulting duplication can raise costs, but this is less of a concern if the MNCs do not face strong pressures for cost reduction or global integration. In most MNCs that pursue an international strategy, the headquarters retain fairly tight control over marketing and product strategy.

Unless aware, MNCs implementing the international strategy can be blindsided by an unexpectedly innovative rival. Google, for example, faces increasingly threat from local rivals whose native sensitivities to local search tendencies pose threats.

2. Global strategy

全球化战略是指跨国公司在其运营的所有国家采用基本相同的竞争模式,在全球销售标准化产品,并努力打造全球品牌,公司总部通常控制和协调其全球行动。采取全球化战略的企业通常面临较高的全球化整合压力和较小的本土响应压力。该战略可以很好地通过标准化来获取规模经济、区位经济和学习效应,降低成本,实现企业的效率目标。

In quadrant 2 of Figure 4-2, the need for integration is high and awareness of differentiation is low. In terms of scale economies, this situation leads to global strategy based on price competition. A global strategy is one in which an MNC employs the same basic competitive approach in all countries where it operates, sells standardized products globally, strives to build global brands, and coordinates its actions worldwide with strong headquarters control. It presents a think-global, act-global approach. This strategy champions worldwide consistency and standardization and focuses on increasing profitability and profit growth by capitalizing on the cost reductions that come from scale economies, learning effects, and location economies. To take advantage of the large-scale operations that provide for economies of scale, manufacturing and other operational activities are centralized. The emphasis on cost may come at the expense of flexibility and responsiveness to national markets. That is to say, MNCs implementing global strategy consider achieving efficiency as its major strategic goal. By using a global integration strategy, the MNC is compelled to find a mix of products for all its foreign markets. Standardization of products among its subsidiaries does not allow for customizing products to national criteria and tastes. Global integration can be based on product or process specialization.

Global strategy is suited to industries that emphasize efficient operations and where local responsiveness needs either are nonexistent or can be neutralized by offering a higher-quality product at a lower price than the local substitute. Many industrial goods industries, like bulk chemicals and semiconductor, usually have global standards and their products often serve universal needs.

Countries whose markets demand local responsiveness reduce the attractiveness of the global strategy. In these markets, the strength of the global strategy, ironically, becomes its weakness. The cost sensitivity and standardization bias of a global strategy gives MNCs little latitude to adapt value creation activities to local conditions. Moreover, disruptive market changes or product breakthroughs can turn a fine-tuned value chain into a misfiring machine.

3. Multidomestic/Localization strategy

多国战略是指跨国公司根据不同国家的消费者偏好和市场条件,改变其产品供应和竞争策略,以实现对不同国家的响应。跨国公司通常在本地响应压力较大而通过全球整合降低成本的压力较低时采用多国战略。与此同时,多国战略也意味着管理、设计、生产和营销活动在各国市场的重复,所以必然会增加成本。

The opposite situation to quadrant 2 in Figure 4-2 is quadrant 3, where the need for differentiation and local responsiveness is high but the concern for integration is low. This quadrant is referred to as multidomestic strategy or localization strategy. A multidomestic strategy is one in which an MNC varies its product offering and competitive approach from country to country in an effort to be responsive to differing buyer preferences and market conditions. It is considered as a think-local, act-local type of international strategy, facilitated by decision making decentralized to the local level. The multidomestic strategy focuses on increasing profitability by customizing the company's goods to meet the needs and preferences of the local market. Therefore, it is the "effectiveness" option rather than "efficiency" through global integration. Subsidiaries are treated as if they are autonomous national companies. They are allowed to respond to local demands as they see fit. The MNC's headquarters maintains overall coordination among various subsidiaries in a way that maximizes the MNC's global performance. Since cost pressures are low, the additional costs that come with customization do not present a problem. In the food industry, it is common for companies to adapt their ingredients in their products and sell the localized versions to cater to country-specific tastes. MNCs applying a multidomestic strategy hold that value-chain design is the prerogative of the local subsidiary, not the unilateral declaration by the home office. Management that chooses the multidomestic strategy believes in customizing value activities to the unique conditions that prevail in different markets. Whereas the competitive advantage of global strategy is based on corporate-wide standardization and similarities among national markets, multidomestic strategy employs the MNC's worldwide resources for a competitive edge.

A multidomestic strategy makes sense when the MNC faces a high need for local responsiveness and low need to reduce costs via global integration. It has other benefits as well, such as minimizing political risk given the local standing of the company, lower exchange-rate risk given reduced need to repatriate funds to the home office, greater prestige given its national prominence, higher potential for innovative products from local R&D, and higher growth potential due to entrepreneurial zeal.

At the meantime, the multidomestic strategy leads to widespread replication of management, design, production, and marketing activities around the world. Customizing products and processes to local markets inevitably increases costs. Different product designs require different materials, production runs become shorter, marketing programs are adapted, distribution requires new channels, and different transactions require different coordination methods. Hence, the multidomestic strategy is impractical in cost-sensitive situations.

4. Transnational strategy

当跨国公司所处的环境中全球整合和本土响应的压力均比较大时,它们通常会选择跨国战略。跨国战略同时具备多国战略和全球战略的特征,它要求企业在通过区位经济、规模经济和学习效应降低成本的同时,也能差异化其产品和服务以满足不同市场的差异化需求。该战略要求企业有较强的全球协调能力和适应能力。

When a company is facing both types of pressures as in quadrant 4 of Figure 4-2, a transnational strategy might be appropriate. A transnational strategy is a think-global, act-local approach that incorporates elements of both multidomestic and global strategies. MNCs pursuing a transnational strategy try to meet demand for low costs by focusing on location economies, economies of scale, and learning effects, while at the same time, differentiate the product to meet the needs of individual markets. In addition, a transnational strategy fosters a multidirectional flow of skills between the subsidiaries within the company's global network. A transnational strategy simultaneously engages pressures for global integration and local responsiveness in ways that leverage insight to improve the company's core competency. The transnational strategy requires a coordination capability, which is an ability to respond quickly to changing situations and to shift different aspects of the operation among countries when circumstances change. For instance, if interventions by host governments create unacceptable conditions, the MNC should have the alternative of shifting its priorities between national subsidiaries.

The learning orientation of the transnational strategy drives many benefits when balancing global integration and local responsiveness. The vitality of learning in the transnational strategy pushes managers to respond to changing environments, configuring resources and coordinating processes without imposing more bureaucracy. Ultimately, these capabilities permit standardizing some links of the value chain to generate the efficiencies warranted by global integration pressures, while also adapting other links to meet pressures for local responsiveness without sacrificing the benefits of one for the other.

The transnational strategy is ambiguous compared with the clarity of the other strategies. It is an option when there is no clear-cut preference for either global integration or host country focus strategies. Limitations arise from complicated agendas, high costs, and cognitive limits. It attempts to trade off the costs and benefits of the other strategies on a case-by-case basis to maximize the overall results.

Strategy evolves over time. A company may start out using an international strategy, but then find that it has to shift to a global standardization strategy or transnational strategy as competition increases. Similarly, a localization strategy might initially give a company a competitive advantage, but competition might also put pressure on price prompting the company to move to a transnational strategy.

关键术语（Key Terms）

战略管理（strategic management）
公司战略（corporate strategy）
业务战略（business strategy）
职能战略（functional strategy）
战略制定（strategy formulation）
外部环境（external environment）
内部环境（internal environment）
价值创造（value creation）
资源（resources）
能力（capabilities）
核心竞争力（core competencies）

竞争优势（competitive advantages）
价值链（value chain）
区位经济（location economies）
规模经济（scale economies）
范围经济（scope economies）
全球整合（global integration）
本地响应（local responsiveness）
国际化战略（international strategy）
全球化战略（global strategy）
多国战略（multidomestic strategy）
跨国战略（transnational strategy）

小结（Summary）

1. There are three levels of strategy: corporate strategy, business strategy and functional strategy. Strategic management is the process by which organizations set goals, formulate strategies to achieve these goals, and then allocate resources to ensure the successful implementation of these strategies. It is a dynamic and iterative process

that requires organizations to continuously assess and adapt to changing environments. The core of strategic management is making wise decisions that align with the organization's mission, vision, and values. For MNCs, strategic management is even more complex because their operations are global in nature. MNCs must conduct their management activities within multiple legal systems, cultural norms, economic conditions, and competitive landscapes.

2. Efficiency is one of the primary strategic objectives for MNCs, and the integration-responsive framework in global strategy well reflects this efficiency goal. Global integration can bring economies of scale to MNCs, requiring them to centrally coordinate and control activities dispersed around the globe. The demand for local responsiveness or differentiation means that MNCs need to adapt to the different tastes and government regulations in various locations.

3. When facing different situations of the two pressures for global integration and local responsiveness, MNCs typically have four basic international strategic choices to achieve the trade-off among location economies, scale economies, and scope economies: international strategy, global strategy, multidomestic strategy, and transnational strategy.

延伸阅读（Further Readings）

习题（Exercises）

第五章
Chapter 5

跨国公司的组织管理
Organizing of Multinational Corporations

Learning Objectives

- To know the concept of organizing of multinational corporations
- To recognize the coordination and control system of multinational corporations
- To be familiar with the basic organizational structures of multinational corporations and their evolution
- To understand the organizational choice and its match with strategy of multinational corporations

第一节 跨国公司组织管理的概念
（The Concept of Organizing of Multinational Corporations）

1. The definition of organizing of multinational corporations

跨国公司在制定战略后,接下来的任务便是如何实现战略,首当其冲的问题是,如何设计合适的组织结构来实施战略。这种思路符合逻辑,即有什么样的战略便有什么样的结构与之匹配,学术界称之为"结构追随战略",由著名企业史学家钱德勒在1962年出版的《战略与结构》一书中提出。然而,与此相反,管理学者安索夫和彼得斯却认为,组织的战略选择会受到其内部的权力结构的影响,组织的结构会影响其战略选择,特别是市场定位和目标市场的选择。这一观点被称为"战略追随结构"。上述两种观点针锋相对,难分高下,直至战略管理大师明茨伯格指出"战略与结构就像人行走时的两只脚,是相互追随的关系"后,战略与组织之间的关系争论才逐渐平息。

After formulating the strategy, the MNCs' next task is how to implement the strategy. The first and foremost issue is how to design a suitable organizational structure to implement the strategy. This idea is very logical, that is, there is a structure that matches the strategy, which is called "structure following strategy" in the academic community. It was proposed by the famous business historian Alfred D. Chandler in his 1962 book *Strategy and Structure*. However, on the contrary, American management scholars Igor Ansoff and Tom J. Peters believe that an organization's strategic choices are influenced by its internal power structure, which in turn affects its strategic choices, particularly in market positioning and target market selection. This viewpoint is known as the "strategy following structure". The above two viewpoints are in sharp opposition and difficult to distinguish between high and low, until strategic management guru Henry Mintzberg (1998) pointed out that strategy and structure are like two feet when walking, and they follow each other. Only then did the debate on the relationship between strategy and organizational structure gradually subside.

本书遵循"结构追随战略"的观点，认为跨国公司的组织结构是为了实现跨国公司的战略目标而形成的公司内部的权力、责任、控制与协调关系的特定形式。跨国公司的组织结构围绕公司内部的工作任务展开，涉及分工与协调两个方面，包括纵向与横向两个维度。纵向维度即确定公司员工的上下级关系，表现为控制系统；横向维度即确保员工之间、部门之间的沟通与合作，表现为协调系统。控制系统的核心是对权威的配置，即集权与分权，又称为垂直差异化。协调系统的核心则是部门划分，即将公司划分为一些正式的子单位，又称为水平差异化。

This book follows the view of "structure following strategy" and believes that the organizational structure of MNCs is a specific form of power, responsibility, control, and coordination within the company formed to achieve the strategic goals of the MNCs. The organizational structure of MNCs revolves around internal work tasks, involving two aspects: division of labor and coordination on vertical and horizontal dimensions. The vertical dimension determines the hierarchical relationship of company employees, manifested as the control system. The horizontal dimension ensures communication and cooperation between employees and departments, manifested as a coordinated system. The core of a control system is the configuration of authority, namely centralization and decentralization, also known as vertical differentiation. The core of the coordination system is departmental division, which divides the company into formal subunits, also known as horizontal differentiation.

Vertical differentiation refers to the allocation of authority. When decision-making power is concentrated in the hands of top-level managers, it is called centralization, and when decision-making power is heavily delegated to middle and lower-level managers, it is called decentralization. There are arguments for both centralization and decentralization. The opinions supporting centralization include the following. First, centralization can facilitate coordination and integration of operations. Second, centralization can help ensure that decisions are consistent with MNCs' objectives. Third, by concentrating power and authority in one individual or a management team, centralization can give top-level managers the means to bring about needed major organizational changes. Fourth, centralization can avoid the duplication of activities that occurs when similar activities are carried on by various subunits within the MNCs. For instance, many MNCs centralize their R&D functions at one or two locations to ensure that R&D work is not duplicated.

Nevertheless, many people support decentralization for the following reasons. First, top-level managers can become overburdened when decision-making authority is centralized, and this can result in poor decisions. Decentralization gives top-level managers time to focus on critical issues by delegating more routine issues to lower-level managers. Second, decentralization can motivate employees to work hard because they are willing to give more to their jobs when they have a greater degree of individual freedom and control over their work. Third, decentralization permits greater flexibility and quicker decisions because decisions do not have to be reported to the higher level managers. Meanwhile, decentralization can result in better decisions since decisions are made closer to the spot by individuals who have better information than managers several levels up in a hierarchy. Fourth, decentralization can increase control. Decentralization can be used to establish relatively autonomous, self-contained subunits within MNCs. Subunit managers can then be held accountable for subunit performance. The more responsibility subunit managers have for decisions that impact subunit performance, the fewer excuses they have for poor performance.

Horizontal differentiation is concerned with how the firm decides to divide itself into subunits. The decision is normally made on the basis of function, type of business, or geographic area. In many firms, just one of these predominates, but more complex solutions are adopted in others. This is particularly likely in the case of MNCs, where the conflicting demands to organize the company around different products and different national markets must be reconciled.

2. Coordination system of multinational corporations

协调系统是组织内部为保持各单位之间及各单位与组织目标之间的一致性而设置的各种机制。在企业中,各个部门的经营取向往往各不相同。例如,生产部门主要关注产能的提升、成本的降低与质量的控制,而营销部门则主要关注产品的价格、销量的增加及市场份额的变化。这些差异会阻碍不同部门之间的沟通,各个部门目标上的不一致甚至可能导致部门冲突。对于在国内外均有多个子公司的跨国公司而言,这类问题尤其突出。尤其是当子公司的经理所在时区、彼此距离和各自国籍各不相同时,各个子公司的行动差异就会更为明显。因此,需要协调来实现各个部门之间的整合,形成公司合力。协调有助于提高技术效率,因为协调保证了水平方向上部门之间的活动一致,可以更好地实现规模经济和范围经济效应。协调还可以降低代理成本,实现代理效率,因为协调保证了垂直方向上各级目标的一致,降低了委托人和代理人之间的不对称性。

A coordination system is a variety of mechanisms established within an organization to maintain consistency between units and between units and organizational goals. In MNCs, the business orientation of each department is often different. For example, the production department mainly focuses on improving production capacity, reducing costs, and controlling quality, while the marketing department mainly focuses on product prices, increasing sales volume, and market share changes. These differences can hinder communication between different departments, and inconsistencies in departmental goals may even lead to departmental conflicts. For MNCs with multiple subsidiaries both domestically and internationally, such issues are particularly prominent. Specifically, when the managers of subsidiary companies are located in different time zones, with different distances from each other, and nationalities, the differences in their actions will be more pronounced. Therefore, coordination is needed to achieve integration between various subsidiaries and form a joint force within the company. Coordination helps to improve technical efficiency, as it ensures consistency of activities between subsidiaries in the horizontal direction, which can better achieve economies of scale and scope. Coordination can also reduce agency costs and achieve agency efficiency, as it ensures consistency of goals at all levels in the vertical direction and reduces asymmetry between principals and agents.

There are three main methods of coordination.

The first method is to coordinate with standards. This method achieves standardization and consistency in operations by specifying the way employees handle work relationships and customer affairs, in order to coordinate the business activities of various departments and reduce operational differences. To this end, organizations will establish various conventions to standardize operational characteristics, covering secular affairs such as dress code and etiquette specified in employee manuals, as well as strategic affairs such as dealing with partners and evaluating potential markets.

The second method is to coordinate through planning. With the intensification of market competition and changes in commercial systems in various countries, it has become increasingly complex and even impractical to coordinate the subsidiaries and departments of MNCs around the world using standards. For example, some MNCs are unwilling to constrain their behavior with various standards in order to improve the flexibility of local response. In this situation, MNCs tend to establish a target list and give interdependent departments greater discretion in coordinating system development. Relying on a list of goals rather than rules and regulations is the foundation for coordinating with plans. As long as they follow the deadline and goals of the plan, these departments have the freedom to adjust their operations. In fact, the specific plan document establishes the framework for the next stage and serves as a guiding action plan for managers to coordinate. However, plans cannot keep up with changes, and no matter how carefully planned, accidents will always occur. The revision of the target list requires constraint and coordination. MNCs usually use a series of executive development plans to familiarize unit heads with the preferred planning format and proactively eliminate potential threats. Other ways include building teams composed of members from different nationalities, consolidating the international and product divisions into one office unit, or bringing foreign staff into senior committees to understand foreign perspectives.

The third method is to coordinate with adjustment. In addition to explicit standards and plans, MNCs also use a series of informal coordination mechanisms. Encouraging colleagues of the same level to communicate about issues of mutual concern in a certain process is called coordinating through mutual adjustment. Usually, the specific ways of coordinating among employees at the same level include direct contact, liaison role, task force, team, full-time integrator, and committee.

Direct contact between subunit managers is the simplest integrating mechanism. By this mechanism, managers of the various subunits simply contact each other whenever they have a common concern. Direct contact may not be effective if the managers have differing orientations that act to impede coordination. Liaison roles are a bit more complex. When the volume of contacts between subunits increases, coordination can be improved by giving a person in each subunit responsibility for coordinating with another subunit on a regular basis. Through these roles, the people involved establish a permanent relationship. Occasionally, a task force is a temporary cross-departmental group established to provide guidance and recommendations for a specific issue. When the need for coordination is greater still, firms tend to use temporary or permanent teams composed of individuals from the subunits that need to achieve coordination. They typically coordinate product development and introduction, but they are useful when any aspect of operations or strategy requires the cooperation of two or more subunits. Product development and introduction teams are typically composed of personnel from R&D, production, and marketing. The resulting coordination aids the development of products that are tailored to consumer needs and that can be produced at a reasonable cost. In addition, full-time integrators can be appointed as managers who are specifically responsible for coordinating work involving multiple functional departments. In huge MNCs, a committee may be established as a specialized organization to provide consultation or make decisions on specific matters.

3. Control system of multinational corporations

控制就是通过指导和监控个体的活动,确保战略如期实施的措施。控制系统调节公司资源的分配和使用,从而便利了协调过程,是组织的基本组成部分。判断控制系统是否有效的标准是能否有效支撑公司战略。控制系统的目的之一是处理业绩模糊性。当子单元性能不佳的原因不清楚时,就会出现业绩模糊性。当一个子单位的绩效部分依赖于其他子单位的绩效时,即当组织内的子单位之间存在高度的相互依存关系时,业绩模糊性就产生了,这种情况并不罕见。绩效模糊性程度是组织中各子单元相互依存的函数。显然,业绩模糊性会增加控制成本。

Control is the measure of ensuring the timely implementation of a strategy by guiding and monitoring individual activities. The control system regulates the allocation and utilization of company resources, thereby facilitating the coordination process, and is a fundamental component of an organization. The criterion for determining the effectiveness of a control system is whether it can effectively support the company's strategy. One of the purposes of a control system is to handle performance ambiguity. Performance ambiguity appears when the causes of a subunit's poor performance are not clear. This is not uncommon that performance ambiguity appears when a subunit's performance is partly dependent on the performance of other subunits, that is, when there is a high degree of interdependence between subunits within the organization. The level of performance ambiguity is a function of the interdependence of subunits in an organization. Obviously, performance ambiguity raises the costs of control.

There are four main control methods: personal control, bureaucratic control, output control, and cultural control.

Personal control is control achieved by personal contact with subordinates. This type of control tends to be most widely used in small firms, where it is seen in the direct supervision of subordinates' actions. However, it also structures the relationships between managers at different levels in MNCs. For instance, the CEO may use a great deal of personal control to influence the behavior of his or her immediate subordinates, such as the heads of worldwide product divisions or major geographic areas. In turn, these heads may use personal control to influence the behavior of their subordinates, and so on down through the organization.

Bureaucratic control is control achieved through a system of rules and procedures that directs the actions of subunits. The most important bureaucratic controls in subunits within MNCs are budgets and capital spending rules. Budgets are essentially a set of rules for allocating a firm's financial resources. A subunit's budgets specifies with some precision how much the subunit may spend. Headquarters uses budgets to influence the behavior of subunits. Most budgets are set by negotiation between headquarters and subunit management. Headquarters can encourage the growth of certain subunits and restrict the growth of others by manipulating their budgets. Capital spending rules require headquarters to approve any capital expenditure by a subunit that exceeds a certain amount. A budget allows headquarters to specify the amount a subunit can spend in a given year, and capital spending rules give headquarters additional control over how the money is spent. Headquarters can be expected to deny approval for capital spending requests that are at variance with overall firm objectives and to approve those that are congruent with firm objectives.

Output control involves setting goals for subunits to achieve and expressing those goals in terms of relatively objective performance metrics such as profitability, productivity, growth, market share, and quality. The performance of subunit managers is then judged by their ability to achieve the goals. If goals are met or exceeded, subunit managers will be rewarded. If goals are not met, headquarters will normally intervene to find out why and take appropriate corrective action. Thus, control is achieved by comparing actual performance against targets and intervening selectively to take corrective action. Subunits' goals depend on their role in the firm. Self-contained product divisions or national subsidiaries are typically given goals for profitability, sales growth, and market share. Functions are more likely to be given goals related to their particular activity. Thus, R&D will be given product development goals, production will be given productivity and quality goals, marketing will be given market share goals, and so on.

Cultural control exists when employees share the norms and value systems of the firm. When this occurs, employees tend to control their own behavior, which reduces the need for direct supervision. In a firm with a strong culture, self-control can reduce the need for other control systems.

In order to make the above control methods effective, MNCs often establish the following control mechanisms. Firstly, reporting, where subordinates report work progress to supervisors, which has become an important basis for many companies to allocate resources, monitor performance, and provide rewards. Secondly, inspection, which refers to the headquarters inspecting subsidiaries or supervisors inspecting subordinate departments. For MNCs that rely on mutual adjustment for coordination and cultural control, inspections can help obtain first-hand information that cannot be obtained from reporting, leading to better decisions and instructions. Thirdly, management performance evaluation, which refers to the separate evaluation of subsidiary managers to avoid punishing or rewarding uncontrollable factors. If a subsidiary cannot take risk management measures to eliminate the negative impact of parent company decisions, especially when sacrificing individual subsidiary profits for the overall performance of the company, the management personnel of the subsidiary should be evaluated separately. Fourthly, comparability between costs and accounting, which clearly states that the impact of differences in costs and accounting practices should be considered when comparing performance. Fifthly, the evaluative scale, which refers to establishing comprehensive rather than single evaluative indicators, while taking into account both financial and non-financial indicators.

第二节　跨国公司的基本组织结构
（Basic Organizational Structures of Multinational Corporations）

　　一般而言,企业在国际化的初期很少改变其组织结构。绝大多数以出口方式进入海外市场的企业都会使用与其在国内销售中基本相同的结构、程序和人员来完成订单。即使是更大规模的直接出口,公司也会尽量避免改变基本的组织结构,因为组织结构的变革往往伤筋动骨,耗时费力且不一定能成功。于是,更多的企业会选择学习利用同行知识和经验来管理其出口业务。类似地,选择许可方式进行跨国经营对公司的组织结构也没有太大冲击。仅当海外业务对企业的成功至关重要时,企业才会开始建立适当的组织结构管理其跨国经营活动。可用于企业进行跨国经营的组织结构主要有出口部、国际分部、全球地理结构、全球产品结构、全球混合或矩阵结构、跨国网络结构和元国家网络结构。

Generally speaking, firms rarely change their organizational structure in the early stages of internationalization. The vast majority of firms that enter overseas markets through export use the same structure, procedures, and personnel as they do in domestic sales to complete orders. Even for larger scale direct exports, firms will try their best to avoid changing their basic organizational structure, as changes in organizational structure are often painful, time-consuming, and may not necessarily succeed. Therefore, more firms will choose to learn and utilize peer knowledge and experience to manage their export business. Similarly, choosing a licensing method for cross-border operations does not have a significant impact on the firm's organizational structure. Only when overseas business is crucial to the success of a firm, will it begin to establish appropriate organizational structures to manage its cross-border operations. The following are types of organizational structures that can be used by firms for cross-border operations: export department, international division, worldwide geographic structure, worldwide product structure, worldwide hybrid and matrix structure, transnational network structure, and metanational network structure.

1. Export department

当出口占公司销售的很大比重并且公司希望对其出口经营实施更大的控制时,管理者经常建立独立的出口部。独立的出口部门表明高层管理相信,投资于出口的人力资源与财务资源是支持和扩大国际销售所必需的。出口部负责所有产品的出口,出口部经理经常控制着公司产品在国际市场上的定价与促销。出口部员工具备特定国家或产品的专门知识,出口部经理有责任处理与出口管理公司、国外分销商和国外客户之间的关系。当公司成立出口部专门负责出口业务时,其他国家的销售代表需要向出口部经理报告工作。图 5-1 是设有出口部的组织结构图。

When exports account for a significant proportion of a firm's sales and the firm wishes to exercise greater control over its export operations, managers often establish independent export departments. The establishment of the independent export department indicates that headquarters believe that investing in human and financial resources for exports is necessary to support and expand international sales. The export department is responsible for the export of all products, and the managers of the export department often control the pricing and promotion of the firm's products in the international market. The personnel of the export department have specialized knowledge of specific countries or products, and the managers of the export department are responsible for handling relationships with export management companies, foreign distributors, and foreign customers. When an MNC establishes an export department specifically responsible for export business, sales agents from other countries need to submit reports to the export department manager. Figure 5-1 is an example of an MNC's organizational structure with an export department.

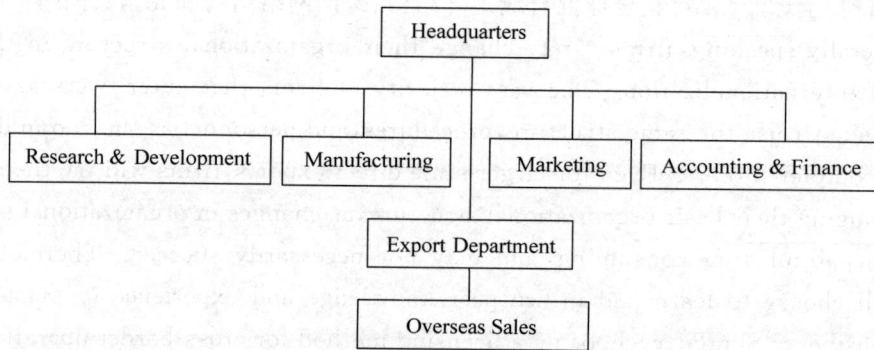

Figure 5-1　Organizational structure with an export department

The biggest advantage of the organizational structure of the export department is the emphasis on exports, which facilitates better management and development of export business. Due to the limited overseas sales force that can be directly managed by the export department, and the limited variety of products directly responsible for export and the number of overseas markets covered, the organizational structure of the export department is generally only applicable to small and medium-sized firms that have just begun international operations.

2. International division

随着企业扩大其销售力量的规模并在其他国家开展生产经营,出口部门通常随之成长为国际分部。国际分部在许多方面不同于出口部门,它一般规模较大,除管理出口和销售力量之外,还监督具有多种职能的国外子公司,其中绝大多数是销售单位。国际分部还拥有国际经验丰富的员工,他们可以履行多项职能,包括洽谈许可经营与合资协议、海外促销等。图5-2是某总部在美国的跨国公司的国际分部组织结构图。图中显示,其国际分部负责在欧洲及中国的子公司的所有产品,并控制亚洲其他地区的总体销售力量。

As firms expand their sales force and engage in production and operation in other countries, the export sector typically grows into an international division. The international branch is different from the export department in many ways. It is generally larger in scale and, in addition to managing export and sales forces, also supervises foreign subsidiaries with multiple functions, the vast majority of which are sales units. The international branch also has internationally experienced employees who can perform multiple functions, including negotiating licensing and joint venture agreements, overseas promotions, etc. Figure 5-2 shows the organizational structure of international branches of a company headquartered in the U.S. As shown in the figure, the international branch is responsible for all products of its subsidiaries in Europe and China, and controls the overall sales force in other regions of Asia.

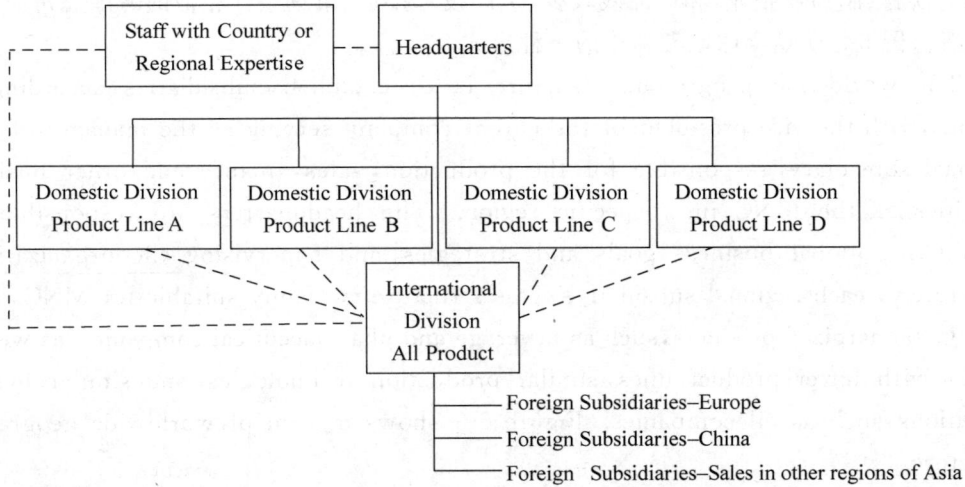

Figure 5-2　One company's international division structure

The popularity of international division in large companies has declined. For MNCs engaged in diversified product operations in multiple countries, international divisions are not an effective organizational structure. But for medium-sized companies with limited product varieties and limited involvement in overseas markets, international divisions are still a universally effective organizational structure. The main reason why the organizational structure of international divisions is increasingly not adopted by MNCs are as follows. First, too many product varieties exceed the management capacity of the international division. For example, in terms of sales, employees in the international division have difficulty mastering the entire product line and its sales worldwide. Second, when the number of overseas markets involved increases, it is difficult for international divisions to make regional adjustments, and distant corporate headquarters cannot understand local needs and make corresponding adjustments. Third, it is difficult to implement international strategies that utilize global product or location advantages, as the international division separates the headquarters from the firm's foreign subsidiaries, making it difficult for these overseas branches to view the entire global market as a whole. Even the home country and its product divisions find it difficult to view the global production and research development locations as a global platform. On the contrary, for the vast majority of firms that establish international divisions, the domestic market is the focus, and international issues are only the "problems" of the international division.

3. Worldwide geographic structure

全球地理结构就是按照地区设立分部,由母公司副总经理担任各地区分部经理,负责企业在某一特定地区的生产、销售、财务等业务活动,而总公司负责制定全球性经营目标和战略,监督各地区分部执行的组织结构。这种结构主要适用于那些产品高度标准化的企业如饮料、制药业企业，和产品线较少、生产技术接近、市场条件相似的跨国公司如石油企业等。图 5-3 就是全球地理结构的一种形式。

The worldwide geographic structure is to establish subsidiaries according to regions, with the vice president of the parent company serving as the manager of each regional subsidiary, responsible for the production, sales, finance and other business activities of the MNC in a specific region. The headquarters are responsible for formulating global business goals and strategies, and supervising the organizational structure of each regional subsidiary. This structure is mainly suitable for MNCs with highly standardized products, such as beverage and pharmaceutical companies, as well as MNCs with fewer product lines, similar production technologies, and similar market conditions, such as oil companies. Figure 5-3 shows a form of worldwide geographic structure.

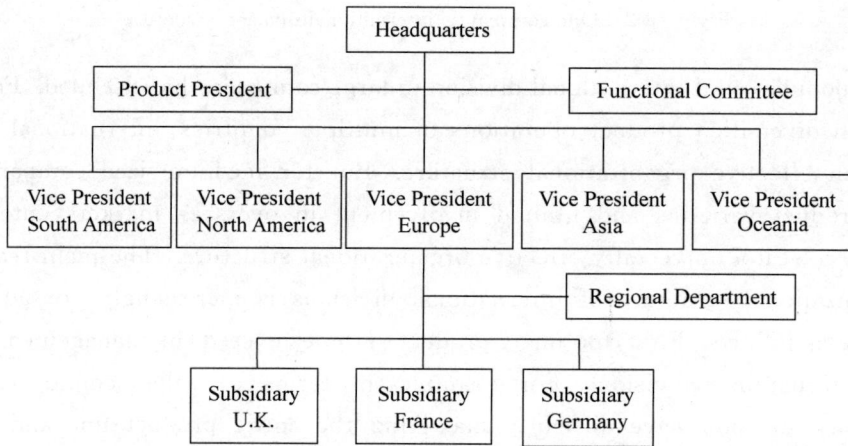

Figure 5-3　Worldwide geographic structure

The worldwide geographic structure is often adopted by firms that pursue a multidomestic strategy. The structure gives regional and country managers a high degree of autonomy to change their product strategy to adapt to the unique environment of the host country or region. This has enabled the MNCs to quickly adapt to the local market. Country level divisions can only exist when the market size or importance is sufficient to support independent organizations, and independent divisions are meaningful for large market countries such as the United States, China, Germany, or Japan. Regional divisions group similar small countries together, such as Italy, Spain, and Portugal into the Southern European division. This combination is mainly based on a balance between the similarity of customer needs and the efficiency of a single product. Under the regional division structure, the vast majority of business activities are dispersed to the countries where the MNCs participates in competition. The evaluation of local subsidiaries in multiple countries generally adopts a profit center standard that focuses on results, rather than whether they comply with the policies of the headquarters. Usually, locals are appointed as national managers, and the turnover of management personnel is relatively slow. Each subsidiary has its own characteristics and personality, forming its own internal strategy. The responsibilities of a national manager are similar to those of the president of headquarters, except that their geographic area of activity is limited.

The advantages of worldwide geographic structure include the following. First, MNCs can coordinate the production and sales of products in the same regional market, and adopt flexible marketing mix strategies according to the characteristics and changes of the regional market, which is conducive to simplifying the management of global business by the president of headquarters. Second, MNCs are easily able to invest and expand their marketing efforts to a new host country within the geographical jurisdiction of the region. Third, using regional divisions as profit centers is beneficial for coordination among subsidiaries within the region. In addition, for many MNCs, the worldwide geographic structure captures the vast majority of efficiency advantages brought by globalization, with only relatively few activities truly requiring global scale to maximize their economic benefits. The worldwide geographic structure generally has fast delivery, allows customization, and has less inventory.

The disadvantages of this structure are as follows. First, it is difficult to obtain economies of scale brought about by specialized division of labor. Second, each regional subsidiary is based on its own interests, and there are inconsistencies in management. The contradictions in production standards and price transfer are also difficult to resolve, which is not conducive to the implementation of the overall business strategy of the enterprise. Third, when the diversification of MNC production deepens, the worldwide geographic structure will hinder the transfer of new products and technologies between regions, as well as production cooperation between regions. Fourth, the autonomy of regional subsidiaries does not help MNCs learn from each other. The greater the autonomy of subsidiary companies in regions, the less likely excellent experience and products can be disseminated and utilized. Lastly, the worldwide geographic structure can also easily lead to overlapping personnel and institutions within the MNC, thereby significantly increasing its management costs.

4. Worldwide product structure

全球产品结构适用于那些规模庞大、生产技术要求高、产品多样化程度高、消费市场又较为分散的跨国公司。这种结构把企业经营的重点放在产品市场和技术诀窍上，认为各种产品的差异性比东道国的差异性更为重要，因此以全球作为目标市场，按照产品种类设立分部门，以产品部作为该产品在全球范围内产销活动的基本组织单位。图5-4就是全球产品结构的一种形式。

Worldwide product structure is suitable for MNCs with large scale, high production technology requirements, high product diversification, and relatively dispersed consumer markets. This structure places the focus of business operations on product markets and technological know-how, believing that the differences in various products are more important than those in the host country. Therefore, the global market is taken as the target market, and subsidiaries are established according to product types, with the product department as the basic organizational unit for global production and sales activities of the product. Figure 5-4 shows a form of worldwide product structure.

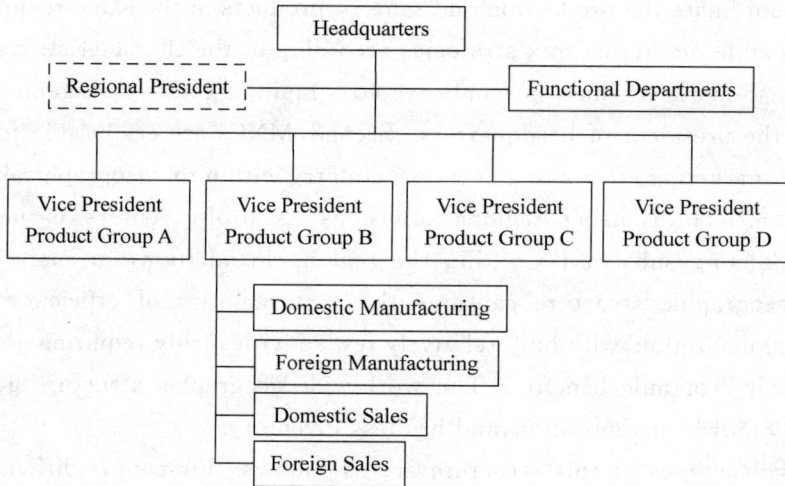

Figure 5-4　Worldwide product structure

The worldwide product structure is usually aligned with the globalization strategy of MNCs. When MNCs seek resources globally, product managers can set up activities based on differences in costs and technology across countries. Under the worldwide product structure, some activities are dispersed, such as component processing and assembly, while others are centralized, such as research and development activities. In order to reduce costs, European and American firms usually transfer some labor-intensive activities to countries with low wage levels and skilled workers, as well as tax-free areas. With the worldwide product structure, the overall goals and business strategies of the firm are determined by the headquarters, and each product department develops its own business plan based on the headquarters' business goals and strategies. The operation of affiliates does not have much autonomy. They become a part of the global organization. The products produced by affiliates are certain models or components for the whole company. The design and description of products are rarely determined by affiliates. In these cases, coordination between the parent company and its affiliates becomes crucial, usually achieved by appointing expatriates from the parent company to the affiliates for 3-5 years. Because specialization is the core of globalization strategy, each affiliate should prioritize service and be evaluated as a cost center.

Affiliates have almost no strategic autonomy and do not take spontaneous actions.

The main advantages of the worldwide product structure include the following. First, it serves as the organizational guarantee for MNCs to integrate their industrial and supply chains on a global scale. Second, it encourages firms to reduce manufacturing costs globally. Third, it is beneficial for MNCs to standardize the production of similar products globally. Fourth, it is useful for the internal transfer of production technology for the same product between different regions. Fifth, it benefits the global sales of products.

The main drawbacks of the worldwide product structure are as follows. Firstly, MNCs establish multiple institutions in specific regions based on types of products, resulting in overlapping institutional settings and excessive management personnel. Secondly, it is difficult to coordinate between different product groups in the same region because the region in this structure does not serve as a profit center, but a cost center, which is difficult to make timely and effective adjustments to marketing activities for different products within that region. As shown in Figure 5-4, suppose the product group A spent a lot of money to commission a European company to produce product A in order to expand the European market. At the same time, the product group B happened to have a factory in Europe and incurred losses due to insufficient production tasks. Originally, due to technological similarities, this factory could easily switch to product A. However, due to the closed information between various product groups, the overall economic interests of the MNC suffered losses. In order to overcome this obstacle, MNCs have gradually introduced regional management systems on the basis of their product groups. The dashed box in the figure represents the regional president, who is not directly responsible for the MNC's profits. His main responsibility is to enable each product group to understand the operating conditions of a certain region. Thirdly, affiliates will become increasingly dependent on the parent company over time, lacking substantial ideas, creativity, and flexibility.

5. Worldwide hybrid and matrix structure

全球产品结构与全球地理结构对于实施跨国战略都各有优劣势。全球产品结构最适合利用世界范围内低成本原料来源和全球营销来开拓全球产品的战略；全球地理结构最适合利用管理人员对当地需求的敏感来进行适应性调整的战略。绝大多数跨国公司的战略既包括对本地响应的考虑，又包括对全球化的产品发展的考虑。因此，几乎所有的跨国公司都拥有混合结构。产品的全球化程度和市场的复杂性及差异决定公司的重点是在产品维度还是地理维度。

Both worldwide product structure and worldwide geographic structure have advantages and disadvantages in implementing cross-border strategies. The worldwide product structure is most suitable for developing a global product strategy by utilizing low-cost raw material sources and global marketing worldwide, while the worldwide geographic structure is most suitable for utilizing the sensitivity of management personnel to local needs for responsiveness. The strategies of the vast majority of MNCs include considerations for both responsiveness and global product development. Therefore, almost all MNCs have a hybrid structure. The globalization degree of the product and the complexity and differences of the market determine whether the MNC's focus is on the product dimension or the geographic dimension.

为平衡地区结构与产品结构的利益或协调混合结构的产品与地理的下属单位,有些跨国公司建立了全球矩阵结构。与大多数混合结构不同,全球矩阵结构是一个对称性组织结构,如图 5-5 所示,它在产品类型和地理分部两个方面具有相同的授权路线。矩阵结构为公司同时实施地方性战略和全球性战略提供了理想的组织结构,地理分部注重国别的反应能力,而产品分部注重全球效率。只有当对地区反应力方面的需要与同规模经济相关的产品标准化方面的需要趋于相等时,矩阵结构才能最好地发挥作用。如果没有这些接近等同的需要,跨国公司就将根据哪一方面对竞争优势更为重要而演变成产品结构或地理结构。

Some MNCs have established a worldwide matrix structure to balance the interests of geographic and product structures, or to coordinate the interests of mixed structure products and regional subsidiaries. Unlike most hybrid organizational structures, the worldwide matrix structure is a symmetrical organizational structure, as shown in Figure 5-5, which has the same authorization route in terms of product types and geographic divisions. The matrix structure provides an ideal organizational structure for the company to implement both local and global strategies simultaneously, with geographic divisions focusing on the specific responsiveness of different countries, while product divisions focusing on global efficiency. The matrix structure can only function best when the need for responsiveness tends to be equal to the need for standardization of products related to economies of scale. Without these nearly equivalent needs, MNCs will evolve into product or geographic structures based on which aspect is more important for competitive advantage.

In theory, worldwide matrix structure produces high-quality decisions because two or more managers need to reach a consensus on how to balance local and global needs. Managers at the junction of product and geographic divisions are called "dual leadership managers" because they have supervisors from the MNC in both product and geographic aspects. Product supervisors tend to emphasize goals such as efficiency and global products, while geographic supervisors tend to emphasize adjustments in the local market. These conflicts of interest mean seeking a balance between pressures from globalization and regionalization. Therefore, for managers at all levels, the worldwide matrix structure requires constant compensation for product and geographic needs. To successfully balance the inherent conflicts between global and local needs, the worldwide matrix structure requires extensive resources for communication among managers.

World Headquarters	European Division	Asian Division	United States Division
Product Division A	Country Manager France	Country Manager China	Regional Manager West
Product Division B	Country Manager Germany	Country Manager Japan	Regional Manager Northeast
Product Division C	Country Manager Italy	Country Manager India	Regional Manager South

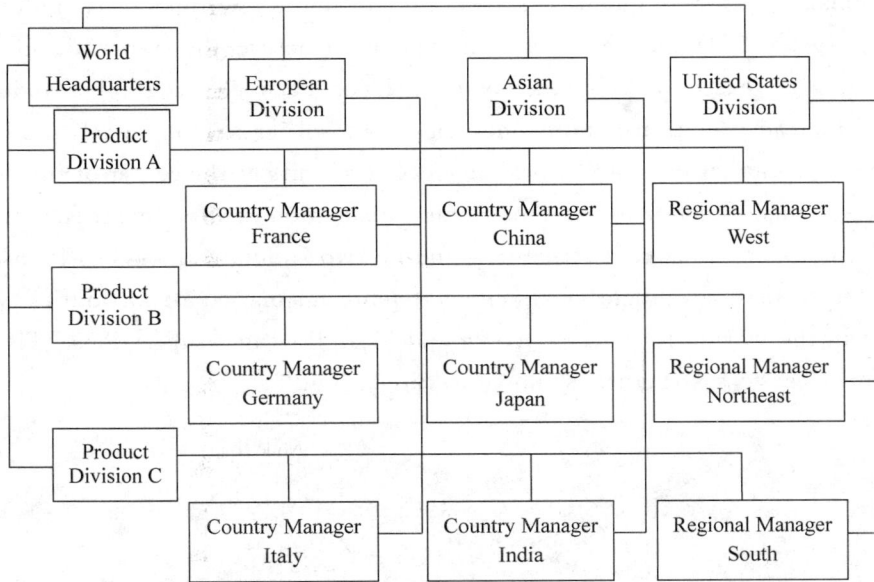

Figure 5-5　Worldwide matrix structure

Middle and upper level managers must possess good interpersonal skills in order to resolve unavoidable personnel conflicts arising from conflicts of interest between products and regions. Middle level managers must also learn to get along with dual supervisors who usually have competitive interests, while headquarters are prepared to resolve conflicts between geographic managers and product managers. In the 1980s, the worldwide matrix structure was widely adopted. But in recent years, the worldwide matrix structure has been criticized, as consistency decisions between product managers and geographic managers have been proven to be slow and cumbersome. In a word, dual leadership is the biggest drawback of the worldwide matrix structure.

6. Transnational network structure

跨国网络结构代表着对具有本地响应、利用地方优势如全球规模经济、寻找全球知识来源的复杂需要的一种最新的解决办案。与全球矩阵结构一样,跨国网络结构试图获取各种组织结构的所有优势,整合职能制、产品制和地理制的下属单位。与具有对称性的矩阵结构不同的是,跨国网络结构不具有基本形式以及地理分部与产品分部之间的对称和平衡。相反,跨国网络连接世界范围内不同类型的子公司,处于网络中心节点的单位协调产品、职能和地域信息。不同的产品类型单位与地区单位具有不同的结构,通常没有两个下属单位是相似的。跨国单位的演变是为了利用其所在地区的资源、人才和市场机会,资源、员工和想法可以全方位地流动。典型的跨国网络结构如图 5-6 所示。

The transnational network structure represents a latest solution to the complex needs of having local responsiveness, utilizing local advantages such as global economies of scale, and seeking global knowledge sources. Like the worldwide matrix structure, the transnational network structure attempts to capture all the advantages of various organizational structures, integrating subordinate units of functional, product, and geographic systems. Unlike the symmetric matrix structure, the transnational network structure has no basic form, symmetry or balance between geographic and product divisions. Instead, the transnational network links different functional, product, and geographic subsidiaries dispersed worldwide. Nodes, units at the center of the network, coordinate product, functional and geographic information. Different product types and geographic units have different structures, and no two subunits are alike. Transnational units evolve to take advantage of resources, talent and market opportunities wherever they exist in the world. Resources, people and ideas flow in all directions. The typical transnational network structure is shown in Figure 5-6.

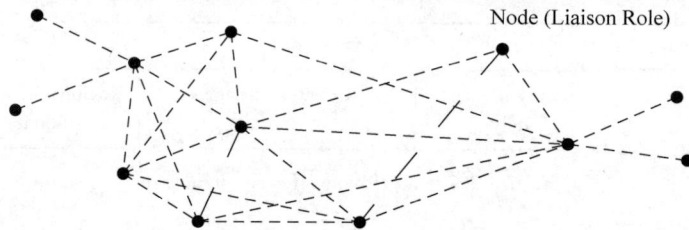

Node (Liaison Role)

Figure 5-6　Transnational network structure

The basic structural framework of the transnational network has three components. The first is dispersed subunits, which are subsidiaries located anywhere in the world they may benefit the firm. The second is specialized operations, which are subunits that specialize, whether in product lines, research or marketing. The third is interdependent relationships, which must exist to manage the dispersed and specialized subunits which share resources and information continuously.

The transnational network structure represents an attempt to concurrently capture all of the advantages of geographic and global product division structures. In transnational network structures, configuration and coordination of activities are mixed, and affiliates play leadership roles for some activities and supporting roles for others. Decisions in transnational network structures are based on maximizing the use of company skills and competencies, irrespective of the activity location or affiliate nationality. MNC acts essentially as a network of activities with multiple headquarters spread across different countries. Affiliate roles of transnational network structures shift over time and learning and sharing are emphasized. In addition, it emphasizes extensive horizontal linkages, effective communication and extreme flexibility.

7. Metanational network structure

如今,一种新的结构正在出现,称为元国家网络结构。这种结构是由能够利用隐藏的创新、技术和市场,特别是全球新兴市场的大型创业跨国公司创建的。元国家网络结构是跨国网络结构的演变,它发展了广泛的系统来鼓励组织学习和创业活动。元国家网络结构类似于跨国网络结构,因为它是一个网络化但无中心的组织,决策权在于子单位。与此同时,元国家网络结构与跨国网络结构的不同之处在于,它的首要目标是向世界任何地方学习,并与公司中的每个人分享这些知识。此外,元国家网络结构使用最新的虚拟连接技术将全球团队成员联系起来。

Nowadays, a new structure called the metanational network structure is emerging. This structure is created by large entrepreneurial MNCs which are able to tap into hidden pockets of innovation, technology and markets, especially emerging markets worldwide. The metanational network structure is an evolution of the transnational network structure that develops extensive systems to encourage organizational learning and entrepreneurial activities. The metanational network structure is similar to the transnational network structure because it is a networked but centerless organization, and decision-making resides with the subunits. Meanwhile, the metanational network structure is different from the transnational network structure in that it has an overriding objective to learn from anywhere in the world, and to share that knowledge with everyone in the company. Morevoer, the metanational network structure uses the latest technology in virtual connectivity to link team members worldwide.

The characteristics of the metanational network structure include the following. First, it has nonstandard business formulas for any local activity. Second, it is looking to emerging markets as sources of knowledge and ideas, not just for local labor. Third, it is creating a culture and advanced communication system that supports global learning. Fourth, it has extensive use of strategic alliances to gain knowledge for varied sources. Fifth, it has high levels of trust between partners to encourage knowledge sharing. Sixth, it has centerless structure that moves strategic functions away from headquarters to major markets. Lastly, it decentralizes decision making to managers who serve key customers and strategic partners.

第三节 跨国公司组织结构的演进与选择
（The Evolution and Choice of Organizational Structures of Multinational Corporations）

1. The evolution of organizational structures of multinational corporations

Due to the significant impact of the organizational structure of MNCs on their business performance, early scholars were committed to finding a formal structure that was applicable under various conditions. To this end, Stopford and Wells proposed a stage model for the structure of MNCs in 1972, as shown in Figure 5-7.

This model has gained widespread recognition in the academic community and is known as a general model for the evolution of organizational structure of MNCs, becoming a benchmark for subsequent research. The vertical axis in the figure

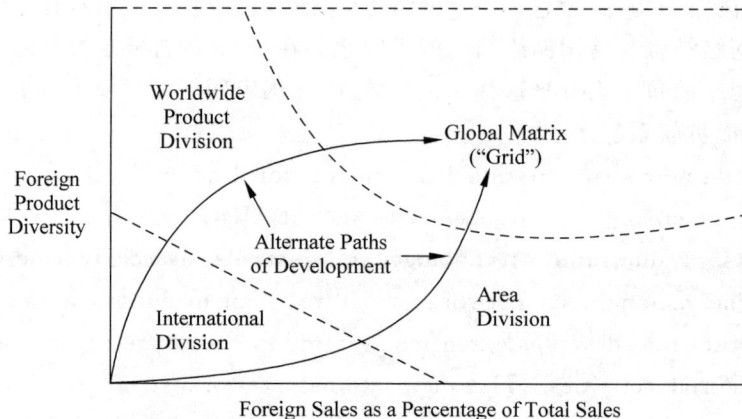

Figure 5-7　The Stopford and Wells stage model of MNC structure

Source：Stopford，John M.，Wells，Louis T.（1972），*Strategy and Structure of the Multinational Enterprise*，New York：Basic Books.

represents the foreign product diversity，indicating the number of products sold overseas by MNCs. The horizontal axis represents the foreign sales as a percentage of total sales，indicating the importance of foreign sales to MNCs. According to this model，in the early stages of overseas expansion，when foreign sales and product diversity are limited，MNCs generally operate internationally through an international division. Subsequently，MNCs that have expanded their foreign sales volume but have not significantly increased the diversity of products sold abroad generally adopt a worldwide geographic structure，while other MNCs that expand by increasing the diversity of products sold abroad tend to adopt a worldwide product structure. Finally，when foreign sales and product diversity are high，MNCs adopt a worldwide matrix structure. However，due to the inherent flaws of dual leadership，the global matrix structure ultimately evolves into an organizational quagmire，forcing many companies to retreat and instead attempt other organizational structures such as transnational network structure.

2. The match of strategies with organizational structures of multinational corporations

　　跨国公司的战略选择与其组织结构具有很强的相关性。如图 5-8 所示，跨国公司的组织结构的变革与跨国经营战略相适应，需要进行动态的匹配。国家与地区反应能力的战略要求使用全球地理结构。国际战略要求管理者采用产品组织结构并拥有全球产品。绝大多数公司利用出口部或国际分部来支持其早期的国际化。随后，公司发展到全球产品结构或全球地理结构阶段，这分别与公司的全球战略或多国战略相匹配。由于本地响应与全球化的双重需要，许多公司转向矩阵结构或跨国网络结构，这与公司的跨国战略相匹配。然而，很多公司都从未达到纯粹的矩阵或跨国网络结构境界，他们采用的都是具有矩阵和跨国性质的混合结构。近年来，由于更多的产品全球化以及来自全球产品的竞争效率，出现了大公司赋予产品分部更大权力和设立跨国性更强的子公司的增长趋势。一些强调组织学习的大型创业跨国公司则开始尝试元国家网络结构。

The choices of MNCs' strategy are strongly correlated with their organizational structure. As shown in Figure 5-8, the organizational structure transformation of MNCs needs to be dynamically matched to adapt to their strategies. The strategic requirement for national and regional responsiveness requires the use of geographic structures. International strategy requires managers to adopt a product structure and possess global products. The vast majority of companies utilize export departments or international divisions to support their early internationalization. After that, the MNC has developed into a stage of worldwide product structure or worldwide geographic structure, which match globalization strategy or multidomestic strategy respectively. Due to the dual pressure of local responsiveness and globalization, many MNCs have turned to matrix structure or transnational network structure, which match transnational strategy. However, many MNCs have never reached the realm of pure matrix or transnational network structure, and they adopt a hybrid structure with matrix and cross-border properties. In recent years, due to the globalization of more products and the competition efficiency from global products, there has been a growing trend of large MNCs granting greater power to product divisions and establishing subsidiaries with stronger cross-border characteristics. Some large entrepreneurial MNCs that emphasize organizational learning have begun to experiment with metanational network structures.

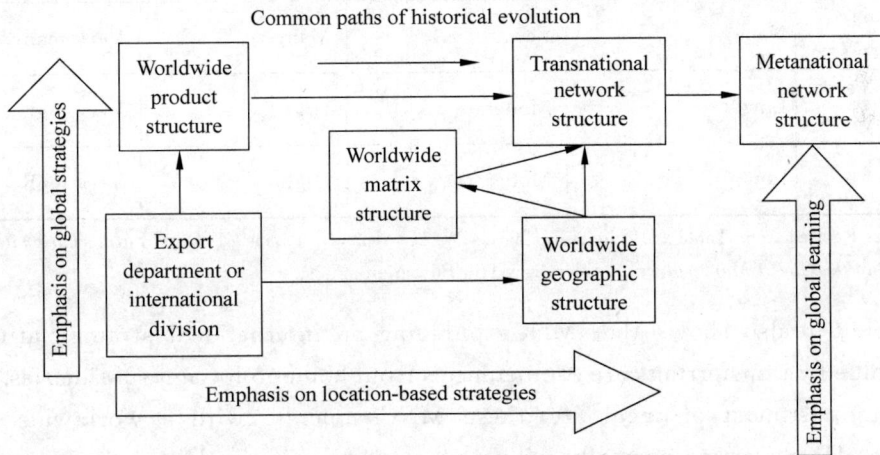

Figure 5-8　The match of strategies with organizational structures of MNCs

Source: Based on White, Roderick E., and Poynter, Thomas A. 1989. "*Organizing for worldwide advantage*." Business Quarterly. Summer: 84-89. Daft, Richard L. 2004. *Organization Theory and Design*. Minneapolis/St. Paul: West.

Based on Figure 5-8, a synthesis of MNC strategy and organizing can be described by Table 5-1.

As shown in Table 5-1, MNCs pursuing a multidomestic strategy focus on local responsiveness. Such firms tend to operate with worldwide geographical structures, within which operating decisions are decentralized to functionally self-contained country subsidiaries. The need for coordination between subunits is low. This suggests that firms pursuing a multidomestic strategy do not have a high need for integrating mechanisms to knit together different national operations. The lack of interdependence implies that the level of performance ambiguity in such enterprises is low, as are the costs of control. Thus, headquarters can manage foreign operations by relying primarily on output and bureaucratic controls and a policy of management by exception. Since the need for integration and coordination is low, the need for organizational culture is also quite low.

Table 5-1   A synthesis of strategies, structures and control systems

Organizing	Strategies			
	Multidomestic	International	Global	Transnational
Vertical differentiation	Decentralized	Core competency more centralized; rest decentralized	Some centralization	Mixed centralization and decentralization
Horizontal differentiation	Worldwide geographical structure	Worldwide product structure	Worldwide product structure	Matrix structure
Need for coordination	Low	Moderate	High	Very high
Integrating mechanisms	None	Few	Many	Very many
Performance ambiguity	Low	Moderate	High	Very high
Need for cultural control	Low	Moderate	High	Very high

Source: Revised from Table 14. 2 in Hill, Charles W. L. , Hult, G. Tomas M. (2017), *International Business: Competing in the Global Marketplace*, 11e, McGraw-Hill Education. P329.

Table 5-1 also shows that MNCs pursuing an international strategy attempt to create value by transferring core competencies from home to foreign subsidiaries. If they are diverse, as most of them are, these MNCs operate with a worldwide product structure. Headquarters normally maintains centralized control over the source of the firm's core competency, which is most typically found in the R&D and/or marketing functions of the firm. All other operating decisions are decentralized within the firm to subsidiary operations in each country. The need for coordination is moderate in such firms, reflecting the need to transfer core competencies. Thus, although such firms operate with some integrating mechanisms, they are not that extensive. The relatively low level of interdependence in this structure translates into a relatively low level of performance ambiguity. These firms can generally get by with output and bureaucratic controls. The need for a common organization culture is not that great. Overall, although the organization required for an international strategy is more complex than that of firms pursuing a multidomestic strategy, the increase in the level of complexity is not that great.

MNCs pursuing a global strategy focus on the realization of location and experience curve economies, as shown in Table 5-1. If they are diversified, as many of them are, these firms operate with a worldwide product structure. To coordinate the firm's globally dispersed web of value creation activities, headquarters typically maintains ultimate control over most operating decisions. In general, such firms are more centralized than MNCs pursuing a multidomestic or international strategy. Responding to the coordination of the various stages of the MNC's globally dispersed value chains, integration in these firms is also in great need. These MNCs tend to operate with an array of integrating mechanisms. The resulting interdependencies can lead to significant performance ambiguities. As a result, in addition to output and bureaucratic controls, MNCs pursuing a global strategy tend to stress the need to build a strong organizational culture that can facilitate coordination and cooperation. On average, the organization of such firms is more complex than that of MNCs pursuing a localization or international strategy.

In addition, Table 5-1 indicates that MNCs pursuing a transnational strategy focus on the simultaneous attainment of location and experience curve economies, local responsiveness, and global learning. These firms may operate with matrix structures in which both product divisions and geographic areas have significant influence. The need to coordinate a globally dispersed value chain and to transfer core competencies creates pressures for centralizing some operating decisions, particularly production and R&D. At the same time, the need to be locally responsive creates pressures for decentralizing other operating decisions to national operations, particularly marketing. Consequently, these MNCs tend to mix relatively high degrees of centralization for some operating decisions with relatively high degrees of decentralization for other operating decisions. The need for coordination is high in these MNCs. This is reflected in the use of any array of integrating mechanisms. The high level of interdependence of subunits implied by such integration can result in significant performance ambiguities, which raise the control costs. To reduce these, in addition to output and bureaucratic controls, MNCs pursuing a transnational strategy need to cultivate a strong culture that promotes cooperation between subunits.

关键术语（Key Terms）

垂直差异化（horizontal differentiation）

水平差异化（vertical differentiation）

协调系统（coordination system）

直接接触（direct contact）

联络员角色（liaison role）

工作组（task force）

团队（team）　　　　　　　　　　出口部（export department）

专职整合者（full-time integrator）　国际分部（international division）

委员会（committee）　　　　　　　全球地理结构（worldwide geographic structure）

控制系统（control system）　　　　全球产品结构（worldwide product structure）

业绩模糊性（performance ambiguity）全球混合结构（worldwide hybrid structure）

个人控制（personal control）　　　全球矩阵结构（worldwide matrix structure）

行政控制（bureaucratic control）　　跨国网络结构（transnational network structure）

产出控制（output control）　　　　元国家网络结构（metanational network structure）

文化控制（cultural control）

小结（Summary）

1. This book follows the view of "structure following strategy" and believes that the organizational structure of MNCs is a specific form of power, responsibility, control, and coordination within the company formed to achieve the strategic goals of MNCs. The organizational structure of MNCs revolves vertical differentiation and horizontal differentiation. The vertical differentiation deals with centralization and decentralization, relating to control system such as personal control, bureaucratic control, output control, and cultural control. The horizontal differentiation relates to coordinated system such as direct contact, liaison role, task force, team, full-time integrator, and committee.

2. The vast majority of firms that enter overseas markets through export use the same structure, procedures, and personnel as they do in domestic sales to complete orders. Even for larger scale direct exports, firms will try their best to avoid changing their basic organizational structure, as changes in organizational structure are often painful, time-consuming, and may not necessarily succeed. MNCs can organize their structure in the following form: export department, international division, worldwide geographic structure, worldwide product structure, worldwide hybrid structure, worldwide matrix structure, transnational network structure, and metanational network structure. Each way of organizing has its advantages and disadvantages. There is no one best organizational design.

3. The organizational structure transformation of MNCs needs to be dynamically matched to adapt to their strategies. The vast majority of companies utilize export departments or international divisions to support their early internationalization. After that, the MNC has developed into a stage of worldwide product structure or worldwide geographic structure, which match globalization strategy or multidomestic strategy respectively. Under the dual pressure of local responsiveness and globalization, many MNCs have turned to matrix structure or transnational network structure, which match transnational strategy. Some large entrepreneurial MNCs that emphasize organizational learning have begun to experiment with metanational network structure.

延伸阅读（Further Readings）

习题（Exercises）

第六章
Chapter 6

跨国公司的营销管理
Marketing of Multinational Corporations

Learning Objectives
- To know the concept of international marketing and marketing orientation
- To recognize international market segmentation and target market selection
- To understand international marketing mix and standardization choice
- To be familiar with factors influencing product adaptation
- To be familiar with pricing factors and three pricing strategies
- To be familiar with factors influencing distribution channel choice
- To be familiar with the four elements of the promotion mix
- To identify the pull and push strategies

第一节　跨国公司市场营销概述
（The Overview of Marketing of Multinational Corporations）

1. The definition and characteristics of marketing of MNCs

营销是规划和落实创意、商品和服务的构思、定价、推广和分销,以创造满足个人和组织目标的交换的过程。跨国公司的营销,也称为国际市场营销,是这些活动过程跨越国界的延伸。在国外开拓新市场的公司必须应对不同的政治、文化和法律制度,以及陌生的经济条件、广告媒体和分销渠道。

Marketing is the process of planning and executing the conception, pricing, promotion, and distribution of ideas, goods, and services to create exchanges that satisfy individual and organizational objectives. The marketing of MNCs, also known as international marketing, is the extension of these activities across national boundaries. Firms expanding into new markets in foreign countries must deal with different political, cultural, and legal systems, as well as unfamiliar economic conditions, advertising media, and distribution channels.

Compared to domestic marketing, international marketing has the following characteristics:

（1）Differences in marketing environment

There are certain differences in politics, economy, culture, and other aspects among countries, so market demand varies greatly, requiring marketing decisions to be tailored to local conditions.

(2) Diversity of marketing methods

The domestic marketing methods are controllable, while the methods of international marketing are relatively more complex and diverse.

(3) Complexity of marketing systems

The participants who make up the international marketing system include those from their own countries, host countries, and third countries, and they are more complex than domestic marketing.

(4) Difficulty of marketing management

International marketing activities require unified planning, control, and coordination of marketing operations in various countries, so that the marketing activities of the parent company and its subsidiaries scattered in various countries around the world become a whole, achieving maximum overall benefits. Therefore, compared to traditional domestic marketing activities, international marketing management activities are more difficult.

(5) Risks of marketing processes

Due to differences in international marketing environments and more complex management, international marketing carries greater risks compared to domestic marketing.

2. Marketing orientations of MNCs

营销导向是一种以市场需求为基础，通过生产适销对路的产品并全面满足顾客需求来获取利润的经营理念。跨国公司的营销导向可分为五类：生产导向、销售导向、客户导向、战略营销导向和社会营销导向。

Marketing orientation is a business philosophy based on market demand, which aims to generate profits by producing products that are suitable for the market and fully meet customer needs. Marketing orientation of MNCs can be classified into five types: production orientation, sales orientation, customer orientation, strategic marketing orientation, and social marketing orientation.

(1) Production orientation

With production orientation, companies focus primarily on production—either efficiency or high quality—with little emphasis on marketing. There is little analysis of consumer needs; rather, companies assume that customers want lower prices or higher quality. This orientation, although has almost gone out of vogue, is used internationally in the following cases: commodity sales, especially those for which there is little need or possibility of product differentiation; passive exports, particularly those that serve to reduce surpluses within the domestic market; foreign-market segments or niches that may happen to resemble segments to which the product is aimed at home. MNCs sell many undifferentiated raw materials and agricultural commodities primarily on the basis of price because there is universal demand. However, even for commodities, MNCs have sometimes had positive international sales results through differentiation. Commodity producers also put efforts into business-to-business marketing by providing innovative financing and ensuring timely, high-quality supplies. Many MNCs begin exporting very passively by filling unsolicited requested from abroad. Under this circumstance, they adapt their products very little, if at all, to foreign consumers' preferences. This practice suffices for many companies that view foreign sales only as a means to dispose of excess inventory they can't reasonably sell domestically. In fact, if fixed costs are covered from domestic sales, they can quote lower export prices to liquidate inventories without disrupting their domestic markets. An MNC may aim a product at a large share of its domestic market and then find that there are a few consumers abroad who are also willing to buy that product. An MNC may also take a production orientation when selling in countries with only a small market potential, particularly in small developing countries. In effect, the market size does not justify the alteration expense.

(2) Sales orientation

Internationally, sales orientation means an MNC tries to sell abroad what it can sell domestically, and in the same manner, on the assumption that consumers are sufficiently similar globally. Of course, MNCs constantly introduce new products or variations of old ones. Once they are operating within a country, a strong information exchange between the foreign subsidiary and headquarters can facilitate the development of products that can be sufficiently standardized and still fit the needs of consumers in different countries. This orientation differs from the production orientation because of its active rather than passive approach to promoting sales. However, there is much anecdotal evidence of foreign-marketing failures because MNCs merely assume without sufficient research that product acceptance will be the same as at home or that heavy sales efforts abroad can overcome negative foreign attitudes toward the product, its price, or method of distribution. Even so, there are successful examples of marketing abroad with little or no research on what foreign consumers want. Of course, there are products other than commodities that need no adaptation on a country basis. For other products, however, an MNC may succeed best with a sales orientation by selling to countries where culture and customer characteristics are similar to those at home and where there is also a great deal of spillover in product information.

(3) Customer orientation

An MNC with sales orientation usually asks the question where the MNC can sell more of product X. In this case, the product is held constant and the sales location is varied. In contrast, an MNC with customer orientation usually asks the questions what and how the MNC can sell in foreign country A. In this case, the country is held constant and the product and methods of marketing it are varied. An MNC may most likely take this approach because it finds the country's size and growth potential attractive. In the extreme of this approach, a company would move to completely different products—an uncommon strategy that some MNCs nonetheless have adopted. Business-to-business suppliers may be primarily concerned with promoting their production capabilities, prices, and delivery reliability rather than determining what will sell in foreign markets. Instead, they depend on other MNCs' purchasing agents to give them product specifications.

（4）Strategic marketing orientation

Most MNCs committed to continual rather than sporadic foreign sales adopt a strategy that combines production, sales, and customer orientations. MNCs that don't make changes to accommodate the needs of foreign customers may lose too many sales, especially if aggressive competitors are willing to make desired adaptations. Meanwhile, they must consider their competencies, lest they deviate too much from what they can do well. Thus, they tend to make marketing variations abroad without deviating very far from experience.

（5）Social marketing orientation

MNCs with social marketing orientations realize that successful international marketing requires serious consideration of potential environmental, health, social, and work-related problems that may arise when selling or making their products abroad. Such groups as consumer associations, political parties, and labor unions are becoming more globally aware—and vocal. They can quell demand when they feel a product in some way violates their concept of social responsibility. MNCs must increasingly consider not only how a product is purchased but also how it is made and disposed of and how it might be changed to be more socially desirable.

3. Segmenting and target market selection of MNCs

（1）Market segmentation

市场细分是指企业通过市场调研，根据顾客对产品或服务不同的需要和欲望、不同的购买行为与购买习惯，把某一产品的整体市场分割成需求不同的若干个市场的过程。分割后的每一个小市场称为子市场，也称为细分市场。市场细分的标准主要包括地理变量、人口变量、社会文化变量和心理变量等。跨国公司的市场细分，也称国际市场细分，是指跨国公司按照一定的细分标准，把整个国际市场细分为若干个需求不同的子市场，其中任何一个子市场中的消费者都具有相同或相似的需求特征，以便跨国公司从中选择其国际目标市场。

Market segmentation refers to the process whereby businesses, through market research, divide the overall market for a particular product into several smaller markets with distinct needs and demands, based on customers' varying needs and desires for products or services, as well as their purchasing behaviors and habits. Each of these smaller markets is referred to as a submarket or segment. Markets can be segmented in numerous ways: by geography, demography (including gender, age, income, race, education level), sociocultural factors (including social class, values, religion, lifestyle choices), and psychological factors such as personality. Because different segments exhibit different needs, wants, and patterns of purchasing behavior, firms often adjust their marketing mix from segment to segment. Thus, the precise design of a product, the pricing strategy, the distribution channels used, and the choice of promotion strategy may all be varied from segment to segment. The goal is to optimize the fit between the purchasing behavior of consumers in a given segment and the marketing mix, thereby maximizing sales to that segment. Market segmentation of MNCs, also known as international market segmentation, refers to MNCs dividing the entire international market into several submarkets with different demands according to certain segmentation standards, where consumers in any submarket have the same or similar demand characteristics, in order for MNCs to choose their international target market from them.

When MNCs consider market segmentation in foreign countries, they need to be cognizant of two main issues: the differences between countries in the structure of market segments and the existence of segments that transcend national borders. For instance, some MNCs are inclined to target a country with a number of different product options based on the multiple unique market segments in a country. Other MNCs prefer to target one unique market segment in a country that also has parallels in other countries. A segment that spans multiple countries, transcending national boarders, is often called intermarket segment. Strategically, MNCs have marketing mix options with these two choices. Targeting one country and its multiple potential market segments with multiple marketing mixes allows an MNC to focus on the cultural characteristics of one country. Targeting many countries and the intermarket segment with characteristics that are largely the same across countries allows a company to focus on cultural characteristics that are universal of certain customers across countries.

These are important choices because the structure of many potential market segments may differ significantly from country to country and also within countries. In fact, an important market segment in a foreign country may have no parallel in the firm's home country, and vice versa. In such a case, the focus cannot be on an intermarket segment, at least not one involving the home-country market. The firm may have to develop a unique marketing mix to appeal to the needs, wants, and purchasing behavior of a certain segment in a given country.

In contrast, the existence of market segments that transcend national borders clearly enhances the ability of an international business to view the global marketplace as a single entity and pursue a global strategy—selling a standardized product worldwide and using the same basic marketing mix to help position and sell that product in a variety of national markets. For a segment to transcend national borders, consumers in that segment must have some compelling similarities along important dimensions—such as age, values, lifestyle choice—and those similarities must translate into similar needs, wants, and purchasing behavior. If this is true, the MNC can globalize its marketing mix efforts by adopting the so-called intermarket segment to target customers' needs, wants, and purchasing behavior. Although such segments clearly exist in certain industrial markets, they have historically been rarer in consumer markets. The forecast, however, is that these intermarket segments will become more and more common with the increased globalization among younger consumers in the developed-and emerging-country markets.

There are three basic approaches to international market segmentation: segmentation by country, segmentation by global consumers, and segmentation by multiple criteria.

Segmentation by country means an MNC may decide to go for the time being only to one country because of its population size and purchasing power. It will then need to segment this country market and decide whether to target a single segment or multiple segments within this country, whether to use the same marketing mix to sell to all segments, whether to tailor the products separately to each segment, and whether to vary the promotion and distribution separately for the different segments. Although this approach may lead to success within this country, it overlooks the possible similarities of various market segments with those in other countries. Thus, there may be little opportunity of gaining economies through standardization to serve market segments that cut across countries.

Segmentation by global consumers means an MNC may identify some segments globally, such as segments based primarily on income. Thus, each country may have some people within this same segment, but the proportional size of each segment will vary by country. Although this may bring about economies of standardization, an MNC may still need to prioritize by country of entry, may have to delay tapping bigger markets in some countries, and may face high entry costs in other countries where the targeted segment is small.

Segmentation by multiple criteria means an MNC may combine the above first by looking at countries as segments, second by identifying segments within each country, and third by comparing these within-country segments with those in other countries. Once a company makes this determination, it can determine similarities for targeting the most promising cross-country segments, gain efficiencies through standardization, and still tailor other aspects of its marketing mix so they are compatible with the needs of each country's market. Actually, an MNC may hold one or more elements of these marketing functions constant while altering the others.

Meanwhile, most MNCs have multiple products and product variations that appeal to different segments. As usual, the MNCs must decide which to introduce abroad and whether to target them to mass markets versus niche segments. Sales to a mass market may be necessary if a company is to gain sufficient economies in production and distribution. Because the percentage of people who fall into any segment may vary substantially among countries, a niche market in one country may be a mass market in another. An MNC may be content to accept a combination of mass and niche markets. However, if it wishes to appeal to mass markets everywhere, it may need to change elements in its marketing program.

(2) Target market selection

目标市场选择过程涉及将潜在的国家市场缩小到可行数量的国家和其中的细分市场。跨国公司不是试图吸引所有人,而是通过确定潜在的进入市场,并随着时间的推移有选择地向那些被认为有吸引力的市场扩张,以最好地利用他们的资源。

The process of target market selection involves narrowing down potential country markets to a feasible number of countries and market segments within them. Rather than try to appeal to all, MNCs must best utilize their resources by identifying potential markets for entry and expanding selectively over time to those deemed attractive.

There are four stages in screening and analyzing foreign markets, including preliminary screening, estimation of market potential, estimation of sales potential, and identification of segments. Each stage should be given careful attention. For instance, in the first stage it is not appropriate to merely reduce the number of alternatives to a manageable few for the sake of reduction, even though the expense of analyzing markets in depth is great. Unless care is taken, attractive alternatives may be eliminated.

The process of screening and analyzing foreign markets starts with very common criteria and ends with product-specific market analyses. The data and the methods needed for decision making change from secondary to primary as the steps are taken in sequence. If markets were similar in their characteristics, the MNC could enter any one of the potential markets. However, differences among markets exist in three dimensions: physical, psychic, and economic. Physical distance is the geographic distance between home and target countries; its impact has decreased as a result of recent technological developments. Psychic, or cultural, distance refers to differences in language, tradition, and customs between two countries. Economic distance translates into the target's ability to pay. Generally, the greater the overall distance or difference between the two countries, the less knowledge the MNC has about the target market. The amount of information that is available varies dramatically. For example, although the MNCs can easily learn about the economic environment from secondary sources, invaluable interpretive information may not be available until the MNCs actually operate in the market.

The first stage of target market selection progress is preliminary screening. The preliminary screening stage must rely chiefly on secondary data for country-specific factors as well as product-and industry-specific factors. Country-specific factors typically include those that would indicate the market's overall buying power, including population, gross national product in total and per capita, total exports and imports, and production of cement, electricity, and steel. Product-specific factors narrow the analysis to the MNC's specific areas of operation. The statistical analyses must be accompanied by qualitative assessments of the impact of cultural elements and the overall climate for foreign firms and products. A market that satisfies the levels set becomes a prospective target country.

The second stage of target market selection progress is estimating market potential. Total market potential is the sales, in physical or monetary units, that might be available to all firms in an industry during a given period under a given level of industry marketing effort and given environmental conditions. The MNC needs to assess the size of existing markets and forecast the size of future markets. A number of techniques, both quantitative and qualitative, are available for this task.

If the data are available for product-specific analysis, the simplest way to establish a market-size estimate is to conduct a market audit, which adds together local production and imports with exports deducted from the total. However, in many cases, data may not exist, be current, or be appropriate. In such cases, market potentials may have to be estimated by methods such as analogy. This approach is based on the use of proxy variables that have been shown either through research or intuition to correlate with the demand for the product in question. The market size for a product in country A is estimated by comparing a ratio for an available indicator for country A and country B, and using this ratio in conjunction with market data available on another related product in country B. In some cases, a time lag in demand patterns may be seen, thus requiring a longitudinal analysis. In similar fashion, a country or a group of countries may be used as a proxy for an entire region.

Despite the valuable insight generated through these techniques, caution should be excercised in interpreting the results. All of the quantitative techniques are based on historical data that may be obsolete or inapplicable because of differences in cultural and geographic traits of the market. In addition, with the advancement of technology, lags between markets are no longer at a level that would make all of the measurements valid. Furthermore, the measurements look at a market as an aggregate, with no regional differences taken into account. Consequently, even in the least developed countries, segments exist with buying power rivaled only in the richest developed countries.

In addition to these quantitative techniques that rely on secondary data, MNCs can use various survey techniques. They are especially useful when marketing new technologies. A survey of end-user interest and response may provide a relatively clear picture of the possibilities in a new market. Surveys can also be administered through a web site or through e-mail.

The third stage of target market selection progress is estimating sales potential. Even when the MNC has gained an understanding of markets with the greatest overall promise, the MNC's own possibilities in those markets are still not known. Sales potential is the share of the market potential that the MNC can reasonably expect to get over the longer term. To arrive at an estimate, the MNC need to collect product—and market—specific data. The data should be related to the following aspects. First, competition, such as strength and likely reaction to entry. Second, market, like the strength of barriers. Third, consumers, such as the ability and willingness to buy. Fourth, product, including degree of relative advantage, compatibility, complexity, trialability, and communicability. Lastly, channel structure, like access to retail level.

The last stage of target market selection progress is identifying segments. Within the markets selected, individuals and organizations will vary in their wants, resources, geographical locations, buying attitudes, and buying practices. Initially, the firm may cater to one or only a few segments and later expand to others, especially if the product is innovative. Segmentation is indicated when segments are indeed different enough to warrant individualized attention, are large enough for profit potential, and can be reached through the methods that the MNC wants to use.

第二节　跨国公司营销组合与产品策略
（Marketing Mix and Product Strategy of Multinational Corporations）

1. Marketing mix and standardization choice of MNCs

在选定目标市场后,下一步是确定适当水平的营销工作。国际营销中的一个关键问题是营销组合的要素应在多大程度上标准化。跨国公司还面临着调整国际市场中每个混合要素的具体挑战。跨国公司的市场营销组合,也称国际市场营销组合,是指跨国公司根据国际市场的营销环境,针对性地制定产品策略、价格策略、促销策略和渠道策略等,并将它们进行组合,使这些策略能够相互配合,发挥出最大的作用,以满足国际市场上不同消费者的需求,并实现企业的市场目标和战略。

After target market are selected, the next step is the determination of marketing efforts at appropriate levels. A key question in international marketing concerns the extent to which the elements of the marketing mix should be standardized. MNCs also face the specific challenges of adjusting each of the mix elements in the international marketplace. The MNC's marketing mix, also known as international marketing mix, refers to the tailored combination of product strategy, pricing strategy, promotion strategy, and distribution strategy formulated by an MNC based on the marketing environment of the international market. These strategies are combined and coordinated to maximize their effectiveness in satisfying the diverse needs of consumers in the international market, thereby achieving the company's market objectives and strategies.

The MNC must first decide what modifications in the mix policy are needed or warranted. Usually, there are three alternatives in approaching international markets. Firstly, make no special provisions for the international marketplace but, rather, identify potential target markets and then choose products that can easily be marketed with little or no modification, also known as standardization approach. Secondly, adapt to local conditions in each and every target market, also known as multidomestic approach. Lastly, incorporate differences into a regional or global strategy that will allow for local differences in implementation, also known as globalization approach.

The trade-offs between standardization and adaptation are clear. Standardization allows a firm to achieve manufacturing, distribution, and promotional efficiencies and to maintain simpler and more streamlined operations. However, the firm may suffer lost sales if its products fail to meet the unique needs of customers in each market. Adaptation allows a firm to tailor its products to meet the needs of customers in each market, although the MNC may sacrifice cost efficiencies by doing so. In essence, standardization focuses on the cost side of the profit equation; by driving down costs, the MNC's profits are enhanced. Adaptation focuses on the revenue side of the profit equation; by attending to the unique customer needs in each market, the MNC is able to charge higher prices and sell more goods in each market. In practice, most firms avoid the extremes of either approach. Many successful MNCs have adopted a strategy of "think globally, act locally" to gain the economies of scale of a global marketing mix while retaining the ability to meet the needs of customers in different national markets.

The degree of standardization or adaptation an MNC adopts depends on many factors, including product type, the cultural differences between the home country and the host countries, and the host countries' legal systems. An MNC may adopt one approach for one element of the marketing mix and another for a second element. Often MNCs standardize product designs to capture manufacturing economies of scale but customize advertisements and the channels of distribution to meet specific local market needs. The degree of standardization also may be influenced by the MNC's perception of the global marketplace.

Nowadays, standardization usually means cross-national strategies rather than a policy of viewing foreign markets as secondary and therefore not important enough to have products adapted for them. Ideally, the MNC should think globally and act locally, focusing on neither extreme: full standardization or full localization. Global thinking requires flexibility in exploiting good ideas and products on a worldwide basis regardless of their origin. Table 6-1 summarizes some factors that may lead a firm to adopt standardization or adaptation for all or part of its international efforts.

Table 6-1   Advantages and disadvantages of standardized and adapted international marketing

	Advantages	Disadvantages
Standardized international marketing	• Reduces marketing costs • Facilitates centralized control of marketing • Promotes efficiency in R&D • Results in economies of scale in production • Reflects the trend toward a single global marketplace	• Ignores different conditions of product use • Ignores local legal differences • Ignores differences in buyer behavior patterns • Inhibits local marketing initiatives • Ignores other differences in individual markets
Adapted international marketing	• Reflects different conditions of product use • Acknowledges local legal differences • Accounts for differences in buyer behavior patterns • Promotes local marketing initiatives • Accounts for other differences in individual markets	• Increases marketing costs • Inhibits centralized control of marketing • Creates inefficiency in R&D • Reduces economies of scale in production • Ignores the trend toward a single global marketplace

Source: Revised from Table 11.1 in Griffin, Ricky W., Pustay, Michael W. (2013), *International Business*, 7th Edition, Pearson Education, Inc. P286.

2. Factors influencing product adaptation

跨国公司的大多数产品都必须以某种方式为国际市场做出改变。这些改变既包括较小的变动,如用户手册的翻译,也包括较大的变化,如更经济的产品版本。这些改变通常会影响包装、计量单位、标签、产品成分和特征、使用说明,以及在较小程度上影响徽标和品牌名称。以下三个因素会影响产品对特定市场的适应性:市场环境、产品特性和公司政策。

The majority of MNCs' products have to be modified for the international marketplace one way or another. The changes vary from minor ones, such as translation of a user's manual, to major ones, such as a more economical version of the product. Changes typically affect packaging, measurement units, labeling, product constituents and features, usage instructions, and, to a lesser extent, logos and brand names. The following three factors have an impact on product adaptation for a given market: market environment, product characteristics, and company policies.

(1) Market environment

Typically, the market environment, especially regional, country, and local characteristics, mandates the majority of product modifications. The most stringent requirements come from government regulations. Some requirements may serve no purpose other than a political one such as protection of domestic industry or response to political pressures. Due to the country sovereignty, the individual MNCs must comply, but they can influence the situation either by lobbying directly or through industry associations to have the issue raised during negotiations. Government regulations may be spelled out, but MNCs need to be ever vigilant for changes and exceptions.

Product decisions made by marketers of consumer products are especially affected by local behavior, tastes, attitudes, and traditions. A knowledge of cultural and psychological differences may be the key to success. Often no concrete product changes are needed, only a change in the product's positioning, which is the perception by consumers of the MNCs' brand in relation to competitors' brands. In other words, positioning is the mental image a brand, or the MNC as a whole, evokes.

Although nontariff barriers include product standards, testing or approval procedures, subsidies for local products, and bureaucratic red tape, the nontariff barriers affecting product adjustments usually concern elements outside the core product.

The monitoring of competitors' product features, as well as determining what has to be done to meet and beat them, is critical to product-adaptation decisions. Competitive offerings may provide a baseline against which resources can be measured. For instance, they may help to determine what it takes to reach a critical market share in a given competitive situation.

In addition, an MNC must take into account the stage of economic development of the overseas market. As a country's economy advances, buyers are in a better position to buy and to demand more sophisticated products and product versions. On the other hand, the situation in some developing markets may require backward innovation. When the market require a drastically simplified version of the MNC's product because of lack of purchasing power or of usage conditions, the backward innovation occurs. Economic conditions may shift rapidly, thus warranting change in the product or the product line.

（2）Product characteristics

Product characteristics are the inherent features of a product, whether actual or perceived. The inherent characteristics of products, and the benefits they provide to consumers in various markets make certain products good candidates for standardization, and others not.

An MNC must ensure that its products do not contain ingredients that might violate legal requirements or religious or social customs. Packaging is an area where MNCs generally make modifications. Due to the longer time that products spend in channels of distribution, MNCs, particularly those marketing food products, have used more expensive packaging materials and/or more expensive transportation modes for export shipments. The promotional aspect of packaging relates primarily to labeling. The major adjustments concern legally required bilinguality. Other government requirements include more informative labeling of products for consumer protection and education. Inadequate identification, failure to use the required languages, or inadequate or incorrect descriptions printed on the labels may all cause problems. Increasingly, environmental concerns are having an impact on packaging decisions. On the one hand, governments want to reduce the amount of packaging waste by encouraging marketers to adopt the four environmentally correct Rs: redesign, reduce, reuse, and recycle. On the other hand, many markets have sizable segments of consumers who are concerned enough about protecting the environment to change their consumption patterns, which has resulted in product modifications such as the introduction of recyclable yogurt containers.

Brand names convey the image of the goods or service. Offhand, brands may seem to be the most standardizable items in the product offering. However, the establishment of worldwide brands is difficult. How can an MNC establish world brands when the MNC sells nearly 1,000 products in more than 150 economies, while most of them are under different names? Standardizing the name to reap promotional benefits is difficult because names have become established in each market, and the action would lead to objections from local managers or even governments. In response, MNCs have standardized all other possible elements of brand aesthetics including color, symbols, and packaging. However, brand aesthetics have to take market-specific realities including culture into account.

The product offered in the domestic market may not be operable in the foreign market. When a product that is sold globally requires repairs, parts, or service, the problems of obtaining, training, and holding a sophisticated engineering or repair staff are not easy to solve. If the product breaks down and the repair arrangements are not up to standard, the product image will suffer. In some cases, products abroad may not even be used for their intended purpose and thus may require modifications not only in product configuration but also in service frequency.

The country of origin of a product has considerable influence on quality perceptions. The perception of products manufactured in certain countries is affected by a built-in positive or negative assumption about quality. Hence, measures must be taken by the MNCs to overcome or at least neutralize biases. It is especially important for developing countries that need to increase sales in developed countries. Some countries have started promotional campaigns to improve their overall images in support of investment.

(3) Company policies

Company policies will often determine the presence and degree of adaptation. Whether product adaptation is of value or not depends on the MNC's ability to control costs, to correctly estimate market potential, and, finally, to secure profitability. The decision to adapt should be preceded by a thorough analysis of the market. Formal market research with primary data collection and/or testing is warranted. From the financial standpoint, some MNCs have specific return-on-investment levels to be satisfied before adaptation. Others let the requirement vary as a function of the market considered and also the time in the market—that is, profitability may be initially compromised for proper market entry.

Most MNCs aim for consistency in their market efforts. This means that all products must fit in terms of quality, price, and user perceptions. Consistency may be difficult to attain, for instance, in the area of warranties. Warranties can be uniform only if use conditions do not vary drastically and if the company is able to deliver equally on its promise anywhere it has a presence.

第三节　跨国公司定价策略
（Pricing Strategies of Multinational Corporations）

1. Factors influencing pricing strategies

制定有效的定价政策是任何跨国公司成功的关键决定因素。定价策略直接影响跨国公司的收入规模。这些策略也是一种重要的战略武器，使跨国公司能够塑造其开展业务的竞争环境。

Developing effective pricing policies is a critical determinant for the success of all MNCs. Pricing strategies directly affect the revenues of an MNC. The strategies also serve as an important strategic weapon by allowing the MNC to shape the competitive environment in which it does business.

Compared with domestic companies, pricing for an MNC is more complex. To begin with, an MNC's business operation costs vary widely by country. Differences in transportation charges and tariffs cause the landed price of goods to vary by country. Differences in distribution practices also affect the final price the end customers pay. In addition, exchange rate fluctuations can create pricing problems.

In some countries, an MNC may have many competitors and thus little discretion in setting its prices. In other countries, it may have a near monopoly situation, which allows it to exercise considerable pricing discretion by using any of the following tactics: a skimming strategy, charging a high price for a new product by aiming first at consumers willing to pay the price, and then progressively lowering the price; a penetration strategy, introducing a product at a low price to induce a maximum number of consumers to try it; a cost-plus strategy, pricing at a desired margin over cost. Country-of-origin stereotypes also limit pricing possibilities. For instance, MNCs from developing economies often compete primarily through low prices because of negative perceptions about their products' quality. However, it is dangerous by lowering prices in response to adverse stereotypes since a lower price may reduce the product image even further.

An MNC must consider the above factors in developing its pricing strategies for each national market it serves. It must decide whether it wants to apply consistent prices across all those markets or customize process to meet the needs of each. In reaching this decision, an MNC must remember that competition, culture, distribution channels, income levels, legal requirements, and exchange rate stability may vary widely by country.

2. Specific pricing strategies

跨国公司通常采用以下四种定价策略之一：标准定价、双重定价、市场定价和转移定价。

An MNC generally adopts one of the following four pricing strategies: standard pricing, dual pricing, market pricing, and transfer pricing.

（1）Standard pricing

Standard pricing implies that an MNC charges the same price for its products and services regardless of where they are sold or the nationality of the customer. Firms selling goods that are easily tradable and transportable often adopt this pricing approach out of necessity. Standard pricing is based on average unit costs of fixed, variable, and export-related costs.

（2）Dual pricing

Dual pricing means an MNC sets one price for all its domestic sales and a second price for all its international sales. An MNC that adopts a dual pricing policy commonly allocates to domestic sales all accounting charges associated with research and development, administrative overhead, capital depreciation, and so on. The firm then can establish a uniform foreign sales price without having to worry about covering these costs. Indeed, the only costs that need to be covered by the foreign sales price are the marginal costs associated with foreign sales, such as the product's unit manufacturing costs, shipping costs, tariffs, and foreign distribution costs. Hence, the foreign sales price is far in excess of domestic prices. This is called price escalation.

Dual pricing is often used by domestic firms just beginning to internationalize. In the short run, charging foreign customers a price that covers only marginal costs may be an appropriate approach for such MNCs. However, an MNC that regards its foreign customers as marginal rather than integral to its business is unlikely to develop the international skills, expertise, and outlook necessary to compete successfully in the international marketplace. MNCs that adopt a dual pricing policy are also vulnerable to charges of dumping. Dumping is the selling of a MNC's products in a foreign market for a price much lower than that charged in the MNC's domestic market—an outcome that can easily result from a dual pricing system. Most major trading countries have issued regulations intended to protect domestic firms from dumping by foreign competitors.

（3）Market pricing

Among the four pricing strategies, market pricing is the most complex and most commonly adopted. An MNC utilizing market pricing customizes its prices on a market-by-market basis to maximize its profits in each market. Two conditions must be met if an MNC is to successfully practice market pricing. One is that the MNC must face different demand and/or cost conditions in the countries in which it sells its products. This condition is usually met because taxes, tariffs, standards of living, levels of competition, infrastructure costs and availability, and numerous other factors vary by country. The other is that the MNC must be able to prevent arbitrage. The MNC's market pricing policy will unravel if customers are able to buy the MNC's products in a low-price country and resell them profitably in a high-price country. Because of tariffs, transportation costs, and other transaction costs, arbitrage is usually not a problem if country-to-country price variations are small. If prices vary widely by country, however, arbitrage can upset the MNC's market pricing strategy. When the two conditions are met, the MNC can set higher prices where markets will tolerate them and lower prices where necessary to remain competitive. It also can directly allocate relevant local costs against local sales within each foreign market, thereby allowing corporate strategist and planners to better allocate the MNC's resources across markets. Nevertheless, such advantages come with a cost. To capture the benefits of market pricing, local managers must closely monitor sales and competitive conditions within their markets so that appropriate and timely adjustments can be made. Also, corporate headquarters must be willing to delegate authority to local managers to allow them to adjust prices within their markets.

Except exposure to complaints about dumping, an MNC adopting market pricing policy takes the following three risks: damage to its brand name, development of a gray market for its products, and consumer resentment against discriminatory prices. The MNC needs to ensure that the prices it charges in one market do not damage the brand image it has carefully nurtured in other markets. An MNC adopting market pricing policy also risks the development of gray markets for its products as a result of arbitrage. A gray market is a market that results when products are imported into a country legally but outside the normal channels of distribution authorized by the manufacturer. This phenomenon is also known as parallel importing. A gray market may develop when the price in one market is sufficiently lower than the price the MNC charges in another market that entrepreneurs can buy the product in the lower-price market and resell it profitably in the higher-price market. Thus, the MNC that has large price differences among markets is vulnerable to having these differentials undercut by gray markets. Gray markets frequently arise when MNCs fail to adjust local prices after major fluctuations in exchange rates. Products commonly influenced by gray markets include big-ticket items such as automobiles, cameras, computers, ski equipment, and watches. Gray markets are also more prevalent in free-market economies, where fewer government regulations make it easier for gray markets to emerge. Gray market sales undermine an MNC's market pricing policy and often lower the MNC's profits. Gray market sales also cause friction between the MNC and its distributors, who lose sales but are often stuck with the costs of either providing customer support and honoring product guarantees on gray-market goods or explaining to unhappy customers why they will not do so. The last risk lies in consumer resentment. Consumers in the high-priced country may feel they are being gouged by such pricing policies.

(4) Transfer pricing

MNCs usually involve a large number of transfers of goods and services between the parent company and foreign subsidiaries and between foreign subsidiaries, which is particularly likely in MNCs adopting global and transnational strategies because these MNCs are likely to have dispersed their value creation activities to various optimal locations around the world. The price at which goods and services are transferred between entities within the MNCs is so called transfer price. Transfer prices can be used to position funds within an MNC. For instance, funds can be moved out of a particular country by setting high transfer prices for goods and services supplied to a subsidiary in that country and by setting low transfer prices for the goods and services sourced from that subsidiary. Conversely, funds can be positioned in a country by the opposite policy: setting low transfer prices for goods and services supplied to a subsidiary in that country and setting high transfer prices for the goods and services sourced from that subsidiary. This movement of funds can be between the MNCs' subsidiaries or between the parent company and a subsidiary.

There are at least four advantages of adjusting transfer prices. Firstly, an MNC can reduce its tax liabilities by using transfer prices to shift earnings from a high-tax country to a low-tax one. Secondly, an MNC can use transfer prices to move funds out of a country where a significant currency devaluation is expected, thereby reducing its exposure to foreign exchange risk. Thirdly, an MNC can use transfer prices to move funds from a subsidiary to the parent company when financial transfers in the form of dividends are restricted or blocked by host-country government policies. Lastly, an MNC can use transfer prices to reduce the import duties it must pay when an ad valorem tariff is in force—a tariff assessed as a percentage of value. In this case, low transfer prices on goods or services being imported into the country are required. Since this lowers the value of the goods or services, it lowers the tariff.

In addition, the most significant strategic use of transfer prices is to reduce an MNC's total income tax payments. Table 6-2 shows the strategic use of transfer prices. Suppose an MNC operates in two countries, one with high corporate income tax rates and another with low rates. The MNC can raise the transfer prices charged to the subsidiary in the high-tax country and lower those charge to the subsidiary in the low-tax country. Doing this will reduce the profitability of the first subsidiary, as measured by its accounting records, while increasing the profitability of the second. The net effect is to shift the location of the MNC's profits from the high-tax country to the low-tax country, thereby reducing the MNC's overall tax burden.

Table 6-2　Strategic use of transfer prices

Goal	Technique	Effect
Decrease tariffs paid on components imported from a subsidiary	Lower transfer prices charged by the subsidiary	Lowering the price on which an ad valorem tariff is based decreases total amount of import tariffs
Decrease overall corporate income tax	Raise transfer prices paid by subsidiaries in high-tax countries and/or lower transfer prices charged by those subsidiaries Lower transfer prices paid by subsidiaries in low-tax countries and/or raise transfer prices charged by those subsidiaries	Reported profits of subsidiaries in high-tax countries decrease, and reported profits of subsidiaries in low-tax countries increase Total corporate tax burden decreases
Repatriate profits from a subsidiary located in a host country that blocks repatriation	Raise transfer prices paid by the subsidiary Lower transfer prices charged by the subsidiary	Cash flows from the subsidiary to other units, circumventing restriction on repatriation

Source: Revised from Table 13. 4 in Griffin, Ricky W. , Pustay, Michael W. (2013), *International Business*, 7th Edition, Pearson Education, Inc. P355.

However, significant problems are associated with adopting a transfer pricing policy. First of all, when transfer prices are used to reduce an MNC's tax liabilities or import duties, most governments feel they are being cheated of their legitimate income. Similarly, when transfer prices are manipulated to circumvent government restrictions on capital flows such as dividend remittances, governments perceive this as breaking the spirit of the law. As a result, many governments now limit MNCs' ability to manipulate transfer prices in the manner described. In many countries, the correct transfer price is an arm's-length price which would prevail between unrelated MNCs in a market setting. Such a strict requirement of transfer prices theoretically limits an MNC's ability to manipulate transfer prices to achieve the benefits above.

The second problem associated with transfer pricing is related to management incentives and performance evaluation. Transfer pricing is inconsistent with a policy of treating each subsidiary in the MNCs as a profit center. When transfer prices are manipulated by the MNC and deviate significantly from the arm's-length price, the subsidiary's performance may depend as much on transfer prices as it does on other pertinent factors, such as management effort. A subsidiary told to charge high transfer prices for goods supplied to another subsidiary will appear to be doing better than it actually is, while the subsidiary purchasing the goods will appear to be doing worse. Unless this is recognized when performance is being evaluated, serious distortions in management incentive systems can occur. For instance, managers in the selling subsidiary may be able to use high transfer prices to mask inefficiencies, while managers in the purchasing subsidiary may become disheartened by the effect of high transfer prices on their subsidiary's profitability.

Despite these problems, research suggests that not all MNCs use arm's-length pricing but instead use some cost-based system for pricing transfers among their subunits, typically cost plus some standard markup. Only market and negotiated prices could reasonably be interpreted as arm's-length prices. The opportunity for price manipulation is much greater with cost-based transfer pricing. Although an MNC may be able to manipulate transfer prices to avoid tax liabilities or circumvent government restrictions on capital flows across borders, this does not mean the MNCs should do so. Since the practice often violates at least the spirit of the law in many countries, the ethics of engaging in transfer pricing are dubious at best. In addition, there are growing tendencies that tax authorities in many countries are strengthening their scrutiny of this practice in order to stamp out abuses.

第四节　跨国公司分销策略
（Distribution Strategies of Multinational Corporations）

1. Factors influencing distribution strategies

分销策略是将产品交付给消费者的手段，它是跨国公司营销组合的关键要素。国际制造公司的基本分销渠道包括五个组成部分：创建产品或服务的内部或外部制造商，从制造商那里购买产品和服务然后将其转售给零售商的批发商，从批发商那里购买然后转售给客户的零售商，购买产品或服务以供最终消费的最终客户，以及从外部制造商那里购买产品然后将其直接出售给批发商、零售商或客户的进口代理商。影响分销系统的因素主要有四个：零售集中度、渠道长度、渠道排他性和渠道质量。

Distribution strategy is the means for delivering the product to the consumer. It is a critical element of the marketing mix for an MNC. Figure 6-1 shows the basic channel options used by most international manufacturing companies. There are five basic parts in Figure 6-1: the inside or outside manufacturer that creates the product or service, the wholesaler that buys products and services from the manufacturer and then resells them to retailers, the retailer that buys from wholesalers and then sells to customers, the final customer who buys the product or service for final consumption, and the import agent who buys the products from the outside manufacturer and then sells them to wholesalers, or retailers, or customers directly. There are four main differences in distribution systems: retail concentration, channel length, channel exclusivity, and channel quality.

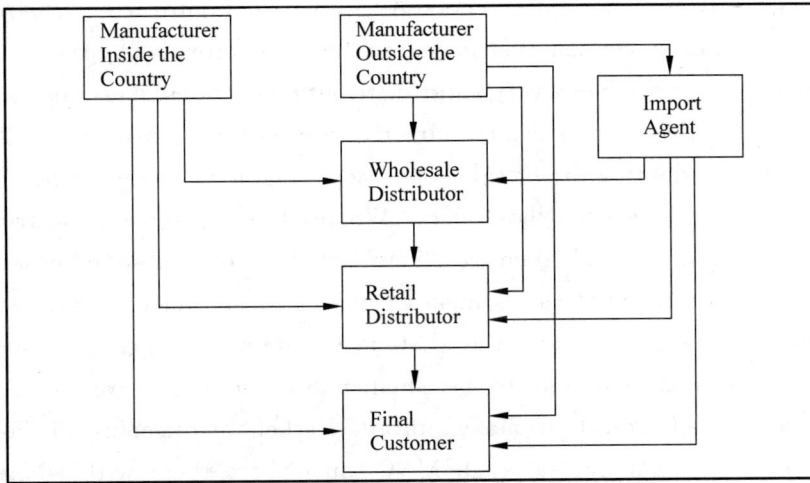

Figure 6-1　A typical distribution system

Source: Hill, Charles W. L., Hult, G. Tomas M. (2017), *International Business: Competing in the Global Marketplace*, 11e, McGraw-Hill Education. P414, Figure 18.1

（1）Retail concentration

In some countries, the retail system is very concentrated, while in other countries it is fragmented. In a concentrated system, a few retailers supply most of the market. In a fragmented system, there are many retailers, no one of which has a major share of the market. Many of the differences in concentration are rooted in history and tradition. There is a tendency for greater retail concentration in developed countries. The factors contributing to this tendency are the increases in car ownership, the number of households with refrigerators and freezers, and the number of two-income households. All these factors have changed shopping habits and facilitated the growth of large retail establishments sited away from traditional shopping areas. On the contrary, retail systems are very fragmented in many developing countries, which can make for interesting distribution challenges.

（2）Channel length

Channel length is the number of intermediaries between the producer and the consumer. When the producer sells directly to the consumer, the channel is very short. When the producer sells through an import agent, a wholesaler, and a retailer, a long channel exists. The more fragmented the retail system, the more expensive it is for a firm to make contact with each individual retailer. Fragmented retail systems tend to have longer channels of distribution, sometimes with multiple layers. In some countries, the channel length is shortening because of the entry of large discount superstores including Walmart, Costco, and Carrefour. The business model of these retailers is, in part, based on the idea that in an attempt to lower prices, they cut out wholesalers and instead deal directly with manufacturers. As shown in Figure 6-1, an MNC can sell directly to its customers, which then pays the business directly, bypasses wholesalers and retailers and therefore has a very short distribution channel. This approach is called direct sales because the MNC is dealing directly with its final consumer. Dell Computer is the typical MNC adopting direct sales approach. The longest distribution channel in Figure 6-1 involves the use of wholesalers. Wholesalers are separate distributors that buy from manufacturers and then resell to retailers or, in some cases, to other wholesalers. The use of wholesalers makes it easier to market in countries with little retail concentration and also allows the MNC to maintain a smaller sales staff. On the other hand, profit margins tend to be smaller because there are more businesses involved, each of which expects to make a profit. Rather than keeping all the profits for itself, as in the case of direct sales, an MNC must share them with wholesalers and retailers.

（3）Channel exclusivity

An exclusive distribution channel is one that is difficult for outsiders to access. For instance, it's often difficult for a new firm to get access to shelf space in supermarkets. This occurs because retailers tend to prefer to carry the products of established manufacturers of foodstuffs with national reputations rather than gamble on the products of unknown firms. The exclusivity of a distribution system varies among countries. Japan's system is an example of a very exclusive system. In Japan, relationships among manufacturers, wholesalers, and retailers often go back decades. Many of these relationships are based on the understanding that distributors will not carry the products of competing firms. In return, the distributors are guaranteed an attractive markup by the manufacturer. The close ties that result from this arrangement can make access to the Japanese market difficult.

（4）Channel quality

Channel quality refers to the expertise, competencies, and skills of established retailers in a nation, and their ability to sell and support the products of international businesses. The quality of retailers is good in most developed countries, but is variable at best in emerging markets and less developed countries. A poor-quality channel can impede market entry, particularly in the case of new or sophisticated products that require significant point-of-sale assistance and after-sales services and support. When channel quality is poor, an MNC may have to devote considerable attention to upgrading the channel by providing extensive education and support to existing retailers and by even establishing their own channel.

The choice depends on the relative costs and benefits of each alternative. Each intermediary adds its own markup to the products, so there is a link between channel length and profit margin. The longer a channel, the greater the aggregate markup, and the higher the price that consumers are charged for the final product. To ensure that prices do not get too high as a result of markups by multiple intermediaries, a firm might be forced to operate with lower profit margins. If price is important, a shorter channel is better. If a retail sector is very fragmented, a long channel is better. The benefit of using a longer channel is market access—the ability to enter an exclusive channel.

2. Selection of transportation modes

The most obvious issue an MNC's distribution managers must address is the selection of a mode or modes of transportation for shipping the MNC's products from their point of origin to their destination. Faster modes of transportation, such as air freight and motor carrier, are more expensive than slower modes, such as ocean shipping, railroad, pipeline, and barge. However, the transportation mode selected affects the MNC's inventory costs and customer service levels, as well as the product's useful shelf life, exposure to damage, and packaging requirements. International air freight, for example, scores high on each of these dimensions, whereas ocean shipping ranks very low.

Consider the impact of transportation mode on the MNC's inventory expenses and the level of customer service. If the MNC relies on slower modes of transportation, it can maintain a given level of inventory at the point of only by maintaining higher levels of inventory in transit. If the MNC selects unreliable modes that make it difficult to predict when shipments will actually arrive, the MNC will have to increase buffer stocks in its inventory to avoid stock-outs that will lead to disappointed customers. Slower modes of transportation also increase the MNC's international order cycle time—the time between the placement of an order and its receipt by the customer—for any given level of inventories. Longer order cycle time lowers the MNC's customer service levels and may induce its customers to seek alternative supply sources.

The product's shelf life affects the selection of transportation mode. Goods that are highly perishable because of physical or cultural forces—such as cut flowers or fashionable dresses—are typically shipped by air freight because of their short shelf life. Less perishable products, such as coal, crude oil, or men's socks, are shipped using less expensive modes. In some cases, the transportation mode may affect the product's packaging requirements. For instance, goods sent on long ocean voyages may need special packaging to protect them from humidity and damage due to rough seas; the MNC could avoid the extra costs of packaging if it chose a faster mode such as air freight.

E-commerce, the ability to offer goods and services over the Web, is growing drastically. MNCs planning to enter e-commerce will not have to do it on their own.

Hub sites, also known as virtual malls or digital intermediaries will bring together buyers, sellers, distributors, and transaction payment processors in one single marketplace, making convenience the key attraction. Once customers have the ability to access a company through the Internet, the MNC itself must be prepared to provide 24-hour order taking and customer service, have the regulatory and customs-handling expertise to deliver internationally, and have an in-depth understanding of marketing environments for the further development of the business relationship. The instantaneous interactivity users experience will also be translated into an expectation of expedient delivery of answers and products ordered. The challenge faced in terms of response and delivery capabilities can be overcome through outsourcing services or by building international distribution networks. Transactions and the information they provide about the buyer allow for more customization and service by region, market, or even by individual customer. A number of hurdles and uncertainties are keeping MNCs out of global markets or from exploiting them to their full potential. MNCs have to be sensitive to the governmental role in e-commerce. No real consensus exists on the taxation of e-commerce, especially in the case of cross-border transactions. In addition, any product traded will still be subject to government regulations. Governments will also have to come to terms with issues related to security, privacy, and access to the Internet. The private sector argues for the highest possible ability to safeguard its databases, to protect cross-border transmission of confidential information, and to conduct secure financial transactions using global networks. This would require an unrestricted market for encryption products that interoperate globally. Privacy issues have grown exponentially as a result of e-business. For industries such as music and motion pictures, the Internet is both an opportunity and a threat. The Web provides a new efficient model of distribution and customization of products. Meanwhile, it can be a channel for intellectual property violation through unauthorized posting on websites where they can be downloaded.

第五节　跨国公司促销策略
（Promotion Strategies of Multinational Corporations）

促销包括跨国公司为提高其产品在潜在买家中的吸引力所做的一切努力。尽管许多促销活动都是专门针对买家的,但成功的跨国公司认识到,他们还必须与分销商和公众沟通,以确保对跨国公司本身及其产品的好感。由于促销依赖于与东道国受众的沟通,因此,它是营销组合中最受文化约束的部分。跨国公司必须特别注意确保东道国受众收到的信息实际上是跨国公司想要发送的信息。为此,跨国公司必须有效地融合和利用促销组合的四个要素——广告、人员推销、销售促进和公共关系——来激励潜在客户购买他们的产品。

Promotion encompasses all efforts by an MNC to enhance the desirability of its products among potential buyers. Although many promotional activities are specifically targeted at buyers, successful MNCs recognize they also must communicate with their distributors and the general public to ensure favorable sentiment toward the MNCs themselves and their products. Because promotion relies on communication with audiences in the host country, it is the most culture bound of the marketing mix. Thus, an MNC must take special care to ensure that messages host country audiences receive are in fact messages the MNC intend to send. MNCs must therefore effectively blend and utilize the four elements of the promotion mix—advertising, personal selling, sales promotion, and public relations—to motivate potential customers to buy their products.

1. Advertising

For most MNCs, especially those selling consumer products and services, advertising is the most important element in the promotion mix. The key decision-making areas in advertising are: media strategy, the promotional message, and the organization of the promotional program.

Media strategy is applied to the selection of media vehicles and development of a media schedule. The media is the communication channel used by the advertiser to convey a message. An MNC must alter the media used to convey its message from market to market based on availability, legal restrictions, standards of living, literacy rates, the cultural homogeneity of the national market, and other factors. Media spending varies by market. Media regulations will also vary. Some regulations include limits on the amount of time available for advertisements. Countries often outlaw the use of certain media for advertising products that may be harmful to their societies. Global media vehicles have been developed that have target audiences on at least three continents and for which the media buying takes place through a centralized office. These media have traditionally been publications that, in addition to the worldwide edition, have provided advertisers with the option of using regional editions. Furthermore, the Internet provides the MNC with a global medium. One way of getting started is to choose a few key languages for the web site. If the MNC elects to have a global site and region-specific sites, the look should be similar, especially in terms of the level of sophistication of the global site. Another method is to join forces with Internet service providers. In additional to personal computers, smart phones and interactive TV will become delivery mechanism.

The message of an advertisement is the fact or impression the advertiser wants to convey to potential customers. The choice of the message is an important reflection of the way the firm sees its products and services and the way it wants them to be seen by customers. The promotional message is the message chosen by the MNC to express the consumer's motivation to buy its product, which varies depending on: the diffusion of the product, service, or concept into the market, the criteria on which the consumer will evaluate the product, and the product's positioning.

As far as the organization of the promotional program is concerned, the ideal situation is to have a world brand—a product that is manufactured, packaged, and positioned the same around the world. However, a number of factors will force companies to abandon identical campaigns in favor of recognizable campaigns. Many MNCs customize the advertising copy to appeal the local market. Moreover, many MNCs are staffed and equipped to perform the full range of promotional activities. In most cases, however, they rely on the outside expertise of advertising agencies and other promotions-related companies such as media-buying companies and specialty marketing firms. Usually, local agencies tend to forge ties with foreign advertisement agencies for better coverage and customer service, and thus become part of the general globalization effort. MNCs are choosing specialized interactive shops over full-service agencies for Internet advertising. However, a major weakness with the interactive agencies is their lack of international experience.

2. Personal selling

Personal selling means making sales on the basis of personal contacts. The use of sales representatives, who call on potential customers and attempt to sell them a firm's products or services, is the most common approach to personal selling. Because of the close contact between the salesperson and the potential customer, sellers are likely to rely on host country nationals to serve as their representatives. An MNC just starting internationalization often will subcontract personal selling to local sales organizations that handle product lines from several firms. As the MNC grows and develops a sales base in new markets, it may establish its own sales force.

The importance of personal selling as an element of the promotion mix differs for industrial products and for consumer products. For industrial products such as complex machinery, electronic equipment, and customized computer software, customers often need technical information about product characteristics, usage, maintenance requirements, and availability of after-sales support. Well-trained sales representatives are often better able to convey information about the intricacies of such products to customers than are print or broadcast media. For consumer products, personal selling is normally confined to selling to wholesalers and to retail chains. Most consumer product firms find that advertising, particularly in print and broadcast media, is a more efficient means of communicating with consumers than is personal selling. However, personal selling can be used to market some goods. Actually, personal selling has the following advantages for MNCs. Firstly, MNCs hiring local sales representatives can be reasonably confident that those individuals understand the local culture, norms, and customs. Secondly, personal selling promotes close, personal contact with customers.

Customers see real people and come to associate that personal contact with the MNC. Lastly, personal selling makes it easier for the MNC to obtain valuable market information. Knowledgeable local sales representatives are an excellent source of information that can be used to develop new products and/or improve existing products for the local market. Nevertheless, personal selling is a relatively high-cost strategy. Each sales representative must be adequately compensated even though each may reach relatively few customers. An industrial product sales representative, for instance, may need a full day or more to see just one potential customer. After a sale is closed, the sales representative may still find it necessary to spend large blocks of time with the customer explaining how things work and trying to generate new business. Most larger MNCs also find it necessary to establish regional sales offices staffed by sales managers and other support personnel, which add more sales-related costs.

跨国公司必须在推动策略和拉动策略之间做出选择。推动策略强调人员推销，而拉动策略强调大众媒体广告。选择取决于：相对于消费者成熟度的产品类型、渠道长度和媒体可用性。

MNCs must choose between a push strategy and a pull strategy. A push strategy emphasizes personal selling, whereas the pull strategy emphasizes mass media advertising. The choice depends upon product types relative to consumer sophistication, channel length, and media availability.

The product type relative to consumer sophistication is the first factor influencing the choice of a pull or push strategy. Consumer goods firms trying to sell to a large segment of the market tend to prefer a pull strategy, whereas industrial product firms or makers of other complex products favor a push strategy. Direct selling allows the firm to educate potential consumers about the features of the product. This may not be necessary in advanced nations where a complex product has been in use for some time, where the product's attributes are well understood, where consumers are sophisticated, and where high-quality channels exist that can provide point-of-sale assistance. However, customer education may be important when consumers have less sophistication toward the product, which can be the case in developing nations or in advanced nations when a new complex product is being introduced, or where high-quality channels are absent or scarce.

Channel length is the second factor influencing the choice of a pull or push strategy. The longer the channel, the more intermediaries involved. It can be expensive to use direct selling to push a product through many layers of a distribution channel. Hence, a firm may try to pull its product through the channels by using mass advertising to create consumer demand. Once demand is created, intermediaries will feel obliged to carry the product.

Media availability is the third factor influencing the choice of a pull or push strategy. A pull strategy relies on access to advertising media. In many developing nations, the mass media of all types are typically limited. Consequently, a firm's ability to use a pull strategy is limited in these countries by media availability. In such cases, a push strategy is more attractive. Meanwhile, media availability is limited by law in some countries. For example, few countries allow advertisements for tobacco and alcohol products on television and radio, though they are usually permitted in print media. Similarly, while advertising pharmaceutical products directly to consumers is allowed in the United States, it is prohibited in many other advanced nations. Under this circumstance, pharmaceutical firms must rely heavily on advertising and direct-sales efforts focused explicitly on doctors to get their products prescribed.

In conclusion, a push strategy is common for industrial products or complex new products when distribution channels are short, and when few print or electronic media are available. Meanwhile, a pull strategy tends to be common for consumer products when distribution channels are long, and when sufficient print and electronic media are available to carry the marketing message.

3. Sales promotion

Sales promotion has been used as the catchall term for promotion that is not advertising, personal selling, or publicity. Sales promotion comprises specialized marketing efforts such as coupons, in-store promotions, sampling, direct mail campaigns, cooperative advertising, and trade fair attendance. Sales promotion activities focused on wholesalers and retailers are designed to increase the number and commitment of these intermediaries working with the firm. Many MNCs participate in international trade shows to generate interest among existing and potential distributors for the MNCs' products. Participation in international trade shows is often recommended as a first step for firms wanting to internalize their sales. MNCs also may develop cooperative advertising campaigns or provide advertising allowances to encourage retailers to promote the MNCs' products. Sales promotion activities may be narrowly targeted to consumers and/or offered for only short time before being dropped or replaced with more permanent efforts. This flexible nature of sales promotions makes them ideal for a marketing campaign tailored to fit local customs and circumstances.

4. Public relations

Public relations consists of efforts aimed at enhancing an MNC's reputation and image with the general public, as opposed to touting the specific advantages of an individual product or service. Public relations means both internal and external communication. Internal communication is important for MNCs to create an appropriate corporate culture. External campaigns can be achieved through the use of corporate symbols, corporate advertising, customer relations programs, the generation of publicity, as well as getting an MNC's view to the public via the Internet. Some material on the MNC is produced for special audiences to assist in personal selling. Increasingly, the United Nations is promoting programs to partner MNCs and NGOs to tackle issues such as healthcare, energy, and biodiversity. The consequence of effective public relations is a general belief that the MNC is a good "corporate citizen", that it is reputable, and that it can be trusted. Savvy MNCs recognize that money spent on public relations is money well spent because it earns them political allies and makes it easier to communicate the MNCs' needs to the general public. They also recognize that, as "foreigners", they are often appealing political targets; thus, the MNCs attempt to reduce their exposure to political attacks. The impact of good public relations is hard to quantify, but over time an MNC's positive image and reputation are likely to benefit the MNC in a host country. Consumers are more likely to resist "buy local" pitches when the foreign firm is also perceived to be a good guy. Good public relations can also help the MNC when it has to negotiate with a host country government for a zoning permit or an operating license or when it encounters a crisis or unfavorable publicity.

关键术语（Key Terms）

国际市场营销（international marketing）

生产导向（production orientation）

销售导向（sales orientation）

客户导向（customer orientation）

战略营销导向（strategic marketing orientation）

社会营销导向（social marketing orientation）

国际市场细分（international market segmentation）

国际市场营销组合（international marketing mix）

标准定价（standard pricing）

双重定价（dual pricing）

市场定价（market pricing）

转移定价（transfer pricing）

零售集中度（retail concentration）

渠道长度（channel length）

渠道排他性（channel exclusivity）

渠道质量（channel quality）

广告（advertising）

人员推销（personal selling）

销售促进（sales promotion）

公共关系（public relations）

推动策略（push strategy）

拉动策略（pull strategy）

小结（Summary）

1. Marketing is the process of planning and executing the conception, pricing, promotion, and distribution of ideas, goods, and services to create exchanges that satisfy

individual and organizational objectives. International marketing is the extension of these activities across national boundaries. Marketing orientation is a business philosophy based on market demand. Marketing orientation of MNCs can be classified into five types: production orientation, sales orientation, customer orientation, strategic marketing orientation, and social marketing orientation. International market segmentation refers to MNCs dividing the entire international market into several submarkets with different demands according to certain segmentation standards. There are four stages in selecting target markets including preliminary screening, estimation of market potential, estimation of sales potential, and identification of segments.

2. International marketing mix refers to the tailored combination of product strategy, pricing strategy, promotion strategy, and distribution strategy formulated by an MNC based on the marketing environment of the international market. The majority of MNCs' products have to be modified for the international marketplace one way or another. The changes vary from minor ones, such as translation of a user's manual, to major ones, such as a more economical version of the product. The following three factors have an impact on product adaptation for a given market: market environment, product characteristics, and company considerations.

3. Developing effective pricing strategies is a critical determinant for the success of MNCs. Pricing strategies directly affect the revenues of an MNC. The strategies also serve as an important strategic weapon by allowing the MNC to shape a competitive environment in which it does business. An MNC generally adopts one of the four pricing strategies: standard pricing, dual pricing, market pricing, and transfer pricing.

4. Distribution strategy is the means for delivering the product to the consumer. It is a critical element of the marketing mix for an MNC. There are five basic parts in MNCs' distribution channel: the inside or outside manufacturer that creates the product or service, a wholesaler that buys products and services from the manufacturer and then resells them to retailers, the retailer that buys from wholesalers and then sells to customers, the final customer who buys the product or service for final consumption, and the import agent who buys the products from manufacturer and then sells them to wholesalers, or retailers, or customers directly. There are four main differences in distribution systems: retail concentration, channel length, channel exclusivity, and channel quality.

5. Promotion encompasses all efforts by an MNC to enhance the desirability of its products among potential buyers. Because promotion relies on communication with audiences in the host country, it is the most culture bound of the marketing mix. Thus, an MNC must take special care to ensure that the message host country audiences receive is in fact the message the MNC intend to send. MNCs must therefore effectively blend and utilize the four elements of the promotion mix—advertising, personal selling,

sales promotion, and public relations—to motivate potential customers to buy their products.

延伸阅读（Further Readings）

习题（Exercises）

第七章

Chapter 7

跨国公司的财务管理
Financial Management of Multinational Corporations

Learning Objectives

- To understand the concept of financial management and financial management goals of MNCs
- To identify the methods of investment decision and the financing sources and costs of MNCs
- To be familiar with the methods to minimize cash balances, reduce transaction costs, and move money across borders
- To know the foreign currency transaction and types of foreign currency exposure
- To understand international taxation and double taxation mitigation
- To differentiate international tax avoidance from international tax evasion

第一节 跨国公司财务管理概述
（The Overview of Financial Management of Multinational Corporations）

1. The definition and goals of financial management of MNCs

跨国公司的财务管理包括三组相关决策：关于为哪些活动融资的投资决策、关于如何为这些活动融资的融资决策，以及关于如何最有效地管理跨国公司财务资源的资金管理决策。关于财务管理的目标，有两个有影响力的论点：股东财富最大化和公司财富最大化。

Financial management of MNCs includes three sets of related decisions: investment decisions about what activities to finance, financing decisions about how to finance those activities, and money management decisions about how to manage the MNCs' financial resources most efficiently. In international businesses, investment, financing, and money management decisions are complicated by the fact that countries have different currencies, different tax regimes, different regulations concerning the flow of capital across their borders, different norms regarding the financing of business activities, different levels of economic and political risk, and so on. Financial managers must consider all these factors when deciding which activities to finance, how to finance those activities best, how to manage the MNCs' financial resources best, and how to protect the MNCs from risks best.

There are two influential arguments on the goals of financial management: stockholder wealth maximization and corporate wealth maximization. MNCs from the U. S. are characterized by maximizing shareholder wealth, also known as stockholder wealth maximization. It dictates that the management of the MNCs should actively seek to maximize the returns to stockholders by working to push share prices up and to continually grow the dividends paid out to those same shareholders. This implies in the extreme, however, that management is not seeking to build value or wealth for the other stakeholders in MNCs such as the creditors, management itself, employees, suppliers, the communities in which these MNCs reside, and even the government. Obviously, the free market capitalism is a near sole focus on building wealth for stockholders alone, and has been frequently interpreted as extremely short-run in focus. However, MNCs from Europe and Japan are characterized by corporate wealth maximization, which directs management to consider the financial and social health of all stakeholders, and not to focus exclusively on the financial returns of the MNC alone. It doesn't mean that the MNC is not driven to maximize its profitability, but it does direct the MNC to consider and balance short-term financial goals against long-term societal goals of continued employment, community citizenship, and public welfare needs.

The above two different philosophies are not necessarily exclusive, and many MNCs attempt to find some balance between the two. The stockholder wealth maximization is in many ways simpler and easier to pursue, having a single objective and in many ways a single client. Although simplistic, and sometimes leading to the abuses that have been so widely reported in recent years, it has led to the development of the relatively more competitive global business. Although in many ways a kinder and gentler philosophy, corporate wealth maximization has the unenviable charge of attempting to meet the desires of multiple stakeholders. Decision making becomes slower, less decisive, and frequently results in MNCs that cannot meet the constantly growing pressures of a global marketplace which rewards innovation, speed, and lower costs. Although sounding good on the public relations releases, the concerns of social impacts such as environmental responsibility and sustainable development impose heavy burdens on MNCs trying to compete in a wireless, internet-based marketplace.

The ultimate goal of the financial management of an MNC is to increase the value of the shareholders' investment as much as possible. As a conglomeration of many subsidiaries operating in a multitude of economic environments, the MNC must determine for itself the proper balance among three primary financial objectives. The first is the maximization of consolidated, after-tax income. The second is the minimization of the MNC's effective global tax burden. The third is correct positioning of the MNC's income, cash flows, and available funds. These goals are frequently contradictory, in that the pursuit of one goal may result in a less-desirable outcome for another. Management must make decisions about the proper trade-offs among goals and their effects in the future.

2. Investment decision

跨国公司的投资资金有限，而且往往有无穷无尽的项目可供选择。财务经理必须建立机制，以开发、筛选和选择跨国公司将进行重大新投资的项目。评估投资项目的方法有很多，但最常用的方法包括净现值法、内部收益率法和投资回收期法。

MNCs have limited funds for investment and often a seemingly endless set of projects from which to choose. Financial managers must establish mechanisms for developing, screening, and selecting projects in which the MNC will make significant new investments. Numerous approaches for evaluating investment projects are available, but the most commonly used methods include net present value, internal rate of return, and payback period.

（1）Net present value

The net present value approach is based on a basic precept of finance theory that a dollar today is worth more than a dollar in the future. To calculate the net present value of a project, an MNC's financial managers estimate the cash flows the project will generate in each time period and then discount them back to the present. Any investment is financially justified if the present value of expected cash inflows is greater than the present value of expected cash outflows; in other words, if it has a positive net present value (NPV) which is defined as follows:

$$NPV = \sum_{t=1}^{n} \frac{FCF_t}{(1+k)^t} - IO$$

Where FCF_t = the annual free cash flow in time period t

k = the appropriate discount rate; that is, the required rate of return or cost of capital

IO = the initial cash outlay

n = the project's expected life

The construction of a capital budget is the process of projecting the net operating cash flows of the potential investment to determine if it is indeed a good investment. For many projects, the cash flow in the early years will be negative because the MNC must outlay cash for the initial investment and be prepared to suffer start-up operating losses in the first year or two. In later years, of course, the MNC expects cash flows to be positive. Financial managers must decide which interest rate, called the rate of discount, to use in the calculation, based on the MNC's cost of capital. For instance, if the MNC's cost of capital is 10%, then financial managers will use an annual interest rate of 10% to discount the cash flows generated by the project through time in order to calculate the present value. The MNC will undertake only projects that generate a positive net present value. The net present value approach can be used for both domestic and international projects. However, several additional factors must be considered when determining whether to undertake an international project. These factors are risk adjustment, currency selection, and choice of perspective for the calculations.

As a foreign project may be riskier than a domestic project, MNCs may adjust either the discount rate upward or the expected cash flows downward to account for a higher level of risk. The amount of risk adjustment should reflect the degree of riskiness of operating in the country in question.

The determination of the currency in which the project should be evaluated depends on the nature of the investment. If the project is an integral part of the business of an overseas subsidiary, use of the foreign currency is appropriate. For foreign projects that are more properly viewed as integrated parts of an MNC's global procurement strategy, translation into the home country currency may make sense.

Another factor is determining whether the cash flows that contribute to the net present value of the capital investment should be evaluated from the perspective of the headquarters or that of the subsidiary project. Practically, some MNCs analyze the cash flows of the subsidiary project, others focus on the project's impact on headquarters, and some others do both. The cash flows to the headquarters can differ from those to the subsidiary for several reasons. MNCs often impose arbitrary accounting charges on the revenues of their operating units for the units' use of corporate trademarks or to cover general corporate overhead. These arbitrary charges may reduce the perceived cash flows generated by the project but not the real cash flows returned to the headquarters. For instance, suppose that when the headquarters accountants are calculating a subsidiary's profitability, they routinely assess a 5% fee against revenues for general corporate and administrative expenses. This technique may be a reasonable mechanism for allocating general corporate expenses across all the MNC's operations. The 5% charge, however, does not represent a true drain on the cash flow generated by the subsidiary. Thus, the charge should be ignored in the calculation of the net present value to the parent of a project the subsidiary proposes. Similarly, fees assessed against the subsidiary for the use of corporate trademarks, brand names, or patents should not be considered in the present value calculation because the headquarters incurs no additional costs regardless of whether the subsidiary undertakes the project. Financial managers also must consider any governmental restrictions on currency movements that would affect the MNC's ability to repatriate profits when it wants. A project proposed by a foreign subsidiary may be enormously profitable, but if the profits can never be repatriated to the headquarters, the project may not be desirable from the perspective of the headquarters and its shareholders. The importance of currency controls in determining the attractiveness of a project also may be a function of headquarters' overall strategy.

(2) Internal rate of return

The second approach commonly used for evaluating investment projects is to calculate the internal rate of return. With this approach, financial managers first estimate the cash flows generated by each project under consideration in each time period, as in the net present value analysis. They then calculate the interest rate of return that makes the net present value of the project just equal to zero. As with the net present value approach, the financial managers must adjust their calculations for any accounting charges that have no cash flow implications, including intracorporate licensing fees, overhead charges for general corporate and administrative expenses, and so on. They then compare the project's internal rate of return with the hurdle rate which is the minimum rate of return the MNC finds acceptable for its capital investments. The hurdle rate may vary by country to account for differences in risk. The MNC will only undertake projects for which the internal rate of return is higher than the hurdle rate.

(3) Payback period

The third approach for assessing and selecting projects is to calculate a project's payback period—the number of years it will take the MNC to recover, or pay back, the original cash investment from the project's earnings. The payback period technique has the virtue of simplicity: all one needs is simple arithmetic to calculate the payback period. This approach ignores, however, the profits generated by the investment in the longer run. A project that earns large early profits but whose later profits diminish steadily over time may be selected over a project that suffers initial start-up losses but makes large continuous profits after that. Because of simplicity, many MNCs use the payback period technique for a quick-and-dirty screening of projects and then follow with a more sophisticated method for further analysis of those projects that pass the preliminary screening. An MNC may choose more different payback criteria for international projects than for domestic ones. Here too adjustment must be made to eliminate intracorporate charges that have no real effect on corporate cash flows.

All capital budgets are only as good as the accuracy of the cost and revenue assumptions. Adequately anticipating all of the incremental expenses that the individual project imposes on the MNC is critical to a proper analysis. A capital budget is composed of three primary cash flow components. The first is initial expenses and capital outlays. The initial capital outlays are normally the largest net cash outflow occurring over the life of a proposed investment. Since the cash flows occur up front, they have a substantial impact on the net present value of the project. The second is operating cash flows, which are the net cash flows the project is expected to yield once production is underway. The primary positive net cash flows of the project are realized in this stage; net operating cash flows will determine the success or failure of the proposed investment. The final component of the capital budget is composed of the salvage value or resale value of the project at its end. The terminal value will include whatever working capital balances can be recaptured once the project is no longer in operation. The financial decision criterion for an individual investment is whether the net present value of the project is positive or negative. The net cash flows in the future are discounted by the average cost of capital for the MNC. The purpose of discounting is to capture the fact that the MNC has acquired investment capital at a cost. The same capital could have been used for other projects of other investments. It is therefore necessary to discount the future cash flows to account for this foregone income of the capital, its opportunity cost. If net present value is positive, then the project is an acceptable investment. If the project's net present value is negative, then the cash flows expected from the investment are insufficient to provide an acceptable rate of return, and the project should be rejected.

3. Financing decisions

（1）Capital structure

The way an MNC is funded is referred to as its capital structure. If capital is provided by owners of the MNC, it is called equity. If capital is obtained by borrowing from others, such as commercial banking institutions, it is termed debt. Debt must be repaid, with interest, over some specific schedule. Equity capital, however, is kept in the MNC. Any MNC's ability to grow and expand is dependent on its ability to acquire additional capital as it grows. The net profits generated over previous periods may be valuable but are rarely enough to provide needed capital expansion. MNCs therefore need access to capital markets, both debt and equity. The choice of what proportions of debt and equity to use in international investments is usually dictated by either the debt-equity structure of the parent or the debt-equity structure of competitive MNCs in the host country. The MNC's headquarters regard equity investment as capital at risk. Hence, it would usually prefer to provide as little equity capital as possible. Although funding the foreign subsidiary primarily with debt would still put the headquarters' capital at risk, debt service provides a strict schedule for cash flow repatriation to the lender. Equity capital's return—dividends from profits—depends on managerial discretion. Table 7-1 provides the financing alternatives for foreign affiliates.

在表 7-1 中,欧元股票和欧元债券是欧洲货币市场的融资方式。欧洲货币是指货币发行国以外金融机构的任何以外币计价的存款或账户。欧元市场是货币和资本市场,其交易以交易地以外的货币计价,不限于欧洲。

In Table 7-1, Euro-equity and Euro-bond are the financing methods in Eurocurrency market. A Eurocurrency is any foreign currency-denominated deposit or account at a financial institution outside the currency issuing country. Euromarkets are money and capital markets in which transactions are denominated in a currency other than that of the place of the transaction, not confined to Europe.

Table 7-1   Financing alternatives for foreign affiliates

Financing method	Sources	Benefits	Costs
Equity capital	• From the headquarters • From a joint-venture partner in the home or host country, or a share issue in the host country • From a third-country market such as a share issue in the Euro-equity market	• May enhance the borrowing capacity of overseas subsidiaries • The parent company has strong control over the operations of its subsidiaries • Easy to obtain low-cost funds	• Higher foreign exchange exposure risk • Relatively high risk of repatriation of profits and investment capital repayment • High risk of confiscation and nationalization of property
Debt capital	• From the headquarters • From a bank loan or bond issue in the home or host country • From a third-country bank loan, bond issue, or Euro-bond issue	• Paid interest deducted before taxation • May establish good relationships with local businesses and other financial institutions • Easy to repatriate profits and repay capital	• Limited availability of capital • The parent company has weak control over overseas operations • Subsidiaries have higher foreign exchange exposure risks

Source: Revised from Table 9-2 in Czinkota, Michael R., Ilkka A. Ronkainen, Michael H. Moffett (2004). *Fundamentals of International Business*, South-Western, Cengage Learning. P223

(2) External financing sources

MNCs use capital budgeting techniques to allocate their financial resources toward those domestic and international projects that promise the highest rates of return. Having identified such profitable opportunities, MNCs must secure sufficient capital to fund them, from either external or internal sources. In doing so, an MNC wants to minimize the worldwide cost of its capital, while also minimizing its foreign-exchange risk, political risk, and global tax burden.

When raising external financing for their investment projects, MNCs may choose from a rich source of debt and equity alternatives. Investment bankers and security corporations can help MNCs acquire capital from external sources. For instance, if an MNC wants to increase its equity base, such an intermediary can place the MNC's stock with investors in the home or host, or even the other country. To facilitate the raising of equity internationally, many MNCs list their common stock on stock markets in several different countries. Through multiple foreign listings, MNCs assure foreign investors they can easily dispose of their shares should the need arise.

大型跨国公司可能依赖银团短期和中期贷款,其中国际银行集团使用欧洲货币,因为缺乏昂贵的中央银行监管降低了基于欧洲货币的贷款的成本。跨国公司也可能以母国债券、外国债券和欧元债券的形式获得长期贷款。

MNCs also have many opportunities to borrow funds internationally on either a short-term or a long-term basis. They may shop for the best credit terms in their home country market, in the host country market, or in other markets. Larger MNCs may rely on syndicated short-and medium-term loans in which a consortium of international banks use Eurocurrencies because the absence of expensive central bank regulations reduces the cost of Eurocurrency-based loans. MNCs also may secure longer-term loans in the form of home country bonds, foreign bonds, and Euro-bonds.

跨国公司可以发行双货币债券,即以一种货币借款并支付利息,但以另一种货币偿还本金。或者,债券可以以多种货币的篮子计价,也可以兑换成黄金。

Securities corporations and investment banks are continually developing innovative financing techniques to reduce the costs of borrowing for their MNC clients or to exploit gaps in national financial regulations. For instance, an MNC may issue dual-currency bonds, whereby it borrows money and pays interest in one currency but repays the principal in a second currency. Alternatively, bonds may be denominated as a basket of several currencies or be redeemable in gold.

国际资本市场的一个特别重要的方面是掉期市场,在这个市场中,两家跨国公司可以交换其金融义务。掉期是为了改变跨国公司利息义务的成本和性质,或改变其债务的计价货币。

A particular important facet of the international capital market is the swap market, in which two MNCs can exchange their financial obligations. Swaps are undertaken to change the cost and nature of an MNC's interest obligations or to change the currency in which its debt is denominated. For instance, suppose corporation A has a fixed-rate obligation but prefers a floating-rate one, whereas corporation B has a floating-rate obligation and wants a fixed-rate one. The two corporations can swap their obligations. Often an international bank will facilitate such swaps by acting as a broker or by undertaking half of a swap for its own account.

MNCs also often engage in currency swaps to shift their interest and payment obligations from a less preferred currency to a more preferred one. An MNC may consider its net obligations in one currency to be too large or may expect exchange rate fluctuations so adversely affect its loan repayment costs. A swap may be arranged between two corporations that have differing currency preferences. International banks play a key role in the currency swap market. Because they continually monitor foreign-exchange markets as well as their own net currency exposures, they usually can accommodate any MNC's currency swap needs. Most international banks engage in currency swaps with corporate clients on an ongoing basis.

（3）Internal financing sources

Another source of investment capital for MNCs is the cash flows generated internally—for instance，profits from operations and noncash expense such as depreciation and amortization earned by the headquarters and its various subsidiaries. The amount from such sources is significant. Subject to legal constraints，the headquarters may use the cash flow generated by any subsidiary to fund the investment projects of any member of the corporate family. The headquarters may access the cash flow directly via the subsidiary's dividend payments to it. The headquarters then can channel those funds to another subsidiary through either a loan or additional equity investments in that subsidiary. Alternatively，one subsidiary can invest in or lend funds directly to a second subsidiary. Figure 7-1 summarizes the various internal sources of capital available to the headquarters and its subsidiaries.

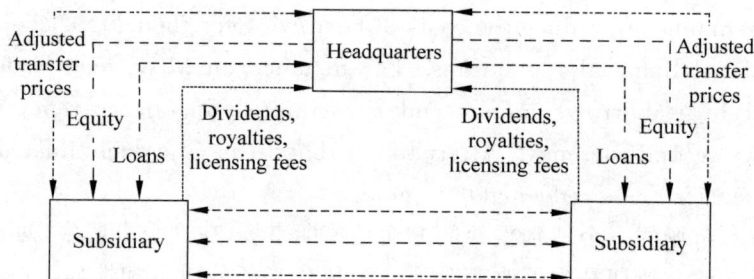

Figure 7-1　Internal sources of capital for MNCs

Source：Adapted from Figure 13. 4 in Griffin，Ricky W. ，Pustay，Michael W. （2013），*International Business*，7th Edition，Pearson Education，Inc. P354

（4）Financing cost

跨国公司的融资方式主要为股权融资和债务融资，依靠股权融资和债务融资的不同比重就构成不同的资本结构，两者的综合成本即为跨国公司的融资成本，又称为加权平均资本成本。

The financing methods of MNCs mainly include equity financing and debt financing. The different proportions of equity financing and debt financing constitute different capital structures. The comprehensive cost of the two is the financing cost of MNCs，also known as the weighted average cost of capital（WACC）. The calculation formula is as follows：

$$K = K_i \times (1-t) \times W_i + K_e \times W_e$$

Where K is WACC

$K_i =$ the cost of debt financing

$W_i =$ the proportion of debt capital in total capital

$K_e =$ the cost of equity financing

W_e = the proportion of equity capital in the total capital

t = the corporate income tax rate

计算加权平均资本成本的关键是求得债务融资成本 K_i 和股权融资成本 K_e。债务融资成本相对容易得到,股权融资成本的计算则比较复杂,一般可通过戈登模型和资本资产定价模型间接估算。

The key to calculating WACC is to obtain the debt financing cost K_i and the equity financing cost K_e. The cost of debt financing is relatively easy to obtain because most corporate debt has fixed interest rates and bank loan interest rates are also very certain. Although the true cost of debt financing for MNCs is not equal to the bond coupon rate and the nominal interest rate of bank loans, the true cost of debt financing can be roughly calculated based on these data. The calculation of equity financing costs is relatively complex, as the level of dividends is uncertain and difficult to know beforehand. The cost of equity financing can generally be indirectly estimated through the Gordon model and the capital asset pricing model (CAPM).

The Gordon model can be expressed as:

$$P_0 = \frac{D_1}{k_e - g}$$

After a simple transformation, the cost of equity financing can be obtained as:

$$K_e = \frac{D_1}{P_0} + g$$

Where K_e = the cost of equity financing

D_1 = the expected dividends for the first year after investment

P_0 = the current market price of the stock

g = the expected annual growth rate of dividends

The CAPM can be expressed as:

$$K_e = r + \beta(K_m - r)$$

Where K_e = the cost of equity financing

r = the risk-free rate of return, such as the interest rate of treasury bills

β = the systematic risk of this stock

K_m = the combined return rate of the stock market

Although the above model's estimation of equity financing costs is not entirely accurate, it can approximately calculate the costs of equity financing and thus calculate the capital costs of MNCs.

第二节　跨国公司的资金管理
(Money Management of Multinational Corporations)

跨国公司的资金管理是指跨国公司试图有效地管理其全球现金资源,即营运资金。这包括三个方面:尽量减少现金余额、降低交易成本和尽量减少公司税收负担。

Money management of MNCs means that the MNCs try to efficiently manage their global cash resources which are actually the working capital. This includes three aspects: minimizing cash balances, reducing transaction costs, and minimizing corporate tax burdens.

MNCs possess both operating cash flows and financing cash flows. Operating cash flows arise from their everyday business activities, such as paying for materials or resources, or receiving payments for items sold or licenses granted. Financing cash flows arise from their funding activities. The servicing of existing funding sources, interest on existing debt, and dividend payments to shareholders constitute potentially large and frequent cash flows. Periodic additions to debt or equity through new bank loans, new bond issuances, or supplemental stock sales may also add to the volume of financing cash flows in the MNCs.

1. Minimizing cash balances

跨国公司可以通过以下方法最大限度地减少现金余额:现金池、提前和延迟结汇、再融资和内部银行。

MNCs can minimize cash balances mainly with the following methods: cash pooling, leads and lags, reinvoicing, and internal banks.

(1) Cash pooling

Every MNC needs to hold some cash balances for servicing accounts that must be paid and for insuring against unanticipated negative variation from its projected cash flows. The critical issue for an MNC is whether each foreign subsidiary should hold its own cash balances or whether cash balances should be held at a centralized depository. A large MNC with a number of subsidiaries operating both within an individual country and across countries may be able to economize on the amount of MNC assets needed in cash if one central pool is used for cash pooling. With one pool of capital and up-to-date information on the cash flows in and out of the various units, the MNC spends much less in terms of foregone interest on cash balances, which are held in safekeeping against unforeseen cash flow shortfalls. Generally, MNCs prefer to hold cash balances at a centralized depository for three reasons.

First, by pooling cash reserves centrally, the MNCs can deposit larger amounts. Cash balances are typically deposited in liquid accounts, such as overnight money market accounts. Because interest rates on such deposits normally increase with the size of the deposit, by pooling cash centrally, the MNC should be able to earn a higher interest rate than it would if each subsidiary managed its own cash balances.

Second, if the centralized depository is located in a major financial center, it should have access to information about good short-term investment opportunities that the typical foreign subsidiary would lack. Also, the financial experts at a centralized depository should be able to develop investment skills and know-how that managers in the typical foreign subsidiary would lack. Thus, the MNC should make better investment decisions if it pools its cash reserves at a centralized depository.

Third, by pooling its cash reserves, the MNC can reduce the total size of the cash pool it must hold in highly liquid accounts, which enables the MNC to invest a larger amount of cash reserves in longer-term, less liquid financial instruments that earn higher interest rates.

However, an MNC's ability to establish a centralized depository that can serve short-term cash needs might be limited by government-imposed restrictions on capital flows across borders, such as controls put in place to protect a country's foreign exchange reserves. Also, the transaction costs of moving money into and out of different currencies can limit the advantages of such a system. Despite this, many MNCs hold at least their subsidiaries' precautionary cash reserves at a centralized depository, having each subsidiary hold its own cash balance for day-to-day needs. The globalization of the world capital market and the general removal of barriers to the free flow of cash across borders particularly among advanced industrialized countries are two trends likely to increase the use of centralized depositories.

（2）Leads and lags

The timing of payments between units of an MNC is somewhat flexible, and this allows the management of payments between the headquarters and its subsidiaries to be much more flexible, allowing the MNC not only to position cash flows where they are needed most, but also to help manage currency risk. A foreign subsidiary that is expecting its local currency to fall in value relative to the U. S. dollar may try to speed up, or lead, its payments to the headquarters. A lead strategy means either collecting foreign-currency receivables before they are due when the foreign currency is expected to weaken, or paying foreign-currency payables before they are due when the foreign currency is expected to strengthen. Similarly, if the local currency is expected to rise versus the dollar, the subsidiary may want to wait, or lag, payments until exchange rates are more favorable. With a lag strategy, an MNC either delays collection of foreign-currency receivables if that currency is expected to strengthen, or delays payables when the currency is expected to weaken. In other words, an MNC usually leads into and lags out of a hard currency and leads out of and lags into a weak currency.

（3）Reinvoicing

MNCs with a variety of manufacturing and distribution subsidiaries scattered over a number of countries within a region may often find it more economical to have one office or subsidiary taking ownership of all invoices and payments between units. The subsidiary literally buys from one unit and sells to a second unit, thereby taking ownership of the goods and reinvoicing the sale to the next unit. Once ownership is taken, the sale/purchase can be redenominated in a different currency, netted against other payments, hedged against specific currency exposures, or repriced in accordance with potential tax benefits of the reinvoicing center's host country.

(4) Internal banks

Some MNCs have found that their financial resources and needs are becoming either too large or too sophisticated for the financial services that are available in many of their local subsidiary markets. One solution to this has been the establishment of an internal bank within the MNC. The internal bank actually buys and sells payables and receivables from various units, which frees the units of the MNC from struggling for continual, working-capital financing, and lets them focus on their primary business activities.

All of these structures and management techniques are often combined in different ways to fit the needs of the individual MNC. Some techniques are encouraged or prohibited by laws and regulations, depending on the host-country's government and stage of capital market liberalization. MNC cash flow management requires flexibility in thinking—artistry in some cases—as much as technique on the part of managers.

2. Reducing transaction costs

交易成本即交换成本。对于一家拥有全球分散的相互依存的价值创造活动网络的跨国公司来说,交易的数量可能会特别高。多边净额结算可以减少跨国公司子公司之间的交易数量和交易成本。

Transaction costs are the costs of exchange. Every time an MNC changes cash from one currency to another, it faces transaction costs which are the commission fees the MNC pays to foreign exchange dealers for performing the transaction. Most banks also charge a transfer fee for moving cash from one location to another, which is another transaction cost. The commission and transfer fees arising from intrafirm transactions can be substantial. The volume of such transactions is likely to be particularly high in an MNC that has a globally dispersed web of interdependent value creation activities. Multilateral netting can reduce the number of transactions between MNCs' subsidiaries and the number of transaction costs.

Multilateral netting is an extension of bilateral netting. Under bilateral netting, if a Japanese subsidiary owes a Korean subsidiary US $ 5 million and the Korean subsidiary simultaneously owes the Indian subsidiary US $ 2 million, a bilateral settlement will be made with a single payment of US $ 3 million from the Japanese subsidiary to the Indian subsidiary.

Under multilateral netting, this simple concept is extended to the transactions between multiple subsidiaries within an MNC. Suppose an MNC would establish multilateral netting among four European subsidiaries based in Germany, France, Italy, and Spain. These subsidiaries all trade with each other, so at the end of each month a large volume of cash transactions must be settled. Figure 7-2 shows how the payment schedule might look at the end of a given month. Table 7-2 is a payment matrix that summarizes the obligations among the subsidiaries. Note that US $ 48 million needs to flow among the subsidiaries. If the transaction costs including foreign exchange commissions plus transfer fees amount to 1% of the total funds to be transferred, this will cost the parent firm US $ 480,000. However, this amount can be reduced by multilateral netting. Using the payment matrix shown in Table 7-2, the MNC can determine the payments that need to be made among its subsidiaries to settle these obligations. Figure 7-3 shows the results. By multilateral netting, the transactions depicted in Figure 7-2 are reduced to just three: the Italian subsidiary pays US $ 6 million to the French subsidiary, and the German subsidiary pays US $ 2 million to the French subsidiary and US $ 1 million to the Spanish subsidiary. The total funds that flow among the subsidiaries are reduced from US $ 48 million to just US $ 9 million, and the transaction costs are reduced from US $ 480,000 to US $ 90,000, a savings of US $ 390,000 achieved through multilateral netting.

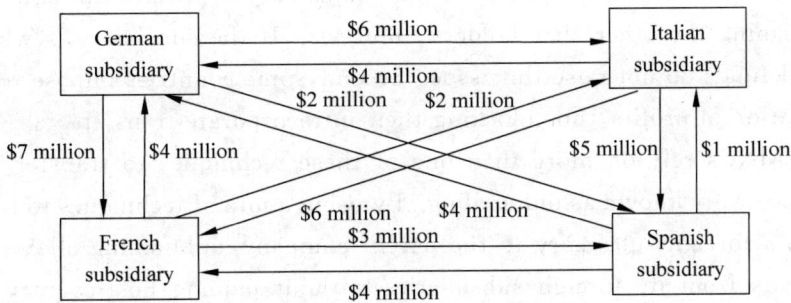

Figure 7-2 Cash flows before multilateral netting

Table 7-2 Calculation of net receipts（Unit：US $ million）

Receiving subsidiary	Paying subsidiary				Total receipts	Net receipts
	Germany	France	Italy	Spain		
Germany	—	4	4	4	12	−3
France	7	—	6	4	17	8
Italy	6	2	—	1	9	−6
Spain	2	3	5	—	10	1
Total payments	15	9	15	9	48	9

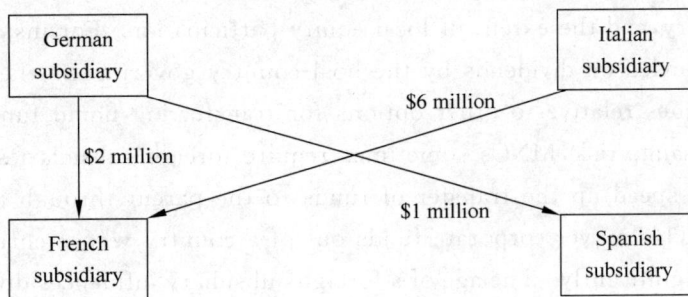

Figure 7-3 Cash flows after multilateral netting

3. Moving money across borders

为了最有效地利用跨国公司的现金资源并最大限度地减少跨国公司的全球纳税义务,跨国公司需要能够将资金从全球一个地方转移到另一个地方。跨国公司使用多种技术跨境转移流动资金,包括股利返回、特许权使用费和费用、预付贷款。

Pursuing the objectives of utilizing the MNC's cash resources most efficiently and minimizing the MNC's global tax liability requires the MNC to be able to transfer funds from one location to another around the globe. MNCs use a number of techniques to transfer liquid funds across borders including dividend remittances, royalty payments and fees, and fronting loans.

Two legal constraints may affect the headquarters' ability to shift funds among its subsidiaries. First, if the subsidiary is not wholly owned by the headquarters, the headquarters must respect the rights of the subsidiary's other shareholders. Any intracorporate transfers of funds must be done on a fair-market basis. This ensures that the headquarters does not siphon off the subsidiary's profits through self-dealing, thereby harming the other shareholders' interests. If the subsidiary is wholly owned, transfers of funds do not raise this issue. Second, some countries impose restrictions on the repatriation of profits, thus blocking their intracorporate transfer.

Some MNCs rely on more than one of these techniques to transfer funds across borders, practically known as unbundling. By using a mix of techniques to transfer liquid funds from a foreign subsidiary to the parent company, unbundling allows an MNC to recover funds from its foreign subsidiaries without piquing host-country sensitivities with large dividend drains. An MNC's ability to select a particular policy is severely limited when a foreign subsidiary is part-owned either by a local joint-venture partner or by local stockholders. Serving the legitimate demands of the local co-owners of a foreign subsidiary may limit the MNC's ability to impose the kind of dividend policy, royalty payment schedule, or fronting policy that would be optimal for the parent company.

(1) Dividend remittances

Dividend remittance is the most common method of transferring funds from subsidiaries to the parent company. The dividend policy typically varies with each subsidiary depending on such factors as tax regulations, foreign exchange risk, the age of the subsidiary, and the extent of local equity participation. For instance, the higher the rate of tax levied on dividends by the host-country government, the less attractive this option becomes relative to other options for transferring liquid funds. With regard to foreign exchange risk, MNCs sometimes require foreign subsidiaries based in high-risk countries to speed up the transfer of funds to the parent through accelerated dividend payments. This moves corporate funds out of a country whose currency is expected to depreciate significantly. The age of a foreign subsidiary influences dividend policy in that older subsidiaries tend to remit a higher proportion of their earnings in dividends to the parent, presumably because a subsidiary has fewer capital investment needs as it matures. Local equity participation is a factor because local co-owners' demands for dividends must be recognized.

（2）Royalty payments and fees

Royalties represent the remuneration paid to the owners of technology, patents, or trade names for the use of that technology or the right to manufacture and/or sell products under those patents or trade names. It is common for a parent company to charge its foreign subsidiaries royalties for the technology, patents, or trade names it has transferred to them. Royalties may be levied as a fixed monetary amount per unit of the product the subsidiary sells or as a percentage of a subsidiary's gross revenues. A fee is compensation for professional services or expertise supplied to a foreign subsidiary by the parent company or another subsidiary. Fees are sometimes differentiated into "management fees" for general expertise and advice and "technical assistance fees" for guidance in technical matters. Fees are usually levied as fixed charges for the particular services provided. Royalties and fees have certain tax advantages over dividends, particularly when the corporate tax rate is higher in the host country than in the parent's home country. Royalties and fees are often tax-deductible locally because they are viewed as an expense, so arranging for payment in royalties and fees will reduce the foreign subsidiary's tax liability. If the foreign subsidiary compensates the parent company by dividend payments, local income taxes must be paid before the dividend distribution, and withholding tax must be paid on the dividend itself. Although the parent can often take a tax credit for the local withholding and income taxes it has paid, part of the benefits can be lost if the subsidiary's combined tax rate is higher than that of the headquarters.

（3）Fronting loans

A fronting loan is a loan between an MNC and its subsidiary channeled through a financial intermediary, usually a large international bank. In a direct intrafirm loan, the MNC headquarters lends cash directly to the foreign subsidiary, and the subsidiary repays it later. In a fronting loan, the headquarters deposits funds in an international bank, and the bank then lends the same amount to the foreign subsidiary. Thus, a Chinese MNC might deposit US $ 1 million in a New York bank. The New York bank might then lend that US $ 1 million to a Spanish subsidiary of the MNC. From the bank's point of view, the load is risk-free because it has 100% collateral in the form of the headquarters' deposit. The bank "fronts" for the headquarters, hence the name. The bank makes a profit by paying the headquarters a slightly lower interest rate on its deposit than it charges the foreign subsidiary on the borrowed funds.

MNCs use fronting loans for two reasons. In the first place, fronting loans can circumvent host government restrictions on the remittance of funds from a foreign subsidiary to the headquarters. A host government might restrict a foreign subsidiary from repaying a loan to its headquarters in order to preserve the country's foreign exchange reserves, but it is less likely to restrict a subsidiary's ability to repay a loan to a large MNC. To stop payment to an international bank would hurt the country's credit image, whereas halting payment to the headquarters would probably have a minimal impact on its image. As a result, MNCs sometimes use fronting loans when they want to lend funds to a subsidiary based in a country with a fairly high probability of political turmoil that might lead to restrictions on capital flows.

In the second place, fronting loans have certain tax advantages. For instance, a tax haven subsidiary that is 100% owned by the headquarters deposits US $2 million in a New York international bank at 9% interest. The bank lends the US $2 million to a foreign operating subsidiary at 10% interest. The country where the foreign subsidiary is based taxes corporate income at 50%, as shown in Figure 7-4. Under this arrangement, interest payments net of income tax will be as follows. First, the foreign operating subsidiary pays US $200,000 interest to the New York bank. Deducting these interest payments from its taxable income results in a net after-tax cost of US $100,000 to the foreign operating subsidiary. Second, the New York bank receives the US $200,000 for its services and pays US $180,000 interest on the deposit to the tax haven subsidiary. Lastly, the tax haven subsidiary receives US $180,000 interest on its deposit tax-free. The net result is that US $180,000 interest in case has been moved from the foreign subsidiary to the tax haven subsidiary. Since the foreign subsidiary's after-tax cost of borrowing is only US $100,000, the headquarters has moved an additional US $80,000 out of the country by using this arrangement. If the tax haven subsidiary had made a direct loan to the foreign operating subsidiary, the host government may have disallowed the interest charge as a tax-deductible expense by ruling that it was a dividend to the headquarters disguised as an interest payment.

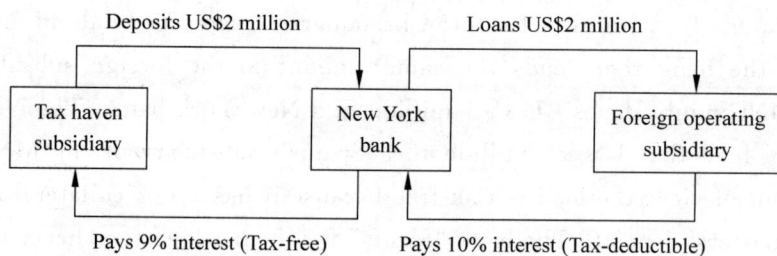

Deposits US$2 million　　　　Loans US$2 million

| Tax haven subsidiary | | New York bank | | Foreign operating subsidiary |

Pays 9% interest (Tax-free)　　　Pays 10% interest (Tax-deductible)

Figure 7-4　An example of the tax aspects of a fronting loan

第三节　跨国公司的外币与外汇风险管理
（Foreign Currency and Exchange Exposure Management of Multinational Corporations）

1. Foreign currency transaction management

外币交易是指跨国公司使用常见外币或功能货币以外的货币进行的交易。将外币财务报表折算为外币主要有两种方法：时间法和当前汇率法。

Foreign currency transactions refer to transactions conducted by multinational corporations using foreign currencies or currencies other than functional currencies. Such transactions may be the purchase of goods or services, the payment of payables or the collection of receivables. In accounting, the currency in the main economic environment in which the business is operated is called the bookkeeping standard, which usually refers to the currency in the economic environment in which the company mainly receives and pays cash. If the subsidiary is just the extension of headquarters, the domestic currency is selected as the functional currency. If the subsidiary operations are relatively concentrated and the business is mainly concentrated in the country where the subsidiary is located, the local currency will be selected as the functional currency.

There are mainly two methods of translating foreign currency financial statements in foreign currency: temporal method and current exchange rate method.

Temporal method is good to reflect changes in exchange rates. If the items in the balance sheet are measured with the past value, the historical exchange rate shall still be used in the financial statement. If the value is measured by the present value, the real exchange rate shall be used in the financial statement. In terms of the income statement, depreciation and amortization expense shall be translated at the historical exchange rate of the corresponding asset at the time of acquisition, while other income and expense items shall be translated at the average exchange rate of the reporting period. The translation difference generated by exchange rate changes is included in the consolidated net income of the current year. However, the exchange rate change cannot be directly reflected in the current profit and loss. It is argued that temporal method ignores overseas operations as an independent entity, and the excessive exchange rate translation increases the workload of financial personnel.

The current exchange rate method has different requirements for the three financial statements. The assets and liabilities items in the balance sheet are translated at the spot exchange rate on the balance sheet date, also known as the closing exchange rate, except for the undistributed profit items. The owner's equity items use the spot exchange rate that occurred, also known as the historical exchange rate. The income and expenses in the income statement shall be translated at the spot exchange rate on the transaction date. For the difference of translation of financial statements in foreign currency, it shall be listed in other comprehensive income items when preparing consolidated financial statements. For cash flow statements in foreign currency, the spot exchange rate on the date of the cash flow should be used for translation, and the impact on cash due to exchange rate changes should be listed separately as an adjustment item.

The current exchange rate method is simpler than the temporal method, and a more uniform exchange rate is adopted to maintain a basic balance of the financial ratio after conversion. As a result, the current exchange rate method has become the most widely used exchange rate method. However, this method also has obvious disadvantages. For instance, fixed assets are generally measured at historical cost, but need to be adjusted according to the spot exchange rate at the end of the period in the balance sheet.

2. Foreign exchange exposure management

跨国公司意识到利率和汇率在任何时候都可能对任何跨国公司的资产负债表价值和年收益造成重大风险。一般来说,跨国公司有三种外汇风险敞口:交易风险敞口、经济风险敞口和折算风险敞口。

MNCs are aware of the substantial risks to balance sheet values and annual earnings that interest rates and exchange rates may inflict on any MNC at any time. Generally, MNCs have three types of foreign currency exposure: transaction exposure, economic exposure, and translation exposure.

The first is transaction exposure, which is the risk associated with a contractual payment of foreign currency. MNCs that buy or sell internationally have transaction exposure if any of the cash flows are denominated in foreign currency. The second is economic exposure, which is the risk of long-term cash flows affected positively or negatively by unexpected future exchange rate changes. The third is translation exposure, which is the risk arising from the legal requirement that all MNCs consolidate their financial statements of all worldwide operations annually. Any MNC with operations outside its home country, operations that will be either earning foreign currency or valued in foreign currency, has translation exposure. Both transaction exposure and economic exposure are true exposures in the financial sense, which means that they pose potential threats to the value of an MNC's cash flows over time. Different from transaction exposure and economic exposure, translation exposure is a problem arising from accounting.

(1) Transaction exposure

Transaction exposure is the most commonly observed type of exchange rate risk. Only two conditions are necessary for a transaction exposure to exist: a cash flow that is denominated in a foreign currency, and the cash flow will occur at a future date. Any contract, agreement, purchase, or sale that is denominated in a foreign currency which will be settled in the future constitutes a transaction exposure. The risk of a transaction exposure is that the exchange rate might change between the present date and the settlement date. The change may be for the better or for the worse. Transaction exposure is a major problem for MNCs. Many typical international business transactions denominated in a foreign currency can lead to transaction exposure, which includes purchase and sales of goods, services, or asset, credit extension, money borrowing.

交易风险的管理通常通过自然套期保值或合同套期保值来实现。自然套期保值描述了跨国公司如何安排外汇现金流以大致相同的时间和金额流入和流出。风险敞口的管理或对冲是通过匹配抵消的外币现金流来实现的,因此,不需要跨国公司承担异常的金融合同或活动来管理风险敞口。合同套期保值是指跨国公司使用金融合同对冲交易风险。最常见的外汇合约对冲是远期合约,尽管也使用其他金融工具和衍生品,包括期货和期权。远期合约将确保跨国公司在未来的确切日期获得所需两种货币之间的固定汇率。远期合约中的金额将与风险敞口的金额一致。套期保值是一种资产或头寸,其价值与风险敞口金额相同但方向相反。头寸的总价值不会改变,也称为完美套期保值。许多在发展中国家运营的跨国公司选择无保护交易,即在预测汇率变动可能有利的某个特定的日期直接进行交易。

Management of transaction exposures is usually accomplished by either natural hedging or contractual hedging. Natural hedging describes how an MNC arranges to have foreign currency cash flows coming in and going out at roughly the same times and the same amounts. The management or hedging of the exposure is accomplished by matching offsetting foreign currency cash flows and, therefore, does not require the MNC to undertake unusual financial contracts or activities to manage the exposure. Contractual hedging is when the MNC uses financial contracts to hedge the transaction exposure. The most common foreign currency contractual hedge is the forward contract, although other financial instruments and derivatives including futures and options are also used. The forward contract would allow the MNC to be assured a fixed rate of exchange between the desired two currencies at the precise future date. The forward contract would also be for the exact amount of the exposure. A hedge is an asset or a position whose value moves in the equal but opposite direction of the exposure. The total value of the position would not change, also known as a perfect hedge. However, perfect hedges are hard to find, and many MNCs would not use them if they were readily available. The presence of a perfect hedge eliminates all downside risks, but also eliminates all upside potential. Many MNCs accept this two-sided risk as part of their business operations. However, it's generally best to accept risk in the line of business, not in the cash-payment process of settling the business. Table 7-3 summarizes the benefits and costs of different techniques available to manage transaction exposure. Unfortunately, in many developing markets, these techniques are unavailable or very expensive to utilize. As a result, many MNCs operating in such economies choose to go naked, making transaction at a specific date which has been bet to be beneficial on foreign exchange rate variation.

Table 7-3 Strategies for managing transaction exposure

Strategy	Benefit(s)	Cost(s)
Go naked	• No capital outlay • Potential for capital gain if home currency rises in value	• Potential for capital loss if home currency falls in value
Buy forward currency	• Elimination of transaction exposure • Flexibility in size and timing of contracts	• Fees to banks • Lost opportunity for capital gain if home currency rises in value
Buy currency futures	• Elimination of transaction exposure • Ease and relative inexpensiveness of futures contract	• Small brokerage fee • Inflexibility in size and timing of contracts • Lost opportunity for capital gain if home currency rises in value
Buy currency option	• Elimination of transaction exposure • Potential for capital gain if home currency rises in value	• Premium paid up front for option because of its "heads I win, tails I don't lose" nature • Inflexibility in size and timing of option
Acquire offsetting assets	• Elimination of transaction exposure	• Effort or expense of arranging offsetting transaction • Lost opportunity for capital gain if home currency rises in value

Source: Adapted from Table 13. 2 in Griffin, Ricky W. , Pustay, Michael W. (2013), *International Business*, 7th Edition, Pearson Education, Inc. P344

(2) Economic exposure

Economic exposure, also known as operating exposure, is the change on the value of an MNC arising from unexpected changes in exchange rates. Economic exposure emphasizes that there is a limit to an MNC's ability to predict either cash flows or exchange rate changes in the medium to long term. All MNCs that operate in economies affected by international financial events, such as exchange rate changes, are affected. Measuring economic exposure is subjective, and for the most part it is dependent on the degree of internationalization present in the MNC's cost and revenue structure, as well as potential changes over the long run. The impacts of economic exposure are as diverse as are MNCs in their international structure. From the perspective of economic exposure management, the fact that the MNC's total value, subsidiary and parent together, is roughly a wash as a result of the exchange rate change is desirable. Sound financial management assumes that an MNC will profit and bear risks in its line of business, not in the process of settling payments on business already completed. Management of economic exposure is being prepared for the unexpected. Diversification of operations would allow the MNC to be desensitized to the impacts of any one pair of exchange rate changes. Diversification of financing serves to hedge economic exposure much in the same way as it does with transaction exposures. An MNC with debt denominated in many different currencies is sensitive to many different interest rates. If one country or currency experiences rapidly rising inflation rates and interest rates, an MNC with diversified debt will not be subject to the full impact of such movements. Purely domestic MNCs, however, are actually somewhat captive to the local conditions and are unable to ride out such interest rate storms easily. It should be noted that these two kinds of diversification are passive solutions to the exposure problem. It implies that without knowing when or where or what the problem may be, the MNC that simply spreads its operations and financial structure out over a variety of countries and currencies is prepared.

(3) Translation exposure

财务人员可以通过使用资产负债表套期保值来减少折算风险敞口,即会计风险。当跨国公司将其以特定货币计价的资产与其以相同货币计价的负债相匹配时,就会产生资产负债表套期保值。

Translation exposure, also known as accounting exposure, can be reduced by financial officers through the use of a balance sheet hedge. A balance sheet hedge is created when an MNC matches its assets denominated in a given currency with its liabilities in that same currency. This balancing occurs on a currency-by-currency basis, not on a subsidiary-by-subsidiary basis. A controversy exists among financial experts over whether or not firms should protect themselves from translation exposure. Some experts believe managers should ignore translation exposure and instead focus on reducing transaction and economic exposure, arguing that transaction exposure can produce true cash losses to the MNC, whereas translation exposure produces only paper, or accounting, losses. Others disagree, stating that translation exposure should not be ignored. For example, MNCs forced to take write-downs of the value of their foreign subsidiaries may trigger default clauses in their loan contracts if their debt-to-equity ratios rise too high.

第四节 跨国公司的税务管理
(International Tax Management of Multinational Corporations)

1. The definition of international tax

国际税收是两个或两个以上的国家政府凭借其政治权力,对跨国纳税人的跨国所得或财产进行重叠交叉课税,以及由此所形成的国家的税收分配关系。国际税收的管辖权遵循属地原则和属人原则,分为三种类型:地域管辖权、居民管辖权和公民管辖权。

Taxation is a form in which the state, relying on its political power and in accordance with legal standards, distributes a portion of social products free of charge to obtain fiscal revenue, reflecting a specific distribution relationship with the state as the main body. Based on this, international taxation can be understood as the overlapping and cross taxation of transnational taxpayers' transnational income or property by two or more governments using their political power, as well as the resulting tax distribution relationship between countries. International taxation cannot exist independently and must be redistributed through national power. International taxation cannot be separated from multinational taxpayers. Only when the same taxpayer bears the tax obligations of two or more countries at the same time, can tax relationships between countries be established. International tax adjustment refers to the tax distribution relationship between countries.

Taxation involves taxpayers and objects of taxation, and can be divided into many types from different perspectives based on different standards. Common classifications include: direct tax and indirect tax; goods tax and personnel tax; commodity tax, income tax, property tax, etc. The taxpayers of international taxation include transnational natural persons and transnational entities. Transnational natural persons refer to individuals who simultaneously obtain capital gains such as wage income, dividends, debt interest, etc. in several countries. Transnational entities refer to MNCs, including corporate legal persons engaged in any industry. The taxable object of international taxation refers to the transnational taxable income of transnational taxpayers, such as transnational gains, income, transnational general property, etc. The income of transnational taxpayers includes the income of domestic people from foreign countries, as well as the income of non-domestic people in their own country.

The jurisdiction of international taxation follows the principles of territoriality and personality, and is divided into three types. One is territorial jurisdiction, also known as source jurisdiction, which refers to a country's taxation of income originating within its own territory, generally including four aspects: business income, investment income, service income, and property income. The second is resident jurisdiction, which refers to a country's taxation of the income of residents, including legal persons and natural persons, as stipulated in its own tax laws. The standards for determining the resident status of natural persons in various countries include habitation standards, residence standards, and residence time standards. The standards for determining the resident status of legal persons include registration location standards, management organization location standards, headquarters location standards, and election control standards. The third is citizen jurisdiction, which means that a country taxes the income of its citizens who hold its own nationality.

2. Double taxation mitigation

不同的国家有不同的税收制度。许多国家遵循全球原则,即它们有权对设在本国的实体在境外赚取的收入征税。当外国子公司的收入被东道国政府和母国政府都征税时，就会发生双重征税。双重征税可以通过税收抵免、税收协定和递延原则来缓解。

Different countries have different tax regimes. Many nations follow the worldwide principle that they have the right to tax income earned outside their boundaries by entities based in their country. Thus, the Chinese government can tax the earnings of the Indonesian subsidiary of an MNC incorporated in China. Double taxation occurs when the income of a foreign subsidiary is taxed by both the host-country government and the home-country government. However, double taxation can be mitigated by tax credits, tax treaties, and the deferral principle.

A tax credit allows an entity to reduce the taxes paid to the home government by the amount of taxes paid to the foreign government. A tax treaty between two countries is an agreement specifying what items of income will be taxed by the authorities of the country where the income is earned. For instance, a tax treaty between China and Indonesia may specify that a Chinese MNC need not pay tax in Indonesia on any earnings from its Indonesian subsidiary that are remitted to China in the form of dividends. A deferral principle specifies that parent companies are not taxed on foreign source income until they actually receive a dividend.

For MNCs with activities in many countries, the various tax regimes and the tax treaties have important implications for how the MNCs should structure their internal payments system among the foreign subsidiaries and the parent company. As is known, transfer pricing is one of the ways to minimize their global tax liability. Except transfer pricing, the form in which income is remitted from a foreign subsidiary to the parent company including royalty payments and dividend payments can be structured to minimize the MNCs' global tax liability.

目前，一些发展中国家为了通过吸引外资促进经济发展，会在一定程度上和一定时期内对跨国公司来自本国的收入或所得给予免税或减税的优惠，或有选择地向一些特定项目或特定地区的投资提供税收优惠待遇，同时与跨国公司母国协商，对于这部分优惠减免的税收，视同已向东道国政府缴纳的税额而给予饶让抵免，这被称为税收饶让。

At present, some developing countries will provide tax exemptions or reductions for the income or gains of MNCs from their own countries, or selectively provide tax incentives for investments in specific projects or regions to a certain extent and for a certain period of time, in order to promote economic development by attracting FDI. At the same time, they will negotiate with the tax authorities of the home countries of MNCs, and for these tax exemptions and reductions, they will be treated as tax already paid to the host country government and given preferential tax credits, which is known as tax sparing. Tax sparing cannot be unilaterally implemented and must be clearly stipulated through the signing of bilateral tax treaties. The tax sparing from tax credit is the tax that has never been actually paid and has been granted by the host country, hence it is also known as shadow tax credit. For the home country of MNCs, tax concessions and credits are only a form of cooperation with the host country's policies, and do not affect the tax rights of the home country at all, without sacrificing the normal financial interests of the home country government.

3. International tax avoidance and evasion

国际避税是指纳税人利用各国税法规定的差异和税收政策的不同,采取变更经营地点或经营方式等公开的合法手段,最大限度地减轻其国际纳税义务的行为。国际逃税则指跨国纳税人不遵守征税国的有关法律,利用国际税收管理的困难和国际税收合作中存在的漏洞,有意识地采取种种隐蔽或欺诈手段等逃避纳税义务。

International tax avoidance refers to the behavior of taxpayers taking advantage of the differences in tax laws and policies among countries to adopt publicly available legal means such as changing their business location or mode of operation, in order to minimize their international tax obligations. International tax evasion refers to multinational taxpayers who do not comply with the relevant laws of the taxing country, take advantage of the difficulties in international tax management and loopholes in international tax cooperation, and consciously adopt various covert or fraudulent means to evade tax obligations. There are both connections and differences between international tax avoidance and international tax evasion. Their similarity lies in the fact that both lead to tax losses for the relevant countries and distort economic activities. Their main difference lies in the fact that international tax avoidance is legal, while international tax evasion is illegal and is the target of severe crackdowns by tax authorities in various countries. Although international tax avoidance does not violate the provisions of tax laws, it contradicts the legislative intent of tax laws and reduces or loses tax sources, making it a key target for governments around the world to prevent.

国际避税的基本方式有四种:主体转移方式、客体转移方式、转移定价方式及国际避税地方式。一些跨国公司常常利用巴哈马和百慕大等避税地来尽量减少纳税义务。避税地是指所得税非常低或没有所得税的国家。跨国公司可以通过在避税地设立全资非经营性子公司来避免所得税。

There are four basic ways of international tax avoidance: subject transfer, object transfer, transfer pricing, and international tax haven. Some MNCs usually use tax havens such as the Bahamas and Bermuda to minimize their tax liability. A tax haven is a country with a very low, or no, income tax. MNCs can avoid income taxes by establishing a wholly-owned, non-operating subsidiary in the tax haven. These subsidiaries only exist on the registration documents, with only one mailbox or sign, and are therefore also known as mailbox companies, sign companies, or shadow companies. Their main forms include holding companies, financial companies, insurance companies, trading companies, etc.

The tax haven subsidiary owns the common stock of the operating foreign subsidiaries,which allows all transfers of funds from foreign operating subsidiaries to the parent company to be funneled through the tax haven subsidiary. The tax levied on foreign source income by an MNC's home government,which might normally be paid when a dividend is declared by a foreign subsidiary,can be deferred under the deferral principle until the tax haven subsidiary pays the dividend to the parent. This dividend payment can be postponed indefinitely if foreign operations continue to grow and require new internal financing from the tax haven affiliate.

Except the Bahamas and Bermuda,several other smaller countries including the Cayman Islands,the Channel Islands,Liechtenstein,and the Netherlands Antilles also have gone into the business of being the tax haven. To attract MNCs,a tax haven must not only refrain from imposing income taxes but also provide a stable political and business climate,an efficient court system,and sophisticated banking and communications industries. In return,the tax haven is able to capture franchising and incorporation fees and generate numerous lucrative professional jobs far beyond what an economy of its size normally could. Government agencies are well aware of these opportunities to play accounting games. As a result,both home and host countries scrutinize the transfer-pricing policies of MNCs operating within their borders to ensure the MNCs do not evade their tax obligations and that the governments receive their fair share of taxes from the MNCs. A common approach is to use an arm's length test whereby government officials attempt to determine the price that two unrelated firms operating at arm's length would have agreed on. In many cases,however,an appropriate arm's length price is difficult to establish,leading to conflicts between MNCs and tax authorities. Such conflicts are rarely resolved easily or quickly.

The methods of international tax evasion refer to various covert and fraudulent measures taken by multinational taxpayers to exploit the difficulties and loopholes of relevant countries in international tax administration. The common methods of tax evasion include: fabricating false accounts to conceal taxable income,gains,or property; falsifying cost expenses to seek unreasonable deductions; falsifying the total investment amount to extract more depreciation,or inflating the self-owned funds in the investment amount as borrowed funds to expand the deduction items; distributing profits to fictitious partners and transfering income or deductions to other affiliated enterprise declaration forms applicable to lower tax rates; engaging in underground operations to completely evade tax supervision and corporate tax burden. These methods are characterized by concealment,false reporting,misreporting,omission,and fraud.

关键术语（Key Terms）

跨国公司财务管理（financial management of MNCs）

净现值（net present value）

内部收益率（internal rate of return）

投资回收期（payback period）

资本结构（capital structure）

现金池（cash pooling）

提前和延迟结汇（leads and lags）

再融资（reinvoicing）

内部银行（internal banks）

多边净额结算（multilateral netting）

股利返回（dividend remittances）

特许权使用费和费用（royalty payments and fees）

预付贷款（fronting loans）

外币交易（foreign currency transaction）

交易风险敞口（transaction exposure）

经济风险敞口（economic exposure）

折算风险敞口（translation exposure）

国际税收（international taxation）

地域管辖权（territorial jurisdiction）

居民管辖权（resident jurisdiction）

公民管辖权（citizen jurisdiction）

税收抵免（tax credits）

税收协定（tax treaties）

递延原则（deferral principle）

税收饶让（tax sparing）

国际避税（international tax avoidance）

国际逃税（international tax evasion）

避税地（tax haven）

小结（Summary）

1. Financial management of MNCs includes three sets of related decisions: investment decisions about what activities to finance, financing decisions about how to finance those activities, and money management decisions about how to manage the MNC's financial resources most efficiently. There are two influential arguments on the goals of financial management: stockholder wealth maximization and corporate wealth maximization. MNCs have limited funds for investment and often a seemingly endless set of projects from which to choose. Numerous approaches for evaluating investment projects are available, but the most commonly used methods include net present value, internal rate of return, and payback period. The financing methods of MNCs mainly include equity financing and debt financing. The comprehensive cost of the two is the weighted average cost of capital. The cost of equity financing can generally be indirectly estimated through the Gordon model and the capital asset pricing model.

2. MNCs try to efficiently manage their global cash resources which is actually the working capital. This includes three aspects: minimizing cash balances, reducing transaction costs, and minimizing the corporate tax burden. MNCs can minimize cash balances mainly with the following methods: cash pooling, leads and lags, reinvoicing, and internal banks. Multilateral netting can reduce the number of transactions between MNCs' subsidiaries and the number of transaction costs. Pursuing the objectives of utilizing the MNC's cash resources most efficiently and minimizing the MNC's global tax liability requires the MNC to be able to transfer funds from one location to another around the globe. MNCs use a number of techniques to transfer liquid funds across borders including dividend remittances, royalty payments and fees, and fronting loans.

3. Foreign currency transactions refer to transactions conducted by multinational

corporations using foreign currencies or currencies other than functional currencies. There are mainly two methods of translating foreign currency financial statements in foreign currency：temporal method and current exchange rate method. Generally，MNCs have three types of foreign currency exposure：transaction exposure，economic exposure，and translation exposure.

4. International taxation is the overlapping and cross taxation of transnational taxpayers' transnational income or property by two or more governments using their political power，as well as the resulting tax distribution relationship between countries. The jurisdiction of international taxation follows the principles of territoriality and personality，and is divided into three types：territorial jurisdiction，resident jurisdiction，and citizen jurisdiction. Double taxation can be mitigated by tax credits，tax treaties，and the deferral principle. Some MNCs use tax havens to minimize their tax liability. A tax haven is a country with a very low，or no，income tax. MNCs can avoid income taxes by establishing a wholly-owned，non-operating subsidiary in the tax haven. There are both connections and differences between international tax avoidance and international tax evasion.

延伸阅读（Further Readings）

习题（Exercises）

第八章
Chapter 8

跨国公司的全球供应链管理
Global Supply Chain Management of Multinational Corporations

Learning Objectives
- To know the characteristics and content of global supply chain management
- To know the design of a global supply chain management system
- To be familiar with the relationship management in global supply chain
- To understand the procurement management in global supply chain
- To be familiar with the application of information technology in global supply chain

第一节 全球供应链管理概述
（The Overview of Global Supply Chain）

1. The definition and characteristics of global supply chain management

随着 20 世纪末贸易壁垒的降低和信息技术的飞速发展,跨国公司开始意识到传统的生产和分销模式已无法满足日益增长的市场需求。跨国公司需要在全球范围内寻找成本效益更高的原材料供应商、更高效的生产方式以及更快捷的物流配送渠道。这种跨地域、跨行业的资源整合需求催生了供应链管理的概念,它强调通过优化整个产品从原材料到最终用户的流动过程,来提高跨国公司的竞争力。此外,供应链管理的产生也与消费者需求的多样化和个性化紧密相关。在现代市场经济中,消费者对产品的选择更加注重品质、价格、服务和交付速度。为了满足这些需求,跨国公司必须构建一个灵活、高效的供应链体系,以快速响应市场变化,实现产品的快速创新和个性化定制。同时,全球化带来的供应链复杂性也要求跨国公司必须采用更为先进的管理方法和工具,以确保供应链的稳定性和可靠性,从而在激烈的市场竞争中获得优势。全球供应链管理具有跨区性、复杂性和动态性等特点。

With the reduction of trade barriers and advancement of information technology (IT) since the end of the 20th century, MNCs began to realize that traditional production and distribution models could no longer meet the growing market demands. They

186

needed to seek more cost-effective raw material suppliers, more efficient production methods, and faster logistics distribution channels on a global scale. This demand for cross-regional and cross-industry resource integration gave rise to the concept of supply chain management, which emphasizes improving the competitiveness of enterprises by optimizing the entire flow process of products from raw materials to end users. In addition, the emergence of supply chain management is closely related to the diversification and personalization of consumer demands. In modern market economy, consumers pay more attention to quality, price, service, and delivery speed when choosing products. To meet these demands, MNCs must build a flexible and efficient supply chain system to quickly respond to market changes and achieve rapid product innovation and personalized customization. At the same time, the complexity of supply chains brought by globalization also requires MNCs to adopt more advanced management methods and tools to ensure the stability and reliability of the supply chain, thereby gaining an advantage in the market competition.

Supply chain management is an integrative management field with various definitions in academia, but the core concept remains consistent. Supply chain management focuses on not only the flow of raw materials but also the flow of information and funds, as well as how these flows are managed and optimized to enhance the performance of the entire supply chain. The goal of supply chain management is to improve cost-effectiveness, risk management, and customer satisfaction by coordinating various links in the supply chain, ultimately gaining an advantage in the competitive market. Therefore, supply chain management can be defined as an integrated management process that covers the entire process from raw material procurement, product manufacturing, inventory management, logistics distribution to the final delivery of the product to the consumer. Supply chain management, as an integral part of modern business operations, has become increasingly prominent with the deepening of globalization. In today's business environment, supply chain management is no longer confined to a single region or country but spans multiple countries and regions, characterized by trans-regionality, complexity, and dynamism.

（1）Trans-regionality

The trans-regionality of global supply chains refers to the extensive geographical distribution of the supply chain network, covering multiple countries and regions. This layout not only reflects the global characteristics of the supply chain but is also a strategic choice for MNCs to seek optimal resource allocation on a global scale. Through trans-regional supply chain layout, MNCs can optimize various supply chain links such as raw material procurement, manufacturing, and logistics distribution, based on the comparative advantages of different countries and regions. Specifically, trans-regionality enables the supply chain to leverage the cost advantages, technical expertise, and market proximity of different regions.

Trans-regional supply chain layout brings multiple benefits to MNCs. Firstly, it helps to reduce production costs. By searching for the lowest-cost production locations globally, MNCs can reduce overall manufacturing expenses. Secondly, trans-regionality improves the efficiency of the supply chain, allowing MNCs to bring products to the market more quickly to meet consumer demands. Additionally, this layout enhances the enterprise's ability to respond to market changes, enabling it to quickly adjust production and supply chain strategies to adapt to the ever-changing market demands and consumer preferences. However, trans-regionality also brings a series of challenges, such as coordination and integration issues of the supply chain, the complexity of cross-national logistics, and the differences in laws, regulations, and cultures of different countries and regions. Therefore, when implementing a trans-regional supply chain strategy, MNCs are required not only to have a global perspective and strategic thinking but also to be able to cope with the complexity and challenges of trans-regional operations. By optimizing the layout and management of trans-regional supply chains, MNCs can gain advantages in global competition, maximizing cost-effectiveness, efficiency improvement, and market response speed.

A typical case is about Lenovo Group's global supply chain management. As a leading global technology company, Lenovo Group's supply chain management reflects the trans-regional characteristics of global supply chains. Lenovo has 34 production bases and more than 2,000 suppliers worldwide and has established a digital platform for collaborative operation with more than 400 core suppliers. This globally distributed supply chain network not only covers key markets such as Asia, Europe, and the Americas but also achieves optimal allocation of global resources and rapid response to market demands through an efficient supply chain management system. Lenovo's global supply chain layout allows the company to flexibly utilize the resource advantages of different countries and regions around the world to meet market demands. For example, Lenovo has set up R&D centers in the United States, Germany, and China to leverage local technical advantages and talent resources for product innovation; established production bases in countries with lower labor costs such as India and Mexico to reduce production costs; and at the same time, through the global logistics network, achieved rapid product distribution and delivery. In addition, the digital and intelligent transformation of Lenovo's supply chain, through the application of innovative technologies such as predictive analysis, artificial intelligence (AI), and blockchain, has improved the transparency and efficiency of the supply chain and reduced operational risks. This trans-regional supply chain layout and digital management not only enhances Lenovo's global competitiveness but also demonstrates the importance and advantages of global supply chain management in modern enterprise operations.

（2）Complexity

First, the complexity of supply chains is reflected in the diversity of their links, which are composed of multiple stages such as raw material procurement, production manufacturing, inventory management, order processing, and logistics distribution, to the final sales and services of products. Each link not only independently performs specific functions but also has close connections and dependencies with each other, which requires supply chain managers to have a deep understanding and precise control of each link.

Second, the wide range of participants in the supply chain is also a manifestation of complexity. Each link in the supply chain may involve many different economic entities, including raw material suppliers, manufacturers, distributors, retailers, as well as service providers, third-party logistics companies, IT system suppliers, etc. The operational goals and management models of these participants bring additional complexity to supply chain management.

Finally, the complexity of supply chains is also reflected in the diversity of operational models, where different participants may adopt different operational strategies and business models according to market demand and their own strengths, such as lean production, mass customization, agile supply chains, etc. These different operational models focus on improving efficiency, reducing costs, and accelerating response speeds, and they pose higher demands for the overall coordination and optimization of the supply chain. In addition, supply chain managers need to have a high level of coordination ability to ensure that the various links of the supply chain across organizations, regions, and even countries can operate efficiently in coordination. This involves not only the optimization of internal processes but also, more importantly, establishing effective communication, negotiation, and cooperation mechanisms between the various links of the supply chain.

Therefore, in the face of the volatile global market environment and potential supply chain risks, managers need to be able to timely identify and respond to various uncertain factors, such as political turmoil, economic fluctuations, natural disasters, etc. This requires the establishment of a comprehensive risk management and response mechanism to improve the resilience and impact resistance of the supply chain. At the same time, in order to enhance the overall performance and competitiveness of the supply chain, managers also need to continuously explore and adopt new technologies, such as big data analysis, AI, the Internet of Things (IoT), blockchain, etc. The complexity of global supply chains requires managers to have a comprehensive perspective and integrated management capabilities to cope with the ever-changing challenges and demands.

（3）Dynamism

The dynamism of global supply chains is one of its most prominent characteristics, requiring supply chain management to have a high degree of adaptability and flexibility. In the global market environment, the supply chain system is constantly facing challenges from various aspects such as demand fluctuations, technological innovations, shifts in consumer preferences, and macroeconomic fluctuations. These factors together form a constantly changing external environment, which has a profound impact on the operation of the supply chain.

Firstly, the volatility of demand requires supply chain managers to have precise market forecasting capability and the ability to quickly adjust production and inventory to cope with market uncertainty. Secondly, the rapid development of technology has not only changed the way products are produced but also put forward new requirements for the operation model of the supply chain. Supply chain managers need to keep up with technology trends, using advanced information technology and automation technology to improve the efficiency and response speed of the supply chain. Thirdly, the increasingly personalized and diversified consumer preferences have put forward higher requirements for the customization and flexibility of the supply chain. Supply chain managers must deeply understand consumer needs and meet the market's demand for personalized products through flexible supply chain design and operational strategies. In addition, changes in macroeconomic conditions, such as exchange rate fluctuations and trade policy changes, will also have an important impact on the cost structure and operational strategies of the supply chain. Supply chain managers need to monitor market dynamics in real time, using data analysis and intelligent decision-making tools to quickly make decisions that adapt to market changes. For example, in the face of sudden situations such as natural disasters or political events, supply chain managers need to quickly activate emergency plans, adjust logistics routes, find alternative suppliers, and even reconfigure the global production network to ensure the continuity and stability of the supply chain. Therefore, the dynamism of the supply chain requires managers to have strategic thinking, keen market insight, flexible adaptability, and efficient coordination ability. By diversifying supply sources, establishing flexible production capabilities, and logistics networks, the supply chain's ability to resist risks is improved.

The typical case is as follows. The global automotive industry is facing the challenge of supply chain disruption due to the shortage of chips. Due to the shortage of semiconductor chips, many car manufacturers have had to reduce production or temporarily close factories. This dynamism of the supply chain requires car manufacturers to quickly adjust their supply chain strategies to cope with rapid changes in the market and technology; fast fashion brands such as ZARA and SHEIN have demonstrated the dynamism of the supply chain and the ability to respond to market trends. ZARA is known for its rapid replenishment and low inventory strategy, while SHEIN uses data-driven methods to quickly respond to consumer needs, achieving small batches and high-frequency product updates. This model reflects the flexibility of the supply chain and the ability to quickly respond to market changes. These cases show that in global supply chain management, not only efficient operations but also the ability to quickly adapt to the constantly changing external environment are required in the face of market fluctuations, technological progress, changes in consumer behavior, and unpredictable global events.

2. The content of global supply chain management

全球供应链管理涉及规划、组织、协调、监控和优化跨越国界的供应链活动的整个过程。全球供应链管理的主要内容包括：供应链设计、供应商和采购管理、生产和制造管理、库存和物流管理、需求预测、订单处理和客户服务管理、风险和 IT 管理、可持续性和社会责任。

Global supply chain management involves the entire process of planning, organizing, coordinating, monitoring, and optimizing supply chain activities that span national borders. The main contents of global supply chain management include: supply chain design, supplier and procurement management, production and manufacturing management, inventory and logistics management, demand forecasting, order processing and customer service management, risk and IT management, sustainability and social responsibility.

（1）Supply chain design

Supply chain design is the initial stage of building the structure and processes of the supply chain, involving strategic planning for each link in the supply chain. This includes determining the geographical layout of production and storage facilities, optimizing product processes, formulating inventory management strategies, and planning transportation and distribution networks. The design process also needs to consider the flexibility and adaptability of the supply chain to ensure it can respond to market changes and potential risks in time.

（2）Supplier and procurement management

Supplier management is a key link in ensuring the quality and cost efficiency of raw material and component supply. It covers the assessment, selection, development, and ongoing management of potential suppliers. By establishing long-term cooperative relationships, companies can improve the stability and responsiveness of the supply chain and reduce the risk of relying on a single supplier through supplier diversification. Procurement management focuses on obtaining the required materials and services at the lowest cost. This includes optimizing the procurement process and cost control, as well as formulating procurement strategies such as centralized procurement and electronic procurement. Procurement management also needs to ensure the transparency and compliance of the process to prevent ethical risks in the supply chain.

(3) Production and manufacturing management

Production and manufacturing management ensure the efficiency of the production process and product quality. It includes production planning, scheduling, and production efficiency and quality control. Modern production management adopts lean production and agile manufacturing principles to reduce waste, improve production flexibility, and quickly respond to market demand changes.

(4) Inventory and logistics management

Inventory management is a key tool in the supply chain for regulating supply and demand. Effective inventory management strategies can reduce inventory costs and avoid overstock or stockouts. Advanced inventory management technologies, such as real-time inventory tracking, automatic replenishment systems, and economic order quantity models, can improve inventory turnover and reduce inventory holding costs. Logistics management is responsible for the physical flow of products from production to consumption. This includes transportation management, warehouse management, material handling, and distribution activities. By optimizing the logistics network, transportation modes, and distribution plans, MNCs can reduce logistics costs, improve delivery speed, and enhance customer service levels.

(5) Demand forecasting

Demand forecasting is an important part of supply chain management, aiming to help MNCs predict market trends and customer demand. Accurate forecasting can guide production planning and inventory strategies, reducing the risk of inventory backlog and stockouts. Modern demand forecasting methods use statistical analysis, machine learning, and other technologies to improve forecast accuracy.

(6) Order processing and customer service management

Order processing involves the entire process of order reception, processing, and fulfillment. Automated order management systems can improve the speed and accuracy of order processing, provide real-time updates on order status, and enhance customer satisfaction. The efficiency of order processing directly affects the customer's purchasing experience and the company's market response speed. Customer service management ensures that the supply chain can meet customer needs and expectations. This includes providing high-quality after-sales service, handling customer inquiries and complaints, and collecting customer feedback for continuous improvement of products and services. Excellent customer service can enhance customer loyalty and strengthen the company's brand image.

(7) Risk and IT management

Risk management is the process of identifying, assessing, and mitigating potential risks in the supply chain. This includes risks such as supply disruptions, demand fluctuations, price volatility, and technological changes. By developing risk mitigation strategies and emergency plans, MNCs can improve the resilience and impact resistance of the supply chain. IT is the cornerstone of modern supply chain management. The use of Enterprise Resource Planning(ERP) system, supply chain management software, cloud technology, big data analysis, and AI algorithms improves the visibility, data analysis capabilities, decision support, and process automation of the supply chain.

（8）Sustainability and social responsibility

Sustainability and social responsibility require MNCs to consider environmental protection and social responsibility in supply chain management. This includes promoting green supply chain practices, reducing carbon emissions, using sustainable materials, and implementing fair labor practices. A sustainable supply chain can enhance the company's social responsibility image and long-term competitiveness. In the global supply chain, MNCs need to consider cultural differences, laws and regulations, and trade policies of different countries and regions. Ensuring that supply chain activities comply with local and international compliance requirements, and respecting multiculturalism, can reduce legal risks and reputational risks, and improve the company's adaptability in the global market.

3. Global supply chain management system design

In today's globalized economic context, MNCs are facing increasingly complex market environments and ever-changing consumer demands. The design of a global supply chain management system has become a key factor for MNCs to gain competitive advantages. An effective supply chain design not only enhances operational efficiency and reduces costs but also strengthens the company's ability to respond to market changes, improves customer satisfaction, and plays a positive role in social responsibility and sustainability.

全球供应链管理系统的设计要求跨国公司超越传统的地理和组织界限,采用全面和战略性的视角来审查其供应链活动。全球供应链管理系统的设计可以简化为以下五个关键领域:战略和网络设计、流程和技术架构、资源和能力规划、风险和合规管理、绩效和持续改进。

The design of a global supply chain management system requires MNCs to go beyond traditional geographical and organizational boundaries and adopt a comprehensive and strategic perspective to review their supply chain activities. This involves integrated planning and management of logistics, information flow, and capital flow within the supply chain to ensure that every link works in concert to achieve optimal performance of the entire system. The key aspects to consider in the design process include strategy and network design, process and technology architecture, resource and capability planning, risk and compliance management, and performance and continuous improvement.

The strategy and network design of global supply chain is the foundation for building the company's supply chain architecture. This requires MNCs to establish a global strategy for the supply chain based on macro market analysis, internal resource assessment, and long-term development planning. Network design should consider the geographical layout of key nodes such as production, warehousing, and distribution, as well as the integration of logistics, information flow, and capital flow between them. Academic research emphasizes that network design should optimize the total cost of the supply chain while improving service levels and market response speed.

Process and technology architecture are the pillars of supply chain management. Process design focuses on standardizing and optimizing the efficiency of operations at each link in the supply chain, including procurement, production scheduling, inventory control, and order fulfillment. The technology architecture involves the adoption of advanced IT, such as ERP system, SCM platforms, IoT, big data analysis, and AI, to achieve process automation, enhance data-driven decision support, and improve the transparency and collaborative efficiency of the supply chain.

Resource and capability planning is key to ensuring that the supply chain can meet market demands. This includes the assessment and planning of production capacity, inventory levels, human resources, and technological resources. Academically, resource planning is seen as a dynamic process in supply chain management, requiring a comprehensive consideration of demand uncertainty, supply fluctuations, and strategic flexibility to achieve optimal resource allocation.

Risk and compliance management are indispensable parts of the global supply chain design. This requires MNCs to identify and assess potential risks, such as supply disruptions, price volatility, and political instability, and develop corresponding mitigation strategies and emergency plans. Compliance management ensures that supply chain activities comply with international trade regulations, environmental standards, and labor laws. Academic research points out that effective risk management can enhance the resilience and disturbance resistance of the supply chain.

Performance and continuous improvement are the driving forces behind global supply chain management. The performance evaluation system should be based on a series of quantitative and qualitative indicators, such as cost efficiency, delivery time, service quality, and customer satisfaction, to comprehensively assess the performance of the supply chain. The continuous improvement mechanism requires MNCs to establish a data and feedback-based improvement cycle, encouraging innovation and lean management practices to continuously enhance the overall performance and competitiveness of the supply chain.

第二节　全球供应链的关系管理
（The Management of Global Supply Chain Relationship）

在全球经济一体化的浪潮中,跨国公司越来越依赖于复杂的供应链网络来实现其产品与服务的高效流通。供应链已不再是单一线性的实体,而是演化为一个由多个独立但相互依赖的组织构成的复杂网络。这个网络中的每一环节,无论是原材料供应商、制造商、分销商还是最终客户,都是供应链成功的关键。因此,全球供应链的关系管理显得尤为重要,它包括合作伙伴关系的建立与维护、合作伙伴的选择策略,以及客户与供应商关系的有效管理。

In the wave of global economic integration, MNCs increasingly rely on complex supply chain networks to achieve efficient circulation of their products and services. The supply chain is no longer a single linear entity but has evolved into a complex network composed of multiple independent yet interdependent organizations. Every link in this network, whether it is raw material suppliers, manufacturers, distributors, or end customers, is important to the success of the supply chain. Therefore, relationship management in global supply chains is particularly important, which includes the establishment and maintenance of partnerships, partner selection strategies, and effective management of customer and supplier relationships.

Partnership is one of the key factors for the success of global supply chains. It is based on trust, common goals, and the principle of mutual benefit, promoting knowledge sharing, risk sharing, and collaborative innovation through the establishment of strong alliances. The depth and quality of this relationship directly affect the flexibility of the supply chain and its ability to respond to market changes. Partner selection is another important aspect of supply chain relationship management. In the context of globalization, choosing the right partners is important for MNCs to access resources, technology, and market entry. The right choice can significantly enhance the efficiency and effectiveness of the supply chain, reduce operational risks, and bring competitive advantages to the company. Customer and supplier relationship management is the cornerstone of supply chain relationship management. Through effective communication, customized services, and continuous performance evaluation, MNCs can better meet customer needs while motivating suppliers to provide high-quality products and services. The management of this relationship involves not only coordination at the operational level but also strategic cooperation and joint development.

1. Global supply chain partnerships

Against the backdrop of global economic integration, partnerships have become an indispensable part of the global value chain. They are keys for MNCs to acquire resources, expand markets, diversify risks, and enhance competitiveness. The management of partnerships in the global value chain is a multidimensional and cross-cultural complex process, requiring MNCs to have a global perspective, strategic thinking, flexibility, and continuous innovation capabilities. By carefully designing and effectively managing partnerships, MNCs can gain advantages in global competition, achieving long-term stability and sustainable development of the supply chain. With the advancement of technology and innovation in business models, partnerships in the global value chain will continue to evolve, bringing more opportunities and challenges to MNCs.

合作伙伴关系的构建不仅是交易和合同的签订,更是一种战略层面的深度协作,涉及共同目标的设定、资源的整合以及能力的互补。这种关系的建立需要基于相互信任、透明度和战略对接,确保所有合作伙伴都能在价值链中找到自身的定位并发挥最大的效能。维护与发展合作伙伴关系是确保全球价值链持续竞争力的另一个重要方面。这要求跨国公司不仅要在初始阶段投入资源和精力,还要在合作过程中持续地沟通、协调和创新。随着市场环境的变化和业务需求的演进,合作伙伴关系也需要不断地调整和优化。这涉及绩效监控、风险管理、激励机制的建立以及退出策略的规划,以应对未来可能出现的挑战和机遇。

The construction of partnerships is not only about transactions and contract signing but also a strategic level of deep collaboration, involving the setting of common goals, integration of resources, and complementarity of capabilities. The establishment of such relationships needs to be based on mutual trust, transparency, and strategic alignment, ensuring that all partners can find their own position in the value chain and exert the greatest effectiveness. Maintaining and developing partnerships is another important aspect of ensuring the continued competitiveness of the global value chain. This requires MNCs not only to invest resources and effort at the initial stage but also to continuously communicate, coordinate, and innovate during the cooperation process. As the market environment changes and business needs evolve, partnerships also need to be constantly adjusted and optimized. This involves performance monitoring, risk management, the establishment of incentive mechanisms, and planning for exit strategies to address future challenges and opportunities.

(1) Building partnership

Establishing supply chain partnership is the cornerstone of ensuring the long-term success of cooperation. Firstly, strategic alignment requires MNCs to conduct in-depth analysis and understanding of each party's business model, market positioning, and long-term vision. Strategic workshops and joint meetings ensure consistency and complementarity in strategic objectives. Secondly, a comprehensive capability assessment of potential partners is necessary, including financial health, production capacity, technological innovation, and market performance, to ensure that partners can meet specific quality, cost, and delivery standards.

Trust is an indispensable element in partnership, established and deepened through transparent communication and shared business practices. Contract and agreement formulation should cover rights, obligations, and responsibilities, with flexible terms to adapt to future changes and uncertainties. Compliance and standards are the foundations for ensuring partners adhere to international trade regulations, environmental protection regulations, and labor laws. Unified compliance standards and self-inspection mechanisms are established to ensure partners' compliance.

Cultural integration is a key to promoting understanding and respect across different cultural backgrounds, with cultural audits and cross-cultural training programs designed to create diverse and inclusive work teams. Technical and system integration ensures seamless data integration and flow, with the assessment and integration of each party's technology platforms and information systems to design common technical standards and interfaces. Initial cooperation planning clarifies the scope, objectives, resource allocation, timeline, and monitoring mechanisms of the cooperation, laying foundation for the success of the partnership project.

Risk-sharing mechanisms require partners to jointly assess and share potential risks, with a risk management framework designed to identify, assess, monitor, and mitigate risks. Finally, the establishment of communication and coordination mechanisms ensures timely transmission and effective communication of information, with regular meetings, reporting systems, and decision-making processes to maintain coordination among partners. Through these meticulous steps, partnerships in the global value chain can lay a solid foundation, providing support for MNCs in global competition and promoting mutual growth and success.

(2) Maintenance and development of partnership

For the maintenance and development of global supply chain partnership, a comprehensive and systematic approach is required to ensure the long-term stability and effectiveness of the relationship. Firstly, establishing ongoing communication mechanisms is fundamental, which includes a multi-channel communication system and open, honest dialogue to ensure timely transmission and feedback of information. At the same time, shared goals and visions are crucial for partners, ensuring that all stakeholders have a clear understanding of the common objectives and can continuously update them in line with market trends and corporate strategy development.

In terms of joint planning and execution, working with partners on market analysis, demand forecasting, and strategic planning, as well as joint implementation in areas such as new product development and market entry strategies, helps to achieve synergistic effects. Risk-sharing and profit-sharing mechanisms can motivate partners to actively participate, by identifying and addressing potential risks through contract terms and risk management plans, while designing profit-sharing mechanisms to ensure partners receive reasonable returns for their investments.

Performance evaluation and feedback are keys to continuous improvement, monitoring partner performance through quantitative and qualitative performance assessment indicators, and collecting opinions and suggestions from various aspects using a 360-degree feedback mechanism. Technological and process collaboration further promotes seamless integration and collaborative work with partners, by jointly developing and implementing new technologies to enhance the transparency, efficiency, and responsiveness of the supply chain.

Cultural integration and team building are important for promoting the integration of different corporate cultures, improving team collaboration capabilities through cross-cultural training and exchange activities, and establishing cross-functional teams to promote knowledge sharing and innovation. Flexible contract terms can adapt to market and technological changes, including adjustment and exit mechanisms to respond flexibly when necessary.

Incentive and reward programs are designed based on the performance and contributions of partners, enhancing their loyalty and enthusiasm by recognizing and rewarding excellent performance. Continuous improvement and innovation encourage partners to propose suggestions for improvement and innovative ideas, jointly exploring opportunities for supply chain optimization, and investing in R&D and employee training to support these activities.

In response to crises and challenges, a crisis management team and contingency plans are crucial for rapid response to supply chain incidents, working with partners to assess the impact of the crisis and develop response strategies and recovery plans. Social responsibility and sustainability are also important aspects of the partnership, working with partners to share social responsibilities, promote environmental protection and social responsibility practices, and set and implement sustainability goals. Through these coherent measures, global supply chain partnership can be effectively maintained and developed, the competitiveness of the entire supply chain and its ability to adapt to market changes can be enhanced, and long-term success and sustainable development in the global market can be ensured.

2. Partner selection of global supply chain

In the globalized economic environment, the supply chain has expanded from a single enterprise internal process to a complex network on a global scale. To maintain competitiveness, MNCs need to seek out the best partners globally, including raw material suppliers, manufacturers, logistics service providers, and distributors, among others.

合作伙伴选择在全球供应链管理中起着至关重要的作用。合作伙伴选择涉及对潜在合作伙伴的四项评估：战略和核心竞争力一致性、财务稳定性和运营效率、风险管理和合规性、文化兼容性和长期合作前景。

Partner selection plays a crucial role in global supply chain management. Choosing the right partners helps to improve the efficiency of the supply chain, and ensure that each link operates at peak efficiency, thereby reducing costs, shortening delivery times, and enhancing overall response speed. It also helps to ensure the stability of the supply chain, enabling MNCs to better cope with external risks such as political and economic changes. The innovative capabilities of partners can promote continuous improvement and technological upgrades in the supply chain, enhancing the company's market competitiveness. Moreover, partner selection also involves social responsibility and sustainable development, helping MNCs to establish a positive social image and promoting the entire supply chain to move towards a more environmentally friendly and ethical direction. By establishing relationships with multiple partners, MNCs can diversify risks and reduce dependence on a single supplier or market. Overall, partner selection is not only crucial for the immediate operations of a company but also a key factor in ensuring long-term success and sustainable development. Partner selection relates to the four assessments on potential partners: strategic and core competitiveness alignment, financial stability and operational efficiency, risk management and compliance adherence, cultural compatibility and long-term cooperation perspective.

(1) Strategic and core competitiveness alignment

When selecting partners, it is essential to ensure that their strategic goals are highly aligned with the company's strategy, which is the foundation for achieving synergistic effects and long-term cooperation. The strategic direction of the partner should be in line with the company's development vision to promote joint efforts in pursuing common long-term goals. In addition, a thorough analysis of the partners' core competencies is crucial. This includes their expertise in specific technical fields, innovation capabilities, market positioning, and brand influence. These core strengths of the partners should complement the company's existing capabilities to jointly create a unique value proposition and build a lasting competitive advantage in the fierce market competition.

(2) Financial stability and operational efficiency

Financial stability is a key dimension in assessing potential partners, involving profitability, cost control, capital liquidity, and financial transparency. A financially stable partner can provide a stable cooperative environment for the company and reduce financial risks. At the same time, operational efficiency is another important indicator to measure the performance of partners, examining the optimization of their production processes, the efficiency of logistics management, and the response speed of the supply chain. Efficient operations not only ensure the timely delivery of products and services but also directly benefit the company in terms of cost control and quality assurance.

(3) Risk management and compliance adherence

A partner's risk management capabilities directly affect the stability and reliability of the supply chain. The assessment of the partner on its adaptability to market fluctuations, ability to prevent and respond to supply chain disruptions, and maturity of risk diversification and mitigation strategies is not only necessary but also important. In addition, compliance adherence is a prerequisite for protecting the company's reputation and avoiding legal risks. Partners should demonstrate respect for international laws and regulations and actively fulfill corporate social responsibilities in their business practices, including environmental protection, labor rights, and anti-corruption.

(4) Cultural compatibility and long-term cooperation perspective

The compatibility of corporate culture and values is the cornerstone of long-term cooperative relationships. The corporate culture of the partners should be in harmony with the company's own values and business philosophy to promote mutual understanding and trust in cooperation. Assessing the partners' commitment and openness to long-term cooperation, as well as their stance on contract flexibility, market adaptability, and exit mechanisms is indispensable. This helps to ensure that both parties can grow together, adjust flexibly, and terminate the cooperative relationship in order when necessary in the face of market changes and challenges.

By carefully considering these four comprehensive perspectives, MNCs can fully assess the comprehensive strength of potential partners, laying a solid foundation for the stable operation and continuous optimization of their global supply chain.

3. Customer and supplier relationship management of global supply chain

As globalization continues to deepen, the supply chain has expanded to a global scale, involving suppliers, manufacturers, distributors, and retailers from different countries and regions. In this process, the relationships between customers and suppliers in the supply chain have become more complex and diverse. MNCs must not only manage the flow of products and services but also the flow of information, capital, and cooperative relationships with global customers and suppliers. Effective management of these relationships is crucial to ensure the transparency, flexibility, and responsiveness of the supply chain.

客户和供应商关系管理是构建强大、高效和有竞争力的全球供应链不可或缺的一部分。具体而言，全球供应链中的客户和供应商关系管理主要包括以下几个方面：关系建立和维护、合作与协作、绩效评估和反馈、风险管理和持续改进。

The customer and supplier relationship management in the global supply chain is of vital importance to ensure that MNCs remain competitive in today's complex and changing business environment. Effective relationship management can enhance the transparency of the supply chain and improve the speed and flexibility of the enterprise's response to market changes, while reducing operating costs and increasing stability through long-term cooperation. It promotes the exchange of knowledge and technology, drives innovation in products and services, and enhances the competitiveness of the enterprise in the market. Moreover, through close customer and supplier relationships, MNCs can better manage and mitigate risks, establish cooperation based on trust, enhance brand reputation, and address challenges such as laws and regulations and cultural differences in the global market. The deepening of these relationships helps to promote social responsibility practices and achieve sustainability goals throughout the supply chain, ensuring that MNCs are responsible to society and the environment while pursuing economic benefits. In summary, customer and supplier relationship management is an indispensable part of building a robust, efficient, and competitive global supply chain. Specifically, the customer and supplier relationship management in the global supply chain mainly includes the following aspects: relationship building and maintenance, cooperation and collaboration, performance evaluation and feedback, risk management and continuous improvement.

(1) Relationship building and maintenance

Relationship building requires not only establishing clear selection criteria and review processes but also maintaining relationships through long-term cooperation agreements, joint performance goals, and continuous communication mechanisms. In addition, establishing trust and transparency can promote deeper cooperation, such as joint product development and marketing activities.

(2) Cooperation and collaboration

Deepening cooperation and collaboration requires MNCs to take a more proactive role in the supply chain, clarifying the responsibilities and rights of all parties through cooperation framework agreements (CFA). At the same time, using IT, such as supply chain management software and real-time data exchange systems, can enhance collaborative work, optimize inventory management, and reduce uncertainty and inventory backlog in the entire supply chain.

(3) Performance evaluation and feedback

The improvement of the performance evaluation system needs to include the setting of key performance indicators (KPIs), such as order fulfillment rate, delivery time, product quality, and cost-effectiveness. In addition, regular performance review meetings and feedback loops can ensure that supply chain partners are informed of their performance in a timely manner and make necessary adjustments based on feedback.

(4) Risk management and continuous improvement

The formulation of risk management strategies should be based on a comprehensive supply chain risk assessment, including the assessment of suppliers' financial stability, production capacity, compliance, and potential geopolitical risks. Continuous improvement requires MNCs to establish data-based decision-making mechanisms, use supply chain analysis tools to identify opportunities for improvement, and enhance the overall performance of the supply chain through lean management and continuous learning.

In addition, the customer and supplier relationship management in the global supply chain should also consider the following details. One is cultural and regional differences. In cross-cultural and cross-regional supply chains, understanding and respecting business customs and values in different cultural backgrounds is crucial for maintaining good cooperative relationships. The second is technology and innovation. Continuously exploring and adopting new technologies, such as blockchain and AI, can improve the transparency, traceability, and level of automation of the supply chain. The third is environmental and social responsibility. In the global supply chain, MNCs should actively fulfill environmental and social responsibilities, and enhance the ethical standards of the supply chain through sustainable procurement and social responsibility programs. Lastly, compliance and regulatory adherence, ensuring that supply chain activities comply with international trade regulations and the laws and regulations of the target market to reduce legal risks and reputational risks.

第三节　全球供应链的采购管理
（Global Supply Chain Procurement Management）

As globalization continues to deepen, the interdependence between MNCs is increasingly strengthening, making supply chain management the key to modern business competition. Especially in the procurement process, it is not only related to cost control and risk management but also directly affects the enterprise's market response speed and customer satisfaction.

Global supply chain procurement management is a core component of corporate strategic planning. Firstly, it provides cost benefits to MNCs through the optimization of resources on a global scale, while diversifying procurement channels to disperse supply risks. In addition, global procurement promotes the improvement of product quality and drives innovation, enabling MNCs to quickly respond to market changes and accelerate the innovation and launch of products and services. The flexibility of procurement management is crucial for dealing with market fluctuations and demand changes, helping MNCs to achieve agility and adaptability in the supply chain. At the same time, global procurement also emphasizes compliance and social responsibility, promoting MNCs to comply with laws and regulations in international transactions, and pay attention to environmental protection and labor standards, thereby enhancing the enterprise's social image and brand value. By establishing strategic partnerships with global suppliers, MNCs can share information, resources, and market opportunities to jointly develop new growth points. Ultimately, effective global supply chain procurement management can become the core competitiveness of the enterprise, providing a lasting competitive advantage in the global market, and ensuring its sustainable development and long-term success in the ever-changing business environment.

1. Characteristics of supply chain procurement

供应链采购具有跨区域、跨文化和跨时区的特点。它要求跨国公司在全球范围内寻找最佳的供应商资源，同时还要应对不同国家和地区的法律法规、市场条件和文化差异。此外，供应链采购还强调整个供应链的整合与协调，以实现资源的优化配置。

Supply chain procurement is characterized by being cross-regional, cross-cultural, and cross-time zones. It requires MNCs to seek out the best supplier resources on a global scale while also dealing with the laws and regulations, market conditions, and cultural differences of different countries and regions. In addition, supply chain procurement also emphasizes the integration and coordination of the entire supply chain to achieve optimal allocation of resources.

(1) Cross-regional

Cross-regional procurement means that MNCs must cross geographical boundaries to obtain resources and materials from different countries and regions. This feature requires MNCs to have a global perspective, be able to identify and assess suppliers in different areas, and understand the supply capacity and cost structure of various markets. Cross-regional procurement increases the diversity of the supply chain but also brings about logistical complexity, requiring MNCs to have efficient logistics coordination capabilities and risk management strategies to ensure the continuity and stability of the supply chain. For example, Apple Inc. sources electronic components and assembly services globally, with a supply chain that spans Asia, Europe, and the Americas. Apple must manage a complex logistics network to ensure that parts purchased from different regions arrive efficiently and on time at the final assembly locations.

(2) Cross-cultural

Cross-cultural procurement involves communicating and cooperating with suppliers and customers from different cultural backgrounds. This requires MNCs not only to understand the business practices and communication methods in different cultures but also to respect cultural differences and adapt to business practices in different cultural environments. Cross-cultural management skills are crucial for establishing and maintaining international supplier relationships, helping to promote trust and cooperation, reduce misunderstandings and conflicts, and thereby improve the collaborative efficiency of the supply chain. For instance, the German car manufacturer BMW must adapt to the business cultures and working methods when cooperating with suppliers in countries such as China, the United States, and South Africa. BMW ensures effective communication and cooperation with global suppliers through cross-cultural training and localized management teams.

（3）Cross-time zones

Cross-time zone procurement adds time sensitivity to supply chain management. Time zone differences between regions pose challenges to information exchange, decision-making, and logistics scheduling. MNCs need to establish effective communication mechanisms and time management strategies to coordinate operational activities across different regions. Moreover, cross-time zone operations also require MNCs to respond quickly to market changes and customer demands, which often involves adopting advanced IT and automation tools to achieve real-time monitoring and instant communication. For example, as a global e-commerce giant, Amazon boasts supply chain management that can well deal with the challenges across time zones. Amazon has established a global logistics network and uses highly automated warehouse management systems to achieve uninterrupted 24-hour order processing and delivery services to meet the needs of customers in different regions.

In summary, the characteristics of being cross-regional, cross-cultural, and cross-time zones pose high demands for integration and coordination in global supply chain procurement management. MNCs must develop a comprehensive management framework to address the challenges brought by these characteristics and achieve effective allocation of global resources and efficient operation of the supply chain by optimizing the structure and processes of the supply chain.

2. Global procurement

全球采购是供应链管理中的一个重要组成部分,它涉及跨国界的原材料、零部件和服务的采购。跨国公司通过全球采购可以获取更优质的资源、降低成本,并提高供应链的竞争力。然而,全球采购也带来了一系列挑战,如物流复杂性、供应链风险和文化差异等。通常,全球采购战略涉及以下方面:市场和供应商分析、合规和监管遵守、质量和标准管理、成本效益分析、物流和分销管理、文化和沟通战略、技术和信息系统、风险管理和应急计划、持续关系和合作发展。

Global procurement is an essential component of supply chain management, involving the cross-border purchasing of raw materials, components, and services. By engaging in global procurement, MNCs can access higher-quality resources, reduce costs, and enhance the competitiveness of their supply chains. However, global procurement also brings a range of challenges, such as logistical complexity, supply chain risks, and cultural differences. Figure 8-1 shows the World Bank's core procurement principles. These principles should be kept in mind during the entire global procurement process, in particular during the early stages of strategy development and procurement planning, as well as when potential suppliers or contractors are assessed and evaluated. Usually, global procurement strategy involves the following aspects: market and supplier analysis, compliance and regulatory adherence, quality and standard management, cost-benefit analysis, logistics and distribution management, culture and communication strategies, technology and information systems, risk management and contingency planning, ongoing relationships and cooperative development.

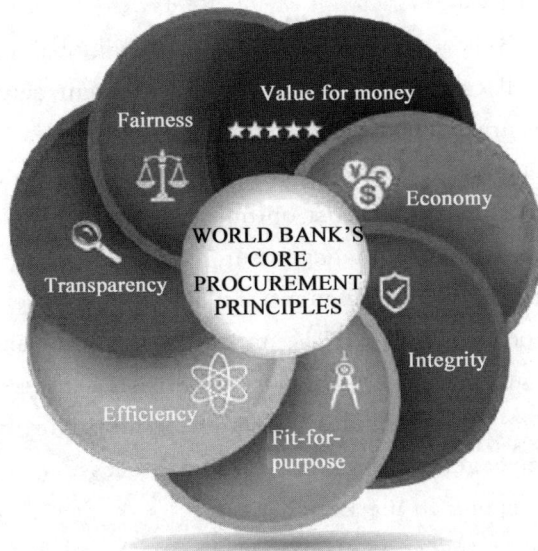

Figure 8-1　The World Bank's core procurement principles

Source: Supply Chain Management, World Bank, 2023

(1) Market and supplier analysis

Market and supplier analysis is the cornerstone of global procurement strategy. MNCs must conduct in-depth research on global markets, assessing the supplier base, production capacity, cost-effectiveness, and potential risks of different countries and regions. This includes a detailed evaluation of suppliers' technical capabilities, quality management systems, delivery reliability, and price competitiveness. Through such analysis, MNCs can identify the best supplier resources and establish a stable and efficient supply chain network.

(2) Compliance and regulatory adherence

Compliance and regulatory adherence are indispensable in global procurement. When engaging in cross-border procurement, MNCs must ensure their activities comply with the laws and regulations of the host country and the international market, including trade agreements, tariff policies, environmental standards, and labor laws. Additionally, MNCs should establish a contractual legal framework to protect themselves from legal risks and ensure the legality and ethics of all business activities.

(3) Quality and standard management

Quality and standard management are crucial for maintaining the consistency and reliability of products and services. Global procurement requires MNCs to establish strict quality control systems to ensure suppliers follow internationally recognized quality standards and management specifications. Through continuous quality improvement and standardization processes, MNCs can ensure the performance and safety of procured products, meeting consumer needs and expectations.

(4) Cost-benefit analysis

Cost-benefit analysis is a key factor in evaluating global procurement decisions. MNCs need to assess all costs associated with procurement activities, including direct costs such as purchase prices and transportation fees, as well as indirect costs such as tariffs, insurance, and potential risk costs. By analyzing the total cost of ownership, MNCs can identify opportunities for cost optimization and minimize supply chain costs.

(5) Logistics and distribution management

Logistics and distribution management are operational essentials for ensuring the success of global procurement. MNCs must design efficient transportation and distribution networks to minimize transportation costs, shorten delivery times, and improve service levels. This includes selecting appropriate transportation modes, optimizing inventory management and distribution processes, and establishing flexible logistics strategies to respond to market changes.

(6) Culture and communication strategies

Culture and communication strategies are vital for partnerships in global procurement. MNCs need to understand and respect business practices and communication styles across different cultural backgrounds, establishing effective cross-cultural communication mechanisms. By fostering cultural sensitivity and communication skills, MNCs can strengthen relationships with suppliers and facilitate accurate transmission and timely feedback of information.

(7) Technology and information systems

Technology and information systems form the technological foundation supporting global procurement activities. MNCs need to utilize advanced IT, such as ERP systems, supply chain management software, and e-commerce platforms, to manage global procurement processes. Through data integration and real-time monitoring, MNCs can improve the efficiency and accuracy of decision-making.

(8) Risk management and contingency planning

Risk management and contingency planning are important to preventing and dealing with uncertainties in global procurement. MNCs need to identify and assess risks that may be encountered in the global procurement process and develop corresponding risk mitigation strategies and emergency response plans. This helps MNCs to act swiftly in the face of political instability, exchange rate fluctuations, or supply chain disruptions, ensuring the stability of the supply chain.

(9) Ongoing relationships and cooperative development

Ongoing relationships and cooperative development are the long-term goals of global procurement strategy. MNCs need to establish long-term strategic partnerships with suppliers, achieving mutual benefit through joint growth and development. This includes innovating cooperation models, sharing market information and technical resources, and establishing trust-and transparency-based cooperative relationships. Through in-depth analysis and strategic implementation in these areas, MNCs can optimize their supply chains in global procurement, enhance competitiveness, and maintain a leading position in the ever-changing global market.

3. Supplier selection

供应商选择是采购管理的核心组成部分。采购供应商的选择涉及质量和合规性评估、成本效益分析、交付和创新能力、合作和风险管理。

Supplier selection is a core component of procurement management. In the context of globalization, MNCs need to assess and choose suppliers who can provide high-quality products, competitive prices, and meet delivery time requirements. The selection of suppliers is not only based on price and quality but also includes their innovation capabilities, willingness to cooperate, and commitment to social responsibility. Procurement supplier selection involves quality and compliance assessment, cost and benefit analysis, delivery and innovation capability, cooperation and risk management.

（1）Quality and compliance assessment

In the quality and compliance assessment phase of suppliers, MNCs need to carefully examine the suppliers' quality management systems, including whether they have passed international quality management standards such as ISO certification, and whether their products meet industry quality and safety standards. In addition, the company's compliance considerations should extend to the suppliers' social responsibility practices, like their performance in environmental protection, labor rights, and anti-corruption. This requires MNCs to conduct thorough background checks and on-site audits to ensure that the suppliers' business operations are not only compliant but also ethical and meet sustainable development requirements.

（2）Cost and benefit analysis

Cost and benefit analysis is a key step in the supplier selection process. MNCs need to assess the total cost of ownership of cooperating with suppliers, including direct procurement costs, transportation and logistics expenses, potential repair and replacement costs, and implicit costs related to quality. By quantifying the analysis of these cost factors, MNCs can determine the most cost-effective supplier options. At the same time, MNCs should also consider the long-term benefits brought by supplier cooperation, such as production efficiency improvements through the adoption of new technologies or process improvements.

（3）Delivery and innovation capability

Delivery capability is one of the important indicators to measure supplier performance. MNCs need to assess the suppliers' production capacity and logistics systems to ensure that they can meet the scheduled delivery times and quantity requirements, while also having the flexibility to cope with urgent orders and demand fluctuations. In addition, innovation capability is essential to the sustainable development of a company; therefore, MNCs should also examine the suppliers' investment in research and development, technical patents, and new product development capabilities, as well as their adaptability to market changes and willingness to jointly innovate products with the company.

（4）Cooperation and risk management

Cooperation and risk management are the foundations for the long-term stability of supplier relationships. MNCs need to assess the suppliers' willingness to cooperate, including their commitment to establishing long-term cooperative relationships, the transparency of communication, and the ability to respond to market changes. At the same time, MNCs must conduct a comprehensive assessment of the supplier's financial stability, legal compliance, and risk management strategies to ensure that they can effectively respond to external risks such as political, economic, and environmental factors. In addition, establishing clear contract terms and exit mechanisms can help MNCs flexibly adjust or terminate cooperative relationships when necessary to protect their interests.

第四节　全球供应链管理与信息技术
（The Management of Global Supply Chain and Information Technology）

In today's globalized economic environment, supply chain management has become a core component of business operations. The rapid development and widespread application of IT have provided new perspectives and tools for global supply chain management. These tools not only optimize the operation of the supply chain but also enhance its transparency and responsiveness. This section aims to explore the application of IT in global supply chain management and analyze how e-commerce interacts with global supply chain management to improve efficiency and competitiveness.

1. Application of IT in global supply chain management

IT 的应用渗透到全球供应链管理的各个方面。从供应链规划、采购、制造、库存管理到物流和客户服务，IT 工具的使用大大提高了供应链的效率和有效性。

The application of IT permeates every aspect of global supply chain management. From supply chain planning, procurement, manufacturing, inventory management to logistics and customer service, the use of IT tools has greatly improved the efficiency and effectiveness of the supply chain. For instance, ERP system, Supply Chain Management （SCM）software, and advanced analytics tools are all indispensable technological support for modern supply chains.

（1）Big data analysis and business intelligence

在供应链管理中，大数据分析和商务智能的应用至关重要，它们使跨国公司能够从海量的数据中提取有价值的信息，从而优化决策过程。具体来说，集成来自供应链各个环节的数据，包括销售点、库存系统、物流跟踪和客户反馈；利用实时数据分析工具监控供应链状态，快速响应市场变化和潜在的供应链中断；应用统计模型和机器学习算法预测需求波动、价格变化和供应链风险；基于数据分析结果优化库存水平、生产计划和运输路线，降低成本并提高服务水平；分析客户行为和偏好，以制定更精准的市场策略和产品开发计划；识别潜在的供应链风险，如供应商不稳定、物流延迟或需求突变，并制定相应的缓解措施。

In supply chain management, the application of big data analysis and business intelligence is crucial. They enable MNCs to extract valuable information from vast amounts of data, thereby optimizing the decision-making process. Specifically, integrating data from all links of the supply chain, including Point of Sale (POS), inventory systems, logistics tracking, and customer feedback; using real-time data analysis tools to monitor the status of the supply chain, and respond quickly to market changes and potential supply chain disruptions; applying statistical models and machine learning algorithms to predict demand fluctuations, price changes, and supply chain risks; optimizing inventory levels, production plans, and transportation routes based on data analysis results to reduce costs and improve service levels; analyzing customer behaviors and preferences to formulate more precise marketing strategies and product development plans; identifying potential supply chain risks, such as supplier instability, logistics delays, or demand changes, and developing corresponding mitigation measures.

For example, as an e-commerce giant, Amazon uses big data analysis to optimize its supply chain. By analyzing consumers' purchase history, search behavior, and feedback, Amazon can predict demand and adjust inventory while providing a personalized shopping experience. Walmart uses business intelligence tools to analyze sales data and consumer trends, thereby optimizing its supply chain network and inventory management. Walmart's efficient supply chain is partly attributed to its data analysis capabilities, enabling it to replenish stocks quickly and reduce inventory backlog. As a fast fashion brand, Zara responds quickly to market trends by analyzing global sales data. Its supply chain can update designs and adjust production in a short time, thanks to its powerful data analysis and business intelligence systems.

These cases show how big data analysis and business intelligence help MNCs achieve higher efficiency, better customer service, and stronger market adaptability in supply chain management. With the advancement of technology, the application of these tools will become more extensive and in-depth, bringing more innovation and value to supply chain management.

（2）AI and machine learning

In supply chain management, the application of AI and machine learning is becoming increasingly critical. They simulate human intelligence to deal with complex problems, optimize forecasting models, and enhance the level of automation. Specifically, AI and machine learning algorithms can analyze historical sales data and other market factors to more accurately predict product demand. Utilizing machine learning models, supply chains can automate certain decision-making processes, such as inventory replenishment, price adjustments, and order processing. AI systems can identify abnormal patterns in supply chain data, providing early warnings of potential quality issues or supply chain disruptions. Machine learning can be used to optimize transportation routes and scheduling, reducing transportation costs and improving delivery efficiency. AI technology can predict equipment failures, reducing production downtime through predictive maintenance. Additionally, AI technology can analyze customer feedback and social media data to gain insights into customer satisfaction and market trends.

For example, the Chinese e-commerce company JD. com uses AI for demand forecasting and intelligent inventory management. JD's AI system can predict the demand for different products in different regions, thereby optimizing inventory distribution and logistics planning. IBM's Watson AI platform is used in multiple aspects of supply chain management, including risk analysis and predictive maintenance. Watson's machine learning capabilities help businesses identify potential supply chain issues and take preemptive measures. General Electric (GE) uses machine learning algorithms to optimize its complex global supply chain. By analyzing a vast amount of supply chain data, GE can predict and mitigate supply chain disruptions, improving operational efficiency. These cases show how AI and machine learning bring intelligent solutions to supply chain management, improving the accuracy of forecasts, optimizing operational decisions, and enhancing the ability to respond to complex supply chain issues. As AI technology continues to evolve, its application in supply chain management will become more extensive, helping businesses achieve higher levels of automation and intelligence.

（3）Blockchain technology

The application of blockchain technology in supply chain management provides a secure, transparent, and tamper-proof way of sharing data, which is significant for enhancing traceability, and increasing the transparency and trust in multi-party collaboration within the supply chain. Specifically, the distributed ledger technology of blockchain ensures that once data is recorded, it cannot be altered, providing a guarantee of data integrity for the supply chain. Blockchain allows MNCs to track every step of a product, from raw materials to finished goods, increasing the transparency of product origin and the process of circulation. Automated smart contracts execute automatically when preset conditions are met, simplifying the transaction process and reducing paper documentation and manual intervention. Blockchain technology promotes collaboration among different participants in the supply chain, improving the efficiency and consistency of information sharing through a shared ledger. By providing transparent data records, blockchain helps to identify and prevent fraudulent activities and risks in the supply chain. Blockchain technology can also improve supply chain financial processes, such as reducing financing costs and improving financing efficiency through transaction records recorded on the blockchain.

For instance, IBM's Food Trust platform is a prime example of blockchain technology applied in the food supply chain. Through this platform, consumers can scan Quick Response (QR) codes on products to obtain information about the food's origin, processing, transportation, and sales, enhancing their confidence in food safety. De Beers' blockchain platform Tracr allows consumers to verify the origin and journey of the diamonds they purchase. This platform ensures the legality and ethics of diamonds, protecting the reputation of consumers and the diamond industry. Walmart in China uses blockchain technology to track the food supply chain, improving traceability, reducing the impact of food safety incidents, and increasing consumer trust in the brand. These cases show how blockchain technology brings increased transparency and efficiency to supply chain management and helps businesses establish a safer and more credible supply chain environment. As blockchain technology continues to develop and mature, its application in supply chain management will become more extensive and in-depth.

(4) Other information technologies

In addition to big data and business intelligence, AI and machine learning, and blockchain technology, other information technologies such as ERP system, warehouse management system (WMS), transportation management system (TMS), and customer relationship management (CRM) system also play a crucial role in supply chain management. They not only improve the efficiency and effectiveness of the supply chain but also reduce operational costs and enhance the competitiveness of MNCs in the market. As technology continues to advance, these tools and systems will continue to evolve, bringing more innovative possibilities for supply chain management.

Specifically, ERP system provides a unified data platform for supply chain management by integrating the core business processes of an enterprise, ensuring the consistency and real-time nature of data, thereby improving the efficiency and accuracy of decision-making. WMS enhances the accuracy and efficiency of inventory management through automated warehouse operations, reducing human errors and operational costs. TMS reduces transportation costs by optimizing routes and modes of transport, and improve the transparency of the supply chain through real-time tracking. CRM system helps

MNCs better understand customer needs by collecting and analyzing customer data, providing personalized services, and enhancing customer satisfaction and loyalty. Cloud technology supports remote collaboration in the supply chain and the scalability of systems by providing flexible data storage and access capabilities. Advanced analytics tools assist MNCs in assessing the potential outcomes of different decision-making scenarios through predictive analysis, simulation, and optimization algorithms, optimizing the decision-making process. Mobile computing technology enables field operations and instant communication in supply chain management through mobile devices and applications, improving the response speed and flexibility of the supply chain.

2. IT in global supply chain management

IT 在供应链管理中扮演着多重角色。它不仅是数据收集和处理的工具，也是决策支持系统的重要组成部分。通过实时数据分析和预测模型，企业可以更准确地预测市场需求，优化库存水平，降低库存积累和过剩的风险。

IT plays multiple roles in supply chain management. It serves not only as a tool for data collection and processing but also as a vital component of decision support systems. Through real-time data analysis and forecasting models, businesses can predict market demand more accurately, optimize inventory levels, and reduce the risks of stock accumulation and excess.

(1) Data collection and processing capabilities

IT is first and foremost reflected in its robust data collection and processing capabilities in supply chain management. Through integrated information systems, MNCs can capture data from various stages of the supply chain in real-time, including order processing, inventory status, and logistics progress. The effective processing of this data provides the foundation for supply chain transparency and traceability, allowing supply chain managers to clearly perceive the entire flow process of products from raw materials to end-users. For example, Walmart uses its advanced supply chain management system to collect and process data from global suppliers, warehouses, and retail stores. Through real-time data analysis, Walmart can optimize inventory management, ensuring ample goods on the shelves while reducing excess inventory.

(2) Decision support systems

IT also serves as an essential component of decision support systems, providing necessary information and analytical tools for supply chain management decision-making. MNCs can utilize advanced analytical tools, such as forecasting analytics, simulations, and optimization algorithms, to support complex decision-making processes. These tools help managers evaluate the potential outcomes of different decision-making scenarios, leading to wiser and more efficient decisions. For instance, Dell uses sophisticated decision support systems to analyze market data and consumer behaviors, thereby formulating its production plans for customized computers. These systems help Dell reduce inventory backlog while quickly responding to market changes.

（3）Market demand forecasting

By applying IT, MNCs can predict market demand more accurately. Forecasting models can predict future market demand using information such as historical sales data, market trends, seasonal factors, and consumer behaviors. This forecasting capability is crucial for optimizing production plans, inventory management, and product distribution, helping to reduce the risks of stock accumulation and excess. For example, Amazon collects and analyzes a vast amount of online consumer data, including search history, purchase behavior, and product reviews, to predict market demand. This enables Amazon to adjust inventory in advance and optimize its logistics network to meet consumer needs.

（4）Inventory optimization and risk reduction

IT enables MNCs to optimize inventory levels based on market demand forecasts. By implementing automated inventory management systems and adopting real-time inventory tracking technologies, MNCs can maintain optimal inventory status, reducing the risks of stock accumulation and excess. At the same time, IT also supports the establishment of safety stock strategies to cope with market uncertainties and potential supply chain disruptions. For example, Zara implements an efficient inventory management system that allows for rapid response to market trend changes. Zara's supply chain uses IT to monitor inventory levels and adjust production plans in a timely manner to reduce the risk of obsolete inventory.

（5）Supply chain collaboration and responsiveness

Furthermore, IT promotes collaboration among various stages of the supply chain. By sharing information platforms, supply chain partners can share data and information in real-time, strengthening collaboration and improving the overall responsiveness of the supply chain. This collaboration not only speeds up the supply chain's reaction time but also enhances the efficiency and effectiveness of the entire supply chain network. For example, Cisco Systems has established an integrated supply chain collaboration platform that enables real-time information sharing with its global suppliers and partners. This platform has improved Cisco's response speed to supply chain disruptions and strengthened the collaborative efficiency of the entire supply chain.

In summary, IT plays an essential role in global supply chain management. It not only enhances the transparency and efficiency of the supply chain but also provides businesses with powerful decision support, helping them better cope with market fluctuations and uncertainties.

3. E-commerce and global supply chain management

电子商务对全球供应链管理的影响是多方面的,主要表现在以下几个方面：市场扩张和客户接触点的增加,订单处理和物流配送的创新,需求预测、风险管理和供应链透明度,技术整合、供应链协作和环境责任。

The rise of e-commerce has further propelled the development of global supply chain management. The emergence of online platforms and digital markets has provided businesses with new sales channels and customer touch points. At the same time, e-commerce also demands that supply chain management can quickly adapt to market changes, achieving more flexible order processing and delivery services. The impact of e-commerce on global supply chain management is multifaceted, mainly manifested in the following aspects: market expansion and increased customer touchpoints; innovation in order processing and logistics distribution; demand forecasting, risk management, and supply chain transparency; technological integration, supply chain collaboration, and environmental responsibility.

(1) Market expansion and increased customer touchpoints

The rise of e-commerce has greatly expanded market boundaries, allowing businesses to enter the global market through online platforms and reach a broader consumer base. This market expansion not only increases sales channels but also provides businesses with valuable customer data and feedback, enabling them to more accurately understand consumer needs and to adjust their supply chain strategies accordingly. At the same time, the interactivity of e-commerce platforms has enhanced customer touch points, offering businesses a direct channel for communication and transaction with consumers.

(2) Innovation in order processing and logistics distribution

Under the e-commerce environment, order processing in the supply chain has become more automated and efficient. Utilizing advanced IT, businesses can quickly process a large number of orders, reduce errors, and improve customer satisfaction. In addition, e-commerce has also driven innovation in logistics distribution services, including express tracking, unmanned delivery, and instant delivery services. These services have improved the speed and reliability of delivery, as well as enhanced the consumer's shopping experience.

(3) Demand forecasting, risk management, and supply chain transparency

The big data generated by e-commerce platforms provides unprecedented insights for supply chain management. Businesses can use this data for more accurate market demand forecasting, optimize inventory management, and reduce inventory backlog. At the same time, e-commerce has also enhanced the transparency of the supply chain, with consumers able to track the status of orders and product information in real-time. This requires all links in the supply chain to provide clear and timely information updates. In addition, e-commerce has also promoted the improvement of risk management, helping businesses to identify and respond to potential market risks in a timely manner.

（4）Technological integration, supply chain collaboration, and environmental responsibility

The development of e-commerce has promoted the application and innovation of technology in supply chain management. The application of technologies such as cloud computing, big data analysis, and AI has made supply chain decision-making more intelligent and automated. The collaborative work of various links in the supply chain has also been strengthened due to e-commerce, improving the efficiency and response speed of the entire supply chain. At the same time, e-commerce has also raised businesses' awareness of environmental and social responsibilities, prompting them to adopt more sustainable and responsible practices in supply chain management to meet the expectations of consumers and society.

In summary, e-commerce has not only changed traditional business models but also had a profound impact on global supply chain management. It has driven innovation and development in the supply chain, enabling businesses to respond more effectively to market changes, improve operational efficiency, and meet consumer needs.

关键术语（Key Terms）

全球供应链管理（global supply chain management）

全球供应链合作伙伴关系（global supply chain partnerships）

采购管理（procurement management）

全球采购（global procurement）

供应商选择（supplier selection）

大数据分析与商务智能（big data analysis and business intelligence）

人工智能与机器学习（artificial intelligence and machine learning）

区块链技术（blockchain technology）

弹性供应链（resilient supply chain）

供应链结构优化（supply chain structure optimization）

多米诺骨牌效应（domino effect）

小结（Summary）

1. Supply chain management is an integrated management process that covers the entire process from raw material procurement, product manufacturing, inventory management, logistics distribution to the final delivery of the product to the consumer. Supply chain management now spans multiple countries and regions, characterized by trans-regionality, complexity, and dynamism. The main contents of global supply chain management include: supply chain design, supplier and procurement management, production and manufacturing management, inventory and logistics management, demand forecasting, order processing and customer service management, risk and IT management, sustainability and social responsibility. The design of a global supply chain management system can be simplified into the following five key areas: strategy and network design, process and technology architecture, resource and capability planning,

risk and compliance management, performance and continuous improvement.

2. Relationship management in global supply chains includes the establishment and maintenance of partnerships, partner selection strategies, and effective management of customer and supplier relationships. Partner selection relates to the four assessments on potential partners: strategic and core competitiveness alignment, financial stability and operational efficiency, risk management and compliance adherence, cultural compatibility and long-term cooperation perspective.

3. Supply chain procurement is characterized by being cross-regional, cross-cultural, and cross-time zones. Global procurement strategy involves the following aspects: market and supplier analysis, compliance and regulatory adherence, quality and standard management, cost-benefit analysis, logistics and distribution management, culture and communication strategies, technology and information systems, risk management and contingency planning, ongoing relationships and cooperative development. Procurement supplier selection involves quality and compliance assessment, cost and benefit analysis, delivery and innovation capability, cooperation and risk management.

4. The application of IT permeates every aspect of global supply chain management. From supply chain planning, procurement, manufacturing, inventory management to logistics and customer service, the use of IT tools has greatly improved the efficiency and effectiveness of the supply chain. IT plays multiple roles in supply chain management. It serves not only as a tool for data collection and processing but also as a vital component of decision support systems. The impact of e-commerce on global supply chain management is multifaceted, mainly manifested in the following aspects: market expansion and increased customer touch points; innovation in order processing and logistics distribution; demand forecasting, risk management, and supply chain transparency; technological integration, supply chain collaboration, and environmental responsibility.

延伸阅读(Further Readings)

习题(Exercises)

第 九 章

Chapter 9
跨国公司的人力资源管理
Human Resource Management of
Multinational Corporations

Learning Objectives

- To define international human resource management
- To understand the orientations of international human resource management and their matching with MNCs' strategies
- To explain how expatriate managers are recruited and selected
- To know the training types and rigor of expatriates
- To identify performance appraisal steps
- To understand how expatriates should be compensated

第一节　国际人力资源管理的概念
（The Concept of International Human Resource Management）

1. The term of international human resource management

跨国公司的人力资源管理也称为国际人力资源管理,是跨越国境的人力资源管理活动。国际人力资源管理不是国内人力资源管理的简单延伸,因为国际人力资源管理是服务于不同跨国公司战略的一项职能管理。当跨国公司制定了不同的战略时,国际人力资源管理也会相应采取不同的管理导向。与国内人力资源管理类似,国际人力资源管理的主要活动包括:人力资源规划、人员招聘与选拔、培训与开发、绩效评价、薪酬设计、劳资关系管理等,即选人、育人、用人、留人。

The main activities of human resource management（HRM）include recruitment, selection, training and development, performance appraisal, compensation, and labor relations. HRM deals with the overall relationship of the employee with the organization. Its major goals are managing and developing human assets. The following are the basic HRM functions: First, recruitment, which means the identification of qualified individuals for a vacant position. Second, selection, which refers to choosing an individual for the position. Third, training, which means providing opportunities to help the individual perform. Fourth, performance appraisal, which means assessing the individual's performance. Fifth, compensation, which refers to providing the adequate reward package. Lastly, labor relations, which means dealing with the relationship between the individual and the company.

International human resource management (IHRM) involves all the HRM functions adapting to the international setting. There are two added complexities compared to domestic HRM. One is the mixture of workers of different nationalities. Another is the necessary to decide how much HRM policies should be adapted to national culture, business culture, and social institutions. Types of employees in MNCs are as follows. The first type is expatriates, the employees who come from a country that is different from the one in which they are working. The second is home-country nationals, the employees who come from the parent company's home country. The next is host-country nationals, local workers who come from the host country where the unit is located. Fourth, third-country nationals, expatriate workers who come from neither the host nor home country. Fifth, inpatriates, the employees from foreign countries who work in the country where the parent company is located. Sixth, flexpatriates, the employees who are sent on frequent but short-term international assignments. Lastly, international cadres, the managers who specialize in international assignments. More MNCs are seeking internationally experienced managerial talent to run their operations in the global market. The key ingredient of any successful strategy of MNCs includes using compatible HRM policies. Given the high cost of expatriate assignments, flexpatriates and short-term assignments are currently becoming more popular.

2. Characteristics of international human resource management

国际人力资源管理与国内人力资源管理的最大区别在于对外派员工的管理,这是国内人力资源管理所没有的职责。

The biggest difference between IHRM and domestic HRM is the management of expatriate employees, which is a responsibility that domestic HRM does not have. Compared to domestic HRM, IHRM has the following characteristics.

(1) Complex external environment

Due to significant differences in economic, political, legal, cultural, and business systems between the home country and host country of MNCs, their operations and management are undoubtedly more influenced by external factors compared to domestic enterprises. This clearly has a direct or indirect impact on IHRM. For example, most developed countries require MNCs to comply with rules and regulations such as trade unions, taxation, health, and safety, but developing countries have incomplete or vastly different laws and regulations in these areas, which requires human resource managers to understand and be familiar with local business practices and behavioral norms as much as possible.

(2) More management functions

In addition to managing expatriates, the human resources department of MNCs is also responsible for handling responsibilities that domestic HRM does not have to undertake, such as understanding host country policies, addressing international taxation, establishing cross-cultural orientation, etc.

（3）Strong global consciousness

Compared to domestic HRM departments, the MNCs' HRM departments face a global talent pool when recruiting personnel. Managers must have a broad global perspective and introduce talents without any restrictions, regardless of the nationality, skin color, gender, mother tongue, religious beliefs, etc. of job seekers.

（4）Outstanding overseas risks

Currently, the international environment is complex and ever-changing, with outbreaks of diseases, terrorist attacks, and localized wars occurring from time to time. Incidents of smashing, looting, and burning of MNCs' local offices triggered by populist ideologies in host countries are also not uncommon. This brings great uncertainties and risks to the daily lives, property, and safety of MNCs' expatriates in host countries. Once these risks occur, they will bring huge losses and are important factors that MNCs have to consider when managing expatriates.

（5）Comprehensive personnel care

In addition to daily selection, training, and development, IHRM also requires participation in the personal lives of expatriates, which includes finding suitable accommodation for expatriates in the host country, assisting with the placement or visit of expatriates' families, facilitating enrolling expatriates' children in school, paying taxes at local banks, etc.

第二节　国际人力资源管理导向
（Orientations of International Human Resource Management）

1. The term of IHRM orientation

正如组织结构须追随公司战略一样，作为跨国公司的一项管理职能，国际人力资源管理也需要适应跨国公司所制定的战略。即有什么样的公司战略，就有什么样的国际人力资源管理导向与之匹配。国际人力资源管理导向是指跨国公司在进行人力资源管理时所遵循的哲学理念。国际人力资源管理导向一般可分为民族中心导向、多国中心导向、区域中心导向和全球中心导向四种，每种导向在人力资源管理的具体实践中都有不同的做法。

Just as organizational structure has to follow company strategy, as one of the management functions of MNCs, IHRM also needs to adapt to the strategies formulated by MNCs. IHRM orientation should be matched with the corresponding company strategy. MNCs have several options for developing the appropriate IHRM policies for the implementation of their strategies. One way is to examine its IHRM orientation, or philosophy. IHRM orientation is a company's basic tactics and philosophy for coordinating IHRM activities for managerial and technical workers. There are four basic IHRM orientations such as ethnocentric IHRM orientation, polycentric IHRM orientation, regiocentric IHRM orientation, and global IHRM orientation. Ethnocentric IHRM orientation means all aspects of HRM tend to follow the parent organization's home country HRM practices. However, under regiocentric and polycentric IHRM orientations, HRM is more responsive to the host country differences in practices. Different from these orientations, global IHRM orientation implies the firm assigns its best managers to international assignments, recruiting worldwide.

(1) Ethnocentric IHRM orientation

民族中心的国际人力资源管理导向指对管理者和技术雇员等人力资源管理的各个方面都倾向于遵循母国母公司的人力资源管理习惯。

Ethnocentric IHRM orientation refers to the tendency to follow the HRM habits of the parent company in all aspects of HRM, including managers and technical employees. In recruitment, important management and technical personnel come from their home countries, and host country nationals only occupy low-level and auxiliary positions. In MNCs that adopt an ethnocentric orientation, past performance and technical expertise in the home country determine the selection criteria for overseas assignments. Like the use of home country nationals for management and technical positions, evaluation and promotion also follow home country standards. The subsidiaries adopt the same standards and methods as the home country to evaluate the performance of managers. However, due to differences in national environments, companies may have to adopt different methods when evaluating and promoting local managers in the host country. Unfortunately, such local adjustments often have little impact on the promotion process for employees outside the lowest management level. Therefore, due to the limitations of production institutions and opportunities in the host country, the career development of host country nationals in companies is usually limited. When MNCs with ethnocentric IHRM orientation utilize expatriates, training for international assignments is often limited or non-existent. Except for high-level national or regional positions, most international assignments are short-term, often for marketing and signing sales contracts. The use of evaluation and promotion standards from the parent company, lack of training, and the short-term nature of overseas assignments all limit and hinder the cultural adjustment of expatriates. For example, expatriate managers from their home country rarely understand the language of the local country. In MNCs with ethnocentric IHRM orientation, accepting international positions may hurt the careers of managers and technical professionals. Since MNCs with ethnocentric IHRM orientation often concentrate important decisions in their home country, overseas managers find it difficult to successfully communicate with headquarters on local needs. In addition, expatriates often feel lonely due to being excluded from the core decision-making circle, and they have almost no opportunity to contact senior managers. As a result, expatriates often receive additional compensation, with a salary level higher than their domestic assignments.

（2）Polycentric IHRM orientation

采取多国中心国际人力资源管理导向的公司，对东道国在人力资源管理习惯上差异的反应比较强烈。多国中心导向强调适应各国文化与制度差异，并根据各个东道国的差异调整人力资源管理的具体实践。

Companies that adopt a polycentric IHRM orientation have a stronger reaction to differences in HRM habits in the host country. The polycentric IHRM orientation emphasizes adapting to cultural and institutional differences among countries, and adjusting specific practices of HRM according to the differences of each host country. MNCs with polycentric IHRM orientation treat HRM differently in each host country, and the parent company headquarters generally instructs its subsidiaries in each country to follow local HRM practices. Correspondingly, the company mainly recruits and selects managers from the host country, and the recruitment and selection criteria follow local practices. To enhance communication with the headquarters of MNCs, host country managers typically need to have proficient listening, speaking, reading, and writing skills in the language of the parent company's country. MNCs with polycentric IHRM orientation typically use home country citizens in senior management and technical positions, using home country managers to control overseas operations or transfer technology to overseas production institutions. Like the MNCs with ethnocentric IHRM orientation, MNCs with polycentric IHRM orientation still retain HRM for expatriates from their home countries at their headquarters, and only provide limited cross-cultural adaptation training and language training for home country managers. Unless the headquarters values the unique international experience of certain countries, international employment may still hurt the management careers of home country nationals. Unlike MNCs with ethnocentric IHRM orientation, MNCs with polycentric IHRM orientation tend to adopt local procedures and standards for the assessment and promotion of most host country nationals. The empowerment of headquarters allows host country managers to assess their own human resource needs and establish local assessment and promotion standards. Unlike the parent company, local culture also influences the procedures used by subsidiaries to assess and promote employees. In MNCs with polycentric IHRM orientation, host country employees receive salaries based on the host country's standards, while expatriates from their home country receive additional pay and benefits.

（3）Regiocentric IHRM orientation

区域中心导向的公司按地区调整国际人力资源管理方式，遵循所在区域的人力资源管理习惯，并采用地区范围的人力资源管理政策。

Companies that adopt a regiocentric IHRM orientation also have a strong response to the differences in HRM habits among different regions around the world. MNCs with regiocentric IHRM orientation adjust their HRM methods by region，following the HRM habits of their respective regions and adopting regional HRM policies. Correspondingly，MNCs with regiocentric IHRM orientation mainly adopt the conventions and standards of their respective regions to recruit and select employees，and may also seek important candidates who have already mastered the culture and language of the country in the region from their parent companies. To enhance communication with the headquarters of MNCs，managers of MNCs with regiocentric IHRM orientation must receive limited to moderate cross-cultural adaptation training and business language training，often in English. MNCs with regiocentric IHRM orientation typically use regional or national managers，and below in senior management and technical positions to allow employees within the region to take on these roles. International assignments have neutral to slightly positive career implications for home country nationals. Unlike MNCs with ethnocentric IHRM orientation，MNCs with regiocentric IHRM orientation tend to use the procedures and standards of their respective regions for the assessment and promotion of managers. The empowerment of headquarters allows regional managers to assess their own human resource needs and establish local assessment and promotion standards. Due to longer duration of overseas assignments，MNCs with regiocentric IHRM orientation generally provide less additional compensation for expatriates.

（4）Global IHRM orientation

采用全球中心国际人力资源管理导向的跨国公司将其最优秀的管理者委以国际任职，并在世界范围内任何可能发现优秀合格雇员的国家开展招聘和选拔，更注重管理者是否适合职位要求，而淡化任何对个人国籍或任职国家的考虑。

MNCs with global IHRM orientation entrust their best managers to international positions and conduct recruitment and selection in any country where excellent and qualified employees may be found worldwide，focusing more on whether the managers are suitable for the job requirements and downplaying any consideration of individual nationality or the country of employment. Therefore，capable managers can easily make adjustments to fully adapt to different cultures，and these managers are usually proficient in two or more languages. In addition，in MNCs with global IHRM orientation，international assignment is a prerequisite for a successful managerial career. Due to the fact that employees come from all over the world and often have different cultural backgrounds，the company's cross-border location configuration makes it easy for customers and suppliers with cultural differences to have conflicts. Therefore，MNCs with global IHRM orientation will continuously provide multilingual communication and cross-cultural training to their employees to adapt to cultural differences within and outside the company. In addition to cultural conflicts，managers in MNCs with global IHRM orientation must also meet the coordination and control requirements of the company headquarters. To successfully tackle these challenges，managers need to continuously train in cultural adaptation and develop skills that balance local needs with overall company goals. MNCs with global IHRM orientation evaluate employees based on their contribution to the company，and pay them based on this standard. Only limited adjustments are made to the compensation standards when there are special circumstances in certain regions or host countries.

Table 9-1 shows the application of the four IHRM orientations mentioned above in the IHRM practices for managers and technical workers.

Table 9-1　IHRM orientations and IHRM practices for managers and technical workers

IHRM Practices	IHRM Orientations			
	Ethnocentric	Polycentric	Regiocentric	Global
Recruitment and selection	Home country nationals for key positions selected by technical expertise or past home country performance; host country nationals for low levels of management only	Home country nationals for top management and technical positions; host country nationals for midlevel management positions; selection of home country nationals similar to ethnocentric; selection of host country nationals based on fit with home country culture, e. g. home country language ability	Home country nationals for top management and technical positions; regional country nationals for midlevel management and below	Worldwide throughout the company; based on best qualified for positions
Training for cross-cultural adaptation	Very limited or none; no language requirements	Limited for home country nationals; some language training	Limited to moderate training levels for home country nationals; home and host country nationals use business language, often in English	Continuous training for cultural adaptation and multilingualism
Management development effects of international assignments	May hurt career	May hurt career of home country nationals; host country nationals' advancement often limited to their own country	Neutral to slightly positive career implications; international assignments of longer duration	International assignments required for career advancement

IHRM Practices	IHRM Orientations			
	Ethnocentric	Polycentric	Regiocentric	Global
Evaluation	Home standards based on contribution to corporate bottom line	Host country standards based on contribution to unit bottom line	Regional standards based on contribution to corporate bottom line	Global standards based on contribution to corporate bottom line
Compensation	Additional pay and benefits for expatriate assignments	Additional pay and benefits for expatriate assignments; host country compensation rates for host country nationals	Due to longer assignments, less additional compensation for expatriate assignments	Similar pay and benefit packages globally with some local adjustments

Source: Adapted from Adler, Nancy J., and Ghadar, Fariborz (1990). *International strategy from the perspective of people and culture: the North American context*, Research in Global Business Management, 1: 179-205; Heenan, D. A., and H. V. Perlmutter (1979). *Multinational Organization Development*. Reading, Mass: Addison Wesley.

2. The advantages and disadvantages of IHRM orientations

(1) The advantages and disadvantages of ethnocentric IHRM orientation

The benefits of ethnocentric IHRM orientation include the following. First, there is little need to recruit qualified host country nationals for higher management. When host country has no or very few qualified talents, this orientation works successfully. Second, there has been greater control and loyalty of home country nationals since the key decisions are centralized. Third, there is little need to train home country nationals because their overseas assignments are usually short-term. Nevertheless, ethnocentric IHRM orientation has the following costs. First, it may possibly limit career development for host country nationals as they can only occupy low-level management positions. Second, host country nationals may never identify with the home company because they have no chance to make the key decisions with headquarters. Lastly, expatriate managers are often poorly trained for international assignments and make mistakes.

(2) The advantages and disadvantages of polycentric and regiocentric IHRM orientations

Regiocentric IHRM orientation implies that regionwide HRM policies are adopted, while polycentric IHRM orientation implies that MNCs treat each country-level subsidiary separately for HRM purposes. MNCs with regiocentric or polycentric IHRM orientations are more responsive to the host country differences in HRM practices.

Benefits of polycentric and regiocentric IHRM orientations are as follows. First, they reduce training expenses because most of the subsidiaries will be charged by the host country nationals. Second, due to the same reason, there are fewer language and adjustment issues. Third, there are lessened hiring and relocation costs. Meanwhile, costs of polycentric and regiocentric IHRM policies are as follows. First, the coordination problems with headquarters are very serious because of cultural, language, and loyalty differences. Second, there are limited career-path opportunities for host country and regional managers. Lastly, there are limited international experiences for home country managers since very few of them will be expatriated for overseas assignments.

（3）The advantages and disadvantages of global IHRM orientation

Global IHRM orientation implies recruiting and selecting worldwide, and assigning the best managers to international assignments regardless of nationality. In MNCs with global IHRM orientation, managers are selected and trained to manage cultural diversity inside and outside the company. The benefits of global IHRM orientation include the bigger talent pool, high international expertise, and the development of transnational organizational cultures. However, global IHRM orientation also has costs such as difficulty in importing managerial and technical employees as well as added expense due to the continuous cross-cultural adaptation training and global standard pay and benefits packages.

3. The matching of strategies with IHRM orientations

每一种国际人力资源管理导向都有其优点和缺点，跨国公司对国际人力资源管理导向的选择在很大程度上取决于其跨国战略。表 9-2 展示了跨国公司的不同战略与支持这些战略的国际人力资源管理导向之间的联系。将国际人力资源管理导向与确定的跨国公司战略相配合，是成功地实施战略的主要内容。正如所有的跨国公司战略决策一样，国际人力资源管理决策主要基于跨国公司如何面对全球化与本地响应的两难选择。当跨国公司需要十分了解东道国情况的雇员时，国际人力资源管理决策就关注本地响应。而当跨国公司需要具备世界级竞争力的管理者而不在乎其国籍时，国际人力资源管理的决策就会反映全球化的压力。

Every IHRM orientation has its advantages and disadvantages. Properly matching IHRM to the selected strategy of an MNC is a major requirement for successful strategy implementation. Some IHRM decisions show a concern for local responsiveness when MNCs need people with a superior understanding of host country issues. Other IHRM decisions reflect globalization pressures when MNCs need managers with world-class competence regardless of nationality. The success of any strategy requires the careful assessment of a firm's IHRM practices. Usually no one orientation exactly fits an MNC's strategy, and few companies follow any one orientation completely. Each MNC selects a general approach, combined with specific IHRM practices and procedures from other orientations that, all together, fit its strategic needs, as shown in Table 9-2.

Table 9-2   IHRM orientations and MNC strategies

MNC strategies	IHRM orientations			
	Ethnocentric	Polycentric	Regiocentric	Global
International	√	△	△	△
Multidomestic	×	√	△	×
Global	×	√	√	△
Transnational	×	×	×	√

Notes: "√" means ideal IHRM orientation; "×" means unlikely IHRM orientation; "△" means selected elements from IHRM orientations

As shown in Table 9-2, the international strategy emphasizes globalization upstream of the value chain, where subsidiaries under the centralized control of the home country produce and sell global products that require almost no local adjustments. Due to the need for standardization and centralized control of products, ethnocentric IHRM orientation can provide the most effective and ideal way of human resource management. However, for most companies, a purely international strategy is difficult to achieve success. The vast majority of companies adopting international strategies have products that need to be adapted to regional or local needs, and most of these companies engage in overseas production due to considerations of low cost, customer concentration, or political factors. According to the unique conditions faced by the company, it is necessary to comprehensively utilize polycentric IHRM orientation, regiocentric IHRM orientation, or global IHRM orientation. For example, ethnocentric IHRM orientation is adopted for senior managers, while polycentric IHRM orientation is adopted for local production managers.

MNCs that adopt a multidomestic strategy value their ability to respond to local situations. According to Table 9-2, polycentric IHRM orientation treats each country differently, providing appropriate IHRM guidance for enhancing flexibility at the national level. Especially the extensive use of managers and employees from the host country has laid the foundation for the company to understand the local situation. That is to say, the polycentric IHRM orientation helps to implement multidomestic strategies, as local managers typically have a better understanding of local consumer preferences, distribution channels, government regulations, worker expectations, and other unique characteristics of the local business environment.

Table 9-2 also shows that MNCs adopting global strategy increasingly need to coordinate the activities of their subordinate units located in different countries. As these subordinate units are located in the same country or region, the polycentric or regiocentric IHRM orientation can most effectively support the company's strategic intentions. The ethnocentric IHRM orientation is almost unable to serve MNCs that adopt global strategy. For example, MNCs that emphasize regional coordination in production will find that the polycentric IHRM orientation is very effective. Production institutions located in dispersed host countries can also design HRM methods that are suitable for local conditions, enabling their products to be sold regionally and supplying components for a regional product. In this case, regional senior managers only need to have a regional perspective and utilize regional or global IHRM policies to manage them. In contrast, MNCs that share research and development and product knowledge on a regional scale will find that they only need to utilize regional or global IHRM methods to recruit, select, and develop personnel with certain abilities. In this situation, qualified managers at all levels need to possess knowledge about regional markets, governments, national culture, language, and social systems.

From Table 9-2, it can be seen that MNCs that adopt transnational strategy almost invariably adopt a global IHRM orientation. MNCs require a highly flexible organization to maximize their location advantages along their value chain. In this way, MNCs must select and train managers with different national backgrounds to be competent for positions around the world. Managers of MNCs must actively embrace global corporate culture, enabling them to flexibly approach different cultures and national social systems.

跨国公司任何一种战略的实施都必须认真评估其国际人力资源管理导向。成功的跨国公司对国际人力资源管理导向的选择主要取决于它是否能最好地支持其跨国战略的实施。任何国际人力资源管理导向都不能准确地恰好适合跨国公司的战略,很少有跨国公司完全遵循一种国际人力资源管理导向。

The implementation of any strategy of an MNC requires a careful evaluation of its IHRM orientation. The choice of IHRM orientation by a successful MNC mainly depends on whether it can best support the implementation of its strategy. No IHRM orientation can accurately and precisely fit the strategy of MNCs, and few MNCs fully follow just one IHRM orientation. The usual practice is for MNCs to choose a primary IHRM orientation, and then select some specific IHRM methods and procedures from other orientations as auxiliary means according to their strategic management needs. IHRM is the key to supporting all levels of the value chain, therefore, the improper combination of IHRM orientation and MNC strategy will be a fatal mistake.

第三节 外派人员的招聘与培训
（The Recruitment and Training of Expatriates）

1. The recruitment source of expatriates

外派人员是指由母公司任命的在东道国工作的员工,其招聘来源包括母国、东道国和第三国。

Expatriates refer to employees appointed by the parent company to work in the host country, including home-country nationals, host-country nationals, and third-country nationals. Expatriates from different sources have their own advantages and disadvantages, as shown in Table 9-3.

Table 9-3 Comparison of expatriates from different sources

	Advantages	Disadvantages
Home-country nationals	• Suitable for positions in the parent company with advantageous skills and experience • Applicable when the host country lacks suitable candidates • Facilitate control and coordination of the parent company • Facilitate cultivation of management talents in the home country • Beneficial for confidentiality	• High salary costs • May cause dissatisfaction among host country nationals regarding salary differences • Long time to adapt to the host country • Limited career development opportunities for host country nationals • Easy to provoke dissatisfaction from the host country government towards local employment
Host-country nationals	• Easy to communicate, without language or customs barriers • No visa required, low recruitment and labor costs • Long working period, increasing management continuity • Address employment issues that meet the expectations of the host government	• Lack of qualified and experienced host country nationals • Cultural differences may lead to management conflicts between parent and subsidiary companies • Not conducive to the control and coordination of the parent company • Reduced opportunities for home country nationals to gain experience overseas
Third-country nationals	• Lower labor costs compared to home country nationals • Have a better understanding of the host country than home country nationals • Beneficial for shaping international image	• Higher labor costs than host country nationals • Compatibility of ethnic cultures must be considered • The host government may not support it

Source：改编自王增涛，国际投资与跨国公司，清华大学出版社，2024，P205-206，表 10-1

2. The selection of expatriates

The selection of expatriates is very important since expatriate failure rate is quite high, which leads to huge cost. Expatriate failure means the premature return of an expatriate manager to his or her home country. It represents a failure of the firm's selection policies to identify individuals who will not thrive abroad. Expatriate failure results in premature return from an overseas assignment and high resignation rates. The costs of expatriate failure are also high. It is estimated that the average cost per failure to the headquarters can be as high as three times the expatriate's annual domestic salary plus relocation expenditure. Even with such high costs, the success of an expatriate manager is not guaranteed.

One way to reduce expatriate failure rates is by improving selection procedures to screen out inappropriate candidates, including choosing key success factors and selection methods.

U. S. MNCs traditionally assumed that domestic performance predicts expatriate performance. Besides professional and technical competence, other factors are important for success. Key success factors for expatriate assignments include personality traits, relational abilities, family situation, international motivation, stress tolerance, language skills, emotional intelligence, etc. Technical and managerial skills are needed as only managers with excellent technical, administrative, and leadership skills have strong likelihood of success. Personality traits are important because expatriates must be flexible, willing and eager to learn new things, be able to deal with ambiguity, have an interest in other people and cultures, and have a good sense of humor in order to deal with uncertainties and novelty. Relational abilities are included since the expatriates need the skills to be able to adapt to strange or ambiguous situations, as well as to modify their own behaviors and attitudes. Family situation should be considered as the assignments affect spouse and children. International motivation is also a fatal factor because managers must have motivation to accept expatriate assignments. Stress tolerance means the ability to tolerate stress and to maintain composure in the face of extreme stressors, which plays a decisive role in the success of expatriates. Language skills include the ability to speak, read, and write in the host country language. It will enhance other success factors. Emotional intelligence can be understood as being aware of oneself, understanding and relating to others, being empathetic, and managing one's emotions.

Table 9-4 shows some of the key success factors and selection techniques used in the expatriate selection process.

Table 9-4　Key success factors and methods in expatriate selection

Key success factors	Selection methods					
	Interviews	Standardized tests	Assessment centers	Biographical data	Work samples	References
Professional/technical skills • Technical skills • Administrative skills • Leadership skills	√ √	√	√	√ √	√ √	√ √

续表

Key success factors	Selection methods					
	Interviews	Standardized tests	Assessment centers	Biographical data	Work samples	References
Relational abilities						
• Ability to communicate	√		√			√
• Cultural tolerance and empathy	√	√	√			
• Tolerance for ambiguity	√		√			
• Flexibility to adapt to new behaviors and attitudes	√		√			√
• Stress adaptation skills	√		√			
International motivation						
• Willingness to accept the expatriate position	√			√		
• Interest in culture of the assignment location	√					
• Commitment to the international mission	√					
• Fit with the career development stage	√			√		√
Family situation						
• Spouse's willingness to live abroad	√					
• Spouse's relational abilities	√	√	√			
• Spouse's career goals	√					
• Children's educational requirements	√					
Language skills						
• Ability to communicate in local language	√	√	√	√		√

Source: Adapted from Black,J. S. ,Gregerson,H. B. ,and Mendenhall M. E. (1992). *Global Assignments*. San Francisco: Jossey-bass; and Ronen,Simcha (1986). *Comparative and Multinational Management*. New York: Wiley.

　　In addition to choose key success factors and selection methods,expatriate selection should be done by considering assignment characteristics. For overseas assignment with different characteristics,expatriate success factors should be placed different priorities in order to achieve higher success rate. Table 9-5 provides the details. As shown in Table 9-5,priority of success factors depends on four assignment conditions: assignment length,cultural similarity between home and host countries,amount of required interaction and communication with local people,as well as job complexity and responsibility. For instance,although short-term assignments focus primarily on technical and professional qualifications, longer duration of the assignments place a high priority on professional or technical skills. No matter what characteristics the assignment has, international motivation is always paid high priority, implying the importance and necessity of motivation for international assignments.

Table 9-5　Priorities for expatriate success factors by assignment characteristics

Expatriate success factors	Assignment characteristics			
	Longer duration	More cultural dissimilarity	Greater interaction and communication requirements with locals	More complex or responsible job
Professional/technical skills	High	Moderate	Moderate	High
Relational abilities	Moderate	High	High	Moderate
International motivation	High	High	High	High
Family situation	High	High	Moderate	Moderate
Language skills	Moderate	High	High	Moderate

Source: Adapted from Black, J. S., Gregerson, H. B., and Mendenhall M. E. (1992). *Global Assignments*. San Francisco: Jossey-bass; and Tung, Rosalie L. (1981). Selection and training of personnel for overseas assignments. *Columbia Journal of World Business*. 16(1): 68-78.

3. The training types of expatriates

外派人员的培训按照时间顺序,可分为外派前培训、外派期培训、归国前培训和归国后培训。每种培训的内容各有侧重。

The training of expatriates can be divided into pre-expatriate training, tenure training, pre-repatriation training, and post-repatriation training in chronological order. Each type of training has its own focus.

（1）Pre-expatriate training

外派前培训的侧重点包括文化敏感性培训、跨文化沟通培训、随行家属培训和预先访问。

The focuses of pre-expatriate training include cultural sensitivity training, cross-cultural communication training, accompanying family training, and field trip. Cultural sensitivity training can not only enable employees to consciously recognize the cultural attributes and environment of their home country, but also improve the managements' ability to respond to foreign cultures in terms of knowledge and emotions. The main content of cultural sensitivity training includes two aspects. One is the cultural background, core, and differences between the mother country and other countries. Another is the cultural characteristics and essence of the host country. Cultural sensitivity training helps expatriates prepare for cultural shock and alleviate any discomfort and frustration they may face while living in the host country. Cross-cultural communication training mainly includes training in language and nonverbal communication skills. Expatriates must be proficient in at least one foreign language, especially the most widely used English. Nonverbal communication skills are also crucial, including understanding the differences in values related to time efficiency, thinking habits, personal space, eye contact, demeanor, and the meaning of silence in different countries. Accompanying family training mainly includes language training and adaptability training, in order to minimize the negative impact of overseas maladjustment of accompanying families on the work of expatriates. Field trip refers to experiencing life on-site in the host country before being officially dispatched. Field trip can collect a lot of information that cannot be understood domestically, which helps expatriates adapt to the host country's environment in advance and shorten the adjustment period during their deployment.

(2) Tenure training

外派期培训是对外派人员派驻东道国初期所提供的培训，主要包括生活信息提供、职前引导、师徒制、个别辅导、自我训练等。

Tenure training refers to the training provided to expatriates during their initial deployment to the host country, which mainly includes providing life information, pre-employment guidance, mentorship, individual coaching, and self-training. The provision of life information mainly involves the information needed for living in the host country, such as children's enrollment, medical treatment, rental housing, etc. Pre-employment guidance is mainly to assist expatriates in understanding the surrounding environment, work processes, working conditions, and colleagues, so that they can quickly become competent in their work. Mentorship refers to the parent company arranging an experienced manager as a mentor for expatriates in the host country, in order to provide work guidance and necessary life assistance for expatriates. Individual coaching refers to the hiring of cultural advisors by the parent company to provide one-on-one guidance to expatriates and their accompanying family members, assisting expatriates to integrate into the culture and life of the host country more quickly. Self-training refers to the practice of expatriates accepting new cultures and environments with an open mind and attitude through communication and learning with host country employees.

(3) Pre-repatriation training

归国前培训是为了帮助外派人员归国所做的适应性准备。如果外派人员在海外任职时间较长，归国时可能出现对本国文化不适应的现象，即逆文化冲击。

Pre-repatriation training is designed to help expatriates prepare for their return to their home country. If expatriates have been serving overseas for a long time, there may be a phenomenon of cultural shock when they return home, which is known as reverse culture shock, including adapting to new work environment and culture of home office, relearning to communicate with others in home and organizational cultures, and adapting to their basic living environment. To this end, the parent company needs to provide a strategic purpose for the repatriation, and establish a team to help expatriates cope with it, including reintroducing the core of their home country's culture, customs and habits, and company development plans. Some expatriates are even pre-trained before returning to their home country, which implies that they will maintain contact with the headquarters during their tenure, giving them a sense of belonging.

（4）Post-repatriation training

归国后培训主要是帮助外派人员归国后的工作适应与心理调适，培训形式包括工作任务培训、辅助制度和咨询辅导。

Post-repatriation training is mainly aimed at helping expatriates adapt to work and psychological adjustment after returning home. The training includes job task training, auxiliary systems, and counseling. The training for returning work tasks mainly provides the latest job position information and pre-job training for newly returned expatriates, helping them complete job role transitions. The auxiliary system is an unexpected expenditure and an important resource cultivation and accumulation, aimed at reducing losses caused by work accidents or personnel turnover. Counseling can be offline or online, which helps expatriates feel valued and enhance their self-affirmation and self-confidence.

4. The training rigor of expatriates

Cross-cultural training increases the relational abilities of future expatriates and, in some cases, of their spouses and families. Many MNCs still do not invest heavily in cross-cultural training, which accounts for high expatriate failure rate. Nevertheless, a growing number of MNCs pay more attention to expatriate training with different rigor. Training rigor refers to extent of effort by both trainees and trainers required to prepare the expatriate. Low rigor training lasts for a short period and includes techniques such as lectures and videos on the local culture and briefings concerning company operations. High rigor training may last for over a month and contains more experiential learning, extensive language training, and frequent interactions with host nationals. Figure 9-1 shows the techniques and objectives of different training rigor.

But how does the training rigor relate to the basic expatriate assignment conditions? This is the key question of applying different training rigor. The answer can be found in Figure 9-2. As shown in Figure 9-2, high training rigor with more than 160 training hours is needed when the foreign assignment has the following characteristics: long duration, dissimilar culture, high job responsibility, and high need to communicate with host country nationals. On the contrary, low training rigor with only 4 to 20 training hours is enough if the foreign assignment has the characteristics including short duration, similar culture, low to moderate job responsibility, and low need to communicate with host country nationals. Otherwise, moderate training rigor with 20 to 60 training hours is acceptable.

High

Training Rigor

Techniques: Field trips to the host country, meetings with managers in the host country, meetings with host country nationals, intensive language training.
Objectives: Develop comfort with host country national culture, business culture, and social institutions.

Techniques: Intercultural experiential learning exercises, role playing, simulations, case studies, survival language training.
Objectives: Build general and specific knowledge of host country culture, reduce ethnocentrism.

Techniques: Lectures, videotapes, reading background materials.
Objectives: Provide background information on host country business and national cultures, and basic information on company operations

Low

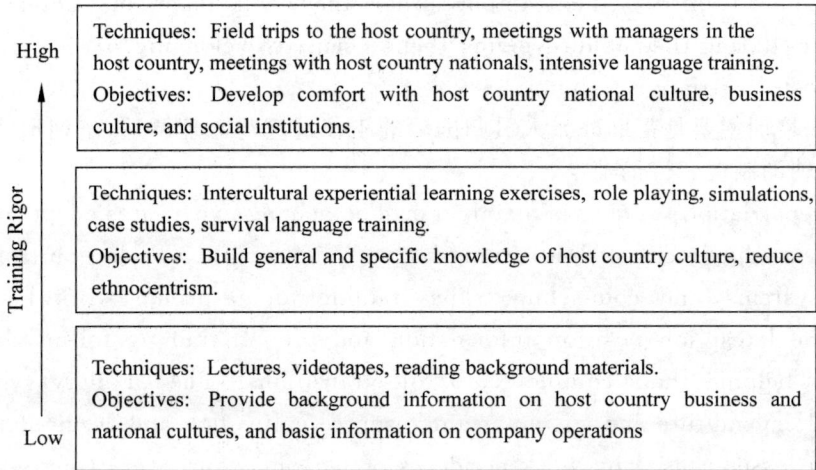

Figure 9-1　Training rigor: techniques and objectives

Source: Adapted from Black, J. S., Gregerson, H. B., and Mendenhall M. E. (1992). *Global Assignments*. San Francisco: Jossey-bass; and Ronen, Simcha (1986). *Comparative and Multinational Management*. New York: Wiley.

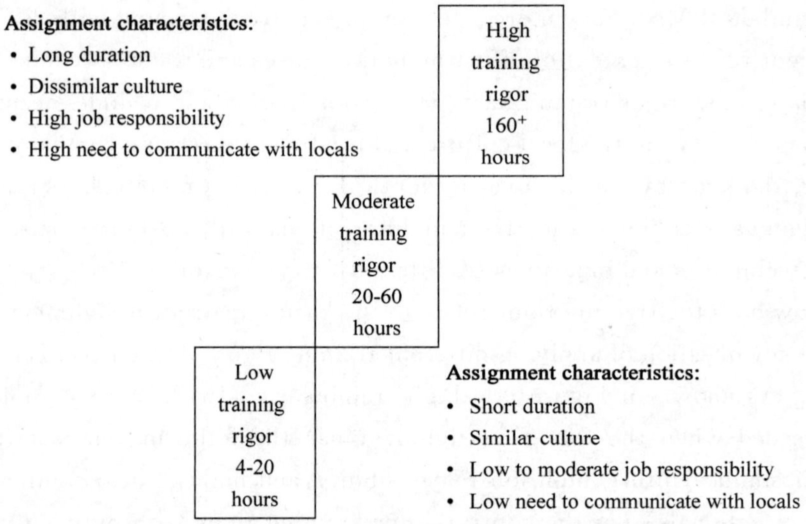

Assignment characteristics:
- Long duration
- Dissimilar culture
- High job responsibility
- High need to communicate with locals

High training rigor 160+ hours

Moderate training rigor 20-60 hours

Low training rigor 4-20 hours

Assignment characteristics:
- Short duration
- Similar culture
- Low to moderate job responsibility
- Low need to communicate with locals

Figure 9-2　How the rigor of training relates to the basic expatriate assignment conditions

Source: Adapted from Mendenhall, Mark E., E. Dunbar, and Gary R. Oddou (1987). Expatriate selection, training and career-pathing: A review and critique. *Human Resource Management*. 26(3): 331-345.

第四节 外派人员绩效评估与薪酬管理
（The Performance Appraisal and Compensation of Expatriates）

1. The performance appraisal of expatriates

（1）The concept of expatriates' performance appraisal

外派人员绩效评估是指跨国公司根据工作目标或绩效标准，采用科学方法评定外派人员工作目标完成情况、工作职责履行程度及外派人员发展情况等，并将评定结果反馈给外派人员的过程。

The performance appraisal of expatriates refers to the process in which MNCs use scientific methods to assess the completion of work goals, fulfillment of job responsibilities, and development of expatriates based on work objectives or performance standards, and provide feedback on the evaluation results to expatriates. On the surface, the performance appraisal of expatriates appears to be only an assessment of their work performance. In fact, similar to the performance appraisal of domestic employees, it is a mechanism for MNCs to control the process of achieving their strategic goals, which is of great significance to both the company itself and expatriates. For MNCs, performance appraisal of expatriates is an important means to improve management efficiency and enhance work performance. Through performance appraisal, MNCs can understand the completion of work goals for expatriates, establish communication channels between managers and employees, express managements' job requirements and expectations for employees, obtain employees' suggestions for management and company development, and jointly explore employees' future development goals. For external personnel, performance appraisal is an important way to improve work and seek development. Through performance appraisal, expatriates can clarify the goals and responsibilities of their work, make the company aware of their work achievements, express suggestions for the company's development, and understand the company's expectations and future job requirements for themselves.

（2）The difficulties of expatriates' performance appraisal

Conducting a reliable and valid performance appraisal is one of the greatest IHRM challenges. Some issues that make expatriate performance appraisals difficult include the following.

First, fit of international operation in MNCs' strategy. For example, MNCs often enter international operations for strategic reasons other than immediate profits. In this case, if short-term assessment indicators such as investment return rate are used, the performance appraisal results of expatriates will be very poor, which makes nonsense.

Second, unreliable data. Local subunit data may not be comparable to home country data or from other international operations. For instance, due to local laws requiring full employment and not allowing overtime, production efficiency appears to be very low. Although it is legitimate to compare subsidiaries against each other on the basis of return on investment (ROI) or other indicators of profitability, it may be inappropriate to use these for comparing and evaluating the managers of different subsidiaries. The manager of a subsidiary in an adverse environment that has an ROI of 5% may be doing a better job than the manager of a subsidiary in a benign environment that has an ROI of 20%. Although the MNC might want to pull out of a country whose ROI is only 5%, it may also want to recognize the manager's achievement.

Third, complex and volatile environments. International environment can change rapidly, resulting in difficulties for expatriates to achieve their original performance goals.

Fourth, time differences and distance separation. Although transportation and communication costs are gradually decreasing and cross-border communication is becoming more convenient, the time and space barrier still poses an intangible obstacle for overseas subsidiaries and parent companies. For the parent company, expatriates are often out of sight, out of mind. This makes it difficult for the parent company to understand the specific situation of its subsidiaries and the performance of its expatriates.

Lastly, local cultural situation. Due to cultural differences, employees in different countries may have different acceptable ways of working. For example, the number of holidays or vacations, expected working hours, and training methods for local employees can directly or indirectly affect the performance of expatriates. Although excellent expatriates can quickly integrate into the local area and adapt to local cultural expectations, the parent company may not necessarily understand the situation of its subsidiaries in the same way. Therefore, good performance appraisal of expatriates must be adjusted based on cultural expectations related to their work.

(3) The improvement steps of expatriates' performance appraisal

To overcome the difficulties of performance appraisal of expatriates, the following steps to improve the process can be taken.

First, fit the evaluation criteria to strategy. MNCs should use appropriate performance appraisal measures to evaluate the expatriate performance. For instance, if the MNC's goal is to enter the market and gain a long-term competitive position, then short-term financial performance evaluation standards will make no sense.

Second, fine tune the evaluation criteria. MNCs should consider carefully all objectives for the international operation and adjust evaluation criteria accordingly. The performance evaluation criteria for expatriates can generally be divided into three categories: hard indicators, soft indicators, and situational indicators. Hard indicators refer to objective, quantitative, and directly measurable standards, such as investment return rate, market share, etc. Soft indicators refer to standards based on relationships or qualities, such as leadership style, interpersonal skills, etc. Situational indicators refer to performance indicators that are closely related to the surrounding environment. These three types of indicators all have their own advantages and disadvantages. MNCs should use these three types of indicators as the basis for performance evaluation and combine them in the evaluation process, rather than relying solely on one indicator.

Third, separate the evaluation of the subsidiary and manager. The evaluation of a subsidiary should be kept separate from the evaluation of its manager. The manager's evaluation should consider how hostile or benign the country's environment is for that business. Furthermore, managers should be evaluated in local currency terms after making allowances for those items over which they have no control, including interest rates, tax rates, inflation rates, transfer prices, and exchange rates.

Fourth, use multiple evaluators with varying periods of evaluation. Complexity of international situation demands more information than similar appraisals done at home. Table 9-6 shows some basic contents of expatriate performance appraisals, including evaluation sources, criteria, and time periods. As shown in Table 9-6, the evaluators include not only on-site supervisors, but also host-country managers, peer expatriates, subordinates, customers and clients. In addition, self-evaluation should also be encouraged. These evaluation sources will use different criteria such as meeting objectives, management skills, project successes, leadership skills, communication skills, subordinates' development, etc. Accordingly, the evaluation time periods vary from six months to one year. The evaluation can also be conducted at the completion of significant projects.

Table 9-6   Evaluation sources, criteria, and time periods for expatriate performance appraisals

Evaluation sources	Criteria	Periods
Self-evaluation	• Meeting objectives • Management skills • Project successes	Six months and at the completion of a major project
Subordinates	• Leadership skills • Communication skills • Subordinates' development	After completion of a major project
Peer expatriates and host-country managers	• Team building • Interpersonal skills • Cross-cultural interaction skills	Six months
On-site supervisors	• Management skills • Leadership skills • Meeting objectives	At the completion of significant projects
Customers and clients	• Service quality and timeliness • Negotiation skills • Cross-cultural interaction skills	Yearly

Source: Adapted from Black, J. S., Gregerson, H. B., and Mendenhall M. E. (1992). *Global Assignments*. San Francisco: Jossey-bass.

At last, pay attention to performance evaluation feedback. Continuous and effective performance evaluation feedback is an important part of the evaluation process. Regular performance evaluation feedback can help employees reduce work errors, learn from lessons, and encourage continuous improvement and enhancement of work performance. It is also an effective means of motivating employees to work hard. If the performance evaluation of expatriates is carried out by home country managers, then appropriate regular feedback is even more important.

2. The components of expatriates compensation

外派人员的薪酬一般由基本薪酬、津贴、奖金、福利和激励薪酬构成。

The compensation of expatriates generally consists of basic salary, allowances, bonuses, benefits, and incentives.

(1) Basic salary

基本薪酬是外派人员薪酬计算的基础,也是外派人员薪酬的保障。基本薪酬的确定标准包括三类,分别是母国薪酬体系、东道国薪酬体系和国际薪酬体系。

Basic salary is the basis for calculating the compensation of expatriates and also the guarantee for their compensation. The criteria for determining basic salary include three categories: headquarters-based compensation, host-based compensation, and global pay systems. The three types of compensation each has its own advantages and disadvantages, and their applicable objects are also different. Headquarters-based compensation implies home country wages paid regardless of location, which is applicable to personnel who have been sent abroad for a short period of time and return to their home country immediately after the completion of their overseas assignment. This compensation is beneficial for expatriates to maintain contact with headquarters and also enables them to quickly regain their original work status after returning home. The drawback is that when the salary in the host country is higher than that of expatriates, it can easily lead to dissatisfaction and even job hopping among expatriates. Host-based compensation implies adjusting wages to local lifestyles and costs of living, which is mainly applicable to those who have been sent abroad for a long time and have a salary level similar to that of their home country. Adopting this compensation is unlikely to cause dissatisfaction among employees in the host country. Global pay systems imply worldwide job evaluations, performance appraisal methods, and salary scales, which is often used for multiple and continual global assignments. It reduces waste from expatriate perquisites, eliminates steep differences in compensation, and maintains compensation equity for long-term international cadre managers.

(2) Allowance

常见的津贴包括以下几类:一是商品与服务津贴,也称消费津贴;二是住房津贴;三是子女教育津贴;四是安家补贴。

Due to significant differences in work and living environments both domestically and internationally，MNCs typically need to pay allowances to expatriate personnel to compensate for their living costs and maintain their standard of living domestically. Common allowances include the following categories. First，goods and services allowance，also known as consumption allowance or cost-of-living allowance. When the prices of goods and services in the host country are higher than those in the home country，MNCs will provide consumption allowances to expatriates. The second is housing allowance. The cost of renting accommodation for expatriates in the host country may be much higher than that in their home country. Therefore，MNCs will pay housing subsidies based on estimates or actual situations. The third is the children's education allowance. Expatriates usually hope that their children can receive education in schools that teach in their mother tongue，and their tuition fees are usually paid by MNCs，which is called school allowance. If expatriates choose to keep their children in their home country for education，MNCs will also provide the cost of attending boarding schools. The fourth is relocation allowances. This is mainly used to compensate for the expenses incurred by expatriates in relocating their families due to working in the host country，often one month's salary paid at the beginning and end of assignment for miscellaneous costs of relocating.

（3）Bonus

跨国公司外派人员的奖金通常以津贴的形式发放，主要包括以下形式：一是海外任职津贴；二是艰苦条件津贴；三是探亲津贴；四是工作期满津贴。

The bonuses for MNCs' expatriates are usually distributed in the form of allowances，mainly including the following forms. One is foreign service premiums，which is designed for accepting the individual and family difficulties associated with an overseas assignment. The amount of the allowance depends on the position of expatriates，the economic development level of the host country，the duration of expatriates，etc. It is generally 10% to 20% of the base salary. The second is the hardship allowance. Hardship conditions refer to harsh weather，poor sanitation，political instability，civil war，and a lack of cultural facilities. MNCs typically provide allowances for expatriates working in areas with harsh conditions. The third is home-leave allowances，covering transportation costs for expatriates and families to return home once or twice a year. The fourth is the allowance upon completion of work. This allowance is issued to employees upon the completion of their contract period to encourage them to work overseas throughout the entire contract period.

（4）Benefit

Compared to domestic employees，the welfare management of expatriates is more complex. Usually，expatriates from American MNCs are entitled to welfare plans in their home country，while expatriates from some countries can only choose local social insurance plans. In this case，MNCs generally have to pay additional fees. In general，

MNCs make good plans for the retirement of employees in their home countries, but do a little worse for employees in third countries.

（5）Incentives

In order to motivate employees to continue accepting overseas assignments, MNCs also provide non-cost related cash incentives for expatriates, which are applicable to all expatriates and are generally paid at 15% of the basic salary along with the monthly salary. Some MNCs also determine this salary as a total bonus amount, called job change funds, which are paid twice at the beginning and end of the expatriate work.

3. The approaches of global pay calculation

计算国际薪酬的方法主要有两种：现行费率法，又称市场费率法；平衡表法，又称累积法。

There are two main methods for calculating global pay: the going rate approach, also known as the market rate approach, and the balance sheet approach, also known as the cumulative approach.

（1）The going rate approach

The going rate approach refers to the salary of expatriates being linked to the salary structure of the host country. MNCs usually first obtain information from the local salary survey company, and then decide whether to take the host country nationals, expatriates of the same nationality, or expatriates from all countries as the reference benchmark. If the going rate system is used in low wage countries, MNCs typically provide additional benefits and allowances in addition to the basic salary. The going rate system will lead to expatriates rushing to demand to be sent to places with favorable treatment, rather than going to areas with less attractive treatment. If the salary level in the host country is higher than that in the home country, the salary should be restored to the latter level when returning home, which will make expatriates extremely unwilling.

（2）The balance sheet approach

The balance sheet approach refers to linking the basic salary of expatriates to the relative home country salary structure. As shown in Figure 9-3, the balance sheet approach attempts to equate purchasing power in the host country with purchasing power in the expatriates' home country. Its aim is that the expatriates should not be treated any better or worse financially as a result of taking the assignment. In order to motivate expatriates, MNCs typically provide additional salary to include adjustments for differences in taxes, housing costs, and basic goods and services. Due to the different basic wages in each country, the balance sheet approach can easily result in different incomes for expatriates engaged in the same or similar work in the same host country. For example, Belgian and Australian employees working at the regional headquarters of a British bank in Japan have the same responsibilities, but due to the difference in basic salary levels between Belgium and Australia, Belgians receive much higher wages than

Australians, which can make employees feel discriminated against. In addition, the difference in the basic wage level will also cause conflicts between expatriates and host country nationals.

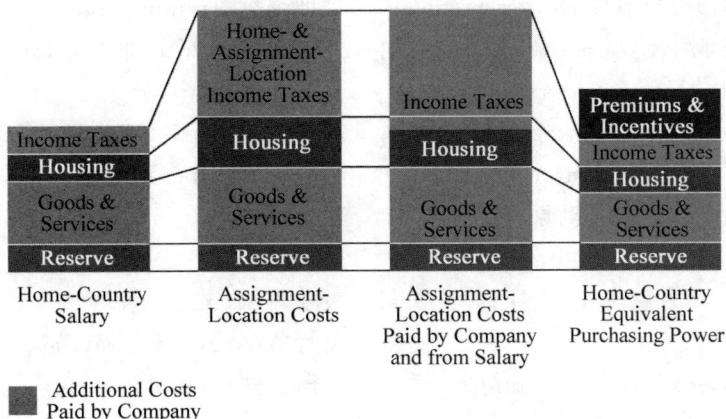

Figure 9-3 The balance sheet approach to expatriate pay

Source: Hill, Charles W. L., Hult, G. Tomas M. (2017). *International Business: Competing in the Global Marketplace*, 11e, McGraw-Hill Education. P. 455

The advantages and disadvantages of the going rate approach and balance sheet approach are shown in Table 9-7.

Table 9-7 **The advantages and disadvantages of going rate approach and balance sheet approach**

	Advantages	Disadvantages
Going rate approach	• Equal treatment between expatriates and locals • Expatriates can determine their compensation in host country • Equal compensation for expatriates of different nationalities	• The compensation of the same employee varies in different dispatch regions • The compensation of expatriates of the same nationality varies in different host countries • Potential repatriation issues
Balance sheet approach	• Equal compensation between different assignments and among expatriates of the same nationality • Facilitating the repatriation arrangements for dispatched employees	• The compensation of expatriates of different nationalities and expatriates and local employees varies • Remuneration management is complex, involving tax, living expenses and different compensation between home country nationals and the other country nationals

Source: 改编自赵曙明、刘燕、道林等，国际人力资源管理（第 5 版），中国人民大学出版社，2012，P144-146，表 7-2，表 7-5

关键术语（Key Terms）

国际人力资源管理（international human resource management, IHRM）

外派人员（expatriate）

母国员工（home-country nationals）

东道国员工(host-country nationals)

第三国员工(third-country nationals)

国际人力资源管理导向(IHRM orientation)

民族中心国际人力资源管理导向(ethnocentric IHRM orientation)

多国中心国际人力资源管理导向(polycentric IHRM orientation)

区域中心国际人力资源管理导向(regiocentric IHRM orientation)

全球中心国际人力资源管理导向(global IHRM orientation)

外派前培训(pre-expatriate training)

外派期培训(tenure training)

归国前培训(pre-repatriation training)

归国后培训(post-repatriation training)

培训强度(training rigor)

外派人员绩效评估(performance appraisal of expatriates)

基本薪酬(basic salary)

津贴(allowance)

奖金(bonus)

福利(benefits)

激励薪酬(incentives)

现行费率法(going rate approach)

平衡表法(cumulative approach)

小结(Summary)

1. The main activities of HRM include recruitment, selection, training and development, performance appraisal, compensation, and labor relations. IHRM involves all the HRM functions adapting to the international setting. Types of employees in MNCs include expatriates, home-country nationals, host-country nationals, third-country nationals, inpatriates, flexpatriates, and international cadre. Compared to domestic HRM, IHRM has complex external environment, more management functions, strong global consciousness, outstanding overseas risks, and comprehensive personnel care.

2. IHRM orientation is a company's basic tactics and philosophy for coordinating IHRM activities for managerial and technical workers. There are four basic IHRM orientations such as ethnocentric IHRM orientation, polycentric IHRM orientation, regiocentric IHRM orientation, and global IHRM orientation. Every IHRM orientation has its advantages and disadvantages. Properly matching IHRM to the selected strategy of MNCs is a major requirement for successful strategy implementation. The usual practice is for MNCs to choose a primary IHRM orientation, and then select some specific IHRM methods and procedures from other orientations as auxiliary means according to their strategic management needs.

3. Expatriates refer to employees appointed by the parent company to work in the host country, including home-country nationals, host-country nationals, and third-country nationals. The selection of expatriates is very important since expatriate failure rate is quite high, which leads to huge cost. Key success factors for expatriate assignments include personality traits, relational abilities, family situation, international motivation, stress tolerance, language skills, emotional intelligence, etc. The training of expatriates can be divided into pre-expatriate training, tenure training, pre-repatriation

training, and post-repatriation training in chronological order. Training rigor refers to extent of effort by both trainees and trainers required to prepare the expatriate.

4. The performance appraisal of expatriates refers to the process in which MNCs use scientific methods to assess the completion of work goals, fulfillment of job responsibilities, and development of expatriates based on work objectives or performance standards, and provide feedback on the evaluation results to expatriates. Conducting a reliable and valid performance appraisal is one of the greatest IHRM challenges. The compensation management of expatriates is relatively complex and influenced by geographic factors, task factors, and personal factors. The compensation of expatriates generally consists of basic salary, allowances, bonuses, benefits, and incentives. There are two main methods for calculating global pay: the going rate approach, and the balance sheet approach.

延伸阅读(Further Readings)

习题(Exercises)

第 十 章
Chapter 10

跨国公司与中国
Multinational Corporations and China

Learning Objectives
- To know the history of MNCs' FDI towards China
- To identify the current situation and characteristics of MNCs' FDI towards China
- To understand the strategy of MNCs' FDI towards China
- To know the development stage of Chinese MNCs
- To identify the development situation and characteristics of Chinese MNCs
- To understand the development mode of Chinese MNCs
- To be familiar with the development trend of MNCs

第一节　跨国公司来华直接投资
（MNCs' FDI Towards China）

1. The history of MNCs' FDI towards China

自 1978 年改革开放以来，中国经济保持了高速、稳定的增长，由此也吸引了越来越多的跨国公司对中国进行直接投资，抢抓市场机遇。跨国公司对中国的直接投资大致经历了探索期、调整期、提升期、稳定期等四个阶段。

Since the reform and opening up in 1978, the Chinese economy has maintained high-speed and stable growth, which has also attracted more and more MNCs to invest directly in China and seize market opportunities. The direct investment of MNCs in China has roughly gone through four stages: exploration, adjustment, promotion, and stability.

（1）Exploration stage：1978—1991

In the early stages of reform and opening up, China's laws and regulations on foreign investment were not perfect, and various infrastructure was relatively backward. MNCs generally held a tentative attitude towards FDI in China. These investments were concentrated in the tertiary industry, mainly led by service-oriented enterprises and real estate development companies with strong funds, advanced technology, and large market

244

share. The investment sources were mainly from Hong Kong，China and Taiwan，China，but there were also some from Japan and European and American countries. The FDI in China from Japan and European and American MNCs was mainly focused on manufacturing industry，and there were many high-tech and high value-added projects. During the exploration stage，China's average annual realized FDI was only US＄1.79 billion. Among them，the amount of realized FDI in 1991 was US＄4.37 billion.

（2）Adjustment stage：1992—2000

In 1992，Comrade Deng Xiaoping delivered a speech on his "Southern Tour". Soon after，China officially decided to build a socialist market economy system. This dispelled the doubts of MNCs，and their FDI towards China began to grow rapidly，causing a certain impact on domestic enterprises in China，and even leading to a certain degree of monopoly in certain industries. In order to gain more profits，MNCs attached greater importance to corporate control and transformed joint ventures into sole proprietorships through capital increase and share expansion. In order to smoothly join WTO，the Chinese government had adjusted and improved the laws and regulations related to foreign investment，greatly increasing transparency，and shifting the emphasis on the utilization of FDI from quantity to quality. Correspondingly，the average scale of MNCs' FDI projects in China had expanded，the funding availability rate had improved，and the number of MNCs entering the high-tech and infrastructure industries had increased significantly. During the adjustment stage，China's average annual realized FDI was nearly US＄36 billion. Among them，the amount of realized FDI in 2000 reached US＄40.72 billion.

（3）Promotion stage：2001—2011

In 2001，China officially joined WTO，which opened up a broad international stage for Chinese products. In order to fully utilize business opportunities，MNCs had unanimously increased their FDI in China，gradually integrating China into their global production and sales networks，and promoting China to become a global manufacturing center. With the intensification of competition，MNCs had not only established production enterprises and sales centers in China，but also set up research and development centers and regional headquarters，and begun to consciously transfer technology. During the promotion stage，China's annual realized FDI exceeded US＄80 billion. Among them，the amount of realized FDI in 2011 reached US＄123.99 billion.

（4）Stable stage：2012 to current

In 2012，the Chinese economy entered a stage so called "new normal"，characterized by a shift from high-speed growth to medium to high-speed growth；continuous optimization and upgrading of economic structure；a shift from factor driven and investment driven to innovation driven. Correspondingly，China has implemented a management model of "pre admission national treatment" and "negative list" for foreign investment,and formulated the *Foreign Investment Law of the People's Republic of China* ,aiming to improve the convenience of foreign investment and establish a higher level of opening up to the outside world,which provides institutional guarantees for foreign investment to enter Chinese market. In this context,MNCs investing in China face greater market opportunities and more intense competition. The scale and quality of investment continue to improve and stabilize at a high level,while accelerating the pace of technology transfer to China. During the stable stage,MNCs' realized FDI in China each year exceeded US $ 120 billion. Among them,the realized FDI in 2022 reached US $ 189. 13 billion.

2. The current situation and characteristics of MNCs' FDI towards China

(1) Scale of realized FDI is steadily increasing

In 2022,China's inflow of FDI continued to maintain a steady growth. As shown in Figure 10-1,the realized FDI amounted to US $ 189. 13 billion,an increase of 4. 5% from 2021. Realized FDI refers to the amount of contractual foreign investment that is actually paid,including the registered capital and working capital that are actually paid by the foreign investor,and the transaction consideration that is actually paid by the foreign investor for the transfer of the equity of the domestic investor. Benefiting from a stable business environment and a large domestic market,China continues to be a hot spot for global cross-border investment,with the realized FDI reaching new records. From 2020 to 2022,China's average annual growth rate in inflow of FDI reached 12. 5%,with an average of 41,574 new foreign-invested enterprises (FIEs). The realized FDI accounted for over 10% of global cross-border investment for three consecutive years.

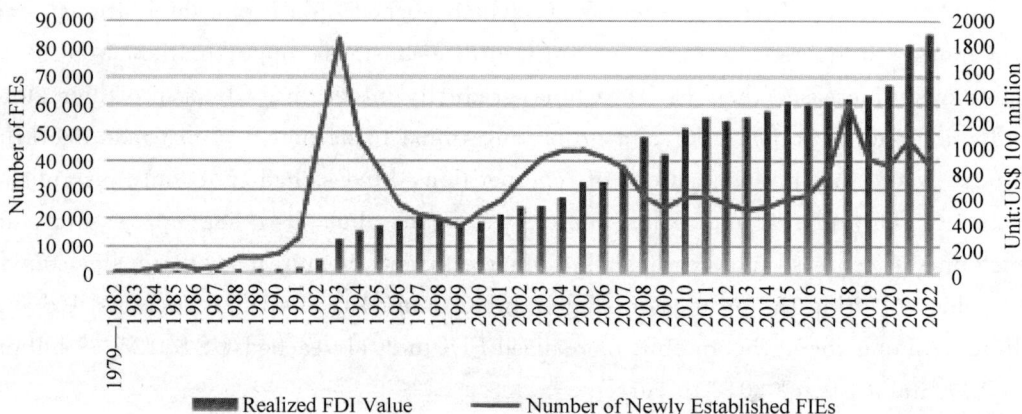

Figure 10-1　FDI in China,1979—2022

Source：Ministry of Commerce of the People's Republic of China (MOFCOM) FDI Statistics

(2) Inflow structure of FDI continues to be optimized

Currently,China has introduced a series of policies and measures to promote high-quality development of the manufacturing industry, and accelerate the integration and development of the service industry and manufacturing industry. As a result, the scale of FDI flowing into the manufacturing industry grows rapidly, and the scale of FDI in the service industry remains basically stable. As shown in Table 10-1, with the scale change of FDI flowing into the three industries from 2005 to 2022, the inflow structure of FDI continues to be optimized.

Table 10-1 FDI by industry, 2005—2022（Unit：US $ 100 million）

Year	Primary Industry		Secondary Industry		Tertiary Industry	
	Number of New FIEs	Realized FDI Value	Number of New FIEs	Realized FDI Value	Number of New FIEs	Realized FDI Value
2005	851	5.7	30027	446.9	13139	271.4
2006	742	4.4	25725	452.7	15029	270.0
2007	887	7.1	20087	428.6	16918	399.5
2008	803	10.6	12299	532.6	14435	539.7
2009	749	12.7	10324	500.8	12369	427.2
2010	796	16.3	11625	538.6	14999	592.5
2011	761	16.7	11630	557.5	15323	665.7
2012	763	18.1	9419	524.6	14752	668.0
2013	629	15.8	7039	495.7	15253	727.7
2014	589	13.0	5649	439.2	17495	832.6
2015	471	11.1	4981	435.9	20888	908.7
2016	449	16.5	4618	402.1	22741	917.8
2017	579	7.9	6017	409.5	29047	945.6
2018	639	7.1	7935	482.7	51986	893.3
2019	424	4.4	6262	422.3	34224	985.5
2020	405	4.2	4607	365.5	33566	1123.7
2021	430	5.4	5613	423.4	41604	1380.8
2022	362	4.7	4608	570.7	33527	1315.9

Source：MOFCOM FDI Statistics

Note：Industry statistics are categorized by sub-sector. Some numbers may only reflect the data by sector, and the sum of primary, secondary and tertiary industry numbers may not equate the annual total of respective years.

In 2022, FDI mainly flowed to manufacturing; leasing and business services; scientific research and technology services; information transmission, software and information technology services; wholesale and retailing; real estate; finance. Newly established FIEs in these seven sectors accounted for 86.3%, and realized FDI value accounted for 91.1%, as shown in Table 10-2.

Table 10-2   FDI by sector，2005—2022（Unit：US $ 100 million）

Sector	Number of New FIEs	Share (%)	Realized FDI Value	Sector (%)
Total	38497	100.0	1891.3	100.0
Agriculture，Forestry，Animal Husbandry and Fishery	420	1.1	12.4	0.7
Mining	28	0.1	15.4	0.8
Manufacturing	3570	9.3	496.7	26.3
Production and Supply of Electricity Heat，Gas and Water	523	1.4	41.5	2.2
Construction	505	1.3	17.9	0.9
Wholesale and Retailing	10894	28.3	145.6	7.7
Transportation，Warehousing and Post	602	1.6	53.2	2.8
Accommodation and Restaurants	828	2.2	5.2	0.3
Information Transmission，Software and Information Technology Services	3059	8.0	238.7	12.6
Finance	353	0.9	68.5	3.6
Real Estate	581	1.5	141.5	7.5
Leasing and Business Services	7473	19.4	330.6	17.5
Scientific Research and Technology Services	7280	18.9	301.8	16.0
Water Conservancy，Environment and Public Facilities Management	96	0.3	7.1	0.4
Resident Services，Repair and Other Services	411	1.1	2.9	0.2
Education	84	0.2	1.2	0.1
Health and Social Work	109	0.3	5.7	0.3
Culture，Sports and Entertainment	1678	4.4	4.5	0.2

Source：MOFCOM FDI Statistics

（3）Location distribution of FDI inflow is unchanging

In 2022，the top ten provinces with the largest number of newly established FIEs were Guangdong，Shanghai，Jiangsu，Zhejiang，Fujian，Shandong，Beijing，Hainan，Sichuan，and Jiangxi，adding up to 86.2% of the national total. The top ten provinces of realized FDI value were Jiangsu，Guangdong，Shanghai，Shandong，Zhejiang，Beijing，Liaoning，Tianjin，Fujian and Hainan，altogether accounting for 86% of the national total，as shown in Table 10-3.

Table 10-3   FDI flows to each province of China in 2022

Province	Number of New FIEs	Share (%)	Realized FDI Value (US $ 100 million)	Share (%)
Total	38497	100.0	1891.3	100.0
Jiangsu	3303	8.6	305.0	16.1
Guangdong	13365	34.7	278.9	14.7

Province	Number of New FIEs	Share (%)	Realized FDI Value (US $ 100 million)	Share (%)
Shanghai	4359	11.3	239.6	12.7
Shandong	2329	6.0	228.7	12.1
Zhejiang	2910	7.6	193.0	10.2
Beijing	1408	3.7	174.1	9.2
Liaoning	644	1.7	61.6	3.3
Tianjin	496	1.3	59.5	3.1
Fujian	2733	7.1	49.9	2.6
Hainan	1352	3.5	37.1	2.0
Hunan	442	1.1	35.3	1.9
Sichuan	755	2.0	35.3	1.9
Hubei	478	1.2	26.5	1.4
Jiangxi	669	1.7	21.7	1.1
Anhui	475	1.2	21.6	1.1
Chongqing	268	0.7	18.6	1.0
Henan	330	0.9	17.8	0.9
Hebei	442	1.1	16.6	0.9
Shaanxi	314	0.8	14.6	0.8
Guangxi	535	1.4	13.7	0.7
Shanxi	91	0.2	8.3	0.4
Yunnan	342	0.9	7.0	0.4
Inner Mongolia	40	0.1	5.4	0.3
Guizhou	105	0.3	5.3	0.3
Xinjiang	38	0.1	4.6	0.2
Jilin	67	0.2	4.5	0.2
Ningxia	22	0.1	3.4	0.2
Heilongjiang	143	0.4	2.3	0.1
Gansu	29	0.1	1.2	0.1
Xizang	2	0.01	0.3	0.02
Qinghai	11	0.03	0.1	0.01

Source：MOFCOM FDI Statistics

（4）Sources of FDI remain stable

In 2022, the main sources of FDI in China remained stable. Categorized by investors' nationality or place of registration（the same below）, newly established FIEs in China by the top 15 sources totaled 25,413, accounting for 66% of the national total. Realized FDI value reached US $ 183.8 billion, accounting for 97.2% of the national total, as shown in Table 10-4.

Table 10-4　Top 15 FDI sources of China in 2022

Country/Region	Number of New FIEs	Share (%)	Realized FDI Value (US $ 100 million)	Share (%)
Total	38497	100.0	1891.3	100.0
Hong Kong (SAR,China)	15814	41.1	1372.4	72.6
Singapore	1176	3.1	106.0	5.6
British Virgin Islands	218	0.6	66.3	3.5
Republic of Korea	1593	4.1	66.0	3.5
Japan	828	2.2	46.1	2.4
Netherlands	103	0.3	44.9	2.4
Germany	422	1.1	25.7	1.4
Cayman Islands	157	0.4	24.2	1.3
United States	1583	4.1	22.1	1.2
United Kingdom	609	1.6	16.0	0.8
Macao (SAR,China)	2313	6.0	12.4	0.7
Malaysia	309	0.8	11.3	0.6
United Arab Emirates	37	0.1	9.6	0.5
France	186	0.5	7.6	0.4
Samoa	65	0.2	7.5	0.4

Source：MOFCOM FDI Statistics

Note：If foreign investors from two or more countries/regions jointly establish an FIE,it will be calculated in the number of new FIEs of each country/region respectively,the total will only be calculated once.

(5) Investment destination status keep constant

After a steep drop in 2020 and a strong rebound in 2021,global FDI declined by 12.4% in 2022. The FDI of China increased by 4.5%,ranking second in the world and first among developing countries for the 31th consecutive year,and accounting for 14.6% of the global total,as shown in Table 10-5.

Table 10-5　Global share of China's realized FDI value,2000—2022 (Unit：US $ 100 million)

Year	Global FDI		Realized FDI Value of China		
	Amount	Growth Rate(%)	Amount	Growth Rate(%)	Share (%)
2000	13566.1	25.8	407.1	1.0	3.0
2001	7727.3	−43.0	468.8	15.1	6.1
2002	5899.1	−23.7	527.4	12.5	8.9
2003	5506.2	−6.7	535.0	1.4	9.7
2004	6925.4	25.8	606.3	13.3	8.8
2005	9477.1	36.8	724.1	19.4	7.6
2006	14035.6	48.1	727.2	0.4	5.2
2007	18917.1	34.8	835.2	14.9	4.4
2008	14900.7	−21.2	1083.1	29.7	7.3
2009	12361.2	−17.0	940.6	−13.2	7.6

续表

Year	Global FDI		Realized FDI Value of China		
	Amount	Growth Rate(%)	Amount	Growth Rate(%)	Share（%）
2010	13962.0	13.0	1147.3	22.0	8.2
2011	16150.8	15.7	1239.9	8.1	7.7
2012	14938.3	−7.5	1210.7	−2.3	8.1
2013	14563.2	−2.5	1239.1	2.3	8.5
2014	14038.6	−3.6	1285.0	3.7	9.2
2015	20323.0	44.8	1355.8	5.5	6.7
2016	20454.2	0.6	1337.1	−1.4	6.5
2017	16448.7	−19.6	1363.2	1.9	8.3
2018	13754.4	−16.4	1383.1	1.5	10.1
2019	17078.3	24.2	1412.2	2.1	8.3
2020	9619.8	−43.7	1493.4	5.7	15.5
2021	14781.4	53.7	1809.6	21.2	12.2
2022	12947.4	−12.4	1891.3	4.5	14.6

Source：MOFCOM FDI Statistics, and *World Investment Report 2023*, UNCTAD

3. Strategies of MNCs' FDI towards China

跨国公司为了争夺中国市场，采取了多种投资战略，主要包括：本土化战略、归核化战略、整体化战略、竞合战略及"中国+"战略。

MNCs have adopted various investment strategies in order to compete for the Chinese market, including localization strategy, refocus strategy, integration strategy, co-opetition strategy, and "China plus" strategy.

（1）Localization strategy

Localization strategy has become a common investment strategy for MNCs in China, mainly manifested in talent localization, procurement localization, brand localization, R&D localization, etc. Talent localization refers to the conscious cultivation of Chinese local managers by MNCs, enabling them to understand the world's cutting-edge technology and the latest management skills through various channels, in order to be competent in various positions of their subsidiaries in China. Once Chinese managers are competent in their respective positions, expatriates previously appointed from the company headquarters will be quickly recalled in order to save management costs, avoid cultural conflicts in the local area, and accelerate market responsiveness. Procurement localization refers to MNCs increasing the proportion of purchasing various intermediate inputs such as components in the Chinese market in order to improve their own flexibility and responsiveness to the global market. Procurement localization enables MNCs to fully utilize China's geographical advantages. Brand localization refers to MNCs not simply applying effective brand management models in domestic or foreign markets to China, but reshaping their brand image based on the characteristics of the

Chinese market and consumer needs. From the Chinese translation of the brand to value appeals, they comprehensively connect with Chinese culture and consumer psychology, and create a brand that is more recognized by Chinese consumers. R&D localization refers to MNCs not only establishing their own R&D centers in China, but also extensively cooperating with Chinese universities, leveraging the technological strength and network relationships of research institutes to study and promote technological achievements. The R&D institutions established by MNCs in China have become an important component of their global R&D network.

（2）Refocus strategy

With the intensification of market competition, MNCs' investments in China are gradually shifting from diversification to centralization. The so-called centralization refers to MNCs focusing their business operations on the most competitive industries, tilting their resources towards the most advantageous links in the value chain, and emphasizing the cultivation, maintenance, and development of their core competencies. The main measures to implement the refocus strategy include: the first is to sell or revoke non-core businesses, and restructure personnel and assets; the second is to acquire enterprises related to value chain advantages and lay off departments and personnel unrelated to core business in the acquired enterprises; the third is to implement strategic outsourcing, which means subcontracting non-core business to other companies.

（3）Integration strategy

Integration strategy refers to the establishment of regional headquarters by MNCs in China, achieving integrated investment management and highlighting the overall investment strategy in the Chinese market. Taking the manufacturing industry as an example, based on China's role as the "global factory", MNCs focus on integrated investment in upstream and downstream, that is, vertical integration. In the upstream of the manufacturing industry, namely in terms of basic raw materials and components, MNCs are increasing their investment efforts to achieve greater localization of procurement and minimize production costs. This is called backward integration. In the downstream of manufacturing, namely market promotion and after-sales service, MNCs have also begun to enter in order to provide better services and brand image for consumers. This is called forward integration. Through the integration of investment management, MNCs have achieved an integrated strategy of "R&D—production—service" in their investments in China, thereby maximizing the rational flow and optimization of production factors such as capital, technology, and personnel, and generating overall benefits.

（4）Co-opetition strategy

Co-opetition strategy refers to the strategy of MNCs investing in China, emphasizing both competition with other MNCs and local Chinese enterprises, as well as potential cooperation with these enterprises. Currently, the Chinese market has already become internationalized, and MNCs from around the world hope to gain a larger market share in the Chinese market. Sole proprietorship is beneficial for MNCs to exclusively enjoy the profits obtained from operating in China, while also facilitating comprehensive competition with other enterprises. But in some industries with huge investment amounts and rapid technological changes, even the strongest MNCs may feel too risky and unable to bear the risk of business failure alone. They are considering forming cross-border strategic alliances with other MNCs or local Chinese enterprises to achieve strong alliances, complementary advantages, and mutual benefit.

(5) "China plus" strategy

The "China plus" strategy refers to MNCs conducting FDI in China while also making similar investments in other Asian countries such as India, Vietnam, Thailand, and Malaysia, forming a "China plus One" pattern. This strategy is mainly driven by the COVID-19 and the game between China and the United States, led by American MNCs, and sought after by European, Japanese and Korean enterprises. These enterprises are influenced by the US government's policies of "decoupling and chain breaking", "small courtyard, high wall" and "de-risk", and are investing and setting up factories in countries outside of China in order to diversify the risks that may arise from excessive dependence on China. However, this investment strategy that violates economic laws exacerbates international tensions, increases global operating costs, and ultimately fails. It has been proven that China's excellent business environment, vast unified market, and complete industrial system still have great appeal to MNCs.

第二节　中国跨国公司的发展
（The Development of Chinese MNCs）

1. Development stage of Chinese MNCs

从新中国成立至 1978 年,中国国有企业在政府主导下从事了较多的对外经济技术援助及对外工程承包和劳务输出的活动。这些境外经济活动不以盈利为目的,因而不是真正意义上的对外直接投资。但这些经营活动为中国企业后续的跨国经营建立了市场联系,培养了跨国人才,积累了经营经验。直到 1978 年改革开放后,中国企业才开始了真正意义上的对外直接投资,大致经历了起步期、调适期、加速期和平稳期等四个阶段。

From the establishment of the People's Republic of China to 1978, Chinese state-owned enterprises, under the leadership of the government, engaged in a significant amount of foreign economic and technological assistance, as well as foreign engineering contracting and labor export. These overseas economic activities are not aimed at profit, so they are not truly outward FDI. However, these business activities have established market connections for Chinese enterprises' subsequent transnational operations, trained transnational talents and accumulated business experience. It was not until the reform and opening up in 1978 that Chinese enterprises began to engage in true outward FDI, which roughly went through four stages: initial stage, adjustment stage, acceleration stage, and stabilization stage.

(1) Initial stage: 1979—1992

On August 13, 1979, the State Council proposed 15 measures for economic system reform, among which the 13th explicitly allowed the establishment of enterprises abroad, thus establishing outward FDI as a national policy for the first time. In November 1979, the Sino Japanese joint venture Jinghe Co. , Ltd. became the first joint venture established by China abroad, marking the beginning of Chinese enterprises' outward FDI. From 1979 to 1983, only state-owned enterprises such as foreign trade enterprises and provincial and municipal international economic cooperation companies in China were allowed to make direct investments overseas, and all investment projects required authorization and approval from the State Council. In October 1984, China proposed a policy of revitalizing the domestic economy and opening up to the outside world. In 1985, the former Ministry of Foreign Trade and Economic Cooperation formulated the approval management measures for establishing non-trade enterprises abroad. Article 2 of the measures stipulates that any economic entity with funding sources, certain technical level and business expertise, and cooperative partners can apply to establish joint ventures abroad. Subsequently, the types and numbers of Chinese enterprises participating in overseas investment have significantly increased, and the investment fields have further expanded. In addition to economic and trade enterprises, industrial enterprises, commercial and trade material enterprises, technology enterprises, and financial and insurance enterprises have also participated in FDI. In 1984, 42 overseas investment enterprises were approved, and the number of approved overseas investment enterprises showed an increasing trend from 1985 to 1991, reaching 355 in 1992. As of 1992, a total of 1,363 overseas investment enterprises had been approved, and the investment areas had expanded to resource development, production and processing, transportation, medical and health care, tourism services, etc.

(2) Adjustment stage: 1993—2001

In 1991, due to unfamiliarity with the international market and foreign laws, as well as insufficient international business experience of some Chinese enterprises and institutions, the expected effects of investing overseas were not significant, and even resulted in losses. This not only caused economic losses to the country, but also had negative political impacts. Therefore, the former National Planning Commission submitted opinions to the State Council on strengthening the management of overseas investment projects. The opinion pointed out that China did not yet have the conditions

is still relatively small, and the proportion of Chinese MNCs' outward FDI in the world is still relatively low. As shown in Figure 10-2, China's outward FDI flow was US $ 177. 29 billion in 2023, an increase of 8. 7% compared with that of the previous year, accounting for 11. 4% of the global share, an increase of 0. 5% from that of 2022. Since the release of annual statistics on outward FDI in 2003, China has ranked among the top three in global outward FDI flows for 12 consecutive years, and its contribution to the world economy has become increasingly prominent, as shown in Figure 10-3. The flow in 2023 was 65. 7 times as much as the flow of 2002, with an average annual growth rate of 22. 1%.

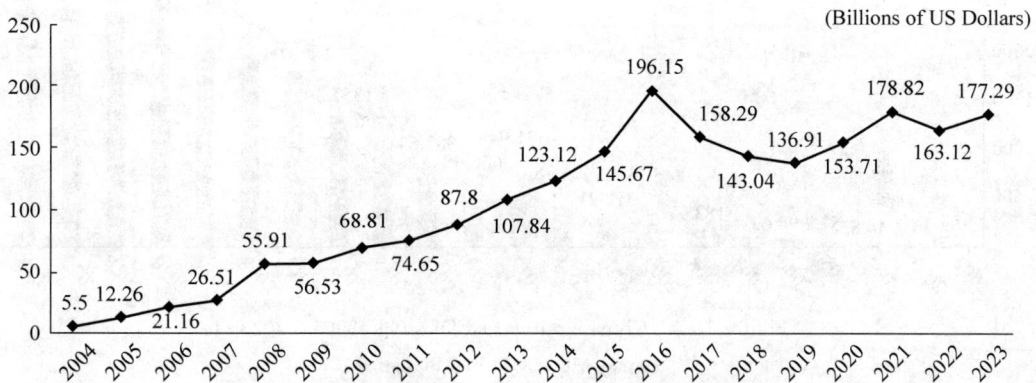

Figure 10-2　China's outward FDI flows, 2004—2023

Source：MOFCOM FDI Statistics

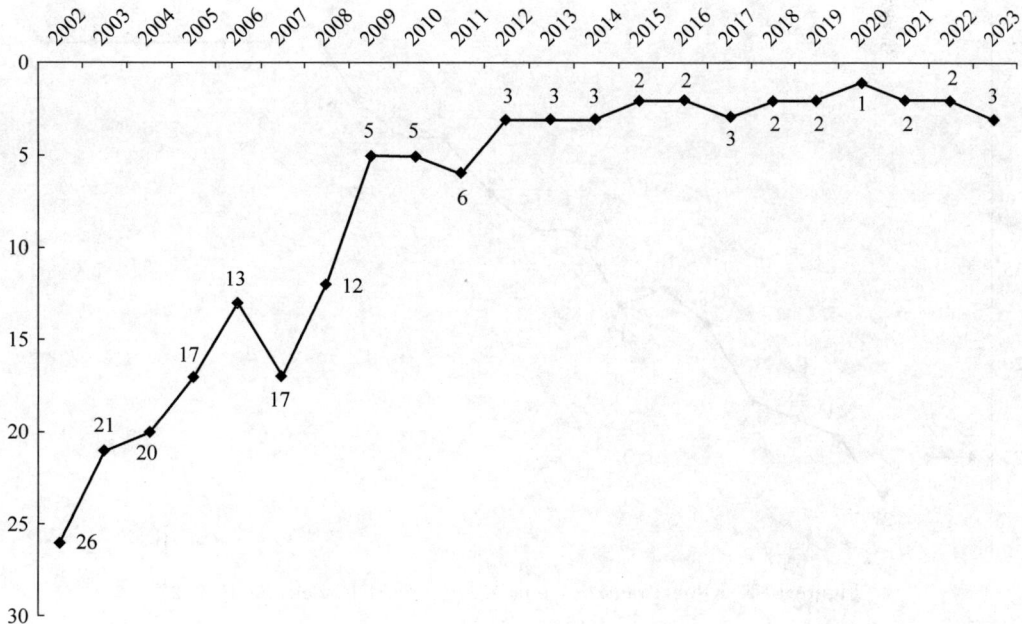

Figure 10-3　Global rank of China's outward FDI flow, 2002—2023

Source：MOFCOM FDI Statistics

As shown in Figure 10-4, at the end of 2023, China's stock of outward FDI was US $ 2,955. 4 billion, accounting for 6. 7% of the global outflow of FDI, up from 0. 4% in 2002. Its ranking climbed from 25th to 3rd, only inferior to the United States (US $ 9. 4 trillion) and the Netherlands (US $ 3. 4 trillion), as shown in Figure 10-5. In terms of stock size, the gap between China and the United States is still significant, only equivalent to 31. 4% of the United States.

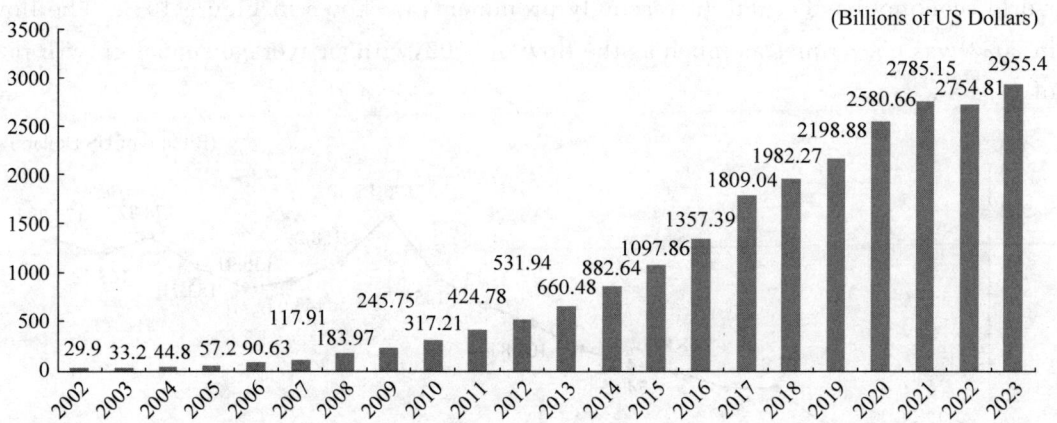

Figure 10-4   China's outward FDI stock, 2002—2023

Source：MOFCOM FDI Statistics

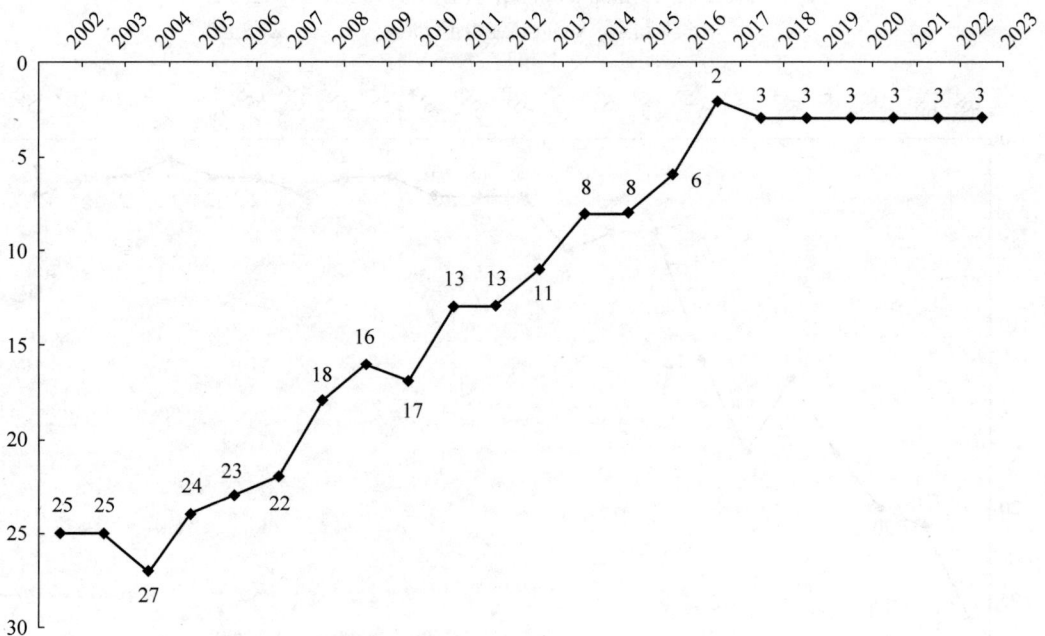

Figure 10-5   Global rank of China's outward FDI stock, 2002—2023

Source：MOFCOM FDI Statistics

（2）Chinese MNCs' outward FDI is dominated by the eastern region, with diversified investment entities

As shown in Table 10-6, local enterprises' outward non-financial FDI flow reached US $ 92.84 billion in 2023, a year-on-year increase of 7.9%. Among them, the eastern region reached US $ 76.05 billion, a year-on-year increase of 14.3%, accounting for 81.9% of local investment flow; the central region reached US $ 9.59 billion, a year-on-year increase of 2.2%, accounting for 10.3%; the western region reached US $ 6.56 billion, a year-on-year decrease of 29.8%, accounting for 7.1%; the three northeastern provinces reached US $ 0.64 billion, a year-on-year decrease of 16.9%, accounting for 0.7%.

Table 10-6　Regional distribution of China's local outward FDI flows in 2023

Region	Flows (US $ Billion)	Year-on-year growth rate (%)	Share (%)
Eastern region	76.05	14.3	81.9
Central region	9.59	2.2	10.3
Western region	6.56	−29.8	7.1
Three northeastern provinces	0.64	−16.9	0.7
Total	92.84	7.9	100

Source: MOFCOM FDI Statistics

Note: 1. The eastern region includes Beijing, Tianjin, Hebei, Shanghai, Jiangsu, Zhejiang, Fujian, Shandong, Guangdong, Hainan.

2. The central region includes Shanxi, Anhui, Jiangxi, Henan, Hubei, Hunan.

3. The western region includes Inner Mongolia, Guangxi, Chongqing, Sichuan, Guizhou, Yunnan, Xizang, Shaanxi, Gansu, Qinghai, Ningxia, Xinjiang.

4. The three northeastern provinces include Liaoning, Jilin, Heilongjiang.

（3）Chinese MNCs' outward FDI is widely distributed in different regions, but unevenly distributed

As shown in Table 10-7, Chinese MNCs' outward FDI is mainly concentrated in Asia, followed by Latin America. In 2023, nearly 80% of investment flowed to the Asian region, with an investment amount of US $ 141.6 billion, accounting for 79.9% of the outward FDI flow that year, an increase of 13.9% from 2022. Among them, the investment in Hong Kong (China) was US $ 108.77 billion, accounting for 76.8% of the investment in Asia; the investment in the 10 ASEAN countries was US $ 25.12 billion, accounting for 17.1% of investment in Asia. The investment in Latin America was US $ 13.48 billion, a year-on-year decrease of 17.6%, accounting for 7.6% of the outward FDI flow that year. The investment in Oceania was US $ 0.51 billion, a year-on-year decrease of 83.4%, accounting for 0.3% of the outward FDI flow that year. In 2023, China's outward non-financial FDI reached US $ 159.07 billion, an increase of 12.8% over the previous year, with a stock of US $ 2.6 trillion in outward FDI, covering nearly 190 countries and regions around the world. The top 20 countries (regions) of Chinese MNCs' investments are Hong Kong (China), Singapore, Cayman Islands, United States, Indonesia, Vietnam, British Virgin Islands, Luxembourg, Thailand, United Arab Emirates, United Kingdom, Kazakhstan, Malaysia, Cambodia, Laos, Mexico, Netherlands, Macao (China), Sweden, Republic of Korea. Among them, the vast majority of investments by Chinese MNCs in the British Virgin Islands and Cayman Islands, as well as nearly one-third of investments in Hong Kong (China), are made through these regions as transit points, ultimately flowing into other economies or "return investment" flows into China.

Table 10-7   Regional distribution of China's outward FDI flows in 2023

Continent	Amount (US $ Billion)	Year-on-year growth rate (%)	Share (%)
Asia	141.6	13.9	79.9
Latin America	13.48	−17.6	7.6
Europe	9.97	−3.6	5.6
North America	7.78	7.0	4.4
Africa	3.96	118.8	2.2
Oceania	0.51	−83.4	0.3
Total	177.29	8.7	100

Source: MOFCOM FDI Statistics

Note: Due to the rounding-off reason, the subentries may not add up to the aggregate totals. The remainder is the same.

(4) Chinese MNCs have a wide and relatively concentrated industry distribution for outward FDI

As shown in Table 10-8, in 2023, Chinese MNCs mainly invested in leasing and business services, wholesale and retail, manufacturing and finance, with investments in these four areas exceeding US $ 100 billion and accounting for nearly 80%. Among them, the leasing and business services industry remained in first place, while the wholesale and retail industry ranked the second place.

Table 10-8   Industry distribution of China's outward FDI flows in 2023

Industry	Flows (US $ Billion)	Year-on-year growth rate (%)	Share (%)
Leasing and business services	54.17	24.6	30.6
Wholesale and retail	38.82	83.4	21.9
Manufacturing	27.34	0.7	15.4
Finance	18.22	−17.6	10.3
Mining	9.88	−34.6	5.6
Transportation, warehousing, and post	8.44	−43.9	4.8
Scientific research and technology services	5.05	4.8	2.8
Production and supply of electricity, heat, gas and water	4.65	−14.7	2.6
Construction	2.86	97.2	1.6

续表

Industry	Flows（US$ Billion）	Year-on-year growth rate（%）	Share（%）
Information transmission，software and information technology services	2.28	34.9	1.3
Agriculture，forestry，animal husbandry and fishery	1.82	256.9	1.0
Real estate	1.42	−35.8	0.8
Resident services，repair and other services	1.05	54.4	0.6
Accommodation and catering	0.95	9500.0	0.5
Water，environment and public facilities management	0.24	33.3	0.1
Health and social work	0.16	−44.8	0.1
Education	0.08	−66.7	—
Culture，sports and entertainment	−0.14	—	—
Total	177.29	8.7	100

Source：MOFCOM FDI Statistics

3. The development mode of Chinese MNCs

根据中国企业过去二十多年"走出去"的实践，大致可以概括为以下九种模式或路径：先难后易、先易后难、借鸡生蛋、借船出海、抱团取暖、品牌共享、资源互补、海外园区、数字复制。每种模式都有各自的优缺点，并无优劣之分。中国企业应根据自身情况选择合适的模式，并在未来结合新的国际形势不断探索总结更多模式，这样才能在全球化过程中少走弯路，发挥更大的作用。

According to the practice of Chinese enterprises' "going global" in the past 20 years，it can be roughly summarized into the following nine models or paths：difficult first，easy later；easy first，difficult later；borrowing hens to lay eggs；borrowing ships to go abroad；huddling for warmth；brand sharing；resource complementation；overseas parks；and digital replication. Each model has its own advantages and disadvantages，and there is no superiority or inferiority. Chinese enterprises should choose appropriate models based on their own situation and continuously explore and summarize more models in the future in combination with the new international situation，so as to avoid detours and play a greater role in the process of globalization.

（1）Difficult first，easy later

This model is for Chinese companies to establish their own production bases overseas based on the location advantages of the host country，directly promote their brands，and establish local corporate images，in order to better sell products and avoid more tariff barriers. Haier，Fuyao and other Chinese enterprises have chosen this model，and they have established production bases in the United States and other places.

This model is mainly driven by the market demand, talent attraction, and technology of the host country, and establishing an R&D center in the host country is an important part. The advantage of this model is that it is easy to gain the trust and welcome of consumers in the host country, but the challenge is high cost, long project construction period, high uncertainty, and high requirements for the strength of MNCs.

(2) Easy first, difficult later

This model refers to Chinese enterprises prioritizing markets in developing countries and regions that are relatively easy to enter during the process of "going global", establishing and developing their own technological systems, forming competitive product and brand advantages, continuously expanding market size, and preparing for future entry into developed country markets. This model can avoid premature confrontation with multinational giants from developed countries, and gain more time and experience for the development of enterprises. The typical representative of this model is Huawei. Huawei has clear international market goals and technological leadership, and focuses on establishing its own technology system, which is a technology oriented model. The challenge of this model is how to sustain technological innovation while avoiding intellectual property disputes.

(3) Borrowing hens to lay eggs

This model refers to Chinese companies achieving internationalization through overseas listings. This is a more effective way for Chinese enterprises to utilize foreign investment in the new situation, not only by "going global" and leveraging foreign markets to bring back new funds, but also by bringing back more standardized business management models. In October 1992, Huachen China Automotive Holdings Co., Ltd. was listed on the New York Stock Exchange in the United States, becoming the first Chinese company to be listed overseas. From 2007 to 2018, the total number of Chinese companies listed overseas reached 1,034, with a financing amount of approximately CNY¥ 1.95 trillion. These companies usually go public in Europe and America first, then use this as a platform to acquire technology companies in Europe and America, and then return to China to operate. Chinese companies going public overseas can not only raise funds and rapidly enhance their competitiveness, but also improve corporate governance and management structure, learn advanced foreign technology and management experience, better attract international talents, discover new strategic cooperation opportunities, and enhance the company's good brand image in the international capital market. Of course, due to differences in finance, law, culture, language, and other aspects, Chinese companies going public overseas will not be smoothly sailing. In recent years, the US government has deliberately targeted Chinese companies for decoupling in the financial sector, forcing many "Chinese concept stocks" listed in the US to delist, making it increasingly difficult to implement this model.

（4）Borrowing ships to go abroad

This model refers to obtaining the brand, resources, technology, etc. of internationally renowned enterprises through mergers and acquisitions, in order to leverage these resources to quickly establish the enterprise in the international market. Lenovo, Sany Heavy Industry and Geely are all typical representatives of this model. This model seems like a gamble, and its success depends crucially on whether the corporate cultures of both parties can be integrated, which is related to the integration ability of the international team of the acquiring company.

（5）Huddling for warmth

The main creators of this model are small and medium-sized enterprises in Wenzhou, also known as the Wenzhou model. It refers to Chinese small and medium-sized enterprises fully utilizing the power of overseas Chinese and overseas Chinese businessmen, and promoting some competitive domestic products to the world through the establishment of "Chinese shopping malls" and other means, achieving the collective "going global" of small and medium-sized enterprises. The challenge of this model is how to strengthen industry coordination, enhance understanding of local culture, and how to conduct orderly management overseas.

（6）Brand sharing

This model refers to Chinese companies combining their unknown brands with internationally renowned brands to drive domestic products to "go global". For example, TCL Corporation combines with well-known German companies such as Snyder, as well as French companies such as Thomson and Alcatel, to drive the enhancement of the TCL brand. The advantage of the brand sharing model is to obtain long-term brand sharing at low cost, but in the long run, companies still need to launch their own well-known brands.

（7）Resource complementation

This model refers to Chinese companies acquiring overseas strategic resources through mergers and acquisitions, joint ventures, and other means in order to make up for the inherent deficiencies in the reserves of some types of mineral resources in China, obtain long-term stable supply of resources and energy, and enhance their bargaining power in negotiations with world mining giants. By sharing the pricing power of resources and energy, the company can reduce its costs. PetroChina, CNOOC, Sinopec, Chinalco, Minmetals, and others are typical representatives of this model. Currently, many large and medium-sized state-owned enterprises in China still need to "go global" in resources such as oil, natural gas, minerals, and forestry to find new resources to support greater domestic economic development, which is an essential model. This model is generally adopted by government-led state-owned enterprises with large investment amounts. Therefore, it is very important to strengthen feasibility studies, enhance supervision, and avoid decision-making errors and losses.

（8）Overseas parks

This model refers to Chinese companies building parks overseas under the guidance of the government, driving more Chinese companies to "go global" and attracting investment from other countries to enter the park. There are two types of overseas park model: one is China's overseas economic and trade cooperation zones guided by the state, and the other is various industrial parks independently built by Chinese enterprises overseas. The biggest advantage of the overseas park model is cluster development, which is efficient and convenient. With the deepening and implementation of the "One Belt and One Road" initiative, China has built more than 100 overseas economic and trade cooperation zones in countries along the "One Belt and One Road", built a platform for enterprise cluster based international development, played a positive role in promoting local economic and social development, and became the fulcrum for achieving sustainable development of the "One Belt and One Road" initiative. In addition to the overseas economic and trade cooperation zones guided by the state, Chinese enterprises, especially private enterprises, have gone overseas and invested in establishing overseas industrial parks, such as Huali, Haier, Hongdou, Kangnai, Huajian, Huihong and other enterprises.

（9）Digital replication

This model refers to that Chinese enterprises, relying on digital technologies such as the Internet, promote their successful business models overseas, and fully tap overseas resources and markets, in order to achieve further development and realize the internationalization of enterprises. Typical representatives of digital replication model include Alibaba, JD. com, and others. These Chinese e-commerce enterprises, relying on the internationally leading Internet technology, have copied the successful experience of the Chinese market overseas, not only bringing shopping platforms and payment methods such as WeChat and Alipay abroad, but also developing powerful logistics services overseas to occupy a larger overseas market.

第三节　跨国公司未来发展趋势
（The Development Trend of MNCs）

1. Triple divergence of FDI patterns

Over the past two decades, MNCs' transformative shifts driven by technological advances, policy developments, and sustainability demands have reshaped globalization. FDI patterns have adapted in two key aspects. First, the growth of FDI and global value chains (GVCs) has lost pace with gross domestic product (GDP) and trade—their growth paths have disconnected. Second, there is a widening gap in investment trends between manufacturing and services sectors. [①]

(1) Long-term FDI stagnation

The long-term trend in MNCs' cross-border investment shows that a slowdown in global FDI already started around 2010. It no longer kept pace with global trade and GDP. Trade within GVCs also slowed, confirming the close link between FDI and GVCs. MNCs' FDI has essentially plateaued from about 2010, well before the onset of trade tensions and recent crises. While global GDP and global trade continued to grow, FDI stagnated. This is different from previous decades, in which FDI grew rapidly in parallel with other macroeconomic indicators.

The comparison with trends in GDP and trade underscores the distinctive nature of the early slowbalisation of cross-border investment. GVC participation, which tracks the trade component of GVCs, shows a similar pattern to FDI. This suggests a connection between the decline in FDI and the slowdown in GVC trade, emphasizing the importance of GVCs in shaping international trade and investment. Since the 2010s, GVCs have undergone a process of prolonged restructuring, partially reversing the trend towards offshoring, fragmentation and unbundling that fueled the concurrent growth of trade and investment in the 1990s and the 2000s. The persistence of this process confirms its structural nature, primarily tied to technological, policy and sustainability factors.

Among the technological trends that are reshaping international production are robotics-enabled automation, enhanced supply chain digitalization, and additive manufacturing. Robotics reduce the share of labor in total costs, increase economies of scale, and can prompt the rebundling and reshoring of fragmented processes. Supply chain digitalization reduces governance and transaction costs, improves coordination, and can enhance access to GVCs for smaller firms through platforms. Additive manufacturing leads to greater geographic distribution of activities, closer proximity to markets, and concentrated value in design phases. Adoption rates of these technologies, however, are affected by trade and investment policies that are trending towards higher levels of interventionism and protectionism, along with a shift from multilateral to regional and bilateral policy frameworks. In particular, after the outbreak of the COVID-19 pandemic and the intensification of geopolitical and trade tensions, major public interventions in developed economies, such as the *Inflation Reduction Act* in the United States and the *Recovery and Resilience Plan* in the European Union, are contributing to reshaping the public policy landscape for MNCs' FDI.

Finally, sustainability concerns, including differences in approach between countries and regions on emission targets and environmental, social and governance (ESG)

---

① Trentini, C., J. de Camargo Mainente and A. U. Santos-Paulino (2022). The evolution of digital MNEs: an empirical note. *Transnational Corporations*, 29 (1): 163-187.

standards, market-driven changes in products and processes, and supply chain resilience measures, are driving further change in international production networks. For example, carbon border adjustment mechanisms are likely to affect trade flows and locational decisions for export-oriented investment. In recent years, FDI has faced additional challenges. Its recovery from the pandemic, slower than that of GDP and trade, reiterates the trend of dual-speed economic globalization. However, it also shows a degree of resilience to shocks, a characteristic long associated with FDI, relative to other international capital flows such as foreign portfolio investment.

Overall, in the analysis of economic fracturing and shifting investment patterns, it is important to note that the long-term trends over the past decade and a half continue to exert a greater and more enduring influence on global investment flows than recent exogeneous shocks—at least until today.

(2) The increasing weight of services

The overall stagnation in FDI conceals sectoral differences. MNCs' cross-border investment in services flourishes while manufacturing lags. This reflects a global shift towards more services-centric and asset-light investment.

The historical trend in cross-border greenfield project announcements, often used to gauge MNCs' FDI patterns, mirrors that of the underlying FDI trend, showing a slowdown followed by long-term stagnation. However, a more dynamic reality can be observed in its composition.

Since the mid-2000s, the share of services in total greenfield projects has increased. This includes investments not only in typical services industries such as banking or consulting but also the services component of traditional manufacturing industries. This service-oriented component is rapidly expanding within traditionally defined manufacturing industries.

Over the course of 20 years, the share of investment in services activities within manufacturing industries has nearly doubled, now representing the majority of projects. This shift underscores a broader trend towards the "servitisation" of manufacturing, enhanced by rapid technological advances. The transition to services has been facilitated by a policy trend favoring investment incentives that promote MNCs' FDI in the service sector. According to UNCTAD's *Investment Policy Monitor Database*, the proportion of investment incentives directed towards the services sector rose from 35% in the period from 2014 to 2018 to 46% in the period from 2019 to 2023.

MNCs' services investments, in particular those linked to digital technologies, are intrinsically more asset-light than investments in manufacturing. Digital economy operations make a physical presence overseas less fundamental, leading to a lighter international production footprint of MNCs.

The obvious corollary of the rise of investment in services is the steep decline in the share of investment in manufacturing activities, which halved over the past two decades (from 26% to 13%). There has also been a decline in greenfield project announcements in other non-services activities or service-sector activities requiring physical investment, such as construction, electricity, extraction and infrastructure. While these activities are not technically part of manufacturing, they share similarities from an FDI perspective as they involve "asset-heavy" investment in tangible assets for material production and transformation as opposed to "asset-light" investment in services activities. The decline in manufacturing activities challenges their traditional centrality in cross-border investment and their role as a cornerstone of FDI-and GVC-based development. Investigating whether this decline is part of an overall process of deglobalization is essential to understanding the changing dynamics of manufacturing investment and its development prospects.

（3）The deglobalization of manufacturing

MNCs' manufacturing FDI, stagnant for two decades, shows negative growth after the outbreak of the COVID-19 pandemic. While global manufacturing activity and investment remain robust, their international component is shrinking, suggesting a trend towards deglobalization. This trend is exacerbated by the growing prevalence of non-equity modes of international production.

Zooming in on the historical patterns of MNCs' greenfield projects in manufacturing and services reveals strikingly different trajectories. The services sector grew rapidly throughout the 2000s. This growth stabilized in the 2010s and showed resilience in the post-COVID phase. In contrast, manufacturing has followed a substantially flat trajectory over the past two decades. In the three years following the outbreak of the COVID-19 pandemic, manufacturing entered negative growth territory, experiencing an annual decline of more than 10%. The year 2023 partially re-balances this post-pandemic narrative, as manufacturing saw a rebound. It remains to be seen whether this rebound signals a structural recovery from the COVID-19 pandemic downturn or merely a temporary fluctuation.

The prolonged struggle of manufacturing and its stark contrast with the growth of the services sector raise questions about a possible manufacturing deglobalization process. Complementary evidence on other indicators, particularly GVC trade data, supports the hypothesis of increasing localization of manufacturing. While manufacturing activity and investment are not declining overall, their international component appears to be shrinking. This is evidenced not only by reduced FDI but also by reduced trade in intermediate inputs. The two indicators reflect two sides of the same coin: as the MNCs, coordinating the international production system reduce their FDI footprint, intra-firm trade of intermediate inputs—a prominent component of GVC trade—also experiences a decline. This broad picture is consistent with a process of reconfiguration of GVCs towards less complex and fragmented structures in the quest for security and resilience.

The stagnation in international production through MNCs' FDI can be explained not only by increased domestic production but also by the increased use of governance modes alternative to FDI, i. e. non-equity modes（NEMs）or contract forms of international production, such as third-party outsourcing or franchise relationships. The data cannot capture the degree to which a shift to NEMs contributes to the negative trend in manufacturing FDI. It is likely that offshore manufacturing is undergoing both a retreat（reshoring）and an evolution towards NEMs simultaneously. The former is likely the main driver of the structural shifts observed in the FDI project data, while the latter potentially acts as an amplifier of these effects.

（4）The growing ends of the smile curve

The transition from manufacturing to services is part of a broader change in the role of MNCs' FDI in global value creation. MNCs' cross-border investment is moving from the center to the two ends of the smile curve, most notably towards business and ICT services upstream and marketing services downstream.

Traditionally depicted as a graphical representation of value addition at various stages of production, the "smile curve" offers relevant insights on the nature of the shift of investment from manufacturing to services. Global investment increasingly targets the upper regions or ends of the curve, both upstream（pre-production）and, to a lesser extent, downstream（post-production）.

MNCs' investment in manufacturing activities at the bottom of the curve has declined from one-third of greenfield projects in the mid-2000s to one-fifth, marking an almost 25% decrease in the absolute number of projects. While the share of the middle layer, encompassing low value-added services like logistics and distribution, remains relatively stable, there is a clear "leap" of projects from the bottom to the upper ends of the smile curve. The share of projects in high-level support functions including business and ICT services has doubled over the past two decades, increasing by more than 150% in absolute terms and now comprising a quarter of all projects. Other high value-added service activities such as concept/R&D/management upstream and marketing downstream have also grown in both share and number.

This highlights the specific set of services increasingly targeted by international investment. It follows that the shift towards services is not merely sectoral but signifies a deeper transformation in the role of MNCs' FDI in global value creation. The pool of low value-added, mainly efficiency-seeking, FDI projects, which traditionally served as entry points for developing countries in GVCs, is clearly narrowing. At the same time, investment at the higher value-added stages of the smile curve, characterized by service-oriented, knowledge-intensive activities, typically accessible only to advanced and emerging economies, is gaining prominence. This presents formidable challenges for policymakers in low-income countries that are still in the early stages of their GVC development path.

（5）Convergence of sectoral patterns across regions

All regions, including developing ones, are feeling the effects of the transition towards MNCs' services-oriented asset-light FDI. Consequently, traditional differences in sectoral patterns between developed and developing regions are increasingly blurring. While the shift towards high value-added services is overall more beneficial to developed economies, it does not exclude developing countries from participating in this transformation. Greenfield data show a notable increase in the number and share of projects in service activities across all regions, including developing ones. Each region on its own replicates the movement towards the upper echelons of the smile curve. As a consequence, traditional distinctions between developed and developing regions regarding the types of FDI they attract are blurring. In 2003, the gap in the share of greenfield projects in service activities between developed and developing regions was still significant, reflecting historical specializations, with developing countries traditionally more focused on commodity processing and manufacturing and developed ones on services. However, two decades later, this gap has been substantially absorbed, with the shares of both developed and developing countries at about 80%.

An analysis at the regional level confirms the convergence among developing regions. The FDI footprints of regions across different development levels are much more similar now than they were two decades ago.

This convergence again has important development implications. It partly explains the continued lackluster growth in absolute project numbers in several developing regions and increasing concentration of investment in economies with the hard and soft infrastructure required to attract investment in the services sector. FDI-based structural transformation—attracting investment to move from the primary sector through manufacturing to higher value-added activities—is increasingly difficult for other developing countries.

2. FDI transition from divergence to fracturing

In recent years, geopolitical differences and global crises have led to FDI transition from divergence to fracturing. This disruption of historical investment patterns is marked by high levels of uncertainty and limited possibilities for countries to strategically benefit from diversification. Geopolitical factors are increasingly driving the location decisions of investors, at times overriding economic considerations.

（1）Unstable investment relationships

Heightened geopolitical tensions are increasing the volatility of investment sources and destinations, and the susceptibility of traditional investment links to disruptions.

Instability in investment relationships limits the capacity of developing countries to strategically capitalize on diversification opportunities arising from shifts in investment patterns.

Since the escalation of trade tensions in 2018, bilateral investment patterns have become increasingly volatile, with indicators of annual change in the geographic distribution of outward investment from the United States, China and Europe showing a significant upward trend. An increase in this indicator implies heightened instability and unpredictability in investment decisions, with geographical patterns changing at a faster pace than their historical evolution. Following a temporary slowdown in 2021, instability shot up further in the last two years.

Significant annual fluctuations in global investment patterns could mean that each year some countries stand to benefit significantly from FDI re-allocation. However, these fluctuations also imply that patterns of winners and losers are less likely to remain steady over time. While isolated shocks can present opportunities for diversification, the presence of long-term uncertainty will generally yield negative effects. An examination of relative gains and losses across recipient regions over the past four years corroborates this perspective.

Some expected shifts can be clearly observed, including the diminishing investment share of China, South-Eastern Europe and Commonwealth of Independent States (CIS) in outward investment from the United States and Europe, and the decline in the United States and Europe's share in Chinese investment. Beyond these shifts, only some countries in Middle East and North Africa (MENA region) have gained share consistently across time and investors in recent years. This region has emerged as a viable alternative for diversifying investment. Current developments in the region though could again alter the outlook, further underscoring the precarious nature of temporary gains in the current unstable global geopolitical landscape.

The picture is less clear for all other regions, with no discernible and consistent diversification pattern across years and investors. Focusing on the past two years only, the broader Asian region, encompassing East Asia (excluding the Chinese mainland and Hong Kong SAR, China), South-East Asia, and South Asia, has also notably benefited from redistributive mechanisms. This trend suggests a potential diversion effect, which had not yet emerged in earlier periods. Prior analyses on greenfield projects before the COVID-19 pandemic have shown that rising trade tensions brought a shift of FDI flows to South-East Asia in specific industries; however, the overall redistributive effect on South-East Asia was still negative.

(2) Fracturing along geopolitical lines

Geopolitical differences are causing a fracturing trend in global FDI, with the reduction in investments between geopolitically distant countries highlighting their significant influence on investors' location choices, overshadowing traditional determinants of FDI.

Tracking investment between countries according to their geopolitical alignment clearly shows the effect of geopolitics on FDI patterns. The first signs of fissures in investment patterns emerged a decade ago already, with investment flows between geopolitically distant countries showing an initial moderate decline. Over the past five years, however, this decline has accelerated, particularly in 2019 amid escalating trade tensions and further in 2022, clearly underscoring the geopolitical nature of the trend. Overall, between 2013 and 2022, the share of FDI projects between geopolitically distant countries decreased by 10 percentage points, from 23% to 13%.

The decline and synchronization with major geopolitical events was even more pronounced in the manufacturing sector, where investment between geopolitically distant countries started to fall sharply in 2019, with the escalation of the trade tensions. Manufacturing investment, inherently more "sticky" than services investment, responded to the geopolitical context with some delay but, at that stage, the response was more pronounced. This trend does not differ substantially for the subset of strategic sectors, including high-tech and semi-conductor industries, despite their additional sensitivity. The year 2023 stands out as an exception to historical patterns. Whether this signals the onset of a structural change or merely reflects a transient rebound remains uncertain. The share of investment between geopolitically aligned countries (linked but not fully complementary to that between geopolitically distant countries) is increasing faster than investment between geographically close ones. The data for 2023 again show a partial reversal of this trend. Geopolitical motivations could thus emerge as primary drivers of investment decisions, potentially overshadowing relevant geographic factors such as near-shoring and regionalization.

3. Sustainability push for FDI

The sustainability imperative and the drive to stimulate investment in the sustainable development goals (SDGs) have opened new opportunities for investment-driven industrial development, particularly in environmental technologies. However, these new opportunities can only compensate in part for the lack of MNCs' FDI growth in other industrial sectors. Many smaller developing countries, and especially the least developed countries (LDCs), are experiencing growing marginalization and vulnerability.

（1）The sustainability imperative driving new FDI sectors

MNCs' FDI in environmental technologies stands out as the main pocket of growth outside services. Since 2010, while manufacturing investment stagnated across all industries, the number of cross-border greenfield projects along the entire value chain of environmental technologies sectors has steadily increased.

One industry has shown significant investment growth in recent years, which is environmental technologies. Since 2010, the number of greenfield projects in environmental technologies has steadily risen. Unlike other industries, such increase was not just confined to services-related activities but occurred along the entire value chain. Projects in environmental technologies have increased from comprising 1% of all greenfield projects in non-services activities in 2003 to 20% in 2023, transitioning from the lowest rank to becoming the leading industry in terms of project numbers outside the services sector.

Furthermore, at the intersection between green energy FDI and technology, the number of FDI projects in the manufacturing of electric vehicles and batteries, while currently still representing a small proportion, has been accelerating at an average annual growth rate of 27% since the middle of the past decade. Beyond the green energy sector, other environmental technology industries are also likely to provide opportunities for industrial development and investment attraction in the coming years, ranging from green hydrogen production to sustainable aviation fuels, battery recycling and material recovery, or eco-friendly packaging solutions.

(2) The increasing concentration of FDI and marginalization of developing countries

Amid historical shifts and economic fracturing, the proportion of MNCs' FDI greenfield projects in smaller developing countries and least developed countries is diminishing. This trend exacerbates their marginalization and vulnerability, as FDI becomes increasingly concentrated in developed and emerging economies.

After netting out the effect of the declining share of China, the share of developing countries in the total number of greenfield projects has been relatively stable. However, the distribution of projects among developing economies has notably shifted towards higher-income and upper-middle income countries.

Over the past two decades, the proportion of projects in countries categorized as low-income and lower-middle income by the World Bank classification has decreased by 15 percentage points, equivalent to a one-third reduction. The share of lower income countries in the total number of greenfield projects in developing economies (excluding China) has decreased to just over 30%. This share encompasses a large number of lower-income developing countries—86 countries classified as low-income and lower-middle income. This trend of increasing marginalization of smaller developing countries is observed across all developing regions. Specifically, in Asia, Latin America and the Caribbean, the decline in the share of projects in lower-income countries has been continuous since the 2000s, while in Africa it has mostly occurred in the last decade. Focusing specifically on the group of LDCs, the number of cross-border greenfield projects in these countries remains alarmingly low, comprising merely 1% of the total. What is particularly concerning is the consistent downward trajectory of this share over the past decade, declining from 3% in the mid-2010s to 2% during 2016 to 2019.

Regrettably, the marginalization of lower income developing countries and LDCs aligns with the broader trend towards increasing FDI concentration. The dynamics of FDI concentration across regions shows that a phase of decline was followed by a reversal towards higher concentration in the last decade. For instance, in Africa, the top 10% of recipient countries accounted for 57% of projects in 2000s, decreasing to 49% by early 2010s before climbing back to 67% in the last three years.

From a development perspective, the emerging narrative is particularly worrisome. While the geographic rebalancing away from China may benefit some developing regions, it primarily favors the largest economies in these regions. These are better positioned to compete with developed economies to attract investment in the fast-growing services sector. Conversely, the decline in manufacturing investment leaves smaller countries increasingly marginalized, with a shrinking pool of efficiency-seeking, lower value-added projects that can support their industrial transformation and their efforts to integrate into GVCs.

关键术语（Key Terms）

本土化战略（localization strategy）
归核化战略（refocus strategy）
整体化战略（integration strategy）
竞合战略（co-opetition strategy）
"中国＋"战略（"China plus" strategy）
先难后易模式（difficult first, easy later model）
先易后难模式（easy first, difficult later model）
借鸡生蛋模式（borrowing hens to lay eggs model）
借船出海模式（borrowing ships to go abroad model）
抱团取暖模式（huddling for warmth model）
品牌共享模式（brand sharing model）
资源互补模式（resource complementation model）
海外园区模式（overseas park model）
数字复制模式（digital replication model）

小结（Summary）

1. MNCs' FDI towards China has roughly gone through four stages: exploration, adjustment, promotion, and stability. MNCs have adopted various investment strategies in order to compete for the Chinese market, including localization strategy, refocus strategy, integration strategy, co-opetition strategy, and "China plus" strategy.

2. Chinese MNCs' outward FDI has undergone four stages such as initial stage, adjustment stage, acceleration stage, and stabilization stage. Chinese MNCs' "going global" has taken the following nine models or paths: difficult first, easy later; easy first, difficult later; borrowing hens to lay eggs; borrowing ships to go abroad; huddling for warmth; brand sharing; resource complementation; overseas parks; and digital replication. Each model has its own advantages and disadvantages, and there is no

superiority or inferiority.

3. FDI patterns have adapted in two key aspects. First, the growth of FDI and GVCs has lost pace with GDP and trade. Second, there is a widening gap in investment trends between manufacturing and services sectors. In recent years, geopolitical differences and global crises have led to a transition from divergence to fracturing. This disruption of historical investment patterns is marked by high levels of uncertainty and limited possibilities for countries to strategically benefit from diversification. The sustainability imperative and drive to stimulate investment in the SDGs have opened new opportunities for investment-driven industrial development. Many smaller developing countries are experiencing growing marginalization and vulnerability.

延伸阅读(Further Readings)

习题(Exercises)

参 考 文 献
（References）

[1] ［美］查尔斯·W. L. 希尔,托马斯·M. 霍特. 国际商务(英文版·第 11 版)[M]. 北京：中国人民大学出版社,2022.

[2] ［美］查尔斯·希尔. 国际商务(第 11 版)[M]. 王蔷,等,译. 北京：中国人民大学出版社,2018.

[3] ［美］查尔斯·希尔著,王蔷改编. 国际商务 (International Business)(英文版·第 11 版)[M]. 北京：机械工业出版社,2019.

[4] 陈立敏,谭力文主编. 跨国企业管理[M]. 北京：清华大学出版社,2012.

[5] 崔日明,徐春祥. 跨国公司经营与管理(第 4 版)[M]. 北京：机械工业出版社,2020.

[6] 韩玉军. 国际商务(第 4 版)[M]. 北京：中国人民大学出版社,2023.

[7] 洪俊杰,郑玮,蓝庆新. 国际商务[M]. 北京：北京大学出版社,2023.

[8] 李林玥. 国际经济合作理论与实务[M]. 北京：清华大学出版社,2023.

[9] ［美］迈克尔·A. 希特,等. 战略管理：竞争与全球化(英文版·第 12 版)[M]. 北京：机械工业出版社,2023.

[10] 卢进勇,等. 跨国公司经营与管理(第 3 版)[M]. 北京：机械工业出版社,2022.

[11] 卢进勇,邸志雄,彭静. 国际投资学(第 2 版)[M]. 北京：中国人民大学出版社,2023.

[12] 任永菊. 跨国公司与对外直接投资(第 2 版)[M]. 北京：清华大学出版社,2024.

[13] 王海文. 国际商务(英文版)[M]. 北京：中国人民大学出版社,2022.

[14] 王炜瀚,王健,等. 国际商务(第 4 版)[M]. 北京：机械工业出版社,2021.

[15] 王允平,陈燕主编. 跨国公司财务管理(第五版)[M]. 北京：首都经济贸易大学出版社,2020.

[16] 王增涛主编,国际投资与跨国公司[M]. 北京：清华大学出版社,2024.

[17] ［英］约翰·邓宁. 多国企业,转引自联合国秘书处《世界发展中的多国公司》中译本. 北京：商务印书馆,1975,附录Ⅱ.

[18] 赵曙明,刘燕,彼得·道林,等. 国际人力资源管理(第 5 版)[M]. 北京：中国人民大学出版社,2012.

[19] Adler, Nancy J., and Ghadar, Fariborz (1990), International strategy from the perspective of people and culture: The North American context, *Research in Global Business Management*, 1: 179-205.

[20] Bartlett, C., Ghoshal S., Birkinshaw, J., Fan, L. (2004), *Transnational Management: Text, Cases, and Readings in Cross-border Management*, McGraw-Hill Companies, Inc.

[21] Basu, R. (2023). *Managing Global Supply Chains: Contemporary Challenges in Supply Chain Management*, London, Routledge.

[22] Black, J. S., Gregerson, H. B., and Mendenhall M. E. (1992). *Global Assignments*. San Francisco: Jossey-bass.

[23] Buckley, P. J. and Casson, M. (1976), *The Future of the Multinational Enterprise*, London, Macmillan.

[24] Buckley, P. J., and Casson, M. (1985), *The Economic Theory of the Multinational Enterprise*. Springer.

[25] Cantwell, J., and Tolentino, P. E. E. (1990), *Technological Accumulation and Third World Multinationals* (No. 139). University of Reading, Department of Economics.

[26] Cullen, John B., Parboteeah K. Praveen (2017), *Multinational Management: A Strategic*

Approach,7e,Thomson Learning Asia.

[27] Czinkota,Michael R.,Ilkka A. Ronkainen,Michael H. Moffett(2004). *Fundamentals of International Business*,South-Western,Cengage Learning.

[28] Czinkota,Michael R.,Ilkka A. Ronkainen,Michael H. Moffett(2008). *International Business*,7th Edition,Cengage learning Asia Pte Ltd.

[29] Doh,Jonathan P.,Fred Luthans(2018). *International Management：Culture,Strategy,and Behavior*,10th Edition,McGraw-Hill Education.

[30] Dunning,J. H.(1979),Explaining changing patterns of international production：in defense of the eclectic theory. *Oxford Bulletin of Economics and Statistics*,41(4)：269-295.

[31] Dunning,J. H.(1981),Explaining the international direct investment position of countries：towards a dynamic or developmental approach. *Weltwirtschaftliches Archiv*,117(1)：30-64.

[32] Dunning,J. H.(1981),*International Production and The Multinational Enterprise*. Allen & Unwin.

[33] Dunning,J. H.,Lundan,S. M.(2008),*Multinational Enterprises and the Global Economy*,Edward Elgar Publishing Limited,Cheltenham,UK.

[34] Ghoshal,S.(1987). Global strategy：An organizing framework. *Strategic Management Journal*,8(5)：425-440.

[35] Griffin,Ricky W.,Pustay,Michael W.(2013),*International Business*,7th Edition,Pearson Education,Inc.

[36] Heenan,D. A.,and H. V. Perlmutter(1979). *Multinational Organization Development*. *Reading*,Mass：Addison Wesley.

[37] Hill,Charles W. L.,Hult,G. Tomas M.(2017),*International Business：Competing in the Global Marketplace*,11e,McGraw-Hill Education.

[38] Hymer,S. H.(1960),*The International Operations of National Firms：A Study of Direct Foreign Investment*(Doctoral dissertation,Massachusetts Institute of Technology).

[39] Ivanov,D.,Tsipoulanidis,A.,Schonberger,J.(2021),*Global Supply Chain and Operation Management*,Springer Cham.

[40] Knight,G. A.,Cavusgil,S. T.(2004),Innovation,organizational capabilities,and the born-global firm. *Journal of International Business Studies*,35(2)：124-141.

[41] McCormick,I. and Chapman,T.(1996). Executive Relocation：Personal and Organization Tactics,in *Managing Across Cultures：Issues and Perspectives*,ed. Pat Joynt and Malcolm Warner London：International Thomson Business Press.

[42] Mendenhall,Mark E.,E. Dunbar,and Gary R. Oddou(1987). Expatriate selection,training and career-pathing：A review and critique. *Human Resource Management*. 26(3)：331-345.

[43] Kindleberger,C. P.(1981),Dominance and leadership in the international economy：Exploitation,public goods,and free rides. *International Studies Quarterly*,25(2)：242-254.

[44] Kojima,K.(1978),*Direct Foreign Investment：A Japanese Model of Multinational Business Operations*,London：Croom Helm.

[45] Lall,S.(1983). *The New Multinationals：The Spread of Third World Enterprises*. Chichester [West Sussex]；New York：Wiley.

[46] Luo,Y.(2021),New OLI advantages in digital globalization. *International Business Review*,30(2),101797.

[47] Luo,Y.,and Tung,R. L.(2007),International expansion of emerging market enterprises：A springboard perspective. *Journal of International Business Studies*,38：481-498.

［48］ Luo, Y. and Tung, R. L. （2018）, A general theory of springboard MNEs, *Journal of International Business Studies*, 49: 129-152.

［49］ Mintzberg, H., Lampel, J., Ahlstrand, B. （1998）, *Strategy Safari: A Guided Tour Through the Wilds of Strategic Management*, Free Press.

［50］ Ronen, Simcha （1986）. *Comparative and Multinational Management*. New York: Wiley.

［51］ Stopford, John M., Wells, Louis T. （1972）, *Strategy and Structure of the Multinational Enterprise*, New York: Basic Books.

［52］ Tolentino, P. E. E. （1993）, *Technological Innovation and Third World Multinationals*, New Fetter Lanc, London.

［53］ Trentini, C., J. de Camargo Mainente and A. U. Santos-Paulino （2022）. The evolution of digital MNEs: an empirical note. *Transnational Corporations*, 29 （1）: 163-187. .

［54］ Tung, Rosalie L （1981）. Selection and training of personnel for overseas assignments. *Columbia Journal of World Business*. 16(1): 68-78. .

［55］ UNCTAD （2017）. *World Investment Report 2017: Investment and the Digital Economy* （United Nations publication. Sales No. E. 17. II. D. 3. New York and Geneva）.

［56］ UNCTAD （2022）. *World Investment Report 2022: International Tax Reforms and Sustainable Investment* （United Nations publication. Sales No. E. 22. II. D. 20. Geneva）.

［57］ UNCTAD （2023）. *World Investment Report 2023: Investing in Sustainable Energy for All* （United Nations publication. Sales no. E. 23. II. D. 17. Geneva and New York）.

［58］ UNCTAD （2024）. *World Investment Report 2024: Investment Facilitation and Digital Government* （United Nations publication. Sales no. E. 24. II. D. 11. Geneva and New York）.

［59］ Vernon, R. M. （1966）, International investment and international trade in the product cycle, *Quarterly Journal of Economics* 80: 190-207.

［60］ Wells, L. T. （1983）, *Third World Multinationals: The Rise of Foreign Investments from Developing Countries*. MIT Press Books.

教师服务

感谢您选用清华大学出版社的教材！为了更好地服务教学，我们为授课教师提供本书的教学辅助资源，以及本学科重点教材信息。请您扫码获取。

》》 教辅获取

本书教辅资源，授课教师扫码获取

》》 样书赠送

国际经济与贸易类重点教材，教师扫码获取样书

清华大学出版社

E-mail: tupfuwu@163.com

电话：010-83470332 / 83470142

地址：北京市海淀区双清路学研大厦 B 座 509

网址：https://www.tup.com.cn/

传真：8610-83470107

邮编：100084